M000315083

Exploring Online Learning Through Synchronous and Asynchronous Instructional Methods

Cynthia Mary Sistek-Chandler
National University, USA

A volume in the Advances in Mobile and Distance Learning (AMDL) Book Series

Published in the United States of America by
    IGI Global
    Information Science Reference (an imprint of IGI Global)
    701 E. Chocolate Avenue
    Hershey PA, USA 17033
    Tel: 717-533-8845
    Fax: 717-533-8661
    E-mail: cust@igi-global.com
    Web site: http://www.igi-global.com

Library of Congress Cataloging-in-Publication Data

Names: Sistek-Chandler, Cynthia Mary, 1958- editor.
Title: Exploring online learning through synchronous and asynchronous instructional methods / Cynthia Mary Sistek-Chandler, editor.
Description: Hershey, PA : Information Science Reference, 2020. | Includes bibliographical references and index. | Summary: """This book explores online learning through the lens of synchronous and asynchronous instructional methods" -- Provided by publisher.
Identifiers: LCCN 2019032966 (print) | LCCN 2019032967 (ebook) | ISBN 9781799816225 (hardcover) | ISBN 9781799816232 (paperback) | ISBN 9781799816249 (ebook)
Subjects: LCSH: Web-based instruction--Design. | Distance education--Computer-assisted instruction--Design. | Instructional systems--Design
Classification: LCC LB1044.87 .E96 2020 (print) | LCC LB1044.87 (ebook) | DDC 371.33/44678--dc23
LC record available at https://lccn.loc.gov/2019032966
LC ebook record available at https://lccn.loc.gov/2019032967

This book is published in the IGI Global book series Advances in Mobile and Distance Learning (AMDL) (ISSN: 2327-1892; eISSN: 2327-1906)

British Cataloguing in Publication Data
A Cataloguing in Publication record for this book is available from the British Library.

For electronic access to this publication, please contact: eresources@igi-global.com.

Advances in Mobile and Distance Learning (AMDL) Book Series

ISSN:2327-1892
EISSN:2327-1906

Editor-in-Chief: Patricia Ordóñez de Pablos, Universidad de Oviedo, Spain

MISSION

Private and public institutions have made great strides in the fields of mobile and distance learning in recent years, providing greater learning opportunities outside of a traditional classroom setting. While the online learning revolution has allowed for greater learning opportunities, it has also presented numerous challenges for students and educators alike. As research advances, online educational settings can continue to develop and advance the technologies available for learners of all ages.

The **Advances in Mobile and Distance Learning** (AMDL) Book Series publishes research encompassing a variety of topics related to all facets of mobile and distance learning. This series aims to be an essential resource for the timeliest research to help advance the development of new educational technologies and pedagogy for use in online classrooms.

COVERAGE

- Ethical Considerations
- Student Achievement and Satisfaction
- Tablets and Education
- E-Books
- Accreditation
- Ubiquitous and Pervasive Learning
- Cloud Computing in Schools
- Virtual Universities
- Mobile Learning
- Online Class Management

IGI Global is currently accepting manuscripts for publication within this series. To submit a proposal for a volume in this series, please contact our Acquisition Editors at Acquisitions@igi-global.com or visit: http://www.igi-global.com/publish/.

The Advances in Mobile and Distance Learning (AMDL) Book Series (ISSN 2327-1892) is published by IGI Global, 701 E. Chocolate Avenue, Hershey, PA 17033-1240, USA, www.igi-global.com. This series is composed of titles available for purchase individually; each title is edited to be contextually exclusive from any other title within the series. For pricing and ordering information please visit http://www.igi-global.com/book-series/advances-mobile-distance-learning/37162. Postmaster: Send all address changes to above address. Copyright © 2020 IGI Global. All rights, including translation in other languages reserved by the publisher. No part of this series may be reproduced or used in any form or by any means – graphics, electronic, or mechanical, including photocopying, recording, taping, or information and retrieval systems – without written permission from the publisher, except for non commercial, educational use, including classroom teaching purposes. The views expressed in this series are those of the authors, but not necessarily of IGI Global.

Titles in this Series

For a list of additional titles in this series, please visit:
http://www.igi-global.com/book-series/advances-mobile-distance-learning/37162

Utilizing a 5-Stage Learning Model for Planning and Teaching Online Courses Emerging Research and Opprtunities
Riad S. Aisami (Troy University, USA)
Information Science Reference • © 2020 • 168pp • H/C (ISBN: 9781799820420) • US $185.00

Managing and Designing Online Courses in Ubiquitous Learning Enironments
Gürhan Durak (Balıkesir University, Turkey) and Serkan Çankaya (İzmir Democracy University, Turkey)
Information Science Reference • © 2020 • 356pp • H/C (ISBN: 9781522597797) • US $185.00

Global Demand for Borderless Online Degrees
Robert P. Hogan (Walden University, USA)
Information Science Reference • © 2020 • 266pp • H/C (ISBN: 9781522589129) • US $185.00

Enriching Collaboration and Communication in Online Learning Communities
Carolyn N. Stevenson (Purdue University Global, USA) and Joanna C. Bauer (Claremont Lincoln University, USA)
Information Science Reference • © 2020 • 319pp • H/C (ISBN: 9781522598145) • US $195.00

Advancing Mobile Learning in Contemporary Educational Spaces
Dominic Mentor (Columbia University, USA)
Information Science Reference • © 2019 • 394pp • H/C (ISBN: 9781522593515) • US $195.00

Student Support Toward Self-Directed Learning in Open and Distributed Environments
Micheal M. van Wyk (University of South Africa, South Africa)
Information Science Reference • © 2019 • 321pp • H/C (ISBN: 9781522593164) • US $195.00

For an entire list of titles in this series, please visit:
http://www.igi-global.com/book-series/advances-mobile-distance-learning/37162

701 East Chocolate Avenue, Hershey, PA 17033, USA
Tel: 717-533-8845 x100 • Fax: 717-533-8661
E-Mail: cust@igi-global.com • www.igi-global.com

Editorial Advisory Board

Table of Contents

Foreword xv

Preface xvii

Acknowledgment xxvii

Chapter 1
Asynchronous/Synchronous Learning Chasm 1
    Peter Serdyukov, National University, USA

Chapter 2
The Importance of Synchronous Sessions in Online Asynchronous Classes 34
    Everett George Beckwith, National University, USA

Chapter 3
Exploring Online Learning Through Synchronous and Asynchronous
Instructional Methods 52
    Jamie Mahoney, Murray State University, USA
    Carol A. Hall, University of Phoenix, USA

Chapter 4
Trifecta of Student Engagement: A Framework for Engaging Students in
Online Courses...77
    Heather J. Leslie, University of San Diego, USA

Chapter 5

The Importance of Social Presence and Strategies for Incorporating It Into an
Online Course 107

Joshua Elliott, Fairfield University, USA

Chapter 6

Using Learning Management Systems to Promote Online Instruction 123

Vaughn Malcolm Bradley, Montgomery County Public Schools, USA

Chapter 7

Instructional Design and Online Standards 151

Lesley S. J. Farmer, California State University, Long Beach, USA

Chapter 8

Process Considerations for the Development and Assessment of Virtual
Education Doctorates 178

Erika Prager, Northcentral University, USA
Barbara M. Hall, Northcentral University, USA
Laurie Wellner, Northcentral University, USA
B. Andrew Riggle, Northcentral University, USA
Robin Throne, Northcentral University, USA

Chapter 9

Precision Education: Engineering Learning, Relevancy, Mindset, and
Motivation in Online Environments..202

Huda A. Makhluf, National University, USA

Chapter 10

The Transition of a School Counseling Program: The Shift From Traditional
to Synchronous to Asynchronous Learning 225

Sladjana Sandy Rakich, National University, USA
Sonia Rodriguez, National University, USA
Ronald Morgan, National University, USA

Chapter 11

A Study on the Effectiveness of College English Blended Learning Under
MOOCs Philosophy in China 247

*Zhaohui Dai, Shanghai University, China & University of Wisconsin,
Madison, USA*

Chapter 12
A Holistic Approach to Integrating ePortfolios as Instructional Methods in
Online Programs 271
    Barbara Miller Hall, Northcentral University, USA
    Miranda R. Regnitz, Northcentral University, USA

Compilation of References 290

About the Contributors 326

Index 331

Detailed Table of Contents

Foreword xv

Preface xvii

Acknowledgment xxvii

Chapter 1

Asynchronous/Synchronous Learning Chasm 1
Peter Serdyukov, National University, USA

Online learning offers generous benefits for learners. Its main attraction, convenience, however, is causing a conflict between asynchronous and synchronous modes of learning which can lead to numerous adverse effects. The shift towards asynchronous at the expense of the synchronous practices are noticeable in some colleges which may deprive students of the two critical benefits of education, personal and social development, and cause deterioration of the learning outcomes. Analysis of these two modes demonstrates advantages and disadvantages of both which calls for a holistic approach to online education realized through an additive interactive model in a blended learning format.

Chapter 2

The Importance of Synchronous Sessions in Online Asynchronous Classes 34
Everett George Beckwith, National University, USA

When online classes began being developed and made available in higher education approximately 20 years ago, the vast majority of the online classes and programs were asynchronous, meaning that instructors did not meet with students in real-time or synchronously. There were few synchronous courses, and this was due to the high expense of video teleconferencing systems and the inability of many computers to handle the high bandwidth and memory required to participate in such synchronous sessions. Now, there has been a significant revolution in video teleconferencing systems and in the computers used to access them. Systems are now affordable and most learning management systems (LMS) even have them embedded. While mobile computers, including handheld devices such as iPhones, Androids, and tablets, can access the synchronous sessions from anywhere they can access the Internet. It is time to reassess the value and effectiveness of having synchronous sessions in online classes that are primarily asynchronous.

Chapter 3
Exploring Online Learning Through Synchronous and Asynchronous
Instructional Methods 52
Jamie Mahoney, Murray State University, USA
Carol A. Hall, University of Phoenix, USA

Teaching and learning in the online environment are challenging. Students and instructors must employ technological tools and strategies to be successful. Merely having a computer and software does not equate to being technologically literate in the 21st century world of work. Learning how to incorporate virtual reality games, webcams, video conferencing, and brainstorming platforms such as Padlet, Bubbl. us, Zoom, Twitter, Instagram, interactive whiteboards, chat rooms, YouTube, and screencasting videos is encouraged. Polleverywhere, Socrative, and Flubaroo are a few assessments to investigate interest by examining the world of synchronous and asynchronous learning environments. The digital natives of today's classrooms are the future employees of tomorrow's real-life world of work; therefore, organizations must take control of the situation and prepare workers to meet future job demands. The question of how to do so effectively will be answered in this chapter.

Chapter 4
Trifecta of Student Engagement: A Framework for Engaging Students in
Online Courses...77
Heather J. Leslie, University of San Diego, USA

This chapter describes a framework adapted from Michael Moore's three essential areas: student-content interaction, student-student interaction, and student-instructor interaction for engaging students in online courses. To be fully engaged in an online course, students need to be engaged with the course curriculum content, with their peers, and with their instructor. When students are engaged in all three areas, it is referred to as the Trifecta of Student Engagement. This chapter incorporates literature on each area of the Trifecta of Student Engagement: student-to-content engagement, student-to-student engagement, and student-to-instructor engagement as well as some suggested synchronous and asynchronous digital tools.

Chapter 5
The Importance of Social Presence and Strategies for Incorporating It Into an
Online Course 107
Joshua Elliott, Fairfield University, USA

As with any mode of course delivery, there are both positives and negatives to online learning. There are the commonly cited positive features of online learning like the removal of geographic restrictions and scheduling barriers. Limitations may include unfamiliarity for those new to online learning and misunderstandings resulting from the transition from primarily face-to-face interactions to only online interactions. One of the nice things about online learning environments is that many of the possible drawbacks can be countered turning them into strength. Building a strong social presence in an online course can help with this. This chapter discusses three categories of strategies for building a social presence; ice breakers, netiquette activities, and discussion activities.

Chapter 6
Using Learning Management Systems to Promote Online Instruction 123
Vaughn Malcolm Bradley, Montgomery County Public Schools, USA

Learning management systems (LMS) reinforce the learning process through online classroom environments. A standard LMS supports an inclusive learning environment for academic progress with interceding structures that promote online collaborative-groupings, professional training, discussions, and communication among other LMS users. Instructors should balance active learning with the use of LMS technological resources and the use of guidelines from the qualified curriculum. As Murcia stated regarding online environments in 2016, instructors can use an LMS to facilitate and model discussions, plan online activities, set learning expectations, provide learners with options, and assist in problem-solving and decision making, supporting learner engagement through their presence in the LMS; facilitators allow students to retain their autonomy, enthusiasm, and motivation. It is vital that stakeholders of the educational community find scientific studies to support their contributions in LMS platforms to assist scholars in learning mathematics and other academic subjects

Chapter 7
Instructional Design and Online Standards 151
Lesley S. J. Farmer, California State University, Long Beach, USA

Online education has a foundation so that beneficial practices can leverage online environments effectively. Besides generic instructional design principles, models of good online instructional design are emerging. These practices and models are codified into online instructional design standards that provide research-based criteria that can be used to measure the degree to which such instructional designs meet those standards and can serve as guidelines of factors to consider when designing online instruction. This chapter provides an overview of instructional design as it applies to online teaching and learning. It also discusses how standards can help improve such instructional design in order to optimize student learning and achievement.

Chapter 8

Process Considerations for the Development and Assessment of Virtual Education Doctorates 178

Erika Prager, Northcentral University, USA
Barbara M. Hall, Northcentral University, USA
Laurie Wellner, Northcentral University, USA
B. Andrew Riggle, Northcentral University, USA
Robin Throne, Northcentral University, USA

This chapter focuses on the use of a customized backward instructional design process used to re-engineer a virtual university's integration of institutional learning outcomes within a practice-based online dissertation process for a doctorate in education (EdD). The EdD will incorporate specialization areas in instructional design, learning analytics, and e-learning and through a lens of best assessment practices for doctoral education. This program will highlight the unique considerations for virtual environments especially those that incorporate asynchronous instructional elements in program and course design. The education doctorate is leadership-based and practitioner-focused to prepare candidates as scholar practitioners who utilize the learning outcomes for research-based decision making and problem solutions within their scope of practice. A new three chapter dissertation allows candidates to solve a practice-based problem as a culminating doctoral learning activity which will be assessed across institutional outcomes and expectations.

Chapter 9

Precision Education: Engineering Learning, Relevancy, Mindset, and Motivation in Online Environments 202

Huda A. Makhluf, National University, USA

Higher education is a pathway to social equality and mobility. Unfortunately, a great number of students who enter Higher Education are not ready to succeed in rigorous college-level courses and fail as a result or drop out. Our nation has entered a transformative period in higher education brought about by the demands of an evidence-based approach that uses rigorous scientific methodologies designed to capture valid and reliable data to drive student success and improve outcomes. Math literacy especially remains a significant challenge for student success in college, in particular for STEM students. Herein, the author describes an innovative solution that leverages technology and data analytics to expand student success, with a special emphasis on engineering an environment for effective learning, mindset, and motivation.

Chapter 10

The Transition of a School Counseling Program: The Shift From Traditional
to Synchronous to Asynchronous Learning 225

Sladjana Sandy Rakich, National University, USA
Sonia Rodriguez, National University, USA
Ronald Morgan, National University, USA

This chapter outlines the evolution of a Master of School Counseling Program
from a traditional in-person model to an asynchronous online program with an
integrated field experience component. It utilizes a case study approach to how
this transition occurred with an overview of the process and strategies used for the
program course redesign presented. The primary goal of the redesign efforts was
to sustain efficient student instructor engagement in an online setting while training
aspiring school counselors for the complex 21st century educational settings. This
chapter also includes a brief literature review of best practices, rubrics used for
program development, progress monitoring, and program assessment. Additionally,
descriptive data that is presented illustrates the perspectives of adjunct faculty and
students in regard to teaching effectiveness, student engagement and satisfaction in
an asynchronous fast paced online program.

Chapter 11

A Study on the Effectiveness of College English Blended Learning Under
MOOCs Philosophy in China 247

Zhaohui Dai, Shanghai University, China & University of Wisconsin,
Madison, USA

This study investigated the effectiveness of college English blended education under
a MOOCs philosophy in China. The findings suggest that many features of MOOCs
philosophy are evident in college English blended education and eight factors
influence effectiveness. Relationships of the influencing factors demonstrate that
interactions and evaluations are highly influencing factors in autonomous learning
and motivations exert high influences on autonomous learning. However, students
have low motivation in interaction and evaluation, for they are more extrinsically
than intrinsically motivated. And also, collaborative learning is the least influencing
factor in the study. To motivate the students, great emphasis should be laid on
interactions and evaluation in student's autonomous learning. Moreover, students'
negative attitude towards autonomous learning hampers their adaptability to college
English blended learning, and, as attitude and motivation are highly related, this
deserves equal attention.

Chapter 12

A Holistic Approach to Integrating ePortfolios as Instructional Methods in
Online Programs 271
        Barbara Miller Hall, Northcentral University, USA
        Miranda R. Regnitz, Northcentral University, USA

The purpose of this chapter is to review a holistic approach to the integration of digital portfolios ("ePortfolios") as an instructional method in online degree programs. The chapter reviews the evidence-based best practices that support four phases to the integration of ePortfolios as an instructional method in online degree programs: scaffolding, tutorials, course integration, and student engagement. Each phase offers a different way to make a lasting impact on students. The innovative instructional method is not the portfolio itself, the supporting tutorials, or any one piece of the ePortfolio project. Rather, the true innovation is the project as a whole, taking a holistic look at how portfolios fit into the program and how to support the development and evaluation of the portfolio for both students and faculty.

Compilation of References 290

About the Contributors 326

Index 331

Foreword

The profound impact of distance education and eLearning over the last quarter century that nearly every academic institution now offers some form of online instruction. Not only has access to education been transformed for the better, but along with the transformation have emerged new ideas and expectations about openness to education. Not surprisingly, such important and dynamic changes require timely and essential resources for practitioners, administrators and scholars who must design, teach and manage delivery of ever-expanding online programs. While the edited volume contained herein is not a textbook on how to teach online, it does offer significant insights into how to better engage and interact with learners and apply learning technologies to educational issues. Accordingly, this volume is timely and instructive, for what has become increasingly clear is that many current online program offerings are not instructionally innovative or characterized by high touch qualities that support interactivity. Rather, as pointed out in the text, with larger and larger online offerings that mimic lecture driven university classrooms, many online programs are cost effective, but student learning suffers. When instruction is relegated to the one-to-many lecture hall model, advances in learning science and instructional design that have accompanied the distant education and eLearning revolution over the same twenty-five-year period are oftentimes ignored. Topics covered in the text respond to these and other issues through the voices of authors from around the world who are experts, practitioners and scholars in the field of eLearning and distance education.

As an applied text, the insights are based on many authors' firsthand experiences in areas like asynchronous and synchronous communication, the utility of learning management systems, standards for online development, and ePortfolios, among numerous others. Many times, through the lens of student engagement and optimal learning, chapters highlight how technology now offers countless tools in an online classroom where students can go beyond typical social media apps such as Facebook and YouTube. Authors go to some length in documenting how any student can use current technologies to record quality videos, make flash cards, or even automate post-it notes to text, graphics and videos. Further emphasized is the impact that ePortfolios can have on student learning through capturing student achievements while also providing a tool to chart career pathways and progress. In another chapter the authors introduce readers to possible forms of student engagement and describe how and to what extent students can engage with content, with other students, and with instructors. Not surprisingly, the authors hold that for ideal learning to occur students need to participate and engage across all three areas. The chapter devoted to uniform online environments and design standards notes how a familiar environment can contribute to the success of online learning, especially when an LMS is employed. Even a standardized course syllabus can improve content engagement because the course structure, requirements, and schedules are clearly stated and easily found. Not to be left out of the discussion is a chapter devoted to analyzing the impact and design features of massive open online courses (MOOCs). Characterized by their mostly asynchronous designs, MOOCs are open to learners from across the globe and often have tens of thousands of students in a single class. An analysis of this seminal, semi-autonomous style of learning is also included in the text.

Whether you work as an instructional designer, administrator of online institutional offerings or are thinking about taking up teaching online I encourage you to read what these contributing experts have to say. I cannot assure that the experience will be as transformational as the changes in distance education and eLearning over the last quarter century, but I can assure the readers of this edited volume that they will be better prepared to incorporate strategies and practices espoused by the chapter authors and editors into their professional practice.

Thomas H. Reynolds
National University, USA

Preface

ONLINE LEARNING: A BRIEF OVERVIEW AND EVOLUTION

Over the last twenty years, online learning, eLearning and distance learning have greatly evolved to adapt to different audiences, addressed various time and spaces, have been customized to meet a variety of subject matter, and have allowed connectivity to content through many modalities. Distance education/online learning has grown dramatically in higher education institutions. According to Seaman, Allen, and Seaman (2018) over 3 million students utilize online-only learning in higher education. In their report published by the Babson Research Group, they state "nearly fifteen percent (14.9%) of all students enrolled in higher education programs participated in distance-only programs (p. 3)." Students taking distance education courses "grew by 5.6% from Fall 2015 to Fall 2016 to reach 6,359,121 students taking at least one distance education course (Seaman et al., 2018 p. 3). That means "31.6% of all students" (p. 3) are now taking distance education courses. With the growing demand for online programs in higher education, demand for online instructors and the demand for the development of quality online curriculum that includes synchronous and asynchronous instructional methods has never been greater.

As the Internet has become ubiquitous, so has access to online education. Online learning has expanded to reach audiences worldwide, in large cities, in developing countries, in rural and urban communities, in the sub-Saharan deserts of Africa, and even in remote islands in the South Pacific. Online learners range from kindergartners to adult learners, and every age group in between. Online courses are designed for undergraduate and graduate degree programs, for certifications, for job training, and for meeting the needs of grade level expectancies in K-12 education. In fact, many high school students are now taking online classes as a form of credit recovery, for Advanced Placement coursework, for enrichment, and even for college credit. Powell from the Aspen Institute states, "Research shows that more than 75% of school districts use blended and online learning for expanded course offerings and credit recovery." Virtual schools are growing at an unprecedented rate and educational institutions as a whole are all embracing online learning as a viable alternative to the traditional, "face-to-face", "on ground" instructional environment. If educational institutions are not currently offering classes online, they will be beyond 2020.

Delivery of Online Learning

Online learning has traditionally been delivered by a learning management system. Learning management systems (LMS) were originally designed as software for the administration, documentation, tracking, reporting, and delivery of online content. The LMS today is much more sophisticated than its early predecessors. In the beginning, all web content had to be in html format and then file transferred or uploaded to a web server. Content was typically "text" only and often replicated content from a textbook. In its early stages, Web 1.0 the "read only" web allowed the learner to access text but without much interaction by the instructor or interaction between peers. In the late 1990's, the LMS later evolved to include discussion boards and forums where learners could post their thoughts and ideas for the instructor and students to read and respond to. These early LMS iterations however lacked the ability to connect the learner through multimedia or through web cameras that allowed for voice and video connection, albeit if these devices were used, they were extremely primitive. As many of the authors have alluded to in this book, this video and voice based online interaction was normally conducted as one dimensional, text-based and written communication and configured one-to-one, teacher-student and student-teacher, and only focused on asynchronous learning.

Then in the mid-1990's with the introduction of online learning materials which included colorful graphics and the transmission and reception of recorded voice and video, it became necessary for educational institutions and students to use powerful computing systems, high-speed modems with tremendous bandwidth which necessitated high-speed Internet connections. These computing systems embraced the graphical user interface (GUI) and needed adequate RAM and graphics cards to read and review the incoming multimedia- infused information. Video streaming was later introduced along with plug-ins for Internet browsers that allowed for video transmission. Web conferencing systems allowed for group meetings to be transmitted by connecting classrooms worldwide. This technological development added to the overall synchronous capabilities and enhanced two-way communication and interactions in online learning.

Later in 1999, with the introduction of Web 2.0 also known as the participatory web or the social web, interaction with Internet delivered materials went beyond "read only". Web 2.0 allowed learners to also write, respond, and collaborate collectively often in real-time. As the Internet grew in its sophistication, the LMS also continued to become more template driven, included more tools for students and professors, and generally became more user friendly (Hiremath & Kenchakkanavar, 2016).

In the future, Web 3.0 will harness the power of metasearch engines and sophisticated tags and algorithms to pinpoint information more quickly and succinctly. These future systems will continue to incorporate artificial intelligence and other types of automated, customized and personalized search and find strategies. The future web will embrace interactions through a variety a media, but especially through live interaction with doctors and medical practitioners (telemedicine), government agencies, subject matter experts, and world-renowned experts. Virtual reality and simulated worlds along with augmented reality will continue to expand the online learning environment.

Some may say that online education has democratized education as a whole. Never in our history of the educational academy has access and opportunity to education been so readily available. Early adopters of online education may also argue there is nothing that cannot be taught online, even dance, music, and participatory performances. We have open access educational courses that are delivered at no cost to the learner from institutions like the Open University in the UK, Coursera, MIT, and Harvard to name a few. Today, online instructors can reach their learners twenty-four hours a day, seven days each week, each term, and each semester. In many cases students text their instructors and connect through other real-time social media-based platforms. In the early nineties, companies like Microsoft launched initiatives that were coined as "anytime, anywhere, any place" learning opportunities. This vision has come to fruition. In our modern-day learning environment, learning is never shut down, and learners are always online, either in an online classroom, accessing self-paced tutorials, or engaging in social networking activities.

As you will discover from several of the chapters in this book, the instructor role has changed and so has the student's ability to interact with content, interact with the instructor, and interact with peers in an online class. The role of the online instructor has expanded to become less of a conveyor of knowledge and a subject matter expert to a more advanced role of an instructional designer, a facilitator, a coach, or even an orchestrator of online learning. Even through massive open online courses (MOOC's), learners can interact and learn content on any subject matter and interact with peers, or with virtual tutors (teacher's assistants) thus increasing the opportunity for hundreds if not thousands of students to take an online class, sometimes without feedback from a central or primary instructor.

Administrators, subject matter experts, instructional designers, instructors, students, and all who are from education who are researching online learning, will benefit from the knowledge base of the experienced chapter contributors. Each author has examined online learning from the perspective of synchronous and asynchronous instruction and learning. This publication serves as an excellent resource that spans innovation of online content, analysis of strategies, description of online tools, online processes and procedures, and shares their journeys, pitfalls and promises of how online learning can meet the needs of learners.

Readers will learn about several innovative content delivery systems through Precision Learning and by a case study of MOOC's from China, as well as learn about the need to use a more traditional learning management system to help guide and contain student artifacts of learning such as an ePortfolio.

Chapter 1

The "Asynchronous/Synchronous Learning Chasm" discusses the attributes of online learning and compares the conflict and congruence of asynchronous and synchronous modes of learning. Dr. Peter Serdyukov provides an analysis of these two modes and demonstrates advantages and disadvantages of both. Dr. Serdyukov has been researching online learning since the late 1980s and has explored asynchronous and synchronous learning throughout his career. His work in this chapter concludes with and calls for a holistic approach to online education as realized through an additive interactive model in a blended learning format. Blended learning offers the students the "best of both worlds" and reinforces various levels of interaction.

Chapter 2

The "Importance of Synchronous Sessions in Online Asynchronous Classes" contains a brief history of online systems used for the delivery of content in the classroom. Beckwith begins by stating, "when online classes began being developed by faculty and supporting course designers and made available in higher education approximately 20 years ago and subsequently were accredited by the various higher education accrediting agencies, the vast majority of the online classes and programs were asynchronous, meaning that instructors did not meet with students in real-time or synchronously." The overall lack of synchronous courses and programs were due to the high expense of video teleconferencing systems and the inability for many computers, especially mobile ones, to handle the high bandwidth and memory required to effectively access and participate in such synchronous sessions. From the initiation of online programs over 20 years ago until the present, there has been a significant revolution in video teleconferencing systems and in the computers used to access them. Dr. Beckwith has been involved with online communication systems since the mid-seventies and from his experience in the military and in public schools in information technology, he shares his view that contemporary systems web conferencing systems are now more affordable for educational institutions. He continues to say that most learning management systems (LMS) have video conferencing systems embedded. Course access has also improved by allowing students to use mobile computers and handheld devices such as iPhones, Android phones, and tablets, allowing all stakeholders to access the synchronous sessions from anywhere they can access the Internet. Beckwith also emphasizes that it is time to reassess the value and effectiveness of having synchronous sessions in online classes that are primarily asynchronous.

Chapter 3

"Exploring Online Learning through Synchronous and Asynchronous Instructional Methods" by Dr. Jamie Mahony and Dr. Carol Hall provides an overview of tools that can be used to support both synchronous and asynchronous instructional methodologies in the online class. As they share, the digital natives of today's classrooms are the future employees of tomorrow's real-life world of work; therefore, the authors suggest that organizations must take control of the situation and prepare workers to meet future job demands. Preparing online learners for the world of work and providing them practice with web tools to expand their proficiencies effectively will be answered in this chapter.

Chapter 4

"Trifecta of Student Engagement: A Framework for Engaging Students in Online Courses," is based on research from Dr. Heather Leslie, and she discusses the framework adapted from Michael Moore's (1989) three essential areas: student-content interaction, student-student interaction, and student-instructor interaction for engaging students in online courses, this chapter further describes how interactions are necessary for learning to take place in an online learning environment. In order to be fully engaged in an online course, students need to be engaged with the course curriculum content, with their peers, and with their instructor. When students are engaged in all three areas, it is referred to as the "Trifecta of Student Engagement." This chapter incorporates literature on each areas of the Trifecta of Student Engagement: student-to-content engagement, student-to-student engagement, and student-to-instructor engagement and includes suggestions for synchronous and asynchronous digital tools.

Chapter 5

"The Importance of Social Presence and Strategies for Incorporating it into an Online Course" by Dr. Joshua Elliott presents the elements of social presence and presents three categories of strategies for building social presence and how these strategies can impact the online learning environment. Elliott states, as with any mode of course delivery, there are both positives and negatives to online learning. There are the commonly cited positive features of online learning such as the removal of geographic restrictions and removal of scheduling barriers however there are also many limitations in online learning that may include unfamiliarity caused by this modality. Online learning sometimes imparts misunderstandings resulting from the transition from primarily face- to-face interactions to only online interactions. One of the bright spots about online learning environments is that many of the possible drawbacks can be countered by turning these issues into strengths. The remedy is to build a strong social presence in an online course. This chapter discusses three categories of strategies for building a social presence; ice breakers, netiquette activities, and discussion activities. Read more to learn how each can build a strong online presence for the instructor and for the students.

Chapter 6

"Using Learning Management Systems to Promote Online Instruction" by Dr. Vaughn Bradley reinforces the learning process through online classroom environments. A standard learning management system supports an inclusive learning environment for academic progress with interceding structures that promote online collaborative-groupings, professional training, discussions, and communication among other standard learning management system users. As Bradley states, instructors need to balance active learning with the use of standard learning management system technological resources and adhere to instructional design guidelines from a qualified curriculum. Instructors can use an standard learning management system to facilitate and model discussions, plan online activities, set learning expectations, provide learners with options, and assist in problem-solving and decision making, supporting learner engagement through their presence in the standard learning management system, facilitators may allow students to retain their autonomy, enthusiasm, and motivation. Lastly, it is vital that stakeholders of the educational community find scientific studies to support their contributions in standard learning management system platforms to assist scholars in learning mathematics and other academic subjects.

Chapter 7

"Instructional Design and Online Standards" contributed by Dr. Lesley Farmer, discusses how online education has stabilized its baseline foundation so that beneficial practices have been identified. These standardized practices can effectively leverage online environments. Besides generic instructional design principles, models of good online instructional design have emerged and are being shared widely. Instructional design practices and models are codified into online instructional design standards that provide research-based criteria that can be used to measure the degree to which such instructional designs meet those standards – and can serve as guidelines of factors to consider when designing online instruction. This chapter provides an overview of instructional design as it applies to online teaching and learning. Farmer also discusses how standards can help improve such instructional design in order to optimize student learning and achievement.

Chapter 8

"Process Considerations for the Development and Assessment of Virtual Education Doctorates" is a collective effort from colleagues Prager, Hall, Wellner, Riggle, and Throne at Northwestern University have shared a case study from a virtual doctoral program they launched at their institution. This chapter focuses on the use of a customized backward instructional design process used to re-engineer a virtual university's integration of institutional learning outcomes within a practice-based online dissertation process for a doctorate in education (EdD). The EdD has incorporated specialized areas in instructional design, learning analytics, and e-learning and through a lens of best assessment practices for doctoral education this program will highlight the unique considerations for virtual environments especially those that incorporate asynchronous instructional elements in program and course design. The education doctorate is leadership-based and practitioner-focused to prepare candidates as scholar practitioners who will utilize the learning outcomes for research-based decision making and problem-solving solutions within their scope of practice. Using a novel approach to the dissertation, a new three-chapter report allows candidates to solve a practice-based problem as a culminating doctoral learning activity which will be assessed across institutional outcomes and expectations.

Chapter 9

"Precision Education: Engineering Learning, Relevancy, Mindset and Motivation in Online Environments" presents a case study written by Dr. Huda Makhulf that reports an institutional innovation at National University. Makhulf shares "higher education is a pathway to social equality and mobility but unfortunately, a great number of students who enter Higher Education are not ready to succeed in rigorous college-level courses and fail as a result or drop out." Precision education has evolved out of the notion that our nation has entered a transformative period in higher education brought about by the demands of an evidence-based approach that uses rigorous scientific methodologies designed to capture valid and reliable data to drive student success and improve outcomes. As Mukhulf states, math literacy especially remains a significant challenge for student success in college, in particular for STEM students. Herein, the author describes an innovative solution that leverages technology and data analytics to expand student success, with a special emphasis on engineering an environment for effective learning, mindset, and motivation.

Chapter 10

"The Transition of a School Counseling Program: The Shift from Traditional to Synchronous to Asynchronous Learning" written by professors of K-12 school counseling Rakich, Rodriguez, and Morgan, outline the evolution of a Master of School Counseling Program from a traditional in person model to an asynchronous online program with an integrated field experience component. This study utilizes a case study approach to how this transition occurred with an overview of the process and strategies used for the program course redesign presented. The primary goal of the redesign efforts was to sustain efficient student instructor engagement in an online setting while training aspiring school counselors for the complex 21st century educational settings. This chapter also includes a brief literature review of best practices, rubrics used for program development, progress monitoring, and program assessment. Additionally, descriptive data that is presented illustrates the perspectives of adjunct faculty and students in regard to teaching effectiveness, student engagement and satisfaction in an asynchronous fast paced online program.

Chapter 11

"A Study on the Effectiveness of College English Blended Learning under MOOCs Philosophy in China" written by Dr. Zhaohui "Bob" Dai shares a study that investigated the effectiveness of college English blended education under MOOCs philosophy in China. The findings suggest that many features of MOOCs philosophy are evident in college English blended education and that eight factors influenced effectiveness. Relationships of the influencing factors demonstrate that interactions and evaluation are the highly influencing factors in autonomous learning and motivation exerts high influences on autonomous learning. However, students who had a low motivation in interaction and evaluation, proved to be more extrinsically than intrinsically motivated. Dai also states that collaborative learning was the least influencing factor in the study. His finding and suggestion, in order to motivate students, a greater emphasis should be laid on interactions and evaluation in a student's autonomous learning process. Moreover, students' negative attitudes towards autonomous learning may hamper their adaptability to college English blended learning, and, as attitude and motivation are highly related, this deserves equal attention.

Chapter 12

"A Holistic Approach to the Integration of Digital Portfolios as an Instructional Method in Online Degree Programs" written by Barbara Hall from North Central University shows us how digital portfolios add promise to enhancing degree programs at her institution. The purpose of this chapter is to review a holistic approach to the integration of digital portfolios "ePortfolios" as an instructional method in online degree programs. The chapter reviews evidence-based practices that support four phases to the integration of ePortfolios as an instructional method in online degree programs: scaffolding, tutorials, course integration, and student engagement. Each phase offers a different way to make a lasting impact on students. In summary, Hall presents an innovative instructional method is not the portfolio itself, but the supporting tutorials, or any one piece of the ePortfolio project as evidence and artifact that represents learning. Rather, the true innovation is the project as a whole - taking a holistic look at how portfolios fit into the program and how to support the development and evaluation of the portfolio for both students and faculty.

CONCLUSION

In conclusion, this book offers a unique analysis of online learning through the lens of synchronous and asynchronous instructional methods and computer/online tools. Over the last twenty years, through my own learning journey as an online instructor, I have directly experienced this great transformation of design and delivery of online learning that has forever changed my role as an online educator and as an instructor. Through this lifelong pursuit of understanding the dynamics of online learning and instruction, I have become more of a coach, and a facilitator in the online classroom. Both synchronous and asynchronous instruction and delivery of content are needed to address student need, to provide humanistic touchpoints to engage students in learning.

Cynthia Sistek-Chandler
National University, USA

REFERENCES

Hiremath, B. K., & Kenchakkanavar, A. Y. (2016). An Alteration of the Web 1.0, Web 2.0 and Web 3.0: A Comparative Study. Imperial Journal of Interdisciplinary Research, (2), 4.

Powell, A., Roberts, V., & Patrick, S. (2015). Using Online Learning for Credit Recovery: Getting Back on Track to Graduation. Promising Practices in Blended and Online Learning Series. *International Association for K-12 Online Learning.*

Seaman, J. E., Allen, I. E., & Seaman, J. (2018). *Grade Increase: Tracking Distance Education in the United States.* Babson Survey Research Group.

Acknowledgment

I would like to acknowledge my online teaching colleagues at National University and those worldwide who have contributed their intellectual merit to this publication. I would particularly like to recognize my colleagues from the Sanford College of Education who have contributed chapters to this book. As one of the first online institutions, our collective experiences have helped to shape this writing.

Chapter 1
Asynchronous/Synchronous Learning Chasm

Peter Serdyukov
https://orcid.org/0000-0002-4921-8225
National University, USA

ABSTRACT

Online learning offers generous benefits for learners. Its main attraction, convenience, however, is causing a conflict between asynchronous and synchronous modes of learning which can lead to numerous adverse effects. The shift towards asynchronous at the expense of the synchronous practices are noticeable in some colleges which may deprive students of the two critical benefits of education, personal and social development, and cause deterioration of the learning outcomes. Analysis of these two modes demonstrates advantages and disadvantages of both which calls for a holistic approach to online education realized through an additive interactive model in a blended learning format.

INTRODUCTION

As much as the automobile liberated people from the oppression of distance and time, technology freed college students from the limitations of distance and time via online education. Yet, as in the case of automobile, technology also presented challenges that require rules and regulations specifying how to use it to benefit the learner and society but without degrading the quality of the learning outcomes or adversely affecting people's lives in any way.

Like with the fascination with a car, learners are drawn to online higher education thanks to its mesmerizing attraction - convenience. Its motto "anywhere, anytime

DOI: 10.4018/978-1-7998-1622-5.ch001

and anyhow" is utterly seductive and promises an easy and stress-free learning experience. No wonder it has been consistently growing in the last two decades. It is truly an ideal opportunity for many people, especially working adults, to get a degree without physically attending the college and on their own schedule. Still, as it often happens, when you get something too easy or too cheap, or choose comfort over hard work, expect consequences. While this format of education has many useful features, convenience has in fact become a cause for a split between the two modes of online interaction, each in its own right: synchronous and asynchronous. This split has far-reaching consequences for educational quality as well as for personal and social development. Here the author presents a discussion of issues related to this chasm to understand how it may affect education and society and try to find a plausible solution.

GENERAL CONCERNS

The demand for online education is constantly increasing (Allen & Seaman, 2017). It is well-known that many students are attracted to online learning primarily because of its convenience which includes, among other things, accessibility, flexibility and speed (Bocchi, Eastman, & Swift, 2004; Serdyukov & Serdyukova, 2006; Mupinga, Nora, & Yaw, 2006; Christensen & Eyring 2011; Cole, Shelley, & Schwartz, 2014). Nowadays, people choose online programs not so much for what they will learn from them but because learning in these programs can be comfortably accommodating to their busy lives: the modern-day learning has to fit in between life and work. As Evan Williams, a co-founder of Twitter, recently put it, "Convenience decides everything…Convenience seems to make our decisions for us, trumping what we like to imagine are our true preferences" (as cited in Wu, 2018).

What online education offered on top of the programs was primarily convenience, the convenience of easy learning. Do we clearly realize its impact on the learner and education in general? We already have convenience stores and convenience food but unable to cook – now we are moving fast towards convenience education. Bill Gates once said, the vision is that "people should have the ultimate in convenience. Being able to get the things they care about on the appropriate device" (Gates, 2019). Young people are attracted to convenience and expediency provided by today's technologies. Students choose convenience over hard work of learning. However, every convenience brings its own inconveniences along with it (Serdyukov 2015). Goik (2018) writes, "The lure of comfort and an easy way of going about life now arguably causes more problems than it solves…though understood and promoted as an instrument of liberation, convenience has a dark side. With its promise of smooth, effortless efficiency, it threatens to erase the sort of struggles and challenges that help give meaning to life. Created to free us, it can become a constraint on what we are willing to do, and thus in a subtle way it can enslave us" (Wu, 2018). Why to brew coffee in your own kitchen if you can buy it at Starbucks? Why walk to the corner Starbucks if you can ride there in a car?

True learning is about the joys of overcoming the difficulties of discovery. It is not designed for the delights of convenience. The joyfulness of learning has disappeared from online classes - what most students want today is just the tangible results like grades, degrees and diplomas (Kerby, Branham, & Mallinger, 2014), as soon as possible, and with the least effort. Why should one sit in the college auditorium if you can take a class online from the comfort of your home? Why waste time on interacting with your instructor and peers if you can do all assignments on your own and on your own time? But do you know how to learn without an effort? Those who take learning seriously don't; moreover, many believe it will atrophy the brain. Learning is difficult work, but it does good to the mind, body and soul prompting them to grow and improve. We learn by overcoming difficulties.

When considering the process, it is worthwhile to remember that while at first online learning was fully asynchronous, after a few exciting initial years of online education revolution educators realized that something was missing there. It was not so much the quality of the learning outcomes, which many researchers argue is comparable or even surpassing conventional, classroom-based education (Ni, 2013, & Wrenn, 2016), though it will definitely take more time and effort to help online students achieve the outcomes similar to the outcomes of the traditional, campus-based learning. It was mostly the lack of live, human, personal, face-to-face interaction with the instructor and peers which brought about the lack of socialization (Ouzts, 2006; Boling 2012), the resulting deficiency of relationships among participants of the learning process, particularly among students (Asfaranjan, 2013), failure to build a learning community in the class or group (Oztoc, 2011), limitations on collaboration and cooperation (Palloff, 2005; Serdyukov & Hill, 2013), formalization of the learning, the ensuing depersonalization of the participants of the learning (Scruton, 2010), fear of being disconnected from other participants and the institution, and every so often, still inadequate quality of the learning and its outcomes.

In later years, thanks to the development of effective teleconferencing technologies (e.g., Blackboard Collaborate, Zoom, WebEx, Google Hangouts) and the growth of social networks, online learning integrated a chance for live, synchronous class sessions which allowed students and instructors to engage in active communication and collaboration in real time. Online learning, like conventional learning, generally counts on the practice of both asynchronous and synchronous interaction within virtual environment (Ku & Chang, 2011). While online learning has always been predominantly an independent, self-regulated, almost exclusively text-based study (despite efforts to infuse visual materials and social networking options into online classes) accomplished by a student one-on-one with the computer and aided by occasional, as needed, instructor's facilitation, technical support from the institution, and scanty interaction among students in threaded discussions, blogs and Wikis, the live, synchronous sessions added a vital opportunity for an enjoyable and productive face-to-face interaction, communication and collaboration.

Recently, however, we started observing a rebound from a dual asynchronous-synchronous mode back to a fully asynchronous one in higher education institutions offering online programs, especially the private ones. A strong push for the entirely asynchronous learning transpires at the expense of the synchronous one which looks like an attempt to sever what little was left there of actual reality and substitute it for a completely virtual one. Communication among participants of the learning process, nevertheless, has always been appreciated by the educators and learners alike. There was even a clause in Title IV Student Aid Regulations, which required institutions to ensure that "regular and substantive interaction" takes place between instructors and students in their online course work. Now the Federal Government reassures institutions that they don't need to provide human interaction, so it is more likely that they'll develop entirely automated programs that are "basically just a textbook, computerized" (Toppo, 2018). Private institutions take advantage of the situation.

What are we going to gain from choosing one alternative over the other instead of keeping this perfect duo together? More enrollment thanks to a wider access to higher education and increased flexibility of learning for students interested in fast results and convenience? But at what price? To have "read-only" students (Nagel 2009)? To boost the ever-growing demand for higher education degrees, some argue that online learning is by definition asynchronous (Matos, 2016) which is undoubtedly an exceptional feature providing for many benefits. Some even go farther claiming that absence of face-to-face communication is one of the advantages of online learning (Russell, 2014). Yet there are numerous instances when using asynchronous mode alone may impair various aspects of the learning as well as human and social development, which are definitely thriving when accomplished synchronously (Maurer, 2015).

The conflict between asynchronous and synchronous modes of interaction is becoming more acute as competition among schools and cost of higher education are growing. The drive behind this asynchronous trend is self-evident: asynchronous programs have more appeal for students, particularly working adults, for whom time is the most critical factor determining the choice of the program. As such, programs are more flexible and time-efficient can boost the enrollment. It looks like institutions of higher learning are following the business trend, which, according to Jeff Bezos of Amazon, is manifested in the obsession with what the customer wants and needs (Premack, 2018). In higher educational institutions, it is a preoccupation with student satisfaction more than with their learning outcomes.

Hence, we can safely assume this push for total asynchronicity of learning is intended to raise profits by catering to customers' (students') demands. Asynchronicity, moreover, paves the way to automation of the learning process (machine learning) which is currently driven by the Precision Learning model (Cook, Kilgus, & Burns, 2017). Its initial purpose is to make education more individualized, more customized, precise and thus more efficient, which will increase enrollments and revenue but, as in many other similar instances, has an additional potential of increasing profits at institutions of higher learning even more by cutting down on the institutions' largest budget item, the faculty payroll. Indeed, though some of online education providers claim they are passionate about access to education for formerly underprivileged population groups through online programs, it does not conceal the ultimate financial reason for awarding prevalence to asynchronous education. Online learning is a big business (Stokes, 2012), but instead of sacrificing education to materialism, we should rather try to turn it back into an authentic, integrated academic endeavor.

When we consider the arguments for asynchronous vs. synchronous learning, leaving business considerations aside, we hear a variety of arguments in favor of some advantages of asynchronous student interaction within an online course, yet we ought to take a holistic approach to education and cogitate each of the approaches from the point of view of pedagogy, psychology and socio-cultural factors, as well as their implications for life, work and social well-being of our students. It is evident technology impacts not only economy and politics, but also culture and social relationships. We should not turn education into the process of consuming the archived content. The real question here is, as always, do we control technology and education, or do we let ourselves be controlled by technology and those who have created and paid for it? "Choose the former," writes Rushkoff, "and you gain access to the control panel of civilization. Choose the latter, and it could be the last real choice you get to make" (Rushkoff, 2010). The raw powers of technology should be harnessed by ultimate interests of society and our students and based on sound pedagogy (Serdyukov, 2017). Learning is not about technology, which is just a tool; it is about acquiring new knowledge, skills and competencies, and preparing for life and work. As one of the students wrote, "We learn not from the computers, we learn from our teachers".

This asynchronous trend causes concern among many educators who fear this process, which focuses exclusively on formal knowledge construction will potentially deprive students of the two critical benefits of education, personal and social development, and cause deterioration of the learning outcomes. There is a considerable concern among many online instructors that online students often tend to lose their social, civic, and humanistic traits and become distanced, solitary, impersonal, and unemotional in the online environment (Serdyukov & Sistek-Chandler, 2015). In this context, it is necessary to raise an eternal question, what is the ultimate goal of education, specifically higher education? Is it just "delivering" the knowledge, as instructors often say, to the "customers", as students are commonly called in online institutions nowadays? (Incidentally, it we deliver education to customers, why not to call what we deliver the "goods", or rather semi-prepared cognitive food, and the university a "knowledge supermarket"?). Is it about granting tangible assets like grades, diplomas and degrees to students by millions? John Dewey in the opening chapter of his classic work Democracy and Education (1916), argued that in its broadest sense education is the means of the "social continuity of life" (Dewey, 1916, p.3). Learning is critical for human self-esteem and self-fulfillment. Should we sacrifice the primary purpose and benefits of education for the secondary ones, even so attractive and powerful as convenience of learning, students' satisfaction, and excitement of playing with captivating gadgets, not mentioning the profit for its providers? It seems like online education is the only transaction where the customers (students) want to receive less, not more for their money just for the sake of convenience. True, they do demand higher grades, but few require more value for the buck as regards quantity and quality of their learning outcomes. Despite all that, nevertheless, university faculty must honorably pursue their obligation to prepare students for wholesome life and work.

College administrations, in truth, do not explicitly ban synchronous communication, but require that online courses be labeled asynchronous (with no mandatory live synchronous sessions) or plain synchronous, the latter overtly scheduling live class sessions at an appointed time and earning a grade for participation. Which of the two, do you think, will the majority of convenience-dependent or time-restricted students choose? Or the instructors are allowed to hold only optional live sessions without a grade, which will definitely give a valid excuse for busy students not to attend them. Administrators also advise instructors to post substantive amounts of announcements or lecture materials, stream videos, engage in back-and-forth discussion boards, respond to students' blogs or journals, provide essential feedback, etc., which they do anyway, but those are all a poor substitute for live synchronous interaction, just an ersatz.

These two modes of online interaction seem to be totally opposite, like fire and ice, but is there anything in common between them? Can't we use the advantages of each for the benefit of online learning? How to resolve this conflicting situation: to uphold the online education quality by providing synchronous sessions and, at the same time, satisfy both consumers' demand for convenience and institutions' drive for asynchronicity? To keep everyone: the administration, faculty and students happy – so to say, have one's cake and eat it too? Let's first compare these two online learning modes. In this paper, the author will discuss both modes of interaction within online learning environment and focus on the significance of synchronous interaction in the online class implemented via telecommunication technology, which affords live communication among all class members.

COMPARISON BETWEEN ASYNCHRONOUS AND SYNCHRONOUS LEARNING

Asynchronicity

Asynchronous learning takes place outside simultaneous interaction. It does not happen at the same time for its participants. It focuses of student's autonomous work on assignments using available resources and offers limited interaction with the instructor and class in a time-delayed format. In asynchronous learning, information exchange is not limited to the same place and time. Asynchronous learning is thus practically an independent enterprise when a student does all his or her course work alone, one-on-one with the computer that is connected to the university through a Learning Management System (LMS), typically Blackboard, Pearson Learning Studio/eCollege, Moodle or other systems. Asynchronous online learning is commonly done within LMS using self-guided lesson modules, course texts, posted lecture notes, pre-recorded lectures and podcasts, video and streaming video content, virtual libraries, and interactions via discussion boards. Methods of communication include high time latency tools like email, threaded discussions, blogs, or social media.

Asynchronicity provides a lot of benefits for students, mainly better access, choice, flexibility, expediency and comfort of homework as it allows learners to take time to accomplish their assignments at their own pace. So, asynchronous learning affords students to make their learning self-regulated, self-paced, on an independent schedule, and spend more time on preparation and reflection when needed, which can contribute to more depth of the learning products, like assignments, discussion posts, and projects. Or, students can do it faster if possible, thus accelerating the achievement of their goals and making it time efficient. Asynchronous tools are helpful in capturing and saving the history of the interactions in a group, letting collective knowledge to be easily shared, distributed and used. Moreover, asynchronous learning boasts of anonymity and invisibility, which students have generally come to enjoy - they love to hide behind the computer screen, as Roger Scruton noted in a bold article "Hiding Behind the Screen" (Scruton, 2010). Asynchronous learning, additionally, is allegedly less expensive than the synchronous one (does not require telecommunication equipment and hypothetically eliminates human instructors).

Asynchronous learning, compared to synchronous learning, is essentially static. Students learn in a virtual isolation chamber and go through a solitary experience.

They must possess elevated intrinsic motivation, highly developed autonomous learning skills, vital purpose and considerable resilience, which are often a deficit among online students. They are disconnected from the instructor and class community, do not develop relationships, seldom collaborate, have limited options to share their ideas and discoveries, unless the instructor allows document sharing but online students don't usually have time for reviewing and learning from their peers' work. Response and feedback are usually delayed, and time of response is unpredictable and long, and error handling is more complex. There is a total loss of human emotions, affection and excitement, except in the case of instructor's critique or getting lower than expected grades. Students receive a scanty feedback, which in an asynchronous class commonly comes in the form of a trivial indication to a content error or a formal positive reinforcement that may lead to a biased self-assessment and distorted self-image. Read-only participants disrupt the formation of a virtual community of learners and compromise learning (Nagel, 2009). Online students are often bored and drop out (Tauber, 2013).

In addition, in online classes, students are willing to rush their progression along the course to reach its completion faster, which may lead to superficial knowledge; on top of that, their time management skills together with usual procrastination in delivering their learning products are notorious. Coupled with a common present-day trait of shrinking attention these factors impede the learning and impair the development of a competence. To crown it all, the instructor's impact on students in asynchronous learning is quickly decreasing and little depends on the instructor's professional quality – quite often online courses are taught by adjunct/part-time instructors who do not possess the necessary qualifications or feel responsible for students' learning outcomes.

Synchronicity

Synchronous learning in the online environment is the learning mode in which interaction among participants occurs at the same time, simultaneously. While there can be various formats of synchronous communication, e.g., telephone conversations or instant messaging, here we mean live, videoconferencing sessions where the whole class or learning group communicate with each other in real time seeing and hearing what is going on and engaging in the process contemporaneously. Students and the instructor work together in a specific virtual place, via a particular online medium (videoconferencing/teleconferencing, live chatting, or live-streaming lectures), at a precise time. In other words, it's not exactly anywhere, anyhow, and anytime.

Thus, synchronous learning is about participation. When students are in participatory learning environments, they experience meaningful learning (Palloff & Pratt, 2013). Synchronicity, as opposed to asynchronicity, provides dynamic experiences, warrants interaction among students, requires direct instructor's involvement in class activities and effective mediation of learning, enables live communication in real time, offers immediacy of response and feedback, helps establish relationships among all participants, which are necessary for productive collaboration, prompts community building and generates class synergy which all together contribute to the success of all and everyone in the class. Synchronous learning often employs classroom-type elements, such as group discussions, teamwork, and common activities. Intellectual energy accumulates in live interaction. It ignites participants with its spontaneity, stimulates everyone by the participants' instantaneous exchange of reaction and feedback, starts a competition of ideas and provokes imagination, deeper thinking and creativity, flares up general excitement, enhances motivation, builds a nourishing learning environment, and inspires students' learning. It helps everyone to learn to express oneself, debate, argue and negotiate. It offers numerous opportunities to learn from each other, build competence from sharing, and jointly construct knowledge. In such collective sessions, students can see other faces as a mirror in which they see their own and learn from role models. It is easy to initiate and maintain, makes error correction immediate and easy, and encourages engagement with the course content and all class members as well as with its potential application. It also evokes a high level of discipline, accountability and engagement as it requires mandatory participation at an appointed time.

Synchronous learning is based on the constructivist theory and a student-centered approach that emphasizes the importance of peer-to-peer interactions (Vygotskiy, 1978). Synchronized experiences, according to the authors of the "resonance theory of consciousness" Tom Hunt and Jonathan Schooler (Livni, 2018), are central to communication and understanding. Synchronous sessions help online students feel like participants rather than isolated individuals and allows students to create learning communities and communities of inquiry. Synchronous learning is perceived by students as more social and helps avoid frustration by asking and answering questions in real time. A number of studies established that social presence, teaching presence, and cognitive presence affect participants' level of engagement (Garrison & Cleveland-Innes 2005, Lehman & Conceição, 2010). When engaging in synchronous learning students find a stable means of communication, tend to stay on task, feel a larger sense of participation, and experience better task/course completion rates (Chen & You, 2007; Mabrito, 2006; Hrastinski, 2010). On the other hand, synchronous learning is definitely more demanding, time-consuming and complex, imposes on students' time and limits choices thus restricting course flexibility to some extent.

COMPARISON

Comparison between synchronous and asynchronous learning is presented in Table 1. It demonstrates advantages and disadvantages of both modes of online learning.

Comparative analysis of asynchronous and synchronous online learning modes demonstrates, as follows from Table 1, that each mode has its own advantages and disadvantages. Each supports different purposes (Hrastinski, 2008). While asynchronous learning is more flexible, time-efficient and helps students to focus on their tasks, synchronous learning expands the role and value of the knowledge, helps to make it more meaningful, allows to enhance it (wide and deep) through interaction with others, and involves students in social processes simulating real situations thus preparing them for life and work after the college. In sum, each mode creates different learning experiences catering to individual preferences.

The nature of communication in asynchronous and synchronous online interactions is qualitatively and quantitatively different. Is it possible to balance synchronicity and asynchronicity in learning? Can we marry water and fire? Both modes offer substantial benefits; in many instances, they complement each other. Conversely, using only one or the other may adversely affect various aspects of the learning. Maybe we should sacrifice a small chunk of convenience for a larger good. In order to choose an optimal path and combine them for more effective learning, we have to carefully weigh each and decide what will be the best option for achieving the planned learning outcomes.

STUDENTS' VOICES

To make the right decision, it is important to know how students themselves assess synchronous and asynchronous modes of online learning. To learn of students' opinions regarding their preferences between these two modes the author conducted a survey of students in graduate programs at the College of Education of National University in the fall of 2018. The survey had one question, "Do you believe synchronous live sessions in the online course are useful for you or not? Explain your reasoning for either response based on your experiences with synchronous and asynchronous learning." We received a total of 92 responses which are noteworthy (students' responses are not edited).

The majority of responders (52.9%) found synchronous sessions useful. They gave several reasons for that:

Table 1. Synchronous vs. asynchronous: advantages and disadvantages

Synchronous (real time)		Asynchronous (delayed)	
Advantages	**Disadvantages**	**Advantages**	**Disadvantages**
Same place, same time	Limitation on flexibility; time zone inconvenience	Any place, any time, easier access; flexibility	Procrastination, can affect quality of work
Simultaneous/real-time/ instantaneous/synchronized	Requires alertness; incomplete answer	Separated in time/time lag	Delayed response, fading signal
Social learning	Time-consuming	Independent learning	Time-efficient
Dynamic learning	Can be stressful	Socially static	Social deprivation
Dialogue/polylogue	Low autonomy	Silent monologue	High autonomy
Discourse, debate, discussion	Pulls students out of their comfort zone; some input can be superficial	Self-study	Lack of live interaction
Common socio-cultural space/ context	Diversity and character conflict	Convenience	No social engagement, depersonalization
Shared experiences, learning from each other, knowledge construction; visibility, mirroring	Forces engagement, comparison, competition	Sole experience, reduces social dominance	Solitude, inhibition, lack of competition, potential for distraction; biased self-assessment and distorted self-image
Collaborate/teamwork, feeling of participation and engagement	Some students prefer independent work	Better access to education	Requires autonomous learning skills and self-sufficiency; can affect learning quality
Communication & social skills development	Some can be silent and unengaged	Self-study	No communication & social skills development
Immediate feedback and clarification, convenient Q&A	Less time for independent learning	No need to engage in open interaction; more time on task and reflection	Delayed response, limited feedback
Reactiveness in interaction, alertness	Can cause anxiety and stress	Deeper learning	No opportunity for reactiveness
Diverse situations	Can be overwhelming	Monosituation/sameness of independent learning environment	Monotony
Motivating, exciting, inspiring, passionate, enthusiastic; socio-emotional development	Requires motivation, social skills & effort for face-to-face interaction	Self-control over learning, self-paced	Hard to create enthusiasm and inspire; unemotional, demotivating
Regularity, frequency, discipline, continuity and consistency; holistic learning	Limitation on flexibility	Flexible, time efficient; low pressure, lack of stress, little anxiety	Requires effective time management, accountability; can lead to lower discipline, apathy, comp-lacency, procrastination and plagiarism
Knowing your instructor and peers; less opportunity for plagiarism	No anonymity and high visibility	Hiding behind the screen; anonymity, invisibility	Few opportunities for connecting, networking, interacting and competing
Staying in touch with the instructor and peers, role modeling	Imposes on time	Autonomy	Scarce guidance and support, little instructor and peer impact
Confirms instructor's credibility and helps identify the character & teaching style	Requires careful planning and preparation	Self-efficacy	Requires self-discipline and sense of accountability
Organized and facilitated by instructor	Requires everybody's engagement	Self-sufficient	High time management expectations, risk of procrastination
Accommodating to various learning preferences	Overwhelming for some students	Potential for automation	Irrelevance of human element
Improved quality of learning outcomes	Higher cost	Low cost	Can impair quality of learning
Saved log of discussions, keeps history of interaction	-	Saved log of discussions, keeps history of interactions	-

General Comments from Students

"I find these live sessions worthy because I not only get to communicate with my teacher one on one and hear their thoughts, but I also am afforded the chance to learn from other students who are invested in the same material as I am. The argument from the other side will be "time", lack of time in particular. We value our "free time" in this country and tend to lose sight of prioritizing and become selfish with it. What we're discussing is a time management issue, and if we are to expect our own students to arrive to our classes on time and give them advice about managing time wisely we should be heeding it ourselves."

"From a student's perspective, eliminating synchronous communication would devalue the course and subsequently the reputation of the university."

Clarification

Students generally regard synchronous sessions as an opportunity to receive answers to their questions about the course:

"Synchronous, live sessions are a useful and valuable tool for students, a convenient middle ground for students who need immediate clarification and reduction of course complexities."

"Meeting live is a direct approach to asking and answering questions, which gives students and instructor an opportunity to meet and discuss course-related information."

"I think that collaborate sessions can be valuable in learning answers to questions you may not have even realized needed to be asked. In my past experiences my classmates have asked questions that I had not thought about during these sessions and the answers have helped guide my work through the course."

Communication and Collaboration

Many students also argue that synchronous sessions are an effective way to establish relationships, communicate and collaborate in the class as a community, and learn:

"Synchronous sessions are the only face-to-face interaction in an online class where we can establish and maintain that human connection."

"Live communication opens peer interaction, allows us to commiserate with other students and learn about your classmates which helps to know who you want to partner with in collaborate assignments."

"Synchronous meetings can be advantageous due to the discourse that can come about. You also get a chance to hear different perspectives of the information, which help me expand my knowledge of the given information."

"Live sessions contribute to developing communication and social skills."

Accommodation to Different Learning Abilities

Some students are concerned that asynchronous only learning may create difficulties for them:

"As an auditory learner, I definitely learn best via listening to people speak."

"We speak in our classes about multiple means of representation and including technology as a means of reaching all learners and yet this option may disappear in the asynchronous mode. Personally, I am a learner that needs visual and auditory reinforcement and it becomes mundane to do all academic interaction in online classes with one's own keyboard. If it is eliminated, it will be cutting off a vital learning modality and if the University is a proponent of reaching ALL learners, stopping this would be in opposition to this."

Character of Interaction

A few responders pointed to the specific character of live, synchronous communication:

"When you are face-to-face with your partner or opponent, you must be able to find the right words and formulate your argument spontaneously, you have no time to ponder on the answers. This is critical in real life situations."

A smaller group of responders (22.9%) preferred asynchronous sessions due to the following reasons:

Busy schedule: "I signed up for purely online classes so I could be the ultimate decision maker when I work on assignments and with everything else being assigned."

Not helpful: "They do not help me in regard to course content. I only feel that they are helpful when it comes to clarifying assignments or specific questions, which could technically most times be answered over email."

Poor peer participation: "Synchronous meetings can be advantageous due to the discourse that can come about, but I have found that most of the time that doesn't happen. Take our course for example, it was usually myself, Michael, and 1-2 others that participated. I find that's that norm in synchronous sessions. Student contribution usually doesn't add much to my knowledge".

Having confidence in one's own abilities: "I don't see it as a learning opportunity because I have always done the learning on my own."

Almost a quarter of responders (24.2%) stated they could learn both with and without synchronous sessions depending on situation:

"Whereas I recognize the synchronous live sessions do somewhat contribute to learning, I think it is a difficult requirement to make. Many students choose online classes because it allows for flexibility in the work schedule."

"I prefer asynchronous learning over synchronous live sessions in most classes. I enjoy being able to manage my work on my own time, but I can also appreciate the value that synchronous live sessions hold."

While the majority of students appreciate the value of synchronous sessions, one of the main reasons for the synchronous sessions to be unpopular among quite a few students is the instructors' inadequate skills at conducting live communication with students. Educators quickly unlearned to work with students directly in a convenient online environment, possess a lack of inspiration, and low level of responsibility for the students' learning outcomes.

Many students expressed their dissatisfaction with the way instructors set up and run synchronous sessions:

"While I think I could benefit from synchronous sessions, I notice that not all instructors are willing to get to know their students and interact or discuss important class topics/issues."

"Sadly, out of all my 13 classes only 5 instructors had the live meetings."

"Most of them (live sessions), unlike yours, were only about watching a PowerPoint and asking Q's at the end. We can read most PowerPoints on our own."

"The live session for this course was the first live session I've ever heard that actually discussed the content of the course and not just assignment requirements."

As follows from this survey, due to a number of benefits ranging from a general positive attitude towards the learning and communication to the appreciated worth of live interaction and collaboration, the majority of respondents favor synchronous live sessions, and also accommodation to different learning preferences. A group of students, who are very concerned about their own time and certain aspects of synchronous sessions, including some of the instructors' unprofessional handling and peers' poor participation, prefers asynchronous learning mode. One of the reasons for students to not favor synchronous interactions is their peers' passive attitude and poor engagement with the class during live sessions. It should be noted that students' inactive involvement in synchronous sessions could be attributed not only to students' preferences but also to the instructors' inability to organize active, inspiring and useful interactions in the sessions. Ineffective facilitation of live sessions by some instructors' negatively impacts students' opinion of synchronous learning events and diverts them from attending these sessions. So, it looks like students would participate more actively in synchronous sessions had those not limited the flexibility of online learning and offered more value.

STUDENT INDEPENDENCE OR SOCIAL PARTICIPATION IN ONLINE LEARNING?

The debate about asynchronous versus synchronous learning boils down to the choice between independent learning and social participation. Online learning is almost exclusively an autonomous enterprise, as we mentioned before. Success in the online class heavily depends on a student's ability to independently and actively engage in the learning process (Wang, Shannon, & Ross, 2013). Online students are expected to be more autonomous, self-regulated and self-sufficient than traditional brick and mortar college students, as the very nature of online education promotes self-directed learning (Serdyukov & Hill, 2013). According to research, however, effective time management, which is one of the attributes of an autonomous learner, is not a typical characteristic of the online learner (Cerezo, Esteban, Sánchez-Santillán, & Núñez 2017). Ineffective time management can jeopardize student's online learning outcomes.

Moreover, fully asynchronous learning drives students further into an obscure room of solitary experience and out of a lighted hall of cheerful social engagement. Students in online learning are already isolated – they have become virtual characters communicating with other virtual participants solely with or via the computer or cell phone, not live members of the team of like-minded collaborators working towards a common goal. While we do need solitude for deep thinking and concentration, learning is more than just an independent study – it is, as we know from Lev Vygotsky, a social process.

Vygotsky argued everything is learned on two levels: first, through interaction with others, and then integrated into the individual's mental structure (Vygotsky,1978). Bandura's social learning theory also suggests that through observation and modeling of behavior of others, a person will develop socially and cognitively (Bandura, 1977). We do learn through communication (Hills, 1979), and the teaching-learning process is essentially an act of communication (Mustea, 2016). According to Moore and Kearsley's transactional distance learning theory (1996), the two critical elements of effective online learning are dialogue and autonomy, both ensuring quality learning. All these theories clearly emphasize the value of synchronous interactions in online learning suggesting that it precedes the asynchronous learning. Independent learning does not predicate the eviction of synchronous communication, socialization and collaboration from online learning. Additionally, active social life, according to research, lowers anxiety and drives evolution (Nolfi & Floreano, 1999). Learning is definitely a form of evolution.

Thus, regarding the learning as a social process we have to consider vital social aspects of online interactions within a learning environment. Productive learning environments are characterized by supportive and warm interactions throughout the class: teacher-student and student-student. (Interpersonal Relationships 2012). Scholars refer to the connectedness one feels toward his or her classmates as social presence. It is defined as "the ability of learners to project themselves socially and affectively into a community of inquiry" (Rourke, Anderson, et al., 1999), or "a measure of the feeling of community that a learner experiences in an online environment (Tu, McIsaac, 2002). Learning communities have been shown to increase student cognitive skills, academic performance, retention rates, and overall satisfaction with college (Arensdorf, Naylor-Tincknell, 2016). Our own research indicated, however, that online students are reluctant to engage in collaboration because they do not trust their potential partners as they do not know them (Serdyukov & Hill, 2013). Trust as the foundation of collaboration emerges in prolonged, close, live relationships.

Yet latest developments in online learning seem to disrupt this social fabric of education and turn the latter into a totally individual enterprise. Though some technology enthusiasts proclaim the end of solitude (Kozak, 2016), in actuality, people are now becoming lonelier even if they are virtually connected to the whole world – the world of strangers with whom relationships are superficial and short-lived: easy to get into and even easier to get out of. Technology has created a new kind of voluntary solitude, which is hiding under a disguise of social networking and unlimited connectedness. Does anyone seriously believe that digital interaction via various technical devices can replace normal, close and warm personal communication and relationships? But solely asynchronous communication in online classes does even worse: it adversely affects the learning by breaking the human link that emerges in synchronous contacts and turns the learning into a completely impersonal, formal and artificial activity with ghost proxies instead of real people. Students, like all people, need human relationships, friendship, affirmation and emotional support which can only be obtained in live, prolonged, face-to-face interactions.

Online college students want to be part of a community. More than half of respondents of one recent study say interaction with classmates and instructors is important to them, and about a quarter of respondents in another study say online courses could be improved by more contact with their instructors and more engagement with classmates (Online college students, 2017). These findings correlate with the author's own research cited above and make a case for sustained, multidimensional interactions and relationships in online learning rather than a solitary, autonomous experience.

TIME FACTOR OF ONLINE LEARNING

Online learning appeal comes not only from its convenience and flexibility but also from the time factor – students, especially working adults, value time more than tuition fees and appreciate any opportunity to save it (Serdyukov, 2008). They also generally maintain that it is less time demanding than onsite, classroom learning, which is essentially true, and hope to complete the courses quickly. Ryan (1991) explains, "Time can be considered an absolute factor that affects a given learning experience. The allocation of time is the single most controllable, and therefore, one of the most powerful operational decisions a school (and students – P.S.) can make". Time factor in online learning in critical, and "a time and process perspective is useful for the improvement of courses in different respects, and these courses can, at the same time, be designed to include students with time and place obstacles to face-to-face participation in classrooms. In a world when communication possibilities constantly improve, and people become accommodated to the communication tools, time factors are likely to gain interest" (Norberg, Stöckel, & Antti 2017, p. 52).

How do students evaluate their time investment in online learning? Students in one study (Online college students 2017) indicate that in order to be able to learn independently they need more time (64.72%) and be able to better organize their time – 50.05%. This response clearly points to the insufficient time adult students have for learning and their concern over their ability to manage the time effectively. Students write, "online classes can be overwhelming when one has a full-time work schedule… "time has a lot to do with my success" (Serdyukov & Serdyukova 2012).

Let's consider the triple function time performance in online learning:

1.   Value for students;
2.   Course logistics and time management of learning;
3.   Simultaneity of learning events.

Time has an utmost value for adult students, as shown above. Convenience of online learning assures that students are controlling their time in it – they are attracted by the flexibility of scheduling their learning and a potential for saving time. Time obstacles, on the contrary, can either avert students from taking courses or affect their performance and learning outcomes. Synchronicity is one of the time obstacles; frequency of the learning events, their duration and deadlines are the others.

Course logistics involves such characteristics as course duration, course structure, frequency of the learning events, schedule of events, number of assignments, estimated time per assignment, time period between them, submission dates, pace of learning and others. Timing of the course events, like mortar, holds the learning together (Serdyukov & Serdyukova, 2012), hence effective time management is key to students' success.

Online courses present distinct challenges for student engagement and effective time management (Miertschin, Goodson, & Stewart 2015). Cereso, Esteban, et al. (2017) confirm the association of time management and academic achievement in the LMS. They show how a more organized learning process can lead to academic success. Shepperd (2002) found time management to be a predictor of student success. He moreover stated poor time management was a reason for dropping distance education courses. Therefore, time management in online learning deserves special attention.

Time management involves the following factors:

- Overall time investment in learning (how much time will it take me to complete the program?)
- Frequency of learning events (how many times do I have to attend class sessions or sit for a task?)
- Time management (how best to fit my learning into an already busy schedule and make good use of it?)
- Pace of learning (how fast do I proceed with the course tasks?)
- Time on task (how much time do I need to accomplish this assignment?)
- Deadline (when do I have to submit my work?)
- Imminence of information exchange (how soon will I receive instructor's response or feedback, or my peers' comments?)
- Time efficiency of learning (how can I minimize my time expenditures in the course?)

The time of the day when communication or learning events take place in the class, task completion (now or later? - Chauhan 2017), instructor's response to a question or concern (now or later) are also significant factors in this debate about asynchronous or synchronous modes of learning.

Synchronicity is associated with simultaneity as the function of time, which is the relation between two events assumed to be happening at the same time in a given frame of reference (now and here in the online course). Simultaneity of interactions within an online course is as much important for its success as the non-simultaneity or deferment between the learning events impacts students' performance in a number of ways, as we have discussed above. It is appropriate to couple simultaneity with synchronicity, and non-simultaneity with asynchronicity in the context of this discourse. The conflict between asynchronous and synchronous learning thus has a temporal dimension based on the simultaneity factor.

It is clear that synchronous learning involves more time than asynchronous learning as it restricts students' flexibility and increases mandatory time on some collective tasks. Communication and collaboration really demand additional time. When selecting between asynchronous and synchronous modes students, especially working adults, tend to look for ways how to minimize the time on learning wherever possible. Many students, as shown in (Serdyukov, Hill 2013), do not want to waste time on establishing relationships necessary for effective teamwork.

Asynchronous learning allows to save time by skipping compulsory class events, like synchronous sessions, improves flexibility of the schedule which lowers the anxiety and easies the stress, and also yields extra time for the more demanding tasks that can be done independently. But this is all about course logistics and time management. Does it help improve the overall time-efficiency of the learning, which is determined by the ratio between the measurable learning outcomes achieved in the program and the time spent? We know that every learning activity requires concentration and a certain time to fulfill, and this time depends on many individual factors, such as attention, abilities, attitude, background knowledge, experience, learning skills, and others. Trying to economize time on some activities may result in the deterioration of the learning outcome quality. Instructors already continuously complain that online students usually skip their announcements, emails, and comments on the assignments, which provide critical guidelines and feedback for effective learning; students do not have time to read them! Moreover, it appears students often do not (a) read the prompts for assignments and discussions, (b) try to understand written directions, (c) follow directions, (d) seek clarification, (e) implement directions, and (f) read course texts or watch assigned videos and PowerPoint presentations in preparation of assignments. As a result, students' performance is often lower than desirable. Synchronous sessions help to cope with these issues.

Similarly, procrastination, which is another time factor, was found to produce a negative impact on completion. Procrastination is an additional destructive aspect of asynchronicity as it affects time on learning. While deadline is usually at some time in the future, in the absence of regular, frequent and required class sessions under the instructor's supervision students tend to lose discipline and start procrastinating. Is there a link between asynchronicity and procrastination? This question brings time into the discussion again because it allows seeing both learning modes in the correct perspective within a scope of their discipline. When a student considers the question when to do the assignment, now or later, asynchronous learning mode may cause a postponement of the activity, especially if the student possesses poor time management skills, which often leads to inadequate learning outcomes. As established in Cereso, Esteban et al. (2017), there is an association between procrastination and student performance. Procrastination is one of the most extended lapses in time management and a common student behavior in every educational stage (Terry 2002, Karatas, 2015). Sánchez (2010) found these behaviors to be present in 80% of university students and it was chronic in 20% of them.

Michinov, Brunot, et al. (2011), furthermore, argue that procrastination and performance in online learning environments is mediated by the level of the learners' participation in discussion forums. In another research it was found that time investment in the course interactions pays off: the time students participate in class discussions ultimately affects their grades: the more they involve themselves, the higher are the grades (Serdyukov & Serdyukova, 2012). This finding validates the importance of sufficient student time allocation for learning and interaction. Interestingly, as was shown in the same research, students' participation in discussions correlates to a considerable degree with the instructor's engagement in these discussions, which emphasizes the importance of instructor's role modelingIt helps understand students' negative attitude towards live synchronous interactions in some cases and discontent with quite a few instructors' lax involvement in synchronous discussions that was discussed earlier.

These time factors clearly underscore the importance of regular and required synchronous class sessions to ensure learning quality as these sessions instill discipline and a certain responsibility among students. Much research demonstrates that synchronous learning needs to be a part of online courses. Koutsabasis, Stavrakis et al. (2011), for example, suggest that the main recommendations that stem out of their study are related to the enhancement of the e-learning platform with more synchronous and "live" content."

The answer to the question "now or later" has far reaching ramifications: what students lose due to the asynchronous "later" participation in the course may be gained in the synchronous "now" interaction. Making teaching and learning more effectual via the clock is a challenge: it calls for productive methods and strategies, stronger instructor's leadership, special online tools, and effective time management. The secret of successful learning is in the efficient use of every moment of the study and keeping students actively engaged in learning activities (Serdyukov & Serdyukova, 2009). Therefore, optimal time management for all learning activities may contribute to a more efficient expenditure of the limited course time and produce better learning outcomes. These issues demonstrate close relationship between qualitative and quantitative aspects of learning as expressed in the time factors, which pertains to all forms of education, especially the online one.

PLAGIARISM AND CHEATING

There is one more disconcerting aspect of online learning, especially in the asynchronous mode, which impacts academic rigor and outcomes: online learning is fraught with plagiarism and peruse of ready-made materials (Roberts, 2008; Evering & Moorman, 2012). The computer screen has a quality of separating the student from the instructor and the rest of the class. It assures invisibility and anonymity. It is easy to cheat when nobody sees you, isn't it? This phenomenon, according to Koran (2017), is pervasive.

Cheating has two conjoint sides, the students' and the instructor's: students may use readymade materials found on the internet and have somebody take the test for them; instructors bamboozle by making formal appearances in online classes and providing superficial teaching. While there are various methods to combat student cheating, it eventually comes down to the instructor how to be a responsible educator and how to react to student's poor performance, and to the administrative control of the instruction. Many instructors, as it was observed through teaching and supervising online classes, do not maintain active presence nor the required rigor in online classes letting students have their own way (Hill & Serdyukov, 2010). They may run a standard, shallow feedback to all students in the class without detailed, critical assessment or pointing to specific individual flaws and mistakes, which doesn't contribute to students' growth.

Fortunately for instructors, today's LMS's are so sophisticated that the instructor's part is already reduced to a minimum – no lectures, no real discourse, and no demanding face-to-face interaction with students when in an asynchronous mode. As opposed to traditional educators who had to prepare and deliver in college lecture halls containing complex course content and conduct challenging live lessons and seminars, online instructors just don't do it anymore, and have gradually unlearned to teach (Serdyukov, 2015). Online delivery offers ample opportunities for instructor's cheating. First of all, teaching asynchronous online class is a huge time saver for the instructors, like to the students. It offers a comfortable opportunity to make some money on the side – a massive demand for part-time teaching online courses by retired educators or active college instructors is a proof of that. Along with students' enjoying convenience of online learning, instructors too fell to the convenience of online teaching - we know today's online college educators are professors only nominally, in actuality they are all facilitators.

What is facilitation? According to a dictionary definition, to facilitate means to make an action or process easier. Thus, the online instructor's role is no longer a leadership one, but a secondary, supportive one, and does not even require classroom management, which is done effectively by the LMS. Hence, interaction with students is cognitively and emotionally less loaded, responsibility for the outcomes is low, and the whole instruction (facilitation) involves only a few actions: introducing students into the course, helping to navigate it, answering students' questions, explaining assignments and occasionally the content, sustaining students' participation in the discussions through random direct engagement, and, finally, grading. There is no need to prepare for the class because students do their learning independently using LMS' instructional functions and uploaded content. Soon, we will need no instructors to perform these limited functions altogether as machine learning systems will take care of all students' needs. True, somebody must develop new courses, but a few experienced faculty members will do it. After that, institutions will have no problem to manage (facilitate) a fully prefabricated instructional product using machines. As of today, instructor facilitation of online learning is generally ineffective. To ensure a higher quality of the learning outcomes online instructors must resume their leadership role, leading by example and role modeling (Hill & Serdyukov, 2010). Quality of teaching, in sum, is a matter of professional expertise, continuous professional development, disposition, responsibility, and, last but not least, administrative quality control.

WHAT TO DO?

As has been established, both asynchronous and synchronous modes of online learning perform a variety of useful functions and each offers numerous advantages. To ensure quality-learning outcomes both ought to be used in concert as these modes function best in a complementary relationship. The goal of successful course management is not to exclude one or the other mode from online learning using a subtractive approach but employ an additive approach instead which allows to integrate both and take advantage of each in effective combinations. This additive approach is supported by seminal works of Vygotskiy, Bandura, Moore and Kearsley, and others; in addition, there are numerous publications which argue for the differentiation of instruction and insist that students be offered multiple means of representation and engagement based on the principles of Universal Design for Learning (Meyer, Rose, & Gordon, 2014).

An example of such a compromise is hybrid or blended learning (BL). BL "refers to a variety of practices and strategies" for enabling students to learn online at least some of the time and maintain a level of control over the "time, place, path or pace of their learning" (Schaffhauser, 2018)). Initially BL related to the integration of face-to-face and online instruction (Graham, 2013) or mixing offline/onsite and online learning and supplementing in-person instruction with digital content and tools. Now this notion of BL is extended to include blended online learning (BOL) as a special case. Whereas in ordinary BL face-to-face classroom instruction is complemented with asynchronous online instruction, BOL adds synchronous online learning to enhance otherwise asynchronous online course (Fadde, 2014).

So, one can identify three major types of blended programs:

1. Combining onsite (in-campus) classes with online asynchronous learning;
2. Integrating synchronous sessions into asynchronous online learning;
3. Merging both types into a hybrid, mixed-mode learning to unite all three approaches: online asynchronous, online synchronous, and onsite (classroom) synchronous live.

Blended learning has been referred to as a catalyst of potential change in institutions of higher education because there is a little bit of old and new mixed together, but it needs a better articulated definition so that higher education institutions can align their strategic goals to be successful at facilitating blended learning (Moskal, Dzinban, & Hartmen, 2013). BL has been found to, not only bring flexibility into student learning, but also to help institutions explore efficient use of space and faculty time (Dziuban, Graham et al., 2018; Yamagata-Lynch, 2014; Bates, 2016). Quite a few investigators have assembled a comprehensive agenda of transformative and innovative research issues for BL that have the potential to enhance effectiveness (Garrison & Kanuka, 2004; Picciano, 2009). Generally, research has found that BL results in improvement of student success and satisfaction, (Dziuban & Moskal, 2011; Means, Toyama et al. 2013) as well as an increase in students' sense of community (Rovai & Jordan, 2004, Dziuban et al., 2018). Combining asynchronous and synchronous modes in right proportions, students will eventually develop autonomous learning competency together with maintaining their social, communication and collaborations skills (McDonald 2016).

An interesting concept of polysynchronous communication which is "a form of a dialogue that takes place via technical functionality that flows flexibly and simultaneously between asynchronous and synchronous potential, and according to individual end-user workflows" is offered by Oztok (Oztok et al. 2014, 158).

Blending various interaction modes requires consideration of a number of factors: course goals, content, structure, instructional methodology, available technology and importance of live interaction for the preset learning outcomes; these factors determine the ratio between asynchronous and synchronous modes. Graham (2006) suggested that BL be not based on percentages of instructional delivery mode, but on what is being blended. Graham referred to instructional modalities/delivery media, methods, and the proportion of online and face-to-face instruction as elements that take a role in defining BL. The use of technology, thus, appears not to be primarily responsible for the learning outcomes. Rather, the biggest effect comes when instructors determine what material they teach and how they teach it (Lederman, 2017; Giesbers, Rienties, Tempelaar, & Gijselaers, 2013).

The goal of the blended program is consequently to identify the most effective combination of instructor, content, and interaction modes to promote student success. Those students who can, participate in live sessions; others who are too far away or too busy to travel, can take part in the sessions via videoconferencing using their computers or mobile devices. In this way we have a synchronous session conducted by an instructor where students can engage both with the instructor and also with all of the class regardless of their location. When offering online classes, institutions must provide opportunities for class meeting onsite whenever possible.

To make synchronous learning an integral part of effective college education we need to institute the rules mandatory for all students, like we do in school: require live participation and collaboration, and teach students better time management skills, appreciation of social learning, live interaction and collaboration in teams. Ground rules, as Yamagata-Lynch (2014) suggested, need to be established and enforced.

Rules:

- Students are expected to participate in all asynchronous and synchronous course interactions: threaded discussions, blogs and live collaborate sessions.
- All interactions are mandatory and graded.
- Students are required to demonstrate meaningful participation through the use of webcams and microphones.
- To ensure effectiveness of live sessions, they must be integrated into the course content and linked to the assignments, course materials, and asynchronous interactions.
- The instructor effectively conducts live sessions and mediates the asynchronous discussions.

Online education should be built, as has been suggested by (Serdyukov & Sistek-Chandler, 2015), on a highly interactive model, one that boosts social presence, active communication, and collaboration; helps establish relationships among all stakeholders, and encourages the creation of a learning community.

CONCLUSION

While it is true that growth of education comes from technological innovations today, it might be wrong to think that letting students and institutions of higher learning to go unchecked regarding online learning will lead to better quality of specialists. Making the learning too easy and too convenient is not the best way to ensure academic excellence, unless we want to make student satisfaction a topmost priority. Pragmatism and consumerism in learning are costly socially.

One of the goals of education is to develop autonomous, efficient, life-long learners who are effective workers, collaborators and active members of society. Online learning can help students develop these qualities, however, while offering students various opportunities to develop independent learning skills, students must also have opportunities for live, synchronous interactions with their peers and instructors, and engage in socialization and collaborative teamwork with their peers and instructors in real time. Similarly, instructors must also engage in class interactions, led by example, inspire, role model and ensure that students develop the necessary qualities of autonomous learners, social communicators and collaborators alike.

To maintain a healthy balance between convenience and academic/social benefits in online college courses, we need to integrate regular synchronous meetings into the predominantly asynchronous routine. A complementary relationship between asynchronous and synchronous modes should be assured: they can smoothly function within the course context even if they pursue different goals and perform diverse functions. An additive approach implemented through blended online learning is undeniably the best option. We must maintain involvement of both students and instructors in the learning process. There are multiple ways to do it so that students could adapt their busy schedule to the course requirements. Where there is a will, there is a way.

REERENCES

Allen, I. E., & Seaman, J. (2017). Digital Compass Learning: Distance Education Enrollment Report 2017. *Babson survey research group*.

Arensdorf, J., & Naylor-Tincknell, J. (2016). Beyond the Traditional Retention Data: A Qualitative Study of the Social Benefits of Living Learning Communities. *Learning Communities: Research & Practice*, *4*(1), 4.

Asfaranjan, Y., Shirzad, F., Baradari, M., Salimi, M., & Salehi, M. (2013). Alleviating the Senses of Isolation and Alienation in the Virtual World: Socialization in Distance Education. *Procedia: Social and Behavioral Sciences*, *93*(October), 332–337.

AZ Quotes. (2019). Bill Gates. *Wise Old Sayings*. Retrieved from https://www.azquotes.com/author/5382-Bill_Gates/tag/vision

Bandura, A. (1977). *Social learning theory*. Englewood Cliffs, NJ: Prentice Hall.

Bates, T. (2016). *Online learning for beginners*: 1. What is online learning? Online Learning and Distance Education Resources. Retrieved from https://www.tonybates.ca/2016/07/15/online-learning-for-beginners-1-what-is-online-learning/

Bocchi, J., Eastman, J., & Swift, C. (2004). Retaining the online learner: Profile of students in an online MBA program and implications for teaching them. *Journal of Education for Business*, *79*(4), 245–253. doi:10.3200/JOEB.79.4.245-253

Boling, E., Hough, M., Krinsky, H., Saleem, H., & Stevens, M. (2012, March). Cutting the distance in distance education: Perspectives on what promotes positive, online learning experiences. *The Internet and Higher Education*, *15*(2), 118–126. doi:10.1016/j.iheduc.2011.11.006

Cerezo, R., Esteban, M., Sánchez-Santillán, M, & Núñez, J. (2017). Procrastinating Behavior in Computer-Based Learning Environments to Predict Performance: A Case Study in Moodle.

Cerezo, R., Esteban, M., Sánchez-Santillán, M., & Núñez, J. C. (2017). Procrastinating Behavior in Computer-Based Learning Environments to Predict Performance: A Case Study in Moodle. *Frontiers in Psychology*, *8*, 1403. doi:10.3389/fpsyg.2017.01403

Chauhan, V. (2017) Synchronous and Asynchronous Learning. *Imperial Journal of Interdisciplinary Research* (IJIR) 3(2), 1345-1348. Retrieved from https://www.stitcher.com/podcast/citr-synchronicity

Chen, W., & You, M. (2007). The Differences Between the Influences of Synchronous and Asynchronous Modes on Collaborative Learning Project of Industrial Design. In *Online Communities and Social Computing: Second International Conference, OCSC 2007* (pp. 275-283). Academic Press. 10.1007/978-3-540-73257-0_31

Christensen, C., & Eyring, H. (2011). *The innovative university: Changing the DNA of higher education from the inside out*. San Francisco, CA: Jossey-Bass.

Cole, M., Shelley, D., & Swartz, L. (2014). Online instruction, e-learning, and student satisfaction: A three-year study. *The International Review of Research in Open and Distributed Learning*, *15*(6). doi:10.19173/irrodl.v15i6.1748

Comprehensive Data on Demands and Preferences. (2017, June 24). *The Learning House, Inc. and Aslanian Market Research*. Retrieved from https://www.learninghouse.com/knowledge-center/research-reports/ocs2017/?utm_source=pressrelease&medium=PR&utm_campaign=OCS2017

Cook, C., Kilgus, S., & Burns, M. (2018). Advancing the science and practice of precision education to enhance student outcomes. *Journal of School Psychology*, *66*, 4–10. doi:10.1016/j.jsp.2017.11.004

Dewey, J. (1916). *Democracy and education: An introduction to the philosophy of education*. New York: Macmillan.

Dziuban, C., Graham, C., Moskal, P., Norberg, A., & Sicilia, N. (2018). Blended learning: The new normal and emerging technologies. *International Journal of Educational Technology in Higher Education, 15*(1), 3. doi:10.118641239-017-0087-5

Dziuban, C., & Moskal, P. (2011). A course is a course is a course: Factor invariance in student evaluation of online, blended and face-to-face learning environments. *The Internet and Higher Education, 14*(4), 236–241. doi:10.1016/j.iheduc.2011.05.003

Evering, L., & Moorman, G. (2012, September). Rethinking Plagiarism in the Digital Age. *JAAL, 56*(1), 35–44. doi:10.1002/JAAL.00100

Fadde, P., & Vu, P. (2014). Blended Online Learning: Benefits, Challenges, and Misconceptions. In P. Lowenthal, C. S. York, & J. C. Richardson (Eds.), *Online Learning: Common Misconceptions, Benefits and Challenges* (pp. 33–48). New York: Nova.

Garrison, D. R., & Kanuka, H. (2004). Blended learning: Uncovering its transformative potential in higher education. *The Internet and Higher Education, 7*(2), 95–105. doi:10.1016/j.iheduc.2004.02.001

Garrison, R., & Cleveland-Innes, M. (2005). Facilitating cognitive presence in online learning: interaction is not enough. *American Journal of Distance Education, 19*(3), 133-148. doi:0.120715389286ajde1903_2

Giesbers, B., Rienties, B., Tempelaar, D., & Gijselaers, W. (2013). A Dynamic Analysis of the Interplay between Asynchronous and Synchronous Communication in Online Learning: The Impact of Motivation. *Journal of Computer Assisted Learning.* doi:10.1111/jcal.12020

Goik, A. (2018, September 6). How Convenience and Comfort Caused the Downfall of Personal Responsibility. *The Accent.* Retrieved from https://theascent.pub/how-convenience-and-comfort-caused-the-downfall-of-personal-responsibility-feebbd6dabed

Graham, C. (2006). Blended learning systems: Definition, current trends, and future directions. In C.J. Bonk & C.R. Graham (Eds.), The Handbook of Blended Learning: Global Perspectives, Local Designs. San Francisco, CA: John Wiley and Sons.

Graham, C. (2013). Emerging practice and research in blended learning. In M. Moore (Ed.), *Handbook of Distance Education* (3rd ed.). New York: Routledge. doi:10.4324/9780203803738.ch21

Hill, R., & Serdyukov, P. (2010). Setting the example: Role modeling in an online class. In *Proceedings of 21ˢᵗ International Conference of the Society for Information Technology and Teacher Education. (SITE).* Academic Press.

Hills, J. (1979). *Teaching and learning as a communication process.* Hoboken, NJ: Wiley & Sons.

Hrastinski, S. (2008). Asynchronous & Synchronous E-Learning. *EDUCAUSE Quarterly*, *4*, 51–55. http://sigproject.pbworks.com/f/sychronous+and+asychrouns+tools.pdf

Hrastinski, S. (2010). The informal and formal dimensions of computer-mediated communication: A model. *International Journal of Networking and Virtual Organizations*, *7*(1), 23–38. doi:10.1504/IJNVO.2010.029869

Karatas, H. (2015). Correlation among academic procrastination, personality traits, and academic achievement. *Anthropologist*, *20*, 243–255.

Kerby, M., Branham, K., Gayle, M., & Mallinger, G. (2014). Consumer-Based Higher Education: The Uncaring of Learning. *Journal of Higher Education Theory and Practice*, *14*(5), 42–54. Retrieved from http://www.na-businesspress.com/JHETP/KerbyMB_Web14_5_.pdf

Koran, M. (2017). 'It's Worse Than You Think': Teachers, Students Say Online Cheating Is Pervasive. *Voice of San Diego*. Retrieved from https://www.voiceofsandiego.org/topics/education/worse-think-teachers-students-say-online-cheating-pervasive/

Koutsabasis, P., Stavrakis, M., Spyrou, T., & Darzentas, J. (2011). *Perceived Impact of Asynchronous E-Learning after Long-Term Use: Implications for Design and Development.* https://pdfs.semanticscholar.org/b5c0/a7efb16813311139468be68d9c8c47 a6b24d.pdf

Kozak, A. (2016) *The End of Solitude: Overtaken by Technology.* Quiet Review. Retrieved from https://www.quietrev.com/the-end-of-solitude-overtaken-by-technology/

Ku, T. D., & Chang, C. S. (2011). The effect of academic discipline and gender difference on Taiwanese college students' learning styles and strategies in Web-based learning environments. *The Turkish Online Journal of Educational Technology, 10*(3).

Lederman, D. (2017) *What Works in Blended Learning.* Inside Higher Ed. Retrieved from https://www.insidehighered.com/digital-learning/article/2017/07/26/researchs-clues-what-works-blended-learning

Lehman, R. M., & Conceição, S. C. O. (2010). *Creating a sense of presence in online teaching: How to "be there" for distance learners.* San Francisco, CA: Jossey-Bass.

Livni, E. (2018, December 11). The science of "vibes" shows how everything is connected. *Quarz,* 2018. Retrieved from https://qz.com/1490276/the-science-of-vibes-shows-how-everything-is-connected/

Mabrito, M. (2006). A Study of Synchronous Versus Asynchronous Collaboration in an Online Business Writing Class. *American Journal of Distance Education,* *20*(2), 93–107. doi:10.120715389286ajde2002_4

Matos, N. (2016). *There's no such thing as asynchronous teaching.* Chronicle Vitae. Retrieved from https://chroniclevitae.com/news/1471-there-s-no-such-thing-as-asynchronous-teaching

Maurer, H. (2015). Is the Internet turning us into dummies? *Communications of the ACM,* *58*(1), 48–51. doi:10.1145/2629544

McDonald, D. (2016). *Asynchronous vs. Synchronous Communication in the Online Classroom. Center for Teaching and Learning.* Learning House. Retrieved from https://ctl.learninghouse.com/asynchronous-vs-synchronous-communication-in-the-online-classroom/

Means, B., Toyama, Y., Murphy, R., & Baki, M. (2013). The effectiveness of online and blended learning: A meta-analysis of the empirical literature. *Teachers College Record,* *115*(3), 1–47.

Meyer, A., Rose, D. H., & Gordon, D. (2014). *Universal Design for Learning, Theory and Practice.* CAST Professional Publishing.

Michinov, N., Brunot, S., Le Bohec, O., Juhel, J., & Delaval, M. (2011). Procrastination, participation, and performance in online learning environments. *Computers & Education,* 2011, 243-252. Retrieved from http://primarythinking.net/EDGE/content/EDGE904/Activity%201%20-%20Reading%201a.pdf

Miertschin, S., Goodson, C., & Stewart, B. (2015). Time Management Skills and Student Performance in Online Courses. In *ASEE Conference and Exposition Proceedings.* Retrieved from 10.18260/p.24921

Moore, M., & Kearsley, G. (1996). *Distance education: A systems review.* Belmont: Wadsworth Publishing Company.

Moskal, P., Dziuban, C., & Hartman, J. (2013). Blended Learning: A Dangerous Idea? *Internet and Higher Education,* *18,* 15–23. doi:10.1016/j.iheduc.2012.12.001

Mupinga, D., Nora, R., & Yaw, D. (2006). The learning styles, expectations, and needs of online students. *College Teaching*, *54*(1), 185–189. doi:10.3200/CTCH.54.1.185-189

Mustea, D. (2016). The Role of Communication Skills in Teaching Process. In *The European proceedings of behavioral and social science*s (pp. 430-434). Academic Press. Retrieved from https://www.futureacademy.org.uk/files/images/upload/ERD2016FA052F.pdf

Nagel, L., Blignaut, A., & Cronjé, J. (2009). Read-only participants: A case for student communication in online classes. *Interactive Learning Environments*, *17*(1), 37–51. doi:10.1080/10494820701501028

Ni, A. (2013). Comparing the effectiveness of classroom and online learning: Teaching research methods. *Journal of Public Affairs Education*, *19*(2), 199–211. doi:10.1080/15236803.2013.12001730

Nolfi, S., & Floreano, D. (1999). Learning and evolution. *Autonomous Robots*, *7*(1), 89–113. doi:10.1023/A:1008973931182

Norberg, A., Stöckel, B., & Antti, M. (2017). Time Shifting and Agile Time Boxes in Course Design. *International Review of Research in Open and Distributed Learning*, *18*(6). Retrieved from https://files.eric.ed.gov/fulltext/EJ1155830.pdf

Online education trends report. (2018). Best Colleges. Retrieved from https://www.bestcolleges.com/perspectives/annual-trends-in-online-education/

Ouzts, K. (2006). Sense of community in online courses. *The Quarterly Review of Distance Education*, *7*(3), 285–295.

Oztok, M., & Brett, C. (2011). Social Presence and Online Learning: A Review of Research. *Journal of E-Learning & Distance Education*, *35*(3). Retrieved from http://www.ijede.ca/index.php/jde/article/view/758/1299

Oztok, M., Wilton, L., Lee, K., Zingaro, D., Mackinnon, K., Makos, A., ... Hewitt, J. (2014). Polysynchronous: Dialogic construction of time in online learning. *E-Learning and Digital Media*, *11*(2), 154–161. doi:10.2304/elea.2014.11.2.154

Palloff, R., & Pratt, K. (2005). *Collaborating Online: Learning Together in Community*. San Francisco, CA: John Wiley and Sons, Inc.

Palloff, R. M., & Pratt, K. (2013). *Lessons from the Virtual Classroom: The Realities of Online Teaching*. San Francisco, CA: Josey-Bass.

Picciano, A. G. (2009). Blending with purpose: The multimodal model. *Journal of Asynchronous Learning Networks, 13*(1), 7–18.

Premack, R. (2018, September 15). Jeff Bezos said the 'secret sauce' to Amazon's success is an 'obsessive compulsive focus' on customer over competitor. *Business Insider*. Retrieved from https://www.businessinsider.com/amazon-jeff-bezos-success-customer-obsession-2018-9

Roberts, T. (2008). *Student plagiarism in an online world: Problems and solutions.* Hershey, PA: IGI Global. doi:10.4018/978-1-59904-801-7

Rourke, L., Anderson, T., Garrison, D. R., & Archer, W. (1999). Assessing social presence in asynchronous text-based computer conferencing. *Journal of Distance Education, 14*, 51–70.

Rovai, A. P., & Jordan, H. M. (2004). Blended learning and sense of community: A comparative analysis with traditional and fully online graduate courses. *International Review of Research in Open and Distance Learning, 5*(2), 1–13. doi:10.19173/irrodl.v5i2.192

Rushkoff, D. (2010). *Program or be Programmed. Ten commands for a digital age.* New York: OR books.

Russell, G. (2014). Absence of face-to-face communication is one of the benefits of online learning. *ValuEd*. Retrieved from http://blog.online.colostate.edu/blog/online-education/absence-of-face-to-face-communication-is-one-of-the-benefits-of-online-learning/

Ryan, M. (1991). Intensive learning: An answer to the dropout crisis. *NASSP Bulletin, 75538*(538), 25–30. doi:10.1177/019263659107553805

Sánchez, A. M. (2010). Procrastinación académica: Un problema en la vida universitaria. *Studiositas, 5*, 87–94.

Schaffhauser, D. (2018) Report: The real role of blended learning in instruction. *The Journal*. Retrieved from https://thejournal.com/articles/2018/03/28/report-the-real-role-of-blended-learning-in-instruction.aspx

Scruton, R. (2010). Hiding behind the screen. *New Atlantis (Washington, D.C.), 28*(Summer), 48–60. Retrieved from https://www.thenewatlantis.com/publications/hiding-behind-the-screen

Serdyukov, P. (2015). Paradox of teacher and student in online education and societal culture. *Proceedings of Global Learn 2015* (pp. 713-723). Association for the Advancement of Computing in Education.

Serdyukov, P. (2017). Innovation in education: What works, what doesn't, and what to do about it? *Journal of Research in Innovative Teaching & Learning, 10*(1), 4–33. doi:10.1108/JRIT-10-2016-0007

Serdyukov, P., & Hill, R. A. (2013). Flying with clipped wings: Are students independent in online college classes? *Journal of Research in Innovative Teaching, 6*(1), 50–65.

Serdyukov, P., & Serdyukova, N. (2006). *Adult learners in an online college class: Combining efficiency and convenience of E-learning. In Education for the 21st century: Impact of ICT and digital resources* (pp. 205–214). NY: Springer.

Serdyukov, P., & Serdyukova, N. (2009). Effective Communication in Online Learning. In *Proceedings of the 9th WCCE IFIP World Conference on Computers in Education*. Academic Press; Retrieved from http://www.wcce2009.org/proceedings/papers/WCCE2009_pap124.pdf

Serdyukov, P., & Serdyukova, N. (2012). Time as Factor of Success in Online Learning. *Journal of Information Technology and Application in Education, 1*(2), 40–46. Retrieved from http://www.jitae.org/paperInfo.aspx?ID=1203

Serdyukov, P., & Sistek-Chandler, C. (2015). Communication, collaboration and relationships in the online college class: Instructors' perceptions. *Journal of Research in Innovative Teaching, 8*(1), 116–131.

Shepperd, R. (2002). *Predictors of Students' Success in Distance Education Courses* [Dissertation]. West Virginia University, Morgantown, WV.

Stokes, P. (2012). In B. Wildavsky, A. Kelly, & K. Carey (Eds.), *What online learning can teach us about higher education? Reinventing higher education: The promise of innovation* (pp. 197–224). Cambridge, MA: Harvard Education Press.

Tauber, T. (2013). The dirty little secret of online learning: Students are bored and dropping out. *Quartz*. Retrieved from https://qz.com/65408/the-dirty-little-secret-of-online-learning-students-are-bored-and-dropping-out/

Terry, K. (2002). *The Effects of Online Time Management Practices on Self-Regulated Learning and Academic Self-Efficacy* [Doctoral dissertation]. Virginia Polytechnic Institute and State University, Blacksburg, VA.

Toppo, G. (2018, August 8). Defining 'Regular and Substantive' Interaction in the Online Era. Inside HigherEd. Retrieved from https://www.insidehighered.com/digital-learning/article/2018/08/08/new-debate-regular-and-substantive-interaction-between

Tu, C. H., & McIsaac, M. (2002). The relationship of social presence and interaction in online classes. *American Journal of Distance Education*, *16*(3), 131–150. doi:10.1207/S15389286AJDE1603_2

Vygotsky, L. (1978). *Mind in Society: Development of Higher Psychological Processes*. Cambridge, MA: MIT Press.

Wang, C., Shannon, D., & Ross, M. (2013). Students' characteristics, self-regulated learning, technology self-efficacy, and course outcomes in online learning. *Distance Education*, *34*(3), 302–323. doi:10.1080/01587919.2013.835779

Wrenn, V. (2016). *Effects of Traditional and Online Instructional Models on Student Achievement Outcomes*. Retrieved from https://digitalcommons.liberty.edu/doctoral/1135

Wu, T. (2018, February 16). The Tyranny of Convenience. *New York Times*. Retrieved from https://www.nytimes.com/2018/02/16/opinion/sunday/tyranny-convenience.html

Wubbels, T., den Brok, P., van Tartwijk, J., & Levy, J. (Eds.). (2012). *Interpersonal relationships in education: An overview of contemporary research* (Vol. 3). Springer Science & Business Media. Retrieved from https://www.springer.com/gp/book/9789460919398

Yamagata-Lynch, L. (2014, April). Blending Online Asynchronous and Synchronous Learning. *International Review of Research in Open and Distance Learning*, *15*(2). Retrieved from http://www.irrodl.org/index.php/irrodl/article/view/1778/2837

Chapter 2

The Importance of Synchronous Sessions in Online Asynchronous Classes

Everett George Beckwith
National University, USA

ABSTRACT

When online classes began being developed and made available in higher education approximately 20 years ago, the vast majority of the online classes and programs were asynchronous, meaning that instructors did not meet with students in real-time or synchronously. There were few synchronous courses, and this was due to the high expense of video teleconferencing systems and the inability of many computers to handle the high bandwidth and memory required to participate in such synchronous sessions. Now, there has been a significant revolution in video teleconferencing systems and in the computers used to access them. Systems are now affordable and most learning management systems (LMS) even have them embedded. While mobile computers, including handheld devices such as iPhones, Androids, and tablets, can access the synchronous sessions from anywhere they can access the Internet. It is time to reassess the value and effectiveness of having synchronous sessions in online classes that are primarily asynchronous.

INTRODUCTION

It was not that long ago—perhaps somewhere around 2000, give or take a few years—that higher education began to undergo a revolution in how it structured and delivered classes. With the reliability and increasing availability of the Internet and

DOI: 10.4018/978-1-7998-1622-5.ch002

the smaller, more capable computers that were mobile and could be used almost anywhere, professors could teach classes from anywhere, and students could take classes from anywhere. Conversion from onsite classes to online classes was not very difficult in that, in most cases, course designers and developers, who often were the professors teaching the class, simply took the lesson plans they used onsite and copied them into online learning management systems (LMS). Working adults made up the initial market for online classes. These working adults were waiting for something like online education with the flexibility to take classes almost anytime from almost any place. Often, these adults needed college degrees to advance in the workplace or who had always wanted to go to college but could not afford to quit their jobs to do so. Since technology at the time did not provide an inexpensive video teleconferencing system for live synchronous classes, and most mobile computers were not capable of handling the large bandwidth that video conferencing demanded, most online classes were asynchronous. For those colleges and universities already structured to support adult learners, adding an online system for teaching classes was relatively inexpensive with the only major expense being buying/obtaining an LMS to which they could move their existing classes. Obtaining additional instructors to teach the classes was relatively simple since they did not have to move and could do teach in the evening, allowing them to keep their full-time jobs.

Learning Management Systems (LMS)

A search of Online Education History reveals no definite date for the beginning of online education because there were so many variations of online education systems and tools that a beginning date can only be established if one specifies what systems/tools are included in the definition. A case can be made, however, that online education became the system as we know it today around 2000, when the first LMS's were developed and began full operation. Blackboard, perhaps the largest LMS today, was founded in 1997, and eCollege, a competitor, was developed in 1999 (History of LMS, 2020). National University (NU), where the author is a faculty member, has used both Blackboard and eCollege LMS's for its programs and courses and therefore, these are the two LMS's with which the author has the most experience and knowledge (16 years). In this paper, the author will use Blackboard and eCollege along with research findings at other colleges and universities that have online programs as examples of online classes and programs. Another factor to be taken into consideration regarding the online programs at NU is that NU is an "open enrollment" university, which means anyone can apply if they meet the basic University requirements. While the rise of online distance education has expanded learning opportunities for all students, it is often most attractive to nontraditional students, who are more likely to have employment and family obligations that make attending traditional face-to-face classes difficult (Xu, 2013). Perhaps as a consequence, online learning enrollments have increased particularly quickly at two-year colleges where a large proportion of the population are nontraditional students. The National Center for Education Statistics (2002) defines a nontraditional student as one who has any of the following seven characteristics: (1) part-time attendance, (2) full-time employment, (3) delayed postsecondary enrollment, (4) financial independence, (5) having dependents, (6) being a single parent, and (7) not possessing a high school diploma.

Course Design Considerations

Synchronous and asynchronous systems depend on commercial systems purchased by the college, university, or school/school district for use in teaching their particular curricula. The three major online learning management systems are Blackboard, Canvas, and Moodle, although there are many other systems available. These systems are primarily asynchronous platforms with synchronous system embedded in them, such as Collaborate, WebEx, Zoom, and Adobe Connect. The asynchronous platform is normally a template upon which a given education entity superimposes their chosen design. Most education institutions that contain a large portion of their academic offerings online develop some type of design standard or checklist that denotes the elements that each course will contain. For example, most online courses have a syllabus or course outline to include summary of the course content, course description, attendance requirements, instructor information, grading criteria, and provisions for students with special needs. There is usually a synchronous system like those named above embedded in the course with instructions on required equipment, like a headphone/microphone and webcam. Instructions specify the minimum bandwidth or Internet speed required for satisfactory participation in synchronous sessions. The online asynchronous part of the course is designed to teach, as closely as possible, the same academic curricula as would be found in an onsite course.

Online Asynchronous and Synchronous Course Components

These curricula elements include components like reading requirements, recorded lectures, assignments with related directions, and grading rubrics. In addition, there is usually an asynchronous threaded discussion in which students respond to specific subject topics or answer questions on the topic being considered in a given time frame. The synchronous sessions follow a similar academic topic approach as the threaded discussions but in real-time, which allows for peer-to-peer feedback on a given topic and provides interaction between students and between students and the professor. If the synchronous sessions are supportive of an asynchronous class that is advertised primarily as an asynchronous course, the course design as well as the instructional approach to the curricula should provide an appropriate balance between the asynchronous and synchronous components. Consideration should be given for accommodation between the freedom of an asynchronous class that allows the students to do their work at a time and place of their choosing and the synchronous requirement to be in that class at a specific time utilizing a specific video teleconference system. For those students who cannot be in class at a specific time and/or may not be in a place where the Internet connectivity supports video teleconferencing, there must be an alternative, which usually means requiring the student to review the recording of the session and submit a brief written report on the its content.

Online Asynchronous Tools

The online course provides some tools that the traditional onsite course does not. For example, an online course provides a grade center or gradebook where student grades are compiled and computed and a test or quiz component that allows the instructor to develop a quiz or test that is administered and graded by the system. The potential of electronic books addresses one of the historic problems of students obtaining the required course texts on time because an electronic book can be obtained and downloaded to a mobile device, like a smart phone, tablet, or Kindle-like device for immediate use. Additionally, there is the capability of recording lectures for students to view later and the potential of providing in-course videos on any number of subjects and topics. Instructors can also embed grading rubrics with each assignment developed by a rubric tool provided by the LMS software. Most LMS rubric systems also provide an analysis function that identifies whether a given assignment meets the learning outcomes of the courses as well as, in many cases, the learning outcomes of the academic program. The data from this analysis can be integrated into the assessment system of the college, university, and/or school to assist the faculty and administration in directing and utilizing their academic funding and support.

Online Synchronous Tools

The synchronous systems provided by learning management systems provide several great teaching support tools for maximizing the limited time devoted to real-time sessions. Not only do the synchronous systems provide real-time interaction and promote interpersonal relations by allowing students and the professor to see, hear, and learn, and observe the personal characteristics of those in the class, but they also provide the professor with presentation tools that permit display of information and data that allow delivery via the Internet to anywhere in the world. The system also provides a means for students to give presentations to the professor and/or the class. This includes the capability of the instructor to divide the class into smaller groups for research and development of academic projects in which students can develop leadership skills and learn how to work and problem-solve in groups.

BACKGROUND

The asynchronous instructional mode was an initial advantage for both instructors and students in that the any time and any place environment of learning was convenient for their schedules. When technology improved the effectiveness and capability of video teleconferencing systems (VTS) while significantly reducing the VTS costs, synchronous class sessions became possible. Over time, the cost and capability of video teleconferencing in support of synchronous sessions in largely asynchronous classes became one of a balance between allowing the students to do most of their work when and where they chose with periodic requirements to be in synchronous sessions at a specific date and time. The increasing amount of research (Xu & Smith, 2013) showed some clear and significant advantages of having some synchronous sessions between instructors and students as well as between students and students. As a result, there are currently three basic modalities of online academic courses: those that are primarily asynchronous, those that are primarily synchronous, and those that are a hybrid that are primarily asynchronous but includes some synchronous sessions. This chapter will explore the importance of synchronous sessions in online asynchronous classes to include the research and rationale for including both asynchronous and synchronous content in academic classes. The question that will be addressed is, "How much is appropriate and how much is too much in an online program that is advertised as a program that is primarily asynchronous?"

Many online classes have a live component where students communicate through videoconferencing. Jordan Friedman (2017), a New York-based higher education freelance reporter, captured the essence of synchronous vs. asynchronous online programs in describing ten facts about student interaction in online programs.

First, Friedman observed that face-to-face communications enhance the online experience and provide for better learning experiences, which allow the student to develop a personal relationship with the faculty and other students. Second, many online classes assign group projects that help students prepare for the workforce, according to Ray Schroeder, associate vice chancellor for online learning at the University of Illinois (Friedman, 2017). In such group projects, students learn how to use valuable online tools, such as Google Docs for editing text and Skype and online chat rooms for problem-solving and discussions. A third subject that students learn about interaction comes from their learning of what tools/equipment they need to be effective in online environments, whether the mode be synchronous or asynchronous.

They learn about the advantage of using a headset with a microphone for the best communications rather than built-in speakers and built-in microphones. Built-in components tend to create noise and poor fidelity while also allowing room noise to interfere with both microphone and speaker clarity (Friedman, 2017). Fourth, discussion boards or threaded discussion sessions in asynchronous online use permit students to respond to questions and voice their views in dialogue with their classmates and instructor. Compared to synchronous sessions where students have to respond to questions and discussion issues quickly, asynchronous sessions allow students the opportunity and the time to think before responding. Fifth, some online degree programs, such as nursing and health, require face-to-face sessions in which they must participate in activities and attend specified lectures. Sixth, online students who live near a college or university campus can meet in real-time, face-to-face while also attending synchronous online discussions, as well as, performing tasks asynchronously, thus gaining personal experience with classmates both online and in-person. Seventh, students readily use social media systems in communicating with their classmates and professors. They have the potential for creating virtual communities and using such communities to simulate reality for learning purposes. This potential is particularly valuable in teaching situations that could be dangerous in real life such as teaching safety where you would not actually want the student to fall off a ladder or slip on a floor. Eighth, online capabilities and applications allow students to participate in college or university extracurricular activities and connect via Facebook and various video conferencing software. Just because the students' major or course of study is online does not mean that they cannot participate in campus activities that can be accessed via the Internet or a variety of social media systems. Ninth, due to the worldwide connectivity of the Internet, students are part of an international community when they become online students. Thus, they are exposed to many cultures and a world campus. Tenth, and finally, Internet communications allow students to meet via social media and establish bonds with classmates across their state, the nation, and even foreign countries. Troy Cornell, an online student at the American University stated that via deep and thoughtful discussions about the course curriculum, he realized that the idea that the online format can't be as effective as an in-person format was untrue (Friedman, 2017).

OVERVIEW OF ASYNCHRONOUS PROGRAMS/COURSES

There is little to no information on the national percentage of online college courses that are synchronous versus asynchronous, however, the majority of articles retrieved on the subject referred to online asynchronous courses. The online programs of prestigious colleges, like MIT, Harvard, John Hopkins, and Cambridge are asynchronous. Because fully synchronous programs/courses comprise the minority of courses taught online and because they are very similar to on-site classrooms in their academic approach, the focus here will be on online asynchronous courses and how to improve them. This can be done by using synchronous applications to add the social and emotional advantages on synchronous courses but balancing the number of synchronous sessions so that students still are able, for the most part, to do their work when and where they choose.

The basic structure/design of an asynchronous course, depending on the college/ university and the LMS used, varies. However, in general, when the student signs on to her/his class, they see the name of the class, a welcome message from the professor, and a clickable syllabus link that provides an overview of the class, major objectives of the class, a list of learning outcomes, and college/university, state and federal mandates and requirements. Usually on the left margin here are clickable links to the major content of the course which may be organized into units, weeks, or some other division. Today, most LMS's have an embedded video teleconferencing system for synchronous sessions. Many online classes have a live component where students communicate through videoconferencing.

Fully Asynchronous Courses (Most Instructors' Preference)

According to the Business-Software Site (2019), asynchronous learning environments are one-way systems that do not allow for real-time collaboration or live participation. They do, however, deliver the obvious advantage of leveraging the maximum amount of flexibility and convenience since the student can download and view the sessions at any time, without having to coordinate with anybody.

In a fully asynchronous course, the instructor has little or no real-time interaction with students. This was understandable in the early days of online education when LMS's were just being developed. As was the author's experience at his university, most instructors simply moved their onsite lesson plans, supporting documents, and lectures to the online LMS. The vast majority of these materials and content were text-based. Multimedia and synchronous video teleconferencing were memory-heavy and expensive and, therefore, these sources were limited. In addition, instructors' limited interaction with students significantly reduced the time they had previously experienced in teaching students on-site. The time saved from the student interaction could, of course, be used to enhance and improve the assignments and content of the course, and some instructors used the additional time accordingly. However, some chose to use the time on other academic responsibilities. When the LMS's eventually began embedding video teleconferencing software in their course templates, most universities began pushing instructors to use this synchronous capability. Instructors found that preparing for and conducting these synchronous sessions took more of their time and effort, so many instructors resented this additional workload. Thus, there was a tendency to keep the synchronous sessions to a minimum. Of course, there was often, from day one, the issue of how many synchronous sessions could be held in an asynchronous class without students complaining that they no longer could do their work at their own time and place. In the face of this concern, many instructors cut back significantly on their synchronous sessions, using them only for "office hours" to meet with students rather than using them in assignments and lectures.

Synchronous Sessions Imbedded in Asynchronous Courses

In asynchronous courses containing synchronous sessions, Business-Software found that online learning, when approached with synchronous technology, is very similar to an actual classroom, in that it permits immediate feedback and detailed collaboration both with instructors and fellow students. In synchronous sessions, various real-time activities can be carried out, which provides continuous motivation for students. In addition, as compared to the asynchronous model, synchronous online learning promotes a sense of community between the students and teachers. Designing effective online synchronous sessions can be a challenge. Alyssa Dyar (2016) proposes several for designing such sessions, such as:

- Set expectations and ensure that students know what the instructor expects of them, such as paying full attention (no multitasking) and finding a quiet location from which to participate.
- Provide the students with an understanding of the software they will be using and how to either troubleshoot or obtain other technical assistance if needed.
- Use synchronous sessions primarily for higher-level learning collaboration and activities such as problem-solving issues, generating ideas, and thoughtful discussions.
- Engage the students and do it often, such as every 5 minutes.
- Utilize language that is meaningful to the students to promote interaction and participation.
- Schedule breaks if the session is lengthy so that students can stretch, get something to drink, or go to the restroom.

For the Faculty at San Jose State University (SJSU), the University (2018) provides a guide for preparing and for conducting online synchronous meetings. They include greeting the students as the session begins, share the entire screen, have a prepared agenda, have any URLs that are able to be accessed for instant linking, and know where breaks are planned for asking questions or whether students are to participate. The NU San Jose Faculty (2018) believes that there is a strong case to be made for including weekly synchronous class meetings in online courses because this weekly contact can be the single strongest thread connecting a student to the instructor, classmates, and course content. This provides, according to SJSU, the opportunity to answer questions as they arise rather than delays that may arise on discussion boards. Since these class meetings can be recorded, they can be revisited if needed and are available in cases where a student has a conflict and cannot attend an online meeting.

Synchronous Sessions Research Findings

Until recently, there was inconclusive research to provide insight on the value of synchronous sessions in largely asynchronous courses, but an extensive study provided new, enlightening value of synchronous sessions. The recent event that impacted many of the NU Faculty's view on synchronous sessions in an asynchronous course was an extensive study of a state's community college system by the Community College Research Center at Teachers College, Columbia University (Xu & Smith, 2013). The study contained nearly 500,000 courses taken by over 40,000 community and technical college students in Washington State. The study examined how well students adapted to the online environment in terms of their ability to persist and earn strong grades in online courses relative to their ability to do so in face-to-face courses. In analyzing all of the factors that impacted students in an asynchronous class, researchers found that there was one primary factor that predicted better grades and that was the amount of interaction between the instructor and the student. Furthermore, researchers found that face-to face interactions promoted attendance and success in class at almost twice the rate as in those classes without such instructor and student interaction. These findings suggest that university students require more interaction with their instructors, not less.

There are several things to consider when designing an asynchronous online course with synchronous components. Bali (2014) found that instructors need to consider time zones and family issues because if they have a geographically dispersed set of learners, the time of the synchronous events must consider the time zones of all students. Instructors should set the session times that they are convenient for all concerned. Another approach to accommodate students is to schedule the synchronous sessions at different times while keeping the content the same as much as possible.

In addition, weekends, national holidays, and other important days in which students may be engaged should also be considered in scheduling the synchronous sessions.

Bali (2014) also notes that in scheduling synchronous sessions, instructors should take the dynamics of family life into consideration because instructors often teach primarily non-traditional students who have either jobs or families. Thus, instructors should avoid placing the students in a situation where it may be difficult to attend the meetings. Bali (2014) observes that instructors can record the synchronous sessions and permit students to review the sessions later, but this can cause some students to feel that they are missing out. Perhaps instructors may even lose students' active participation as a result.

Another factor, according to Bali (2014) is the infrastructure where the students reside. For example, if students live in remote/rural areas or in developing countries where bandwidth is very low or even unreliable, then it may be difficult for them to submit their assignments in a timely manner or participate actively in a synchronous discussion. Since the Internet permits worldwide online classes, it is sometimes the case that some learners may not be fluent in or native speakers of the language of instruction, then they may need assistance and accommodations, such as additional time to interpret and reflect before responding (Bali, 2014).

In comparing asynchronous learning with synchronous learning, Bali (2014) found that asynchronous learning promotes deeper reflection and provides opportunities for learners to conduct and contribute research while creating almost unlimited space for each student to participate. This is not the case for synchronous sessions, in which there is limited time available for synchronous interaction. In addition, in synchronous sessions, some students tend to interact more than others, thus putting those who do not participate as actively at a disadvantage. In an asynchronous conversation, such as in a threaded discussion, the communicator cannot be interrupted, as may be case in synchronous sessions, wherein the more aggressive and outgoing student may tend to dominate conversations. In addition, asynchronous conversations are more easily archived and searchable, which is not as easy with recorded synchronous sessions.

Expectations: Students vs. Instructors

The preponderance of research including that by Xu and Smith (2013) also found that online faculty expected their students to be relatively capable learners who could handle the material on their own. In the instructors' view, their students should be capable of managing their time and be independent in learning the course material. Contrary to the expectations of the faculty, students stated that they expected contact with their instructors, especially if they were having difficulty with the course content. This becomes particularly critical in situations like National University and similar universities, where open enrollment exists. Similarly, community or two-year colleges have students who often enter without having the skills and study habits necessary for academic success. This difference in expectations of academic preparation and performance between faculty and students contributes to the low success rates of many students in online courses. Shatkini (2018) found in his research that as instructors plan a synchronous component, they need to be cognizant of the competing demands on their students' time. Depending on the student population, it may be unrealistic to require even a weekly study session. Instructors also need to be aware that, as with any independent group activity, they will need to intervene in the case of student attrition, incompatibility, and conflict. Sandoval (2017) identified several issues. These issues are that students prefer voluntary rather than mandatory synchronous sessions, which are offered less frequently. Students also prefer that instructors primarily address the key points of the subject matter and that recordings of the sessions be made so that when time constraints preclude students from attending, they can still have access to the session.

National University's Experience With Synchronous Assignments

In the Master of Science Program in Educational and Instructional Technology at National University, synchronous sessions are used in a leadership course to teach students how to problem-solve and practice leadership in small groups. The assignment is to develop a technology plan for their school or business, working as a group of from 5 to 7 students. Students are instructed to meet at least once a week in a synchronous online meeting. Each group must organize itself for problem-solving and for communicating. In doing so, students are required to list the role and responsibility of each group member. First, they are informed to elect someone from the group to be the group leader and to list the names of the other members of your group

The group task is to develop a technology plan, so they are asked to list the possible stakeholders at the site or organization for which they are developing the plan and determine who at the site/organization should be part of the technology plan committee. This is a hypothetical list of persons at the site for which the plan is being developed. Students are reminded that it is important that key people at the organization or site have buy-in to the proposed technology plan. They are advised that key important departments should be represented in the group. Without buy-in from key people and departments, they are warned that the technology plan could be doomed to failure. No group at the organization or site should feel slighted or left out of the process. The group must identify the situational gap in the technology existing at the organizational or site and the technology they plan to add or implement.

Group Gap Analysis

The situational gap is the distance between today's reality and the vision for tomorrow regarding the use and availability of technology where the student/students work. With the group, they should discuss via Collaborate video teleconferencing what each member's workplace environment is like, whether that be a school, school district, business, or corporation. What is the current state of the technology environment and what is the vision of how it could be improved or enhanced? After hearing from every team member, the group must decide on which member's workplace the team will select/use to develop a technology plan for this course. In the synchronous discussion, each group must analyze why there is a gap between today's reality and the tomorrow's vision and determine if it is technical, cultural, or instructional. After the team discussion, each member of the group must individually propose how he/she thinks the gap at the selected workplace could be bridged and what her/his personal vision for the team is i.e., what he/she thinks is its capability for developing, by a group, an effective technology plan?. The group must then answer the specific questions noted in the course text. The sessions are recorded so that if one or more of the students cannot attend, they can stay current on the group's progress and actions via the session recording. The instructor does not attend the sessions so that students take full responsibility for scheduling, holding, and recording the meeting. The instructor can also access the recording to monitor the group's progress.

Group vs. Individual Grades

Each week, the group submits a written report for which they receive a group grade. At the end of the course, the students submit an individual essay for which they receive an individual grade. This essay addresses what they learned about their individual leadership effectiveness and style in the weekly synchronous meetings. In the capstone project course, the next course in the program, students use synchronous sessions to periodically show the instructor their progress in the development of their capstone project, which involves the design and development of an online class. At the end of the class, students use the online synchronous system to present their completed capstone online course to the instructor and the class. Several students have reported that they were hired based on their employer's review of their online course.

Student Feedback on Synchronous Sessions

At the end of the leadership class, each student is required to write an essay about participation in the group synchronous sessions and what he/she learned about herself/himself in the group dynamics of the problem-solving challenge. This includes as the interaction within the group from the leadership or follower role that he or she played. The most common comment from students in the essay is that they were surprised how much they learned about their leadership abilities and about how difficult it often is to be convincing or to "sell" their point of view. Although the students do have synchronous sessions in prior courses, this is the first case in which they must communicate with each other in real time for an extended period and achieve a given group goal during the session. Staying on subject is often a challenge as is presenting a point or idea that may not be initially acceptable to the group. In this case, students must re-double their efforts to more clearly explain their positions.

The Value of Integrating Synchronous and Asynchronous Elements

Christopher Pappas (2015) found that integrating many online activities and exercises not only avoids the potential for learner boredom, but it also allows a wide range of learning preferences and styles. As one example, he (Pappas, 2015) notes that offering a text-only online course might turn off learners who prefer to have content that includes videos and simulations. This is a good reason to have a variety of learning materials and modes in an asynchronous course. This would also challenge self-motived and independent learners, attract their interest, and make them less likely to disengage with course content. Pappas further proposes one weakness of asynchronous learning, which is that it does not include face-to-face instruction for those students who may learn best with direct instructor interaction. As such, instructors must have a solid support system in place to assist those who need additional help with the subject matter or even the learning management system. If the students encounter a glitch or cannot log in to the eLearning platform, they should always have a way to get in touch with someone who can help.

Lisa Yamagata-Lynch (2014) conducted a study to explore how synchronous online learning can complement asynchronous learning in higher education settings. She found that there is a place for evaluating online classes to address strategies for facilitating online synchronous learning that complement asynchronous learning. Synchronous online meetings that are supported by well-structured small group meetings can help students feel a stronger sense of connection to their peers and instructor than students who only experience asynchronous courses and remain engaged with course activities (Yamagata-Lynch, 2014). Hrastinski found that while engaged in synchronous learning when compared to asynchronous learning, participants find a stable means of communication, tend to stay on task, feel a larger sense of participation, and tend to experience better task/course completion rates (2010).

Pratt & Palloff (2011) completed research on asynchronous online learning that suggests that students will experience meaningful learning when they are in participatory learning environments if the environments are intentionally designed to help participants develop a sense of community so that they can engage in collaborative discussions. These interactions encourage participants to actively construct new knowledge related to the course content (Conrad & Donaldson, 2011; Lehman & Conceição, 2011). Asynchronous online participatory learning involves a series of highly complex and ill-defined activities that require participants to reflect and question their traditional learning practices while developing a new identity as a learner (Palloff & Pratt, 2011). Yamagata-Lynch (2014) noted some students shared that being part of an online blended synchronous and asynchronous course gave them the opportunity to experience a greater participation in a flexible learning environment where they had no time to be a passive, non-present student. She (Yamagata-Lynch, 2014) also found that through synchronous communications, students were able to engage in spontaneous discussions, while through asynchronous communications, they were able to take the time to reflect and prepare responses for discussion topics that were designed for any given week.

Defining Asynchronous and Synchronous Tools

Asynchronous tools enable communication and collaboration over a period of time through a "different time-different place" mode (Pierce College, 2018). These tools allow people to connect to the class at each person's own convenience and schedule. Asynchronous tools are effective in sustaining dialogue and collaboration over time and providing people with information and resources that are instantly accessible, night or day. These tools also possess the advantage of involving people from multiple time zones. In addition, asynchronous tools are helpful in capturing the history of the interactions of a group, allowing for collective knowledge to be more easily shared and distributed. The primary drawback of asynchronous technologies is that they require the students to be more disciplined when used for ongoing communities of practice (e.g., people typically must take the initiative to "log in" to participate), and these students may less personal interactions than those who prefer higher-touch synchronous technologies.

MODE ADVANTAGES AND DISADVANTAGES

David Tomar (2018) defines the advantages of synchronous and asynchronous in a much more dynamic way. He believes that if the student who likes active discussion, immediate feedback, and personal familiarity and classroom engagement, will find this is only available through real-time interaction, meaning the student is probably a candidate for a synchronous learning experience. Live videoconferencing, lecture broadcasts, or real-time chats can make it easier to have the personal engagement of a classroom.

Regarding asynchronous learning, Tomar (2018) believes students who may have a demanding schedule or irregular hours are probably better suited for asynchronous learning. Learning will typically revolve around materials that can be accessed on the students' own time - often within a set time frame, like a week or two. Content might include text-based lecture notes, self-guided interactive learning modules, or lectures and podcasts that are prerecorded. The student can complete a module on the train ride to work or listen to a lecture on headphones while her/his baby naps. Asynchronous learning gives the student the materials. It is up to the student to complete them at her/his convenience.

The disadvantages of asynchronous and synchronous systems are also very descriptively defined (Tomar, 2018). Synchronous learning may present students who sign up for online learning because of her/his busy and unpredictable work schedule with some challenges to meet at a specific date and time. A major characteristic of this learning experience is its adherence to a specific schedule. Lectures and class discussions will take place at established meeting times. If the student's job keeps her/him on call at strange hours or parenting responsibilities render the student fully occupied during the daytime, the student may have a hard time satisfying the course requirements. If flexibility is the number one reason that the student decided to go the online route, he/she must make sure they can manage the synchronous learning responsibility around a given schedule.

Of course, if the student likes the personal interaction, and excels best when he/she feels like people are actually listening, asynchronous learning can be a lonely experience. Social media and email obviously can't deliver the same kind of personal connections of real face-to-face interaction. The asynchronous environment is also a less collaborative one than a synchronous one. The opportunities to interface, debate, and network with classmates are also not as great as in a synchronous session. In a many ways, asynchronous learning is best when the plan is simply to do the assignments and get a grade., but if the student is looking for the kind of enrichment that comes from discussion, feedback, and social interaction, he/she might be disappointed by the asynchronous learning experience.

CONCLUSION AND RECOMMENDATIONS

In reflection on the advantages and disadvantages of both synchronous and asynchronous modes of online education, it is apparent that some combination of the two that maximizes the advantages and minimizes the disadvantages is the approach that online educators should adapt. A major obstacle to obtaining a college degree prior to online programs was the requirement to be in a classroom for a significant part of the day. This prevented those with full-time jobs to go to class and to fulfill the time required to obtain a degree. Online education first became popular because of its advertisement for doing the work in classes at any time and any place. The fact that asynchronous is the major mode used today validates that flexibility in time and place in taking online courses is a primary reason that online education is taken in the asynchronous mode. In addition to the advantage of flexibility in taking the courses, the ready access via the Internet means that people who were never able to go to college because of lack of access to a college campus or because they had marginal grades that may have prevented their acceptance at a college, have a second chance. They may now apply and obtain a degree because in addition to the anytime, any place promise of online courses, there are many "open enrollment" universities who accept any student with a high school degree and/or bachelor's degree, regardless of the overall GPA obtained.

Given that the flexibility of time and place is a key and primary motivating factor for students who elect to pursue a degree or take courses online, this equates to taking online programs in an asynchronous mode. But this does not mean that the many advantages of the synchronous mode may not be used in asynchronous online programs. The challenge is to integrate synchronous sessions into asynchronous courses in a balanced manner so that students can still do their work largely in their own time and place but agree to set aside limited time in the course where they will interact with the instructor and/or classmates in real-time. In particular, individual synchronous sessions could be invaluable in assisting students who need the kind of one-on-one assistance that only face-to-face meetings with the instructor can provide.

In view of the conclusions stated above, the recommendation is that in online programs synchronous sessions be integrated into asynchronous courses in a balanced manner in which the online students can do their work any time and in any place while having access to synchronous sessions. Students in synchronous sessions, experience the positive social and emotional aspects of a group and thereby preclude the loneliness that is characteristic of strictly asynchronous courses. This balance of asynchronous and synchronous sessions should be decided by the instructor and the students in each class. Over time, however, after balancing the two modes for many classes, an instructor will probably arrive at the best mix of the two modes in a way that students support the modes and gain the best possible academic experience for each and every student.

REFERENCES

Bali, M. (2014). Bringing out the human in synchronous and asynchronous media for learning. Pressbooks. Retrieved from https://humanmooc.pressbooks.com/chapter/bringing-out-the-human-in-synchronous-and-asynchronous-media-for-learning/

Business-Software Site. (2019). Advantages and disadvantages of online synchronous learning. Retrieved from https://www.business-software.com/advantagesand-and-disadvantages-of-online-synchronous-learning

Conrad, R.-M., & Donaldson, J. A. (2011). *Engaging the online learner: Activities and resources for creative instruction* (2nd ed.). San Francisco, CA: Jossey-Bass.

Dyar, A. (2016). Designing an online classroom. Retrieved from https://edtech.sesp

Friedman, J. (2017). 10 facts about student interaction in online programs. US News. Retrieved from https://www.usnews.com/topics/author/jordan-friedman

History of the LMS. (2020) Learning Management Retrieved from https://learning-management.financeonline.com/history-learning-mamagement-system/

Lehman, R. M., & Conceição, S. C. O. (2010). *Creating a sense of presence in online teaching: How to "be there" for distance learners*. San Francisco, CA: Jossey-Bass.

National Center for Education Statistics. (2002). The traditional student defined. Retrieved from https://nces.ed.gov

Palloff, R., & Pratt, K. (2011). *The excellent online instructor: Strategies for Professional Development*. San Francisco, CA: Augsburg University.

Pappas, C. (2015). Synchronous vs. asynchronous learning—Can you tell the difference. Elearning Industry. Retrieved from https://elearningindustry.com/synchronous-vs-asynchronous-learning-can-you-tell-the-difference

San Jose State University. (2018). High demand courses. Retrieved from http://online.sjsu.edu/teachingresources/nextstep_synchronous

Sandoval, Z. (2017). Asynchronous and synchronous sessions in online courses. Retrieved from https://www.academia.edu/35998401/ASYNCHRONOUS_AND_SYNCHRONOUS_SESSIONS_IN_ONLINE-COURSES_GRADUATE_STUDENTS_PERCEPTIONS

Shatkini. (2018). Synchronous study sessions. Oregon State. Retrieved from http://blogs.oregonstate.edu/inspire/2018/1/05/synchronous-study-sessions/

Tomar, D. (2018). Synchronous or asynchronous online education: Which one is right for you? The Best Schools. Retrieved from https://thebestschools.org/magazine/synchronous-vs-asynchronous-education/

Xu, D., & Smith, S. (2013). *Adaptability to online learning: Differences across types of students and academic subject areas.* Teacher's College, Columbia University.

Yamagota-Lynch, L. (2014). Blending online asynchronous and synchronous learning. Irrodl. Retrieved from http://www.irrodl.org/index.php/irrodl/article/view/1778/2837

Chapter 3
Exploring Online Learning Through Synchronous and Asynchronous Instructional Methods

Jamie Mahoney
https://orcid.org/0000-0003-4354-2339
Murray State University, USA

Carol A. Hall
https://orcid.org/0000-0002-9557-6787
University of Phoenix, USA

ABSTRACT

Teaching and learning in the online environment are challenging. Students and instructors must employ technological tools and strategies to be successful. Merely having a computer and software does not equate to being technologically literate in the 21st century world of work. Learning how to incorporate virtual reality games, webcams, video conferencing, and brainstorming platforms such as Padlet, Bubbl. us, Zoom, Twitter, Instagram, interactive whiteboards, chat rooms, YouTube, and screencasting videos is encouraged. Polleverywhere, Socrative, and Flubaroo are a few assessments to investigate interest by examining the world of synchronous and asynchronous learning environments. The digital natives of today's classrooms are the future employees of tomorrow's real-life world of work; therefore, organizations must take control of the situation and prepare workers to meet future job demands. The question of how to do so effectively will be answered in this chapter.

DOI: 10.4018/978-1-7998-1622-5.ch003

INTRODUCTION

The classroom environment for students in the 21st century differs from classroom environments in the 20th century. Some students now attend all or part of their classes online. The instructor need not stand before a group of students to lecture, disseminate questions for homework, and dismiss the students. In a virtual environment, students and teachers use technology to transfer teaching and learning (Hall, 2012).

BACKGROUND

In 2017, one third of the students in colleges and universities reported taking a class online, and 15.4% of students were enrolled entirely online (Lederman, 2018). During the 2014-15 school year, 2.7 million K-12 students were estimated to have been enrolled in digital learning (Herold, 2017). Some states require students to enroll in at least one online class to earn their high school diploma. The question is how might schools, colleges, and universities maximize teaching and learning so all students reach their potential? The pedagogy of online learning versus face-to-face learning is and continues to be a concern for many K-12 and post-secondary educators, particularly student academic preparedness, maturity level, and study skill acquisition (Hall, 2012).

Online teachers must redefine their teaching and learning roles and switch from a disseminator of knowledge to facilitator of learning (Wiesenberg & Stacey, 2008) shared the following:

Given the expanding interest and demand for online learning, coupled with the results of studies showing that higher levels of learning are not easily achieved in online courses, there is an imperative to advance our understanding of how to facilitate effective online learning activities (p. 121).

In the online environment, the responsibility for learning and success shifts from the teacher to the student. Teachers are facilitators and guides (Berge, 2009; Salmon, 2004; Smith, 2005). Teachers are supporters, resource teachers, and guides who supply students with the tools needed to be successful.

Teachers must prepare well-planned syllabi and produce clear instructor policies consisting of rules and expectations. The online students must carefully read and synthesize syllabi and policies. "Reading the documents several times, highlighting pertinent information such as assignment due dates, and examining assignment criteria and rubrics are most important" (Hall, 2012). If a student is unclear of teacher expectations, the student must seek clarification from the instructor. A syllabus quiz provided by Flubaroo or by Google Forms is one formal assessment instructors can use to determine student understandings of course information explicitly outlined in the syllabus during the beginning of a course. Of importance for students is to note is that online instructors are bound by institutional policies they must follow, which may lessen the flexibility for things such as late assignments and personal emergencies.

According to Berge (2009) successful institutions and school systems that embark on establishing online teaching and learning environments encourage and support teamwork. A sense of community can be fostered by encouraging students to work in teams or groups to engage, discuss, and complete projects (Hall, 2012). Through team assignments, students learn how to lead and learn how to follow. The online classroom is one more teaching and learning environment available to help foster learning.

Information literacy is a skill required to acquire knowledge. Information literacy is the ability to search for and locate information, to evaluate and comprehend the information when located, and, most importantly, to use and apply the information to daily living and working experiences. Bruce (2002) described information literacy as "the personal empowerment learners engage in when independently pursuing lifelong learning" (p. 2). As a learner increases in their ability to apply information, the more power the learner has in making life decisions, and the sooner the learner transitions from knowledge acquirer to the scholar who can apply the knowledge learned to daily life experiences. Learners must, however, judge the information located and received and consider whether the information is appropriate for their current usage. A goal of every teacher should be to "transform dependent learners into independent, self-directed, lifelong learners" (Bruce, 2002).

Teachers have a responsibility to our 21st century communities to educate students about the "Seven Ways of Seeing and Experiencing Information: 1) Informational technology for retrieval and communication, 2) Informational sources, 3) Information processes, 4) Information control, 5) Knowledge construction, 6) Knowledge extension, and 7) Wisdom" (Bruce, 2002). Educational exposure to these seven areas allows students to make better decisions dependent upon information gathered when they have a problem in their daily lives.

KEY DIFFERENCES IN TEACHING ONLINE VERSUS FACE-TO-FACE

The two key types of differences between teaching online and teaching face-to-face are pedagogical and operational. Pedagogical procedures in online classrooms are usually asynchronous procedures to include discussions and various means of assessing student learning. The in person synchronous learning lectures paper and pencil assessments are typically employed. Operationally, online classes are in session 24 hours a day. Face-to-face classes occur in specific geographic locations at regularly scheduled times.

Students who attend online classes versus face-to-face classrooms also appear to differ. Online attendees are working adults who live anywhere in the world, whereas in person students live close to the campus they wish to attend. Instructors who teach online serve as facilitators of learning to assist students by guiding them in their acquisition of knowledge. Most in person instructors appear to lecture and attempt to transfer their own knowledge to students.

BEST PRACTICES IN THE ONLINE ENVIRONMENT

Best practices to foster student learning in the online environment continue to evolve. Instructors need to be present in the online classroom daily and make their presence known by asking questions requiring critical thinking, providing answers to students' questions, and clarifying misconceptions in students' learning. Instructors should call students by name, share experiences, provide appropriate feedback on assignments, set clear learning objectives, be supportive of students, and vary types of assignments. Instructors should construct and publish rubrics for assignments. Introducing various forms of media into the classroom can make learning exciting and fun.

Jacobs (2010) reported best practices in teaching technology methods and tools for students to think critically in the online environment are to "develop literacies for students to participate through blogs, wikis, podcasts, video productions on sites such as YouTube, e-mail, text messaging, and shared online photostreams" (p. 82). Outdated learning tools are no longer appropriate for teaching practices to meet the student's needs of the 21st century. As technology improves, teaching practices must change to include these technology tools as best teaching practices and meet students' needs for higher order and critical thinking.

Teaching and learning classroom environments have changed and will continue to change to adapt to the needs of students. Many students choose to attend online classrooms because of the flexibility options provided in meeting work, family, and school responsibilities. Synchronous and asynchronous learning environments through web-enhanced learning options are the choices most students prefer when taking active roles in educational learning experiences (Blau & Shamir-Inbal, 2017).

INSTRUCTIONAL EXPECTTIONS

Online instructor expectations should include the following items to set the mood for the course and help the online student understand course requirements: (a) a welcome note; (b pre-course announcement with email, phone, and time availabilities; (c) participation requirements and point values to be earned; (d) late assignment policy, and (e) grading policies and expectations (Rios et al., 2018). The online student needs to know the instructor is available and willing to offer assistance when the student is confused and needs clarification. So many times, the online student feels alone. According to Rios et al. (2018), the online student needs to acquire "the social presence, cognitive presence and teaching presence" (p. 160) representative of a collaborative learning environment to feel successful.

ESTABLIHING AN ONLINE LEARNING ENVIRONMENT

Ferriter (2010) provided the link to the website www.classroom20.com as a reference for teachers interested in implementing a digital classroom and discussion zone for sharing technology tools for lessons and instruction. Other tools available for use are Skype (a synchronous tool), Screencast-O-Matic (a narrations and writing tool), and Voicethread (an asynchronous tool). Each of these devices can be used in the classroom to assist students in learning using multiple modalities.

Mobile learning is considered a "24/7 informal, spontaneous, and self-directed experience occurring throughout the day" (Evans, 2015, p. 12) providing the flexibility for all participants in various classroom types. Online learning cohorts engage in texting, gaming, website research and review specifically seeking to gain knowledge or learn new skills (Evans, 2015). An equal mixture of males and females populate these cohorts of active learners rather than passive learners where creating and sharing is more important than just reading about the information (Evans, 2015). Technology and digital learning are an expectation for the experience. Learning is a social experience in which the technology tools are being used to collaborate and network with diverse populations around the world (Gast, 2018/19).

Mobile devices no longer require students to be restrained to the desk or geographic locations. Students and teachers can now travel outside the traditional classroom setting to teach and learn, therefore, expanding knowledge and skills (Evans, 2015). Mobile devices include but are not limited to cell phones; more often mobile devices include smartphones, digital readers, tablets, and laptops. The digital tools facilitate learning projects, assignments, assessments, online videos, social networking, and self-directed academic research projects (Evans, 2015). Incorporating videos, photos, sounds, and text into animated movies or slideshows provides students opportunities to demonstrate knowledge rather than respond to simple multiple-choice assessments.

Preparing to teach in the 21st century requires teachers to become comfortable with an array of hardware and software tools such as "interactive whiteboards, webcams, laptops, digital cameras, iPods, web simulations, flip cameras, WebQuests, Wordle, Moodle, Twitter, Blogs, Video Conferencing, electronic field trips and e-interviews" (Jacobs, 2010, p. 24). Professional development is needed to ensure all teachers are capable of incorporating these tools into their teaching repertoire. Curriculum needs to be updated to take advantage of pedagogical, assessment, and mindset changes.

Technology

Teaching with technology is not specifically about learning to use the technology tools per se. "Learning to dig deeper, doing more research, pitching ideas to the team, coming to a consensus, outlining how to best convey the point for attention, making connections with experts in the field, writing, editing, revising, and engaging the audience" (Jacobs, 2010, p. 124) is the purpose of the learning project not learning how to use the technology. Using the technology to make the project is merely the vehicle to motivate and engage the students to complete the project. The same project could be done by writing a paper and orally presenting it. However, this does not prepare our students for the future world of work.

Digital natives, our students in the online classroom, know how to complete these technology-based activities: "upload, download, text, instant message, communicate in social networking sites, blog, post online videos, participate in virtual reality games, operate video cameras" (Jacobs, 2010, p. 134). The online class needs to accentuate and change to meet these skills with a replacement of updated assignments and assessments. The online classroom should incorporate the modern media created literacy curriculum.

STRATEGIES TO SUPPORT ONLINE LEARNING

Online students have multiple options available to take coursework; therefore, choosing the right school requires synchronous and asynchronous learning environments to have these components available for successful movement from a traditional classroom environment to a virtual school. Components needed include course design elements for the online class with individual and group activities, enhanced written or video lectures, clearly defined expectations aligned with syllabi objectives, and assignment product varieties (Rios, Elliott, & Mandernach, 2018). Instructor communication about course procedures, expectations, and instructor contact preferences allow students to plan appropriately for the course (Rios et al., 2018).

Meeting Students' Needs

Preparing to teach in the digital age requires teachers and school systems to revisit the standard ways of working in the classrooms to meet the needs of all students. Teachers in future classrooms must adapt techniques to deliver instruction. Some of the methods available for teachers are podcasts, webinars, collaborative sessions, self-paced tutorials, webcasts, workshops, learning modules, on-demand resources, study skill resources, and motivational videos. Jacobs (2010) reviewed the need for overhauling current outdated curriculum practices to transform educational needs in the areas of content, assessment, program structures, technology, media literacy, globalization, sustainability, and habits of the mind for students of the 21st century. Schools need to become learning organizations to match the times in which students live. Picciano & Seaman (2010) also build a case for traditional high schools to offer more online choices for students.

ADA ACCOMMODATIONS

Students with disabilities in the online classroom environment require accommodations such as closed captioning (CC) be provided for videos such as YouTube or Screencasts. These closed captioning text-based options are equivalencies of the content presented within the videos. Select the closed caption option using advanced Google search option. Once you include the CC option, a transcript of the video will need to be created and provided. The transcript can easily be created and provided by the instructor if necessary, for students who are deaf or hard of hearing require a copy.

Word documents need to have accommodations with alternative text provided as well. Students with visual difficulties will need graphics described using the *alt.text* feature submitted. Word documents can be read aloud for students with visual impairments, but the graphics will be overlooked unless the alt text feature is provided to explain what the graphic is and why it is important to the document.

PowerPoint presentations require descriptive transcripts of all text and graphic content to be provided for students with disabilities. Instructors should create a handout of the presentation in Word format with notes to explain the information presented within the presentation. All educational images, graphics, infographics, and non-educational graphics should be able to be enlarged without any distortion for those students with visual impairments. Alternative text descriptions should be provided explaining the graphics.

SYNCHRONOUS LEARNING TOOLS

Computer aided delivery (CAD) models of online instruction have improved over the years. Video conferencing and virtual meetings (Zoom, WebConnect, GoToMeeting, and Blackboard Collaborate) are synchronous tools enabling classes to communicate as if in brick and mortar classrooms. Webcams with Internet connections offer video conferencing capabilities such as WebConnect, Zoom, Elluminate or GoToMeeting for classrooms to have the synchronous face to face meeting options. Researchers Lowenthal, Snelson, & Dunlap (2017) discussed the importance of synchronous design interventions and planning to include specific options for student success within the implementation process. Students reported video feedback, video tutorials, and online webchats brought a sense of community, and shared getting answers to questions in a quick manner provided from the instructor were the most helpful for a synchronous online classroom.

Yamagata-Lynch (2014) reviewed ground rules for the synchronous online learning environment. Ground rules are important to assist all students in using time efficiently and effectively during the time spent speaking, listening, and discussing the topics pertaining to the lesson of the hour (s) for the timeframe. Off topic discussions waste precious learning opportunities and distract from the purpose of the meeting. Having and using the appropriate hardware and software tools keeps everyone focused and ready to tackle the goals and objectives in a timely manner for the activities, assignments, breakout rooms, and learning targets preventing any troubleshooting and frustration for missing any important missed conversations. Proactive preparation makes coursework smoother and more productive for everyone involved.

COLLABORATION

A social presence is achieved through collaborative chat room activities and group assignments through the sharing of skills and ideas (Gast, 2018/19). Cognitive presence (CP) of shared experiences and ideas is perfect for the online classrooms as the process of (CP) in the online synchronous environment allows everyone the same opportunity to reply and provide feedback to peers in an interactive and engaging method (Gast, 2018/19). Teaching presence in the online classroom is facilitated through individualized and personalized comments for each student within the classroom (Gast, 2018/19).

Research conducted by Yamagata-Lynch (2014) demonstrated students in the online classroom built a better relationship with the instructor when video conferencing methods were used, and class discussions were held in a synchronous manner. Facilitated synchronous instructional opportunities provided the learner with intentional focus, expert guided informational discussions, purposeful participation, and increased completion rates (Yamagata-Lynch, 2014). Synchronous video-conference learning enlists student accountability and involvement within the online classroom environment.

Many new asynchronous online learners develop a sense of ownership from learning to navigate the digital classroom, navigate and complete the web-related assignments, and communicating and collaborating with the instructor through the course tools. The roles and responsibilities in the asynchronous classroom are time and geographically flexible to meet the needs of the working adult (Yamagata-Lynch, 2014). The structure of the course is provided by the instructor and followed by the student.

Online classroom digital device tasks include skills such as the ability to document work through photos or videos then submitting through email attachments. Another task for using digital devices within the classroom includes researching information, crowdsourcing, capturing interviews, and creating digital projects (Tucker, 2015). Devices should help to engage students' creativity, curiosity, and activate interests encouraging communication and collaboration with others (Tucker, 2015). One such collaboration tool students to be used is Padlet (www.padlet.com) allowing students to post and interact in real time.

VIDEO CONFERENCING TOOLS

Technology tools cross both the synchronous and asynchronous classroom environments and many tools often provide the same features and benefits. Personal preferences or institutional products generally decide which products instructors use in classroom instructional practices (see Table 1).

Blackboard Collaborate

Blackboard Collaborate is a synchronous learning management tool used in communication and collaboration allowing everyone to see and speak together from various locations (Yamagata-Lynch, 2014). Gone are the days where everyone has to travel to the same location to have a meeting therefore cutting costs and eliminating the time factor of waiting for everyone to get to the same location. Technology has improved our abilities to communicate and collaborate. Bary and Rees (2006) insisted, "Learning with/from others is linked to activity: it is achieved while doing something else with two or more people together" (p. 76).

Table 1. Technology tools: Synchronous/asynchronous categorization

Technology Tool	Synchronous/ Asynchronous	Features/Benefits
Zoom	Synchronous Recording can be shared and sent for asynchronous learning later.	Peer breakout rooms Interactive whiteboard feature Screensharing Recording (to be shared later) Real time interactive Face-to-face discussions
Blackboard Collaborate	Both	Peer breakout rooms
GoToMeeting	Synchronous	Screensharing Real time interactive Face to face discussions Paid subscription
ScreenCastify	Both	Recording and playback tool Recording of lesson Playback of lesson
ScreenCastOmatic	Both	Recording and playback tool Recording of lesson Playback of lesson
Skype	Synchronous	Collaboration tool Communication
Interactive Whiteboards	Synchronous	Visual Graphic Video clips interactive
VoiceThread	Both	Communicate Collaborate via internet integrated into any LMS such as Blackboard, Moodle, Canvas
PowerPoint/ Prezi	Both	Presentation tools used in both environments.
Padlet	Both	Collaborative Mapping tool Digital media projects
Bubbl.us	Both	Free online mapping tool Collaborative Digital media projects
Khan Academy	Both	Video presentation learning tools Test prep
Flubaroo	Asynchronous	Formative assessment creations
Rubistar	Asynchronous	Rubric makers
Kahoot	Synchronous	Formative assessment
GoSoapBox	Synchronous	Formative assessment

Elluminate (Aka Blackboard Collaborate)

Elluminate provides webinars using both video and audio formats for learners. Schools and businesses rent out virtual rooms or spaces for web conferencing. Elluminate incorporates Voice over IP, teleconferencing, public and private chat, quizzing, chatting, emoticons, whiteboard, application sharing, and file transfer. This application was primarily used for educational purposes but has evolved to a new version, Blackboard Collaborate and Blackboard Ultra.

GoToMeeting

GoToMeeting is an online meeting space for pay (although not the only tool pay-per-use). This paid option provides a secure online meeting space to connect people anywhere and anytime through the Internet. People can get more done saving time and travel costs with a secure log in and one shared link provided by GoToMeeting. All devices work interconnectedly and communication is seamless. Using GoToMeeting allows participants to share screens while presenting PowerPoint, Word or any other documents. Participants are also able to discuss the information shared on the screens. Special software is not required to use GoToMeeting; only the use of the paid subscription and the online link provide by the subscriber.

Skype (Skype in the Classroom, A Microsoft Product)

Skype (www.skype.com) is a synchronous collaborative tool used to connect people from various geographical locations at the same time. Jacobs (2010) discussed Skype used for a collaboration team establishing and maintaining a working relationship via the Internet with classrooms around the world. Students can also connect with experts in multiple fields from around the world to conduct e-interviews while researching topics. This type of person to person interview provides a better connection than trying to write the author or person and wait for a response through traditional postal mail or even email. Any miscommunication can be corrected right on the spot.

Zoom

Zoom is another tool used to video conference allowing the option to teach, discuss, share computer screens, use interactive whiteboards, break into smaller groups in separate rooms for small group activities and discussions and record for those not able to attend. Students can attend from any geographical location with an Internet connection and video capability. Phones, tablets, and computers of any type can be used to participate in Zoom video conferences. Phones provide a drawback when such activities as collaboration with Google Docs or Google Slides are used for assignments as it is difficult to use a phone and complete a document or slide at the same time. Participants and the instructor have the option of a free or premium version of using Zoom (Wang, Quek, & Hu, 2017). Zoom offers several options for instructors and participants to use including an interactive chat box if students didn't want to verbally respond to the instructor's questions and comments. Instructor's must remember to be interactive and engaging using Zoom or participants will decide to turn off the video option and in effect "virtually leave" the classroom discussions (Wang, Quek, & Hu, 2017).

Miscellaneous Tools

Other tools used by some students and instructors within both the asynchronous and the synchronous environment are instructional assessments, assignments, and products, which include blogs, video clips, journals, discussions, podcasts, Microsoft PowerPoints, Prezi, wikis, augmented reality, screen casting, gamification, webinars, and live chats. Digital storytelling incorporates using digital image production and creatively telling the story using technology. Bookcreator is one of those online websites offering students the technology options to digitally create and tell stories in multiple formats. This differentiated assignment tool provides accessories for students with difficulties the ability to write, create, and tell a story not traditionally available through paper and pencil.

Interactive Whiteboards

Interactive whiteboards such as one at miro.com is a useful tool available to project to the synchronous class environment. Using an interactive whiteboard that connects users online, enables all participants to write, publish, and generate ideas for the learning topic at the same time during the class meeting. "Interactive whiteboards, which are large electronic touch screens, make the computer directly interactive for students" (Jacobs, 2010, p. 201). "Using interactive whiteboards in the face-to-face classroom was associated with a 16-point gain in student achievement" (Marzano, 2009, p. 80). Interactive whiteboards use graphics and visuals to represent information including video clips. Students needing these tools in order to learn the information over reading textual content will interact and engage in the lessons better (Marzano, 2009). These findings support research conducted primarily in K-12 classrooms in a f-t-f classroom.

Blogs

Blogs, otherwise known as web logs, are online community chat forums in which people share information and ideas about specific topics, ask and answer questions, and provide solutions for problems. Synchronous learning using blogs as an informal and casual forum for sharing ideas creates a community of learners choosing to share to gain knowledge rather than having to share to earn a grade.

Rodesiler (2017) reviewed blogging as a reflective practice, collaborative inquiry, and a position of professional identity development in an online environment. Blogging activities and assignments in both the synchronous and asynchronous classrooms focus on these purposes of writing "express and reflect; inform and explain; evaluate and judge; inquire and explore; analyze and interpret; and take a stand/propose a solution" (Rodesiler, 2017, p. 352). Using these purposes in blogging for writing activities or assignments gives the student a different perspective and audience to write for and communicate with therefore creating and using higher order thinking skills.

Videos

Video tools, useful in both asynchronous and synchronous environments, enhance the learning activities in both a visual and auditory format. One of the first steps many students take when unclear about how to do or accomplish a task is to search for a video demonstrating what to do on YouTube. Video clips provide the student with a visual learning opportunity to clarify and help students comprehend an assignment or task in the online classroom. Likewise, allowing students to create a video demonstrating steps needed to complete a task or explaining a concept using such tools as Screencast-O-Matic or Screencastify provide the same presentation mode as being in class in person.

Screencast-O-Matic

Screencast-O-Matic is a website tool. With Screencast-O-Matic, teachers are able to video and publish information with sound and sight capabilities. With Screencast-O-Matic, teachers can record screenshots and share the screenshots with students, colleagues, and others for various purposes. Using a few clicks, a screen can be recorded and uploaded. Options include a free basic version, deluxe, or pro versions. Screencast-O-Matic provides instructors with video tools to share videos with students for more in-class discussions.

Screencast-O-Matic allows an instructor to record and send a video or have two-way conversation with a specific student. Want to capture your lessons in an electronic and video format- Screencast-O-Matic is the tool for the instructor to use and send to students. Students can submit assignments using Screencast-O-Matic to be graded on the instructor's time rather than taking up valuable instructional class time.

Screencastify

Screencastify is a light screen recorder designed especially for Chrome and Chromebooks. This web-enabled tool records anything on the desktop, can record an application, and by using the browser can record whatever the webcam is viewing. Using the webcam option allows the participant to personalize the video and narrate with own voice. Recording can be completed offline without an Internet connection until needed to upload to Google Drive or YouTube.

Voicethread

Voicethread allows participants to communicate, collaborate and connect via the Internet with any type of device. Participants do not have to install any software as this is a cloud application. Google Chrome or Mozilla Firefox are the only web browsers working with Voicethread. Over 50 different types of media can be created and shared in Voicethread. Commenting can be completed using voice, text, or audio uploads. Users create, comment, and share by uploading and discussing documents, slides, presentations, audio files, videos. Integrating Voicethread into learning management systems (LMS) includes Blackboard, Canvas, Desire2Learn and Moodle.

PRESENTATION TOOLS

Presentations include tools such as Microsoft PowerPoint or Prezi allow limited information to be included on each slide and require a person to discuss the slides adding more information to provide clarification. One way to prevent the need for synchronous learning is to add audio files to these presentations thus allowing the reviewer to hear the person presenting the presentation speak throughout each slide. This allows for ADA accommodations to be provided for persons with disabilities to use these tools when applicable. PowerPoint has become an overused and monotonous form of technology used within any classroom environment.

Prezi is more engaging and interactive than PowerPoint. People who are not designers can use the pre-made templates to produce a professional presentation without starting from scratch. Easily customizable with charts and graphics, Prezi lends itself to students without high technology experience. With Prezi, there is no time lapse between oral presentation and visual presentation of information.

COLLABORATION TOOLS

Padlet

Padlet is an online, collaborative mapping tool allowing the options of creating a wall, canvas, stream, grid, shelf or backchannel (Tucker, 2015). All of these communication and collaboration spaces exist in real time providing contributors options to create and build digital media projects from multiple locations at the same time. Templates or start from blank can be chosen thus students have preferences depending upon the requirements for the look and style of the assignment. Use of Padlet is an easiest way to create and collaboratively work in the classroom and at home. Padlet serves as a virtual piece of paper on which a blank screen is used to place whatever information is desired. Students are then able to edit using videos on the screen collaboratively with images and documents to create a beautiful finished product.

Bubbl.us

Another online collaboration website allowing students to brainstorm and create a mind map is bubbl.us. Bubbl.us, a free brainstorming website, allows users to create and use technology tools visually to mind map topics. This site is easy to use. Disabled students can see connections between the parent bubbles and student bubbles. Text can be added, and colors changed, which features students find helpful in assisting them acquire organizational skills and understanding the aspects of mind mapping and brainstorming topics. Using this tool to help students plan for writing will help students see the connections to the structure of the writing process.

Scavenger Hunts

Scavenger hunts are engaging methods to get students collectively working on an assignment all the while having fun in completing and engaging activity and learning at the same time. Instagram is a digital tool rarely used in for academic activities or assignments. An Instagram scavenger hunt planned by the teacher to be completed based upon any topic of the content area. For example, plan a scavenger hunt where students find and post pictures and tag you (your hashtag identification for your Instagram) about Australia and Australian-related memorabilia to help everyone learn about Australia (Tucker, 2015).

Twitter

Twitter has become a tool being used in writing and communicating for the real world for right now. The limited character count assists students in learning to be concise and precise with the statements or comments about topics. Twitter is a global communication tool far reaching to address cultural issues faced by everyone. Tweets are publicly posted but can be restricted by users to their own followers. Posts made by twitter users can be followed, liked and retweeted. Users can post group messages together by using the hashtag (#). Trending topics provide people across the country information to understand what is happening and keep current. Global communication tools and social networking such as twitter allow learners to discuss and engage in solving problems.

ASYNCHRONOUS LEARNING TOOLS

Asynchronous learning methods include online discussion boards, self-study, videos on demand, flipped classroom formats, self-paced learning tutorials, learner dictated information, motivation and flexibility, and non-geography locked, and unbiased, cohorts. Time and geographic location flexibility are just two of the reasons students choose the asynchronous online classroom. The working adult with family responsibilities can have the best of both worlds: being able to work full-time and raise a family while going to school after everyone has gone to sleep and not have to leave the comfort of home. This choice is the option of the new high tech 21st century adult. The option to complete a self-paced degree using online discussion boards rather drive to a campus each week, sit through lectures, drive back home and complete other assignments is one of the flexibility of options provided for students in multiple geographical locations further away from college and university campuses (Gast, 2018/19).

Asynchronous learning is student-directed learning in which students make choices for which activities to complete out of a selection of required options, in the limited timeframe of choice, and grading based solely on chosen responses rather than on the physical characteristics of the student. Students are motivated to begin and complete the assignments in a timely manner. Asynchronous text-based learning allows students to read, re-read, take notes, and research independent of other students at their own pace without feeling pressured to keep the same schedule as the rest of the students in the class. Flexible scheduling is one of the benefits of asynchronous learning for the working adult.

Learning Collaboratively and Globally has been a project for Kristen Paino of New York City. Paino and her colleagues (2015) wanted students to be engaged not passive learners of geography; therefore, the creation of Global Book Series featuring collaborative interactive multimedia books from around the globe. Children take an active role to learn and connect with other students from around the world through iPads equipped with these Global Books. Using the SAMR (substitution, augmentation, modification, and reinvention) model and reproducing old practices with new high technology digital tools gives students an interactive and engaging learning experience either synchronously or asynchronously.

Asynchronous learners expressed the desire for instructors to provide contact information, post regular announcements about assignments, expectations, provide explicit details about participation requirements, grading rubrics and specific feedback on improving performance (Rios, Elliott, & Mandernach, 2018). Online students expressed concerns regarding the online presences of instructors. The online instructor needs to actively participate in the discussions with the students. Discussions need to be personalized and reflect real-life experiences related to the specific comments made by the student (Rios et.al, 2018).

Students in an online, asynchronous environment are used to instructors adapting, creating, modifying, and personalizing assignments (Rios et al., 2018). The online classroom contains culturally and geographically diverse populations of students who expect varying learning opportunities for assorted life and work experiences. To make the assignments meaningful and purposeful for students, instructors must be willing to adapt or modify the assignments to meet the needs of the students.

The use of appropriate software will take the learner from their current functioning level and progressively move them along at a successful pace. Each level of mastery can be achieved in a reasonably short amount of time with appropriate guided support provided at each step. Each student is competing with their own abilities and not competing against their peers or against the computer; as with the current Xbox and PlayStation computerized games students engage in at home. Many technology programs contain some of the same aspects and characteristics needed to enhance self-directed learning (Maehl, 2000; Russell, 2006; & Lawler & King, 2000): These programs are interactive, motivational, and autonomous; therefore, the programs provide opportunities for review with immediate feedback for students, as well as, foster retention.

Alternative assignments such as creating digital stories or movies requiring extensive time recordings and videos can use iMovie (for Macs), Movavi (for Windows), or iMotionHD (Ipad app). These options help to create digital movies for students to tell stories using stop motion pictures adding music, text, and sounds just like a regular movie maker. Student creativity and collaboration can be demonstrated using this alternative to writing (Tucker, 2015).

Student Presentation Tools

PowerPoint is only one of the various presentation tools used by students in the online classroom. Other student tools include Prezi, Google Slides, PowToons, Wide, Sparkle, Adobe Spark, and Thing link. Visual presentations are the first mode of learning to which students resort and search for when posed with an assignment. When students do not know about a topic, what do they do? Google it! When asked to present on a topic, students prefer not to write about it but to provide some type of video or other type of presentation. PowToon is a creative and engaging way to captivate the audience. Instructors can create or find videos already made with PowToon. The animation keeps the audience interested while explaining the topics. Another animation tool to use is Wideo. A video scribe such as Sparkol is similar to Wideo and PowToon. Videoscribe empowers students to create their own learning materials in a style that works best for them. Finally, Thinglink creates unique learning experiences with interactive images, videos and media. Thinglink interacts with Virtual Reality headsets.

Khan Academy

Video presentation tools such as Khan Academy are used for teaching and learning such difficult content subjects as advanced math topics in the areas of Algebra, trigonometry, statistics and probability, and calculus. Other content areas Khan Academy provides videos completed by instructors for learners to watch as many times as necessary include physics, chemistry, macroeconomics, government, civics, history, and Test Prep (Chorianopoulos, 2018). Video lectures provide an intimate feeling for learners as if the instructor is teaching specifically to the learner watching the video. This type of visual and auditory demonstration is more individualized and personalized for the asynchronous online classroom. The learner can watch, rewind, review, stop, take notes, watch again, without interfering with any other student in the class.

MOOC's

Massive Open Online Courses (MOOC's), "the contemporary online platforms employing two styles of video instructional tools: speaker-centric and board-centric" (Chorianopoulos, 2018, p. 297). Speaker-centric video instruction maintains a human example present throughout the demonstration. Board-centric video instruction would be most appropriate for math or science related courses where information would need to be presented in a written format as well as a verbal format. The asynchronous learning environment such as MOOC's require video lectures to accommodate all learning styles of students. Not all students can simply read the textbook and comprehend to apply the knowledge further. Chorianopolos (2018) described video lectures for MOOCs provided at such organizations as MIT and TEDed. Video lectures supplanted by assessment quizzes give learners a purpose to maintain focus during the viewing of the lecture and thereafter demonstrate knowledge learned from the material (Chorianopolos, 2018).

Phan (2018) reported characteristics about asynchronous MOOC's pertinent to student success and engagement in the course. These characteristics are presentation skills, strong content, managerial skills, personalization, feedback and fostering learner-centered interaction. Presentation skills include "videos with clearly articulated commentary, warm, friendly tones, and appropriate bodily gestures" (Phan, 2018, p. 98). Presentation without the use of videos also includes documents and graphics. Instructors should be sure all textual material is able to be accessed and read by students. Instructors need to know their content and be able to answer questions and provide relevant resources to students regarding helpful information about content.

The asynchronous online classroom environment arrangement needs an instructor have organized managerial skills. Students need to be able to locate all class materials in a timely manner in order to be successful and not frustrated. Instructors in the asynchronous environment form relationships with students by providing personalized, relevant and helpful feedback so students can make appropriate changes to assignments in a timely manner. Finally fostering a learner-centered environment requires the instructor to respond to student questions with appropriate answers, respond to students' discussion posts with personalized interactions, identifying each student as an active individual in the class and recognizing each student's unique talents. Teachers in the asynchronous classroom should treat each student as if he or she is in the same type of traditional face to face classroom without the constraints of walls and schedules.

Gliffy

Gliffy is an online visual communication and collaboration tool allowing for creations of flowcharts and diagrams. This program is very versatile for any content. Charts such as Venn diagrams for comparing and contrasting can be made and shared among students. Floor plans can be created using Gliffy. Organizational charts, mind maps, SWOT analysis, and network diagrams can be created and shared using the Gliffy website tools.

Piktochart and Smore

Creating newsletters, handouts, flyers, and reports for professional meetings, groups, and assignments requires more than a simple Word document. Piktochart and Smore provide graphics, templates, and sharing. Students can use Piktochart and Smore to collaborate in a professional manner.

FORMATIVE SYNCHRONOUS ASSESSMENT TOOLS

Active and engaging learning needs to be assessed to guide instructional changes. Digital tools to assist teachers with these assessments include but are not limited to "Socrative (www.socrative.com), Poll Everywhere (www.polleverywhere.com), or Google Forms (www.google.com/forms/about) to create surveys, quizzes, or exit tickets" (Daccord & Reich, 2015, p. 23).

Kahoot is a free website tool available for teachers to use as a review or assessment tool when preparing students for a test. Oftentimes, students perceive Kahoot as a game rather than as an assessment tool. Teachers possess the ability to create a quiz, a discussion, or a survey. When asking questions, Kahoot is limited to the use of 95 characters, whereas answers to questions are limited to 60 characters. Students may respond to questions using iPhones, android phones, or computers. Kahoot is a competitive game-based assessment tool used in a synchronous learning environment in which the faster students respond to the questions the more points are earned.

GoSoapBox

GoSoapBox is another digital tool for formative assessment and interaction with your students. This synchronous assessment tool provides the opportunity for students to alert the teacher with the confusion barometer. Teachers can use this tool asynchronously before class begins to generate questions students are interested in asking and answering for discussion points. Polling, discussions and quizzes are part of the options with GoSoapBox. Teachers can export and analyze student assessment results in order to make instructional changes.

ASYNCHRONOUS FORMATIVE ASSESSMENT TOOLS

Flubaroo

The use of Google Forms and Flubaroo are used in an asynchronous learning environment. These formative assessment tools can be made and sent to the students to be completed at any time. Flubaroo (www.flubaroo.com) is a free online webtool allowing teachers to quickly grade multiple choice and fill in the blank quizzes. The computer will automatically average the scores per question and provide teachers with information regarding low-scoring questions to review with those students needing additional instruction. Flubaroo will also provide teachers with a distribution graph and allow individualized feedback to be sent to students. Another option provided by Flubaroo is to email each student a grade and the answer key.

Simulation Exercises

"Simulation exercises are useful in assessing students' knowledge of interactions among multiple variables in a complex system" (Tucker, 2009, p. 51). Assessments using simulations provide instructors information regarding how students problem solve, think, approaches, reflections, steps taken in completing a project, and processing time. This data is important for driving instruction, reviewing lessons, grouping students, interventions and providing feedback. Simulations can be completed multiple times for students to gain mastery as well. "Technology-enhanced environments and virtual worlds are necessary for students to practice and gain feedback in real-life environments" (Tucker, 2009, p. 52).

Rubistar

Creating rubrics for the assignments and assessments can be a daunting task. Students need to know exactly how their work will be graded and what points count for which expectations of the assignment. Rubistar provides templates and guidance for creating high quality and exemplary grading rubrics matching the requirements, expectations, goals, and objectives of the criteria established for each assessment or assignment students will be graded against.

CONCLUSION

Students today want instant access to learning in the online classroom environment. Life is chaotic. Family responsibilities, work responsibilities, and too few class offerings in locations close to home restrict students from attending old and traditional face-to-face classes in brick and mortar settings. Schools must adapt to meet the demands of the students in the ever-changing highly technological world of work. Synchronous and asynchronous classes are the types of classes students request to continue educational learning and program considerations. Traveling with a laptop and a WIFI connections provides students with learning opportunities from anywhere anytime. This is the new mantra of the 21st century student. Educational institutions must concede to their wishes.

Students in the online classroom made the choice to attend the non-traditional environment for multiple reasons and therefore have different classroom expectations. Technology helps classroom facilitators provide differentiated instructional strategies and appropriate activities to meet non-traditional students' specialized needs. Providing the online students with options of choice to demonstrate their knowledge assists in the learning process for the teacher. Academic success of every student in the synchronous and asynchronous online classroom depends upon the preparedness of the instructor. Teachers using technological tools such as Khan Academy, Twitter, Flubaroo, Screencast-O-Matic, Padlet, Bubbl.us, Kahoot, and Zoom can assist these online students in understanding the various instructional programs taught in the asynchronous or synchronous environments.

REFERENCES

Bary, R., & Rees, M. (2006, March). Is (self-directed) learning the key sill for tomorrow's engineers? *European Journal of Engineering Education, 31*(1), 73–81. doi:10.1080/03043790500429021

Berge, Z. (2009). Changing instructor's roles in virtual worlds. *Quarterly Review of Distance Education, 9*(4), 407–415.

Blau, I., & Shamir-Inbal, T. (2018). Digital technologies for promoting student voice and co-creating learning experience in an academic course. *Instructional Science, 46*(2), 315–336. doi:10.100711251-017-9436-y

Bruce, C. (2002, July). Information literacy as a catalyst for educational change: A background paper. In P. Danaher (Ed.). *Lifelong Learning: Whose responsibility and what is your contribution? Proceedings of the 3rd International Lifelong Learning Conference* (pp. 8-19). Australia: Yeppoon, Queensland.

Chorianopoulos, K. (2018). A taxonomy of asynchronous instructional video styles. *International Review of Research in Open and Distributed Learning, 19*(1), 294–311. doi:10.19173/irrodl.v19i1.2920

Daccord, T., & Reich, J. (2015). How to transform teaching with tablets. *Educational Leadership, 72*(8), 18–23.

Evans, J. (2015). A vision for more mobile learning: More verbs, fewer nouns. *Educational Leadership, 72*(8), 10–16.

Ferriter, W. M. (2010, May). Preparing to teach digitally. *Educational Leadership, 67*(8), 88–89.

Gast, N. (2018/19). Introducing live group meetings in an online class: Tips and techniques. *Internet Learning Journal, 7*(1), 49–64.

Hall, C. (2012). Teaching and learning in a virtual environment. *The Journal of Education, Community, and Values, 12*(1).

Herold, B. (2017, June 23). Online classes for K-12 students: An overview. *Education Week*. Retrieved from https://www.edweek.org/ew/issues/online-classes/index.html

Jacobs, H. H. (2010). *Curriculum 21 Essential education for a changing world.* Alexandria, VA: ASCD.

Kreber, C., & Kanuka, H. (2006). The scholarship of teaching and learning and the online classroom. *Canadian Journal of University Continuing Education, 32*(2), 109–131.

Lawler, P. A., & King, K. P. (2000). *Refocusing faculty development: The view from an adult learning perspective. Proceedings from AERC 2000: Adult Education Research Conference.* Vancouver, BC, Canada: New Prairie Press. Retrieved from https://newprairiepress.org/cgi/viewcontent.cgi?referer=https://www.google.com/&httpsredir=1&article=2187&context=aerc

Lederman, D. (2017). Inside digital learning: Online education ascends. *Inside Higher Ed.* Retrieved from https://www.insidehighered.com/digital-learning/article/2018/11/07/new-data-online-enrollments-grow-and-share-overall-enrollment

Lowenthal, P. R., Dunlap, J. C., & Snelson, C. (2017). Live synchronous web meetings in asynchronous online courses: Reconceptualizing office hours. *Online Learning., 21*(4), 177–194. doi:10.24059/olj.v21i4.1285

Maehl, W. H. (2000). *Lifelong learning at its best.* San Francisco, CA: Jossey-Bass.

Marzano, R. J. (2009). Teaching with interactive whiteboards. *Educational Leadership, 67*(3), 80–81.

NACOL, North American Council for Online Learning. (2010, October). National standards for quality online teaching (ver. 2). Vienna, VA: *International Association for K-12 Online Learning.* Retrieved from http://www.inacol.org/research/nationalstandards/iNACOL_TeachingStandardsv2.pdf

Paino, K. (2015). Learning Collaboratively and Globally, New York City. Retrieved from: https://bookcreator.com/2015/01/expand-students-horizons-global-collaboration/

Phan, T. (2018). Instructional strategies that respond to global learners' needs in massive open online courses. *Online Learning*, 22(2), 95–118. doi:10.24059/olj.v22i2.1160

Picciano, A. G., & Seaman, J. (2010). *Class connections: High school reform and the role of online learning.* Retrieved from http://www.babson.edu/Academics/Documents/babson-survey-research-group/class-connections.pdf

Rios, T., Elliott, M., & Mandernach, B. J. (2018). Efficient instructional strategies for maximizing online student satisfaction. *Journal of Educators Online*, 15(3), 158–166. doi:10.9743/jeo.2018.15.3.7

Rodesiler, L. (2017). Sustained blogging about teaching: Instructional methods that support online participation as professional development. *TechTrends*, 61(4), 349–354. doi:10.100711528-017-0164-6

Russell, S. S. (2006). An overview of adult learning processes. *Urologic Nursing*, 26(5), 349–353. PMID:17078322

Salmon, G. (2004). *E-moderating: The key to teaching and learning online.* London, England: Routledge Falmer. doi:10.4324/9780203465424

Smith, T. (2005). Fifty-one competencies for online instruction. *The Journal of Educators Online*, 2(2), 1–18. doi:10.9743/JEO.2005.2.2

Tucker, B. (2009). The next generation of testing. *Educational Leadership*, 67(3), 48–53.

Tucker, C. (2015). 5 tips for managing mobile devices. *Educational Leadership*, 72(8), 25–29.

Wang, Q., Quek, C. L., & Hu, X. (2017). Designing and improving a blended synchronous learning environment: An educational design research. *International Review of Research in Open and Distributed Learning*, 18(3), 99–118. doi:10.19173/irrodl.v18i3.3034

Wiesenberg, F., & Stacey, E. (2008). Teaching philosophy: Moving from face-to-face to online classrooms. *Canadian Journal of University Continuing Education*, *34*(1), 63–69.

Yamagata-Lynch, L. C. (2014). Blending online asynchronous and synchronous learning. *International Review of Research in Open and Distance Learning*, *15*(2), 189–212. doi:10.19173/irrodl.v15i2.1778

Chapter 4
Trifecta of Student Engagement:
A Framework for Engaging Students in Online Courses

Heather J. Leslie
University of San Diego, USA

ABSTRACT

This chapter describes a framework adapted from Michael Moore's three essential areas: student-content interaction, student-student interaction, and student-instructor interaction for engaging students in online courses. To be fully engaged in an online course, students need to be engaged with the course curriculum content, with their peers, and with their instructor. When students are engaged in all three areas, it is referred to as the Trifecta of Student Engagement. This chapter incorporates literature on each area of the Trifecta of Student Engagement: student-to-content engagement, student-to-student engagement, and student-to-instructor engagement as well as some suggested synchronous and asynchronous digital tools.

INTRODUCTION

Student engagement is an important concept when designing and teaching online courses (Meyer, 2014; Wankel & Blessinger, 2012; Everett, 2015). Although there is a lack of agreement on a single definition, student engagement has been associated with positive outcomes such as student success and development (Mayhew, et, al., 2016). According to the Glossary of Education Reform (2016, n. p.), student engagement

DOI: 10.4018/978-1-7998-1622-5.ch004

"refers to the degree of attention, curiosity, interest, optimism, and passion that students show when they are learning or being taught, which extends to the level of motivation they have to learn and progress in their education." Engaging students is a learner-centered teaching approach that has been recognized in education as being effective (Beaudoin, 1990; Darsih, 2018; Schreurs & Dumbraveanu, 2014). The term *engagement* in this chapter will focus on the asynchronous and synchronous strategies aimed at attracting student interest, attention, and motivation to learn as well as some suggested online tools that can facilitate student interaction.

Focusing on student engagement for online courses can impact the course experience for students and can improve their satisfaction, learning, and achievement (Leslie, 2019). In an online teaching professional development program, faculty who utilized teaching strategies that focused on student engagement saw an improvement in student grades, higher scores on teaching evaluations, and had students report that their learning improved. Research states that student engagement has been positively associated with student academic achievement, progression, retention, graduation, satisfaction, and deeper learning (National Survey of Student Engagement, 2017; Zilvinskis, Masseria, & Pike, 2017; Lei, Yunhuo, & Zhou, 2018). Focusing on strategies that engage students, then, can positively impact student success.

BACKGROUND

One of the major conduits of student engagement in online courses is interaction (Wanstreet, 2009). Interaction allows students to exchange ideas and construct meaning individually and with course participants. Further, interaction in online courses has shown to have a direct impact on student satisfaction, student achievement, and learning outcomes (Durrington, et al., 2006; Bernard et al., 2009). In his seminal research, Michael Moore (1989) outlined three types of interaction in online courses: learner-content interaction, learner-learner interaction, and learner-instructor interaction. Student-content interaction is "the process of intellectually interacting with content that results in changes in the learner's understanding, the learner's perspective, or the cognitive structures of the learner's mind" (Moore, 1989, p. 2). Learner-learner interaction is the process of learners collaborating and communicating information with peers, which can be especially valuable in the areas of application and evaluation (Sharp & Huett, 2006). Learner-instructor interaction "is widely considered essential by educators and students alike. This interaction type includes three tasks to be performed by the instructor: to stimulate interest and motivation; to organize application of student learning; and to counsel, support, and encourage each learner" (Sharp & Huett, 2006, p. 4). It is important to note that the quality of interaction, including personalization and meaningful communication, impacts student satisfaction with the overall learning experience (Eom & Wen, 2006). A framework for student engagement, based on the three types of interaction, is referred to as the Trifecta of Student Engagement (Figure 1). This framework proposes that students, to be fully engaged in a course, need to regularly and meaningfully interact with their course curriculum content, with their peers, and with their instructor.

Figure 1. The trifecta of engagement (adapted from Moore, 1989)

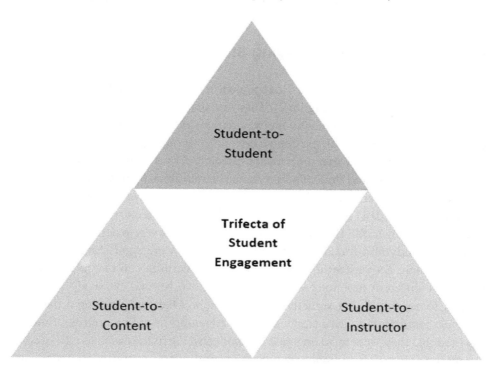

The Trifecta of Student Engagement categorizes student engagement into three areas: student-to-content engagement, student-to-student engagement, and student-to-instructor engagement. Each area of the Trifecta intersects and overlaps with one another in a student-centered online learning community (Hoidn, 2017). The chapter is divided into the following sections:

- The Student-to-Content Engagement section focuses on motivational strategies that challenge and inspire students to engage with content.

- The Student-to-Student Engagement section focuses on social learning theory and constructivist approaches to facilitate student engagement with their peers.
- The Student-to-Instructor Engagement section focuses on building connections with students and faculty through feedback and communication strategies.

The following is a review of the literature for each area of the Trifecta of Student Engagement framework as well as suggested digital tools that can be used in practice.

Review of Literature: Engaging Students with Content

The first area of the Trifecta of Engagement aims to help students engage with course curriculum content (Figure 2). There are many strategies that can encourage students-to-content engagement. One way to get students involved in the learning process and interacting with the course content is through active learning. There is an abundance of research that supports the effectiveness of active learning. Consider one study that compared student performance in traditional lecture courses that used passive methods of content delivery to courses that used active learning techniques. Freeman et al. (2014) found that students in traditional lecture courses were 1.5 times more likely to fail than students who took courses where active learning was used. This study also found that examination scores were significantly higher for students where active learning was used. Active learning can encompass a wide variety of different activities where students move beyond passively absorbing content to actively doing something with content. One study explored the kinds of active learning activities students found engaging in online courses. Students reported that they were most engaged by application activities such as case studies, discussion forums about concepts, labs and group projects, research papers, and current event assignments (Dixson, 2010). Such studies demonstrate that active learning can promote students' engagement with content.

The Australian Survey of Student Engagement (AUSSE), which gathered student engagement data from over 25 Australian and New Zealand higher education institutions, defined active learning as "students' efforts to actively construct their own knowledge" (Coates, 2008, p. vii). This survey found that students were most engaged when challenged to practice higher order thinking and reasoning such as analysis, synthesis, evaluation, and application. Thus, having students complete activities such as solve problems, ask questions, examine assumptions, compare and contrast views, and take part in critical thinking exercises can cultivate deeper learning and engagement with content.

Strategies that challenge students to think deeply and critically can encourage students' engagement with content. One strategy to facilitate deep thinking and inquiry is the use of essential questions. McTighe and Wiggins (2013) describe the purpose of essential questions as challenging students to grapple with big ideas. Essential questions do not have a single "right" answer that students can simply look up or Google. Rather, essential questions can often lead to additional questions, epiphanies, critical insights, and inspired learning. An example of an essential question is: "How do we overcome prejudice and social bias?" Essential questions inspire students to ponder possibilities, solutions, and inquiries which can further their engagement and connection to course content. Essential questions were used in a classroom by a high school history teacher, Mr. P. Mr. P wanted to challenge his students to think more deeply about complex issues of the past and how they connect to the present, as opposed to memorizing an assortment of facts (Lattimer, 2008). Mr. P conscientiously crafted questions that brought to life the issues that would challenge students' assumptions and perspectives. He introduced the unit on personal freedom by connecting it to experiences that students could relate to such as curfew and dress code. Students took a position on issues, which could provide them with a lens for analyzing other issues that would be seemingly less relatable such as women's right to vote, Prohibition, and the rise of the KKK. Throughout the unit, students reflected on essential questions through Socratic seminars, informal discussions, and journal writing. Students' views evolved from "strident certainty to recognizing the tenuous balance between liberty and safety" (Lattimer, 2008, p. 329). Using essential questions as a teaching strategy had positive effects including increased student engagement, more consistent attendance and homework completion, and a 15-point increase in test scores. One student commented in an end-of-course evaluation, "This class made me think more than any other class I've ever had. I learned a lot about history, and I learned even more about how to think about history" (Lattimer, 2008, p. 329). Essential questions that provoke students to think critically and deeply can facilitate students' engagement with content.

Another area that has been studied in depth in terms of engaging students is the use of motivational strategies. There are many different theories that attempt to explain what motivates students and how to tap into students' motivation. Some literature focuses on approaches aimed at specific types of learners such as adults. Adult learning principles suggests that adult learners are engaged by content that is directly tied to their needs and goals (Knowles, 2005). Therefore, some recommend the use of relevancy-based or utility-value interventions that explain the value or relevance of content as a way to motivate students to learn the content (Harackiewicz, Smith, & Priniski, 2016). Some such interventions demonstrated positive outcomes on academic achievement and motivation (Lazowski & Hulleman, 2016). However, there is little consensus as to how to make content relevant and valuable to all students

(Albrecht & Karabenick, 2017). What is relevant and valuable for one student may not be relevant and valuable for another student. Therefore, giving students the opportunity to personalize content and learning may be a useful motivational strategy.

Some authors have advocated for the use of authenticity in course content whereby students are asked to solve real-world problems that hold significance outside the classroom. Newman, Marks, and Gamoran (1996) found that when elementary and middle school students engaged in authentic work that had value beyond school, such as a community project, the quality of their academic work improved. Going further, when students have some autonomy and choice, such as deciding what their project is, what community it will serve, and how they will demonstrate their learning, this can have a positive impact on intrinsic motivation and performance (Zuckerman, Porac, Lathin, Smith, & Deci, 1978). Giving students options to customize projects by following their passions and interests as well as freedom to make decisions in how they demonstrate their learning can allow them to be more creative and self-directed where they take more responsibility for their learning (Merriam & Bierema, 2014). Granting students agency, autonomy, choice, and trust to do work that is authentic and meaningful to them can allow engagement to occur.

A motivational model that has been effective when applied to online courses is the ARCS model (Keller & Suzuki, 2004). In this model, content must gain the attention of learners; bring relevance that connects content with the learner's goals, past experience, and learning style; build confidence so the learner believes they have the self-efficacy to accomplish the task; and satisfaction with the learning experience. This model has been validated in online courses in multiple countries and has been correlated with decreased drop-out rates and positive motivational outcomes (Keller & Suzuki, 2004).

Helping students form a meaningful connection to course content is another strategy to engage students with content. Some have found success in having students construct their own connections to content through activities such as critical self-reflection (Smith, Rook, & Smith, 2010). Smith, Rook, and Smith (2010) conducted a study to test metacognition and affect-based interventions on high school students using a journaling activity for 12 weeks. One group of students answered affective and metacognitive questions in addition to content-based questions from the textbook. Another group of students only answered content-based questions from the textbook. The group of students who answered the affective and metacognitive questions in addition to the content-based questions demonstrated better retention of content material and earned better grades than their counterparts. Engagement can occur when students have the opportunity to personalize course content and build a meaningful connection of course content to their lives.

Another strategy discussed in the literature to motivate students is to trigger their interest in learning the content. Students who develop an interest in the subject matter are more likely to perform better (Hidi & Harackiewicz, 2000). Interest can be developed by a momentary experience of being captivated as well as more enduring affects that lead to further exploration (Harackiewicz, Smith & Priniski, 2016). One method to attract student interest is to use novelty, complexity, or surprise, to trigger attention, excitement, or curiosity (Renninger & Hidi, 2016). One study found the use of inquiry-based learning in a science lesson for ninth graders aroused their interest (Palmer, 2008). The students' level of interest varied throughout the lesson, but the use of novelty, choice, physical activity, and social involvement correlated to the students' interest.

There is no one-size-fits-all approach to motivate students. Student motivation, interest, and perceived utility and relevance of content can vary widely and is dependent on many contextual factors (Albrecht & Karabenick, 2017). Keller and Suzuki (2004) note that student motivation can be influenced but not controlled. Thus, experimenting with methods aimed at attracting student interest and connection to course content are useful for influencing student engagement with content.

Suggested Digital Tools

After examining several strategies for engaging students with content, we can now turn our attention to some practical tools that can be used to facilitate students' engagement with content. Online asynchronous tools that instructors may find useful are blogs and videos.

Blogs

Blogs are like web journals and can be used to promote reflection, self-assessment, and sharing of insights. Blogging, like journaling, can be an effective way for students to connect content to personal experience. Through blogging, students can showcase their learning using text, images, hyperlinks, and media, and their peers can view and comment on their work. There are many free websites that students can use to set up their blogs. Alternatively, some Learning Management Systems have blogging tools included. As students become more proficient in using online technology, tools such as blogs can be a good medium for students to reflect and engage with content. A study examined 350 college students who used blogging as a reflective journaling activity in marketing courses (Muncy, 2014). A majority of students (60 percent) perceived the blogging assignment to be helpful or very helpful in getting them to think about the content. Muncy (2014) notes that several housekeeping items need to be in place for a blogging assignment to be successful including clear instructions that clarify the goals and expectations for the assignment (including reflection versus recitation or summary of content), training for students on how to use the technology, and examples so students can see what constitutes a good blog. The use of blogs for reflective learning can be one way to have students engage with content.

Instructor-Created Videos

Another tool that instructors may find useful to engage students with content is video-creation software. There are many kinds of software to create videos and some institutions have licenses available for instructors. Some examples of video-creation software include Kaltura, Screencast-O-Matic, Camtasia, and Jing. Instructors can use this software to record their computer screen or themselves through a webcam and present content. Presenting content in different formats such as video can appeal to diverse student learning preferences, including audio, visual, and kinesthetic preferences (The National Center on Universal Design for Learning, n.d.). Some students may even prefer that their instructors utilize technology to deliver content in multiple formats such as video (Bork & Rucks-Ahidiana, 2013). Videos can convey instructor presence and add a human element, which are important in online courses. Videos can also be an effective way to demonstrate a procedure, explain a detailed method, or bring a process or idea to life using 3-D images, audio, and graphics. Faculty can use videos to introduce course material or instructions as well as highlight, explain, or reinforce content.

Choi and Johnson (2005) found that the use of instructional videos can be used to motivate learners by attracting their attention and can help with comprehension and retention of information through the use of visual and audio aids. Instructors can also humanize themselves to students (e.g. show that there is a human being on the other side of the screen) through the use of recorded webcam videos (Friend, 2017), which also falls into the area of instructor-to-student engagement. Faculty storytelling, anecdotes, personal experience, and sharing passion for the discipline can provide students with engaging content and make them feel closer to their instructor (Buffo, 2015). Faculty can support the course learning objectives by creating video lessons to teach the course material. Bork and Rucks-Ahidiana (2013) found that students "felt more like they were in a classroom lecture when instructors used audio and video materials. They noted that materials created by the course instructor provided a personal touch, creating a sense of the instructor's presence in the course and giving students a feeling that the instructor was actively teaching them" (p. 21). It is a best practice to limit video length to about three minutes, otherwise engagement can decline (Crawford, 2019). Chunking content into easily digestible bite-sized bits can sustain engagement. Instructors can also have students create their own videos for presentations, reflections, and discussions in order for students to humanize themselves, learn new digital skills, and create engaging content for their peers.

In conclusion, there are numerous ways to engage students with content. Some of the strategies described above for engaging students with content include:

- Using active learning techniques that challenge students to practice higher order thinking.
- Using motivational strategies that frame content as relevant, useful, valuable, and meaningful.
- Using essential questions that provoke students to think critically and deeply.
- Giving opportunities for students to make meaning of content by connecting it to their personal lives using digital tools like blogs for reflective learning.
- Presenting content in multiple formats such as video to appeal to different learning preferences.
- Giving students creative freedom to showcase their learning of content according to their passions and interests.

ENGAGING STUDENTS WITH STUDENTS

The second component of the Trifecta of Engagement is about facilitating student-to-student engagement (Figure 3). Humans are social beings and this affects how we learn. Researchers who have studied psychological well-being note that people have a need to experience a sense of community and belonging (McMillan & Chavis, 1986). In a learning setting, feelings of belonging can positively influence academic persistence and performance (Voelkl, 2012). Being part of a community and having a sense of belonging entails students building relationships with each other, which also improves the learning experience (Hargis, 2005). Student-to-student interactions and relationships have been shown to improve academic performance (Althaus, 1997) and increase student engagement (Voelkl, 2012), motivation (Ryan & Patrick, 2001), and satisfaction (Hiltz & Wellman, 1997).

Vesely, Bloom, and Sherlock (2007) observed that students and instructors perceived community as being very important in online courses, however they also believe it can be more challenging to build community in online courses compared to in-person courses. These authors contend that instructors have a leadership role to play in facilitating community in virtual classrooms. Elements of community that instructors may want to make explicit or co-construct with students include: (1) a shared sense of purpose; (2) an establishment of ground rules or agreements that govern behavior such as netiquette guidelines; (3) norms for interaction and participation; and (4) ensuring an environment of trust, support, and respect among learners. Setting the expectations and climate for students to engage with their peers should also include the rationale for such pedagogies. Namely, that students have a lot to learn from each other and that peer-to-peer interaction contributes to the learning goals. Expectations for interaction can be reinforced and rewarded by providing students with rubrics to evaluate their participation and contribution to the learning community (Vesely, Bloom, & Sherlock, 2007).

When learners interact in a community toward a shared purpose, it is referred to as collaboration (Palloff & Pratt, 1999). Johnson and Johnson (2002) found that collaborative learning helps students achieve more together through collective efforts, than they can by working alone. Collaborative learning means that "learning is not only active but interactive" where learners are "actively involved in constructing knowledge by applying concepts to problems, and/or formulating ideas into words, and these ideas are built upon through reactions and responses of others" (Hiltz, Turoff, & Harasim, 2007, p. 60). The instructor's role in collaborative learning is to encourage students to work together on an academic problem, project, or task that connects to the learning goals or outcomes of the course. Hiltz, Turoff, and Harasim (2007) found that when students work on a shared goal they also have the opportunity to interact socially, which can create a sense of community. This can further motivate students to regularly participate in the class (Hiltz, Turoff, & Harasim, 2007). The instructor can facilitate this process by soliciting students' ideas, thoughts, opinions, and feelings while working on learning tasks (Ryan & Patrick, 2001) and regularly assisting their progress.

Palloff and Pratt (1999) suggest the process of community development mimics the five stages of team development known as forming, norming, storming, performing, and adjourning (Tuckman, 1965, as cited in Palloff and Pratt, 1999). To facilitate this group development process, Palloff and Pratt (1999) recommend creating opportunities for synchronous collaboration such as meeting in person or through web conferencing. According to these authors, indicators of a successful learning community are: (1) active participation, (2) sharing resources among students, (3) socially constructed meaning through questioning or agreement in order to achieve consensus on issues of meaning, (4) expressions of support and encouragement exchanged between students, and (5) a willingness to critically evaluate peers' work (Palloff, Pratt, & Stockley, 2001). Further, they state that a recipe for a successful learning community is honesty, responsiveness, relevance, respect, openness, and empowerment.

In a study that examined graduate students' preferences for interaction, Northrup (2002) found that students thought it was important for online instructors to promote collaboration and dialogue. Further, these types of interactive learning activities enhanced students' motivation and improved academic achievement. Another study also found that online collaboration and dialogue improved undergraduate students' cognitive learning (Krentler & Willis-Flurry, 2005). In addition, Krentler and Willis-Flurry (2005) found that students who collaborated via online class discussions more than 75 percent of the time earned a significantly higher course grade point average (GPA= 2.69) than all other students where the mean course grade point average was 2.49. Collaborative learning, then, can create a sense of connectedness and community in online courses and positively impact learning.

To have a sense of community and make connections, students need to find commonalities in background, motivation, and commitment (Caverly & MacDonald, 2002). To foster these connections, instructors can create opportunities for students to get to know each other through activities such as ice breaker discussions and through meaningful learning activities where students share their prior experience. Incorporating opportunities for student sharing allows students to get to know each other better as the course progresses and tends to result in more authentic conversations. Other practices that can strengthen student-to-student engagement include facilitating camaraderie during deep discussions where the instructor models thoughtful responses and a personal tone (Young & Bruce, 2011). Cultivating such interaction, cohesion, and relationship-building through dialogue can also enhance students' feelings of belonging and can protect against student attrition (Osterman, 2000). Feelings of belonging and being part of a community may be especially beneficial for students who come from marginalized populations (Pittman & Richmond, 2008).

Vesley, Bloom, and Sherlock (2007) found that students ranked instructor modeling as the most important factor in building community in online courses. The idea that students learn from instructor behavior coincides with social learning theory, which suggests that people learn from one another via observation, imitation, and modeling (Bandura, 1977). Instructors can model what has been referred to as *immediacy behaviors*, which "refers to communication behaviors that reduce social and psychological distance between people" (Arbaugh, 2001) or communication behaviors that enhance intimacy between people. Rovai (2001) suggests facilitating two kinds of interactions to promote a sense of community and connectedness among learners: (1) task-driven interactions that align to the learning goals, and (2) socioemotional interactions that enable the well-being of learners and help them develop friendships or bonds. Instructors can demonstrate immediacy by modeling interactions that build relationships. This can include affirming and recognizing students' input or effort, inviting sharing and participation, showing genuine curiosity and interest in students' thoughts and ideas, providing feedback that is personalized and helpful, expressing concern or consideration for students' well-being, and communicating a caring and compassionate attitude (Vesley, Bloom, and Sherlock, 2007). In an online course where students reported feeling a sense of community, the instructor maintained a course presence by posting to the course site daily, mostly through discussion forums (Rovai, 2001). The messages the instructor modeled were encouraging, personalized, and constructive. Instructor messages also mediated issues of student emotional distress, frustration, or confusion. The instructor modeled substantive responses and constructive feedback in discussion forums and invited student suggestions for improvement.

LaRose and Whitten (2000) observed immediacy behaviors that instructors modeled which students, then, replicated in online courses. These behaviors included giving praise, using personal examples, addressing people by name, asking questions, soliciting opinions, and using humor. These behaviors contribute to what is called social presence, which is an essential component of building community. Social presence conveys a feeling of belonging and togetherness that make students feel connected to the class. Social presence theory classifies online interaction according to how well intimacy and warmth are transmitted between course users and their ability to form personal relationships (Lombard & Ditton, 1997). Social presence has also been correlated to improved learning outcomes (Rourke, Anderson, Archer, & Garrison, 1999). Instructors can enhance social presence in online courses in a number of ways including through informal discussion boards. Woods and Ebersole (2003) studied building social presence using informal discussion boards so students could get to know each other and found that students reported feeling more connected to their peers and were more satisfied with the overall course experience. Because there can be a lack of visual cues in online courses, social presence has to be intentional and apparent (Rovai, 2001). One study revealed some instructor immediacy behaviors that enhance social presence and can positively impact the online learning experience. These behaviors include providing frequent and specific feedback and compliments to students, addressing students by name in all correspondence, relating to students on a personal and professional level, and using emoticons to convey emotions and a supportive tone (Gunter, 2007). Gunter (2007) noted that additional research may be needed on immediacy behaviors that take into account differences such as gender.

A case study examining perceptions of feelings of sense of community from students in an online MBA program found positive correlations between feelings of sense of learning community and feelings of belonging, learning engagement, and overall satisfaction with the quality of online courses (Liu, Magjuka, Bonk, & Lee, 2007). Additionally, the results showed that sense of belonging to a learning community was positively associated with instructor presence and facilitation. The use of announcements to broadcast course-related news and instructor feedback was also correlated with the feelings of sense of community. The use of collaborative group work was associated with feelings of sense of community for the individual groups but not necessarily with the class as a whole. Some instructors in the study indicated that they did not see the importance or necessity of building community, stating that such activities were too time consuming. Other instructors seemed to see a need for creating opportunities for robust idea exchange and dialogue to facilitate the learning community. Student survey results showed that 80 percent of students perceived group work was helpful to their learning and 93 percent felt that sharing information and giving feedback to peers contributed to learning. Approximately 86 percent of students felt that collective knowledge is created through group work while taking online courses (Liu, Magjuka, Bonk & Lee, 2007). These results underscore the role that instructors can play in facilitating community as well as how student-to-student interaction and collaboration contributes to a sense of community, belonging, satisfaction, and engagement.

Suggested Digital Tools

After examining instructor strategies for facilitating student-to-student engagement through community building, we can now explore some digital tools for the online classroom that can serve as a medium for interactive student-to-student communication and collaboration. These tools include discussion boards, wikis, and synchronous web conferencing platforms, which may be included in some Learning Management Systems.

Discussion Boards

Discussion boards in online courses are a medium where robust conversations can take place. Because the discussion board is asynchronous, it allows students the time to reflect deeply and craft thoughtful responses (Dawley, 2007). A well-designed discussion board can allow demonstration of knowledge, community building, critical thinking, and reflection. Likewise, a good discussion requires effective facilitation by the instructor. Facilitating discussions that promote critical thinking go beyond asking students to recall information from textbook readings. The use of Socratic questioning techniques and question types can be an excellent resource for facilitators. One study found that the use of Socratic questioning in discussion boards positively impacted students' critical thinking (Lee, Kim, & Kim, 2014). Socratic question types include asking students to: clarify their answers, check their assumptions, provide reason and evidence, examine different viewpoints and perspectives, discuss implications or consequences, or discover the meaning of questions themselves (Lee, Kim, & Kim, 2014).

There are a host of other interactive discussion board activities that can promote student-to-student engagement and critical thinking. Examples include debates, negotiation exercises, role-play scenarios, and student-led discussions. Students can also share their papers, projects, or assignments via the discussion board for peer assessment and peer feedback. Peer assessment can improve students' writing as well as develop assessment and evaluation skills, critical thinking skills, and disciplinary skills (Baker, 2016). This can be beneficial for students' development of writing for readership when work is not just reviewed and created for an instructor's eyes only (Jenkins, 2017). Students can review each other's papers before they submit them or answer questions about a case study, for example, and evaluate each other's answers. These types of peer assessment activities expose students to others' viewpoints, ideas, values, and perspectives. This can enrich the learning experience and give students skills in self-assessment, when a teacher is no longer present, to build skills for lifelong learning (Seifert & Feliks, 2019). The sharing of student work with peers also helps students develop bonds and contributes to the learning community (Hulett, 2019). Whatever discussion or peer assessment activity is chosen should align with the learning objectives of the course. An explanation of the rationale behind the activity and how it connects to the learning objectives can be a strategy to motivate students to engage (Harackiewicz, Smith, & Priniski, 2016).

Wikis

Another asynchronous digital tool that can be used in online courses to promote student-to-student engagement and collaboration is a wiki (Cilliers, 2017). A wiki allows students to collaboratively create and edit a shared post or document. Students and instructors can see all the versions of the post or document to track edits, additions, and changes. This allows the instructor and students to see who contributed to the wiki and what they contributed. A wiki can be used for creating study guides, summaries of what was learned, brainstorming sessions, creative storytelling, concept mapping, annotated bibliographies, or group projects. Su and Beaumont (2010) found that the use of wikis can promote collaborative learning and confidence through formative self and peer assessment by observing others' contributions. However, potential issues with student use of a wiki may include making mistakes such as accidentally deleting peers' posts or intentionally deleting peers' posts (Su & Beaumont, 2010). Su and Beaumont recommend that sufficient training be provided to students on how to use the technology as well as "do's and don'ts" for using the technology.

Web Conferencing Platforms

Synchronous digital technology that can be used to build community in online courses include web conferencing platforms such as Zoom or Blackboard Collaborate. These platforms allow instructors and students to meet virtually in real time and many have a robust set of interactive and collaborative features such as webcam, microphone, polling, white board, chat, and breakout groups. These functions allow the potential to create highly interactive and engaging learning sessions. Additionally, instructors can use web conferencing platforms to host office hours or meet one-on-one with students. McInnery and Roberts (2004) found that synchronous meetings were helpful for building community particularly during the 'forming' stage where students had the opportunity to interact, connect, warm-up to, and get to know each in real time. In order to ensure that synchronous learning sessions run smoothly, instructors should become highly familiar with how to use the various platform tools and plan out their sessions carefully. Additionally, students should be oriented to how to use the different features of the platform and how to participate and contribute meaningfully to the learning community.

There are many ways to engage students with their peers. As previously described, some of strategies for facilitating student-to-student engagement include:

- Setting the tone and expectation for interaction and participation through shared agreements, guidelines, and evaluation methods.
- Fostering a sense of community and belonging through tools such as asynchronous discussion boards and synchronous web conferences.
- Designing opportunities for students to collaborate through activities like group work, peer assessment, and wikis.
- Modeling effective interactions and communications that promote critical thinking and collegiality.

ENGAGING STUDENTS WITH INSTRUCTOR

The third component of the Trifecta of Engagement framework focuses on ways faculty can engage with students. Research has shown that student-faculty relationships have a significant impact on educational outcomes including persistence, satisfaction, effort, achievement, and learning (Pascarella, 1980; Endo & Harpel,1982; Kuh & Hu, 2001). Theories of student engagement have been predicated on student-faculty interaction as being necessary for student integration and success (Spady, 1970; Tinto, 1975).

In one study, Endo and Harpel (1982) categorized faculty interaction as informal or formal. Faculty who interacted informally with students had a friendly relationship and showed concern for students' emotional and cognitive growth. Faculty who interacted formally with students had a professional relationship and focused on academic and vocational topics. Other variables in the study included the quality of faculty advising and the helpfulness of faculty and their impact on students' personal/social outcomes, intellectual outcomes, academic achievement, and satisfaction with education. The results indicated that student-faculty interaction generally affected student outcomes even after controlling for demographic variables. The frequency of informal interactions as well as helpfulness of faculty positively impacted personal/social outcomes, intellectual outcomes, and satisfaction with education. However, neither frequency of informal nor frequency of formal interactions were found to influence academic achievement, although the latter came close. Terenzini and Pascarella (1980) found that the frequency of intellectual and career-oriented student-faculty interactions had an impact on student achievement. Endo and Harpel's (1982) study confirmed that the frequency and quality of student-faculty interaction showed positive effects on personal, intellectual, and academic outcomes.

Another study identified instructor immediacy behaviors that positively influenced student satisfaction in online community college courses. These include an instructor's ability to clearly communicate expectations, the timeliness and accessibility of the instructor, the instructor's ability to provide clear directions about the coursework, and the instructor's expressed enthusiasm for student learning (Jackson, Jones, & Rodriguez, 2010). Other research has demonstrated that successful online instructors are those who provide meaningful and ongoing communication by emailing their students frequently, replying to email promptly, holding regular online office hours, being active in discussions, and using personal touches in the online classroom (Keengwe & Kidd, 2010). In one study, students were asked to rate various instructor practices in online courses. The instructor practices that students rated as most important to them were focused on interpersonal communication needs (such as email, feedback, and responses to discussion board postings) and information communication needs (such as providing course materials, examples, and instructor expectations) (Dennen, Aubteen, & Smith, 2007). Meeting virtually with students one-on-one or in small groups also enhances student-faculty relationships and those relationships have shown to have a positive correlation to student persistence, performance, and satisfaction (Gaytan, 2013).

Bower and Hardy (2004) posited that an online instructor's most essential job is to engage and sustain students in high levels of interaction and involvement. This may require instructors to invest more time into daily management of the online class than would be required for a traditional campus-based setting (Carroll-Barefield, Smith, Prince, & Campbell, 2005). The opportunity to develop more personal interactions with students in a more flexible format can also be a motivating factor for faculty to teach online (Hiltz, Shea, & Eunhee, 2004).

The role of instructor in an online environment is different than in a traditional classroom (Beaudoin, 1990). The focus has shifted from delivering information and transmitting knowledge to facilitating and stimulating the process of learning. This shift in teacher-centered instruction to learner-centered facilitation requires specialized pedagogical skills in anticipating learner needs, coordinating resources, moderating interactions, and mastering technologies (Jackson, Jones, & Rodriguez, 2010). The TPACK framework (Technological, Pedagogical, Content Knowledge) is a useful framework for the kinds of knowledge needed for effective facilitation of learning in an online environment (Harris, Mishra, & Koehler, 2009). Although the instructor role may differ, Chickering and Gamson's (1991) principles for good teaching have been shown to apply effectively to online courses as well (Crews, Wilkinson, & Neill, 2015). The *Seven Principles of Good Practice* are:

1. Encourages reciprocity and cooperation among students
2. Encourages active learning
3. Gives prompt feedback
4. Emphasizes time on task
5. Communicates high expectations
6. Respects diverse talents and ways of learning (Chickering & Gamson, 1991).

Crews, Wilkinson, & Neill (2015) found that these tried and true teaching principles were equally important in online education.

Another theoretical framework that can be used for effective student-instructor engagement is the community of inquiry (CoI) framework (Garrison, Anderson, and Archer, 2000). This model can be used for creating a meaningful (collaborative-constructivist) educational experience through the intentional development of three interdependent components: social presence, teaching presence, and cognitive presence. Social presence enables learners to feel comfortable expressing themselves authentically in terms of their personality and identity. It involves faculty expressing their emotions and creating open communication and group cohesion. Teaching presence involves the design, facilitation, and management of the learning environment to achieve the course learning objectives. It involves direct instruction and helping students build understanding. Cognitive presence enables learners to construct meaning of the learning experience through activities such as reflection and discourse. It involves exploration, integration, and resolution to guide students' thinking (Garrison, 2000). The individual components as well as the overall framework have been examined empirically for effectively building community in online courses (Arbaugh, 2007). Shea, Fredricksen, Pickett, and Pelz (2004) studied the Community of Inquiry framework for 935 online students in the SUNY Learning Network. These researchers found that there was a strong correlation between student satisfaction and high quality and timely feedback on assignments.

One of the most critical areas where instructors engage with students and influence their performance is through giving feedback (Dennen, Darabi, & Smith, 2007). Feedback can be provided in a variety of mediums including written, recorded audio, or video. Prompt feedback allows learners to examine their current knowledge, reflect on their learning, and receive recommendations for improvement. Pyke (2010) notes two types of feedback instructors can use: corrective and motivational. Corrective feedback attempts to provide information to the learner about their performance while motivational feedback focuses on the goals of the learner. It is recommended that feedback be specific, objective, consistent, and timely (Sachdeva, 1996). Sachdeva (1996) suggests that a supportive environment be established with an open dialogue between student and instructor in a collaborative manner with mutually agreed upon goals that are reinforced through follow-up and action plans. Effective feedback is constructive, actionable, encouraging, and personalized, and focuses on specific behavior, effort, or accomplishment, rather than a judgment on student ability (Brookhart, 2008). Additionally, effective feedback targets the task, not the individual or identity, and should focus on the process, not just the results. Faculty can use their comments to teach, rather than justify a grade, focusing on what students should address in future work. Hattie and Timperley (2007) state that effective feedback must answer three major questions for the student: Where am I going? (What are the goals?), How am I going? (What progress is being made toward the goal?), and Where to next? (What activities need to be undertaken to make better progress?). Giving and receiving feedback is an important interactive component between students and faculty that can enhance the student-faculty relationship, improve student performance, increase satisfaction, and enrich the learning experience.

Suggested Digital Tools

Now that we have explored some strategies for enhancing student-to-instructor engagement through immediacy behaviors in the online classroom, we can now consider some digital tools that can be used as a medium for robust communication and instructor presence. These tools include online journals, webcam, and email, which may be included in some Learning Management Systems.

Online Journals

A virtual space where faculty can engage with students and provide personalized feedback is through online journals. Journals allow a space for reflection and metacognition where students can ask questions, share their struggles and successes, think about their learning, and receive one-on-one mentoring, coaching, and support from faculty. Journaling can be one of the most effective exercises to promote self-awareness, improvement, and reflectivity (Herndon, 1996). Reflection is an important part of the learning process and faculty can encourage students to reflect by using online journaling.

Webcam Videos

Another way for instructors to show their presence in an online course by utilizing a webcam. A webcam can humanize faculty to students by showing that there is a human being on the other side of the screen, which can help foster a sense of student-to-faculty closeness (Griffiths & Graham, 2010). Bork and Rucks-Ahidiana (2013) found that "Given the limitations of the asynchronous online environment for creating more personal connections, students found that hearing and/or seeing their instructor helped them to feel a sense of connection to the instructor and the course" (p. 210). Faculty can use webcams to periodically send check-in announcements to the class regarding upcoming assignments, activities, due dates, instructions, or course information. Faculty can also use webcams to give personalized feedback, support, and encouragement to students recorded as video. Webcams can be used in course activities, such as in the discussion board as an alternative to text-based posts. Lastly, webcam videos can be used to enhance instructions on assignments, explain criteria in rubrics, or give examples for students so they can see what constitutes quality work.

Email

Research has shown that students want personal attention from instructors and that students benefit from robust communication from faculty including personal emails (Gaytan, 2015). Sending students email messages can be a proactive strategy to encourage certain behavior (Supiano, 2018). Emails can be used as an intervention to mitigate student attrition and can positively impact student success (Inkelaar & Simpson, 2015). Faculty can send emails to students who have not logged into the course after a certain period of time; to students who are missing assignments or not participating; to students who are low performing; and to students who are high performing, in order to recognize students' effort and reinforce positive behavior. Research has shown that student engagement and retention is less dependent on technology and more dependent on personal connection (Inkelaar & Simpson, 2015). Students need to feel acknowledged, have a sense of belonging, and feel like they are a significant part of the learning community and not just a number or course user (Seidman, 2012). This may seem like common sense, but often students drop out because no one was paying attention to their involvement in the course. This is why it is important for faculty to make it a point to connect with each student in a meaningful way. Oftentimes, the use of personal email can have a positive impact on student-faculty interaction (Young, Kelsey, & Lancaster, 2011).

There are numerous ways to engage students with their instructor. Some strategies for creating student-to-instructor engagement include:

- Adding instructor presence in the online course using webcam videos.
- Communicating regularly and meaningfully with students via email, discussion boards, online journals, and other channels.
- Giving personalized quality feedback.
- Sending email messages to motivate, recognize, and encourage successful student behavior.

FUTURE RESEARCH DIRECTIONS

Utilizing student-centered teaching strategies that engage students in learning continues to be a prominent topic in the literature. The Trifecta of Student Engagement is a useful framework when exploring online asynchronous and synchronous instructional methods. Future research is needed to explore methods and measures of student engagement that can inform teaching practices and pedagogies. In addition, there is a growing body of scholarship dedicated to advancing the understanding of what motivates students to learn and engages them in learning which contribute to advancing the overall field of education towards better learning experiences for students. See Additional Reading section for some titles on this topic.

CONCLUSION

This chapter provided a learner-centered framework for engaging students in online courses. This framework, which places students at the center of all course interaction, proposes that students need to be engaged with the course curriculum content, with their peers, and with their instructor in order to be fully engaged in a learning experience (Moore, 1989). Although this framework dates back thirty years ago when online learning was in its infancy, it is still applicable to online education as it has evolved today. This student engagement framework is still relevant and widely referenced much like TPACK framework (Technological, Pedagogical, Content Knowledge), Community of Inquiry framework, and Chickering and Gamson's (1991) principles for good teaching. New technologies and digital tools have since been developed which can be incorporated into various frameworks, but the foundation by which a meaningful, enjoyable, and valuable learning experience is built remains the same. Each area of the Trifecta of Student Engagement framework focuses on strategies aimed at engaging students. Learning theories, evidence-based teaching practices and models, and empirical research were explored in an attempt to weave together findings from the literature with suggested updated digital tools to use. Those who design and teach online courses may continue to find this framework useful for designing and facilitating online courses.

REFERENCES

Albrecht, J. R., & Karabenick, S. A. (2017). Relevance for learning and motivation in education. *Journal of Experimental Education, 86*(1), 1–10. doi:10.1080/0022 0973.2017.1380593

Althaus, S. L. (1997). Computer-mediated communication in a university classroom: An experiment with on-line discussions. *Communication Education, 46*(3), 158–174. doi:10.1080/03634529709379088

Arbaugh, J. B. (2001). How instructor immediacy behaviors affect student satisfaction and learning in web-based courses. *Business Communication Quarterly, 64*(4), 42–54. doi:10.1177/108056990106400405

Arbaugh, J. B. (2007). An empirical verification of the community of inquiry framework. *Journal of Asynchronous Learning Networks, 11*(1), 73–85.

Baker, K. (2016). Peer review as a strategy for improving students' writing process. *Active Learning in Higher Education, 17*(3), 179–192. doi:10.1177/1469787416654794

Bandura, A. (1977). *Social learning theory*. Englewood Cliffs, NJ: Prentice-Hall.

Beaudoin, M. F. (1990). The instructor's changing role in distance education. *American Journal of Distance Education, 4*(2), 21–29. doi:10.1080/08923649009526701

Bernard, R. M., Abrami, P. C., Borokhovski, E., Wade, A., Tamim, R., Surkes, M. A., & Bethel, E. C. (2009). A meta-analysis of three interaction treatments in distance education. *Review of Educational Research, 79*(3), 1243–1289. doi:10.3102/0034654309333844

Bork, R. H., & Rucks-Ahidiana, Z. (2013, October). *Role ambiguity in online courses: An analysis of student and instructor expectations*. Teachers College, Columbia University.

Bower, B. L., & Hardy, K. P. (2004). From correspondence to cyberspace: Changes and challenges in distance education. *New Directions for Community Colleges, 128*(128), 5–12. doi:10.1002/cc.169

Brookhart, S. (2008). *How to give effective feedback to your students*. Alexandria, VA: Association for Supervision and Curriculum Development.

Buffo, S. (2015, January 9). The power of storytelling in the college classroom. Faculty Focus. Retrieved from https://www.facultyfocus.com/articles/effective-teaching-strategies/power-storytelling-college-classroom/

Carroll-Barefield, A., Smith, S., Prince, L., & Campbell, C. (2005, January 1). *Transitioning from brick and mortar to online: A faculty perspective*. Retrieved from library.educause.edu/resources/2005/1/transitioning-from-brick-and-mortar-to-online-a-faculty-perspective

Caverly, D. C., & MacDonald, L. (2002). Online learning communities. *Journal of Developmental Education, 25*(3), 36–37.

Chickering, A. W., & Gamson, Z. F. (1991). *Applying the seven principles for good practice in undergraduate education. In New Directions for Teaching and Learning*. San Francisco, CA: Jossey Bass.

Choi, H., & Johnson, S. D. (2005). The effect of context-based video instruction on learning and motivation in online courses. *American Journal of Distance Education, 19*(4), 215–227. doi:10.120715389286ajde1904_3

Cilliers, L. (2017). Wiki acceptance by university students to improve collaboration in higher education. *Innovations in Education and Teaching International, 54*(5), 485–493. doi:10.1080/14703297.2016.1180255

Coates, H. B. (2008). *Attracting, engaging and retaining: a new conversation about learning*. Australian Council for Educational Research.

Crawford, S. (2019, March 20). Busting multimedia myths: An evidence-based approach to quality instructional media [webinar]. Quality Matters. Retrieved from https://www.qualitymatters.org/professional-development/free-webinars

Crews, T. B., Wilkinson, K., & Neill, J. K. (2015). Principles of good practice in undergraduate education: Effective online course design to assist student success. *MERLOT Journal of Online Learning and Teaching, 11*(1), 87–103.

Darsih, E. (2018). Learner-centered teaching: What makes it effective. *Indonesian EFL Journal, 4*(1), 33–42. doi:10.25134/ieflj.v4i1.796

Dawley, L. (2007). *The tools for successful online teaching*. Hershey, PA: IGI Global. doi:10.4018/978-1-59140-956-4

Dennen, V., Darabi, A. A., & Smith, L. J. (2007). Instructor-learner interaction in online courses: The relative perceived importance of particular instructor actions on performance and satisfaction. *Distance Education, 28*(1), 65–79. doi:10.1080/01587910701305319

Dixson, M. D. (2010). Creating effective student engagement in online courses: What do students find engaging? *The Journal of Scholarship of Teaching and Learning, 10*(2), 1–13.

Durrington, V., Swafford, J., & Berryhill, A. (2006). Strategies for enhancing student interactivity in an online environment. *College Teaching, 54*(1), 190–193. doi:10.3200/CTCH.54.1.190-193

Endo, J. J., & Harpel, R. L. (1982). The effect of student-faculty interaction on student educational outcomes. *Research in Higher Education, 16*(2), 115–138. doi:10.1007/BF00973505

Eom, S. B., Wen, H. J., & Ashil, N. (2006, July). The determinants of students' perceived learning outcomes and satisfaction in university online education: An empirical investigation. *Decision Sciences Journal of Innovative Education, 4*(2), 215–235. doi:10.1111/j.1540-4609.2006.00114.x

Everett, D. R. (2015). Adding value: Online student engagement. *Information Systems Education Journal, 13*(6), 68–76.

Freeman, S., Eddy, S. L., McDonough, M., Smith, M. K., Okoroafor, H. J., & Wenderoth, M. P. (2014). Active learning increases student performance in science, engineering, and mathematics. *Proceedings of the National Academy of Sciences of the United States of America, 111*(23), 8410–8415. doi:10.1073/pnas.1319030111 PMID:24821756

Friend, C. (2017, June 21). Humanizing the online course experience. Retrieved from https://uslti.bbcollab.com/collab/ui/session/playback/load/1B0DF06FE78A1 1AA56A842F995322 4D3

Garrison, D., Anderson, T., & Archer, W. (2000). Critical inquiry in a text-based environment: Computer conferencing in higher education. *The Internet and Higher Education, 2*(2-3), 87–105. doi:10.1016/S1096-7516(00)00016-6

Gaytan, J. (2013). Factors affecting student retention in online courses: Overcoming this critical problem. *Career and Technical Education Research, 38*(2), 145–155. doi:10.5328/cter38.2.147

Glossary of Education Reform. (2016). Student engagement. Retrieved from https://www.edglossary.org/student-engagement/

Gunter, G. A. (2007). The effects of the impact of instructional immediacy on cognition and learning in online classes. *International Journal of Social, Behavioral, Educational, Economic, Business and Industrial Engineering, 1*(11), 729–735.

Harackiewicz, J. M., Smith, J. L., & Priniski, S. J. (2016). Interest matters: The importance of promoting interest in education. *Policy Insights from the Behavioral and Brain Sciences, 3*(2), 220–227. doi:10.1177/2372732216655542 PMID:29520371

Hargis, J. (2005). Collaboration, community and project-based learning—does it still work online? *International Journal of Instructional Media, 32*(2), 157–162.

Harris, J., Mishra, P., & Koehler, M. (2009). Teachers' technological pedagogical content knowledge and learning activity types: Curriculum-based technology integration reframed. *Journal of Research on Technology in Education, 41*(4), 393–416. doi:10.1080/15391523.2009.10782536

Hattie, J., & Timperley, H. (2007). The power of feedback. *Review of Educational Research, 77*(1), 81–112. doi:10.3102/003465430298487

Herndon, K. (1996). Analyzing mentoring practices through teachers' journals. *Teacher Education Quarterly, 23*(4), 27–44.

Hidi, S., & Harackiewicz, J. M. (2000). Motivating the academically unmotivated: A critical issue for the 21st century. *Review of Educational Research, 70*(2), 151–179. doi:10.3102/00346543070002151

Hiltz, S. R., Shea, P., & Eunhee, K. (2004). Using focus groups to study ALN faculty motivation. *Journal of Asynchronous Learning Networks, 11*(1), 107–124.

Hiltz, S. R., Turoff, M., & Harasim, L. (2007). Development and philosophy of the field of asynchronous learning networks. In R. Andrews & C. Haythornthwaite (Eds.), *The Sage handbook of E-learning research* (pp. 55–72). Los Angeles, CA: Sage. doi:10.4135/9781848607859.n2

Hiltz, S. R., & Wellman, B. (1997). Asynchronous learning networks as a virtual classroom. *Communications of the ACM, 40*(9), 44–48. doi:10.1145/260750.260764

Hoidn, S. (2017). *Student-centered learning environments in higher education classrooms.* New York, NY: Springer. doi:10.1057/978-1-349-94941-0

Hulett, K. H. (2019, March 27). Community from a distance: Building a sense of belonging in an online classroom. Scholarly Teacher. Retrieved from https://www.scholarlyteacher.com/blog/community-from-a-distance-building-a-sense-of-belonging-in-an-online-classroom

Inkelaar, T., & Simpson, O. (2015). Challenging the 'distance education deficit' through 'motivational emails.' *Open Learning: The Journal of Open, Distance and e-Learning, 30*(2), 152-163.

Jackson, L. C., Jones, S. J., & Rodriguez, R. C. (2010). Faculty actions that result in student satisfaction in online courses. *Journal of Asynchronous Learning Networks, 14*(4), 78–96.

Johnson, D., & Johnson, R. (2002). Learning together and alone: Overview and meta-analysis. *Asia Pacific Journal of Education, 22*(1), 95–105. doi:10.1080/0218879020220110

Keengwe, J., & Kidd, T. T. (2010). Towards best practices in online learning and teaching in higher education. *MERLOT Journal of Online Learning and Teaching, 6*(2), 533–541.

Keller, J. M., & Suzuki, K. (2004). Learner motivation and E-learning design: A multinationally validated process. *Journal of Educational Media, 29*(3), 229–239. doi:10.1080/1358165042000283084

Knowles, M. (2005). *The adult learner: The definitive classic in adult education and human resource development.* Burlington, MA: Elsevier. doi:10.4324/9780080481913

Krentler, K. A., & Willis-Flurry, L. (2005). Does technology enhance actual student learning? The case of online discussion boards. *Journal of Education for Business, 80*(6), 316–321. doi:10.3200/JOEB.80.6.316-321

Kuh, G., & Hu, S. (2001). The effects of student-faculty interaction in the 1990s. *The Review of Higher Education, 24*(3), 309–332. doi:10.1353/rhe.2001.0005

LaRose, R., & Whitten, P. (2000). Re-thinking instructional immediacy for Web courses: A social cognitive exploration. *Communication Education, 49*(4), 320–338. doi:10.1080/03634520009379221

Lattimer, H. (2008). Challenging history: Essential questions in the social studies classroom. *Social Education, 72*(6), 325–328.

Lazowski, R. A., & Hulleman, C. S. (2016). Motivation interventions in education: A meta-analytic review. *Review of Educational Research, 86*(2), 602–640. doi:10.3102/0034654315617832

Lee, M., Kim, H., & Kim, M. (2014). The effects of Socratic questioning on critical thinking in web-based collaborative learning. *Education as Change, 18*(2), 285–302. doi:10.1080/16823206.2013.849576

Lei, H., Yunhuo, C., & Zhou, W. (2018). Relationship between student engagement and academic achievement: A meta-analysis. *Social Behavior and Personality, 46*(3), 517–528. doi:10.2224bp.7054

Leslie, H. (2019, June 14). Trifecta of student engagement: A framework for an online teaching professional development course for faculty in higher education. *Journal of Research in Innovative Teaching & Learning*. doi:. doi:10.1108/JRIT-10-2018-0024

Liu, X., Magjuka, R. J., Bonk, C. J., & Lee, S. (2007). Does sense of community matter? An examination of participants' perceptions of building learning communities in online courses. *The Quarterly Review of Distance Education, 8*(1), 9–24.

Lombard, M., & Ditton, T. (1997). At the heart of it all: The concept of presence. *Journal of* Computer *Mediated Communications, 3*(2). Retrieved from http://www.ascusc.org/jcmc/vol3/issue2/lombard.html

Mayhew, M., Rockenbach, A. N., Bowman, N. A., Seifert, T. A., Wolniak, G. C., Pascarella, E. T., & Terenzini, P. T. (2016). *How college affects students: 21st century evidence that higher education works* (Vol. 3). San Francisco, CA: Jossey-Bass.

McMillan, D. A., & Chavis, D. M. (1986). Sense of community: A definition and theory. *Journal of Community Psychology, 14*(1), 6–23. doi:10.1002/1520-6629(198601)14:1<6::AID-JCOP2290140103>3.0.CO;2-I

McTighe, J., & Wiggins, G. P. (2013). *Essential questions: Opening doors to student understanding*. Gale Virtual Reference Library.

Merriam, S., & Bierema, L. L. (2014). *Adult learning: Linking theory and practice*. San Francisco, CA: Jossey-Bass.

Moore, M. (1989). Three types of interaction. In M. Moore (Ed.), *Readings in principles of distance education*. University Park, PA: American Center for the Study of Distance Education.

Muncy, J. A. (2014). Blogging for reflection: The use of online journals to engage students in reflective learning. *Marketing Education Review, 24*(2), 101–114. doi:10.2753/MER1052-8008240202

National Survey of Student Engagement. (2017). *Engagement insights: Survey findings on the quality of undergraduate education-annual results 2017*. Bloomington, IN: Indiana University Center for Postsecondary Research.

Newman, F. M., Marks, H. M., & Gamoran, A. (1996). Authentic pedagogy and student performance. *American Journal of Education, 104*(4), 280–312. doi:10.1086/444136

Northrup, P. T. (2002). Online learners' preferences for interaction. *Quarterly Review of Distance Education, 3*(2), 219–226.

Osterman, K. F. (2000). Students' need for belonging in the school community. *Review of Educational Research, 70*(3), 323–367. doi:10.3102/00346543070003323

Palloff, R. M., & Pratt, K. (1999). *Building learning communities in cyberspace: Effective strategies for the online classroom.* San Francisco, CA: Jossey-Bass.

Palloff, R. M., Pratt, K., & Stockley, D. (2001). Building learning communities in cyberspace: Effective strategies for the online classroom. *Canadian Journal of Higher Education, 31*(3), 175–178.

Palmer, D. H. (2008). Student interest generated during an inquiry skills lesson. *Journal of Research in Science Teaching, 46*(2), 147–165. doi:10.1002/tea.20263

Pascarella, E. T. (1980). Student-faculty informal contact and college outcomes. *Review of Educational Research, 50*(4), 545–595. doi:10.3102/00346543050004545

Pittman, L. D., & Richmond, A. (2008). University belonging, friendship quality, and psychological adjustment during the transition to college. *Journal of Experimental Education, 76*(4), 343–361. doi:10.3200/JEXE.76.4.343-362

Pyke, J. (2010). A closer look at instructor-student feedback online: A case study analysis of the types and frequency. *Journal of Online Learning and Teaching, 6*(1), 110.

Renninger, K. A., & Hidi, S. E. (2016). *The power of interest for motivation and engagement.* New York, NY: Routledge.

Rourke, L., Anderson, T., Archer, W., & Garrison, D. R. (1999). Assessing social presence in asynchronous text-based computer conferencing. *Journal of Distance Education, 14*(3), 51–70.

Rovai, A. P. (2001). Building classroom community at a distance: A case study. *Educational Technology Research and Development, 49*(4), 33–48. doi:10.1007/BF02504946

Ryan, A. M., & Patrick, H. (2001). The classroom social environment and changes in adolescents' motivation and engagement during middle school. *American Educational Research Journal, 38*(2), 437–460. doi:10.3102/00028312038002437

Sachdeva, A. (1996). Use of effective feedback to facilitate adult learning. *Journal of Cancer Education, 11*(2), 106–118. PMID:8793652

Schreurs, J., & Dumbraveanu, R. (2014). A shift from teacher centered to learner centered approach. *International Journal of Engineering Pedagogy, 4*(3), 36–41. doi:10.3991/ijep.v4i3.3395

Seidman, A. (Ed.), *(Year). College student retention: Formula for student success* (2nd ed.). Lanham, MD: Rowman & Littlefield.

Seifert, T., & Feliks, O. (2019). Online self-assessment and peer-assessment as a tool to enhance student teachers' assessment skills. *Assessment & Evaluation in Higher Education, 44*(2), 169–185. doi:10.1080/02602938.2018.1487023

Sharp, J. H., & Huett, J. B. (2006). Importance of learner-learner interaction in distance education. *Information Systems Education Journal, 4*(46), 2–10.

Shea, P. J., Fredricksen, E. E., Pickett, A. M., & Pelz, W. E. (2004). Faculty development, student satisfaction, and reported learning in the SUNY Learning Network. In T. M. Duffy & J. R. Kirkley (Eds.), *Learner-centered theory and practice in distance education* (pp. 343–377). Mahwah, NJ: Lawrence Erlbaum Associates, Inc.

Smith, K. S., Rook, J. E., & Smith, T. W. (2007). Increasing student engagement using effective and metacognitive writing strategies in content areas. *Preventing School Failure, 51*(3), 43–48. doi:10.3200/PSFL.51.3.43-48

Spady, W. (1970). Dropouts from higher education: An interdisciplinary review and synthesis. *Interchange, 1*(1), 64–85. doi:10.1007/BF02214313

Su, F., & Beaumont, C. (2010). Evaluating the use of a wiki for collaborative learning. *Innovations in Education and Teaching International, 47*(4), 417–431. doi:10.1080/14703297.2010.518428

Terenzini, P., & Pascarella, E. (1977). Voluntary freshman attrition patterns of social and academic integration in a university: A test of a conceptual model. *Research in Higher Education, 6*(1), 25–44. doi:10.1007/BF00992014

The National Center on Universal Design for Learning. (n.d.). What is UDL? Retrieved from http://www.udlcenter.org/aboutudl/whatisudl/3principles

Tinto, V. (1975). Dropout from higher education: A theoretical synthesis of recent research. *Review of Educational Research, 45*(1), 89–125. doi:10.3102/00346543045001089

Tuckman, B. W. (1965). Developmental sequence in small groups. *Psychological Bulletin, 63*(6), 384–399. doi:10.1037/h0022100 PMID:14314073

Vesley, P., Bloom, L., & Sherlock, J. (2007). Key elements of building online community: Comparing faculty and student perceptions. *MERLOT Journal of Online Learning and Teaching, 3*(3), 234–246.

Voelkl, K. (2012). School identification. In S. L. Christenson, A. L. Reschly, & C. Wylie (Eds.), *Handbook of research on student engagement* (pp. 193–218). New York, NY: Springer. doi:10.1007/978-1-4614-2018-7_9

Wankel, C., & Blessinger, P. (2012). *Increasing student engagement and retention using online learning activities: Wikis, blogs, and webquests.* Boston, MA: Emerald Group Publishing. doi:10.1108/S2044-9968(2012)6_Part_A

Wanstreet, C. E. (2009). Interaction in online environments. In A. Orellana (Ed.), *The perfect online course: Best practices for designing and teaching* (p. 425). Charlotte, NC: Information Age Publishing.

Woods, R., & Ebersole, S. (2003). Using non-subject-matter-specific discussion boards to build connectedness in online learning. *American Journal of Distance Education, 17*(2), 99–118. doi:10.1207/S15389286AJDE1702_3

Young, S., & Bruce, M. A. (2001). Classroom community and student engagement in online courses. *MERLOT Journal of Online Learning and Teaching, 7*(2), 219–230.

Young, S., Kelsey, D., & Lancaster, A. (2011). Predicted outcome value of email communication: Factors that foster professional relational development between students and teachers. *Communication Education, 60*(4), 371–388. doi:10.1080/0 3634523.2011.563388

Zilvinskis, J., Masseria, A. A., & Pike, G. R. (2017). Student engagement and student learning: Examining the convergent and discriminant validity of the revised National Survey of Student Engagement. *Research in Higher Education, 58*(8), 880–903. doi:10.100711162-017-9450-6

Zuckerman, M., Porac, J., Lathin, D., Smith, R., & Deci, E. L. (1978). On the importance of self-determination for intrinsically motivated behavior. *Personality and Social Psychology Bulletin, 4*(3), 443–446. doi:10.1177/014616727800400317

ADDITIONAL READING

Barkley, E. F. (2010). *Student engagement techniques: A handbook for college faculty*. San Francisco, CA: Jossey-Bass.

Cavanagh, S. R. (2016). *The spark of learning: Energizing the college classroom with the science of emotion*. Morgantown, WV: West Virginia University Press.

Eyler, J. R. (2018). *How humans learn: The science and stories behind effective college teaching*. Morgantown, WV: West Virginia University Press.

Leslie, H. (2019, August 28). National University: A 2019 Blackboard Catalyst Award winner for training and professional development [Blog post]. Blackboard. Retrieved from https://blog.blackboard.com/national-university-a-2019-blackboard-catalyst-award-winner-for-training-and-professional-development/

Meyer, K. A. (2014). *Student engagement online: What works and why*. Hoboken, NJ: John Wiley & Sons.

Chapter 5

The Importance of Social Presence and Strategies for Incorporating It Into an Online Course

Joshua Elliott

https://orcid.org/0000-0003-3899-7769

Fairfield University, USA

ABSTRACT

As with any mode of course delivery, there are both positives and negatives to online learning. There are the commonly cited positive features of online learning like the removal of geographic restrictions and scheduling barriers. Limitations may include unfamiliarity for those new to online learning and misunderstandings resulting from the transition from primarily face-to-face interactions to only online interactions. One of the nice things about online learning environments is that many of the possible drawbacks can be countered turning them into strength. Building a strong social presence in an online course can help with this. This chapter discusses three categories of strategies for building a social presence; ice breakers, netiquette activities, and discussion activities.

INTRODUCTION

Online learning in postsecondary education has grown in frequency and has grown consistently over the last decade (Lederman, 2018). This increase is seen mutually exclusive for both online programs and for students who have taken at least one

DOI: 10.4018/978-1-7998-1622-5.ch005

online course. Almost one-third of college students take an online course as part of their program of study (Protopsaltis & Baum, 2019). Half of those students are enrolled in completely online programs (2019). At the same time, research is mixed about whether achievement or learning tends to be stronger in online or face-to-face learning environments (Cavanaugh & Jacquemin, 2015). A large body of research has found that there no significant difference in learning in online and face-to-face learning environments resulting in the "no significant difference phenomenon (Nguyen, 2015). Students may take online courses because they are what is offered or because of their perceptions of its benefits. They are not taking the courses because they believe they will learn more, as a matter of fact, some students perceive that online courses are easier. Jaggers (2014), in a study with community college students found "most students preferred to take only 'easy' academic subjects online; they preferred to take 'difficult' or 'important' subjects face-to-face."

As with any mode of course delivery both as asynchronous and synchronous, generally there are both positives and negatives to online learning. The most commonly cited positive features of online learning in the literature include the removal of geographic restrictions and scheduling barriers (in asynchronous courses). Limitations may include unfamiliarity for those new to online learning and misunderstandings resulting from the transition from primarily face-to-face interactions to only online interactions, and experiencing isolation. One positive quality of online learning environments is that many of the possible drawbacks can be countered turning them into strengths (Berry, 2018). The previously mentioned absence of face-to-face interaction in online learning environments is an example of this. Face-to-face interaction affords the opportunity to observe facial gestures and body language. Using facial gestures and body language to gain context is not an option in online asynchronous environments. This potential gap in a communication channel can result in misunderstandings that are much easier to avoid or resolve in face-to-face learning environments. In the latter setting; the factors like facial gestures, body language, and the ability to ask quick low-pressure questions diminish the likelihood of many misunderstandings (Hwang & Song, 2018). This does not mean that misunderstandings do not occur in face-to-face classes. It only means that many of the potential misunderstandings can be stemmed before they become an issue. A student can ask a quick informal clarification question or inadvertently show they are not understanding with a confused look letting the instructor know they need to clarify. Asking a question in an online environment is a more formal process and there are no facial gestures or body language to guide understanding except for strategies such as more formal video communications. To ask a question of an online instructor may require a dedicated email, message, or phone call. Although this may not be a big deal, it may be seen as such since it is a more formal process than the quick question option with face-to-face interactions. In a face-to-face class, this may be reserved for bigger issues than those that can be handled with a quick hand raise and question (Molnar, Kearney, & Molnar, 2017). Instructors and course designers can turn this possible issue into a strength with proper planning and forethought. For the purpose of this chapter, only asynchronous online learning environments will be discussed. However, it should be noted that adding synchronous tools to an otherwise asynchronous course is a viable option. Possible tools include chat rooms and video tools like Zoom and Skype. For this chapter, synchronous learning is being defined as a learning environment where learners do not need to be present at the same time. Synchronous learning is being defined as a learning environment in which learners must be present at the same time for learning to occur.

BACKGROUND

The research is mixed on the topic of learning in online versus face-to-face course formats. The results have ranged from improved learning in one area over the other on both sides to no statistically significant difference. One consistent finding is that students who struggle academically or do not see themselves as strong students can have an even harder time in online formats (Cavanaugh & Jacquemin, 2015). One theory for this is that students who do not have academic self-efficacy feel even more isolated in online courses. Establishing a social aspect or "presence" in a class is an important, and sometimes overlooked, part of online teaching (Phirangee & Malec, 2017). Creating a strong social presence in a class can help counter the feeling of isolation that sometimes occur in online learning environments. As stated by Armellini & De Stefani, "The prominence of the social aspects of online learning suggests that social presence is a substantive part of the participants' and tutors' online behaviour." (p. 1205) Social presence has also been linked to cognitive absorption, student interest with content, and to overall student satisfaction with their online courses (Leong, 2011).

The process of establishing a social presence in an online environment is best started in the instructional design stages (Costly, 2016). The instructional design stage is not the only option though. Other simple strategies such as icebreakers and establishing parameters for netiquette can benefit classes in many ways. Using these strategies can proactively make students aware of the limiting factors of lack of facial cues about intent and tone so they are cognizant from the start of class. Just being aware can help diminish the potential of an issue or misunderstanding. Classroom engagement and investment can be optimized through the use of icebreakers. Knowing more about a person than just a name or where they are from can facilitate relationship building. What if instead of just the previously mentioned information, you also saw your classmates and heard their voice through a recorded video piece? What if you saw a brief presentation about where they went on vacation, their hobbies, or what they do with their kids for leisure? These are the things that get mentioned in passing in a face-to-face class without thinking. However, these seemingly trivial interactions also build relationships and make students more enthusiastic (or at least less resistant) to "going to class". Students will see each other as humans they can connect with by learning about and from each other. Students will participate more in a course when they feel like a part of a community. They will be more willing to contribute to a conversation when they feel safe to contribute. This is in contrast to online courses where classmates only know each other by name.

Community of Inquiry Model

The Community of Inquiry (COI) model proposes three types of "presence" must be in place for success in online learning environments. They are teaching presence, cognitive presence, and social presence as seen in Figure 1.

Teaching presence according to Anderson, Rourke, Garrison, & Archer (2011) is defined as:

[the] design, facilitation, and direction of cognitive and social processes for the purpose of realizing personally meaningful and educationally worthwhile learning outcomes. Teaching presence begins before the course commences as the teacher, acting as instructional designer, plans and prepares the course of studies, and it continues during the course, as the instructor facilitates the discourse and provides direct instruction when required. Through adequate teaching presence, formal learning that facilitates personally relevant and educationally defined outcomes is achieved (p. 5).

A social presence calls for a trusting environment to be established within the learning environment so that learners may feel comfortable and participate freely and openly (Horzum & Uyanik, 2015; Thompson, Vogler, & Xiu, 2017). This is done through intentional relationship building activities. "Emotional expression, open communication, and group cohesion are required" for a successful learning environment (Horzum & Uyanik, 2015). Social presence is not the only ingredient for success, but it is just as important as the other ingredients.

Research has shown that a social presence is seen as just as important as a cognitive presence and teaching presence by university students (Haynes, 2016; Taylor, 2016).

Figure 1. The COI model
Retrieved from: https://www.researchgate.net/figure/The-Community-of-Inquiry-Framework-Garrison-Anderson-Archer-2000_fig2_236187779

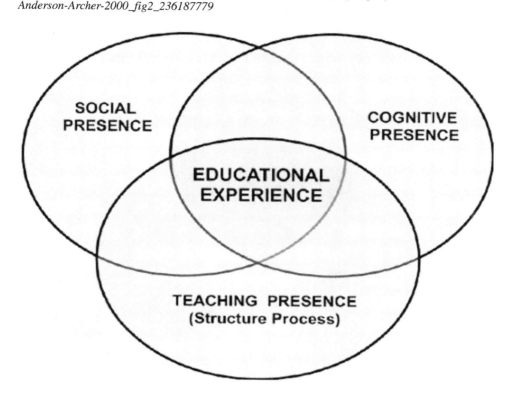

Factors to Consider

There are several factors that can impact what strategies are used in an online course. These include how far into the course design process the strategies are being chosen; whether the course will be synchronous, asynchronous, both; available tools; where the activity falls of the continuum of lower level to higher level learning.

Stages of the Course Development Process

Instructional design models are often used to guide the course development process. One model is the ADDIE model. This model is one of the more commonly used models used. The stages in the ADDIE model are:

1. Analysis
2. Design

3. Development
4. Implementation
5. Evaluation

The model is often shown in a circular model as seen in Figure 2.

Figure 2. ADDIE model, braunschweig, creative commons (2014)

The stages of course development should be considered when reviewing strategies for use. Using the ADDIE model to frame these stages, opportunities for embedding social presence building activities can most often happen during the design or implementation stages. Some teaching strategies can be implemented anytime while teaching the course (Implementation). Other strategies are only effective when embedded in the course during the instructional design stage of course development.

Academic Preparation

Many cite freedom of scheduling as an advantage for online learning. This same factor requires students to be careful about their scheduling to ensure that they stay current with their work. There is no class meeting time to maintain scheduling structure. Although advantageous for some, this structure is beneficial for many students. Students who struggle in traditional courses may find online learning even more difficult. This can result from difficulty with self-discipline with scheduling for students with poor academic preparation (Protopsaltis & Baum, 2019). This can exacerbate rather than alleviate performance gaps.

Synchronous Versus Asynchronous Course Delivery

Another advantage of online learning is that it removes the constraints of geography (Wilson, Watson, Thompson, Drew, & Doyle; 2017). Time constraints can also be removed if the course meets asynchronously (Darling-Hammond, Hyler, & Gardner; 2017). However, meeting synchronously opens up opportunities for people to talk to have a live dialogue via tools like video conferencing tools (Skype, Facetime, Zoom) and chat tools. This creates a trade-off situation. In one scenario, students communicate with each other in "real time" but have to work with each other's schedules. In the other scenario, instructors have more control over scheduling without the live dialogue.

Strategies

Strategies for building a social presence can be categorized to provide structure to the discussion. The three categories outlined and discussed in this chapter are icebreakers, netiquette activities, and discussion activities. All of these categories can be embedded in the course during the instructional design process. Some of them can also be implemented after the course has begun.

Icebreakers

Many online icebreaker activities simply mimic face-to-face icebreaker activities. However, face-to-face instructional activities cannot always be simply moved online. Making the transition to online teaching requires planning and forethought (Chiasson, Terras, & Smart; 2015). This should be considered when creating an icebreaker activity. Traditional icebreaker activities like "two truths and a lie" or "speed dating" can be very effective in face-to-face learning environments. However, much of the strengths in these types of activities lie in the ability for students to build a rapport that builds off of the immediate dialogue resulting from these activities. This immediate response is inherently missing in asynchronous learning activities. Online icebreaker activities should be less reliant on immediate responses so peers can respond over longer periods of time without the effectiveness of either the initial prompt or the resulting responses diminishing. An "About Me" presentation can be very effective. To offer variety, different tools can be used to create the presentation. Tool options include:

- Video Creation Tools
  - Apple iMovie
  - Apple Quick Time
  - Adobe Spark Video
- Presentation Tools
  - Microsoft Sway
  - Google Slides
  - Atavist
- Webpage Creation Tools
  - Spark Page
  - Wix
  - Weebly
  - Google Sites
- Cartoon Generators
  - Powtoon

Instructors who teach multiple online sections should consider creating more than one About Me presentation. The content could be similar using different presentation tools such as Spark Page and Atavist. This would prevent their presentations from becoming stale to students who are taking more than one class with them. Simply creating the presentations using different tools can help resolve this potential issue.

Netiquette Activities

Everyone is open to misunderstandings in online environments regardless of their proficiency with technology. This includes online instructors. It is important to maintain a high level of standards in regards to netiquette for all participants. Netiquette, or Internet etiquette, refers to how one should behave in online environments. There are nine elements to digital citizenship and Netiquette can overlap between multiple elements depending on how one views it. Choi (2016) pooled the nine elements together and broke them down into four categories: Ethics, Media and Information Literacy, Participation/Engagement, and Critical Resistance. How individuals manage their behavior in online environments falls under the ethics category (Guest Editorial, 2018). Under this category, aspects of communication in online environments can include, but are not limited to, appropriate windows for response time, the use of sarcasm, awareness and appreciation for different perspectives. It is important to consider netiquette building activities during the design phase. However, opportunities to build netiquette awareness often occur throughout the course. Instructors should seek these opportunities to model appropriate behaviors. It is also beneficial to draft policies to ensure that these factors are considered in online communications.

Discussion Activities

Social interaction between peers is important in learning environments (Mezirow, 2018). However, research indicates that more traditional asynchronous discussion forums can ultimately limit discussions (Aloni & Harrington, 2018; Kent, 2016). Asynchronous discussion threads are great for maintaining structure in a conversation. This allows users to stay aware of who is responding to who. These same discussion threads can also be restrictive in their nature so conversations may not flow freely. This can result in students posting just enough to meet the requirements of the assignment. This is in contrast to face-to-face conversations where people can banter back and forth freely often resulting in a more dynamic conversation. It may be beneficial for instructors to seek out other forms of communication that more closely resemble common modern communication mediums while maintaining an asynchronous format. Some research indicates that other communication tools like those found in social media may foster more dynamic and engaging discussions (Kent, 2016). These can include, but are not limited to:

- Class Twitter Chats using a hashtag for tracking purposes
- Course Facebook groups
- Dedicated social media tools like NING
- Alternative collaborative tools like Quip and Google Apps

Twitter is a prominent tool for professional growth in education (Colwell & Hutchison, 2018). This includes Twitterchats. Instructors should consider selecting a class hashtag. This will allow them and their students to track conversations. It may also allow the conversation to continue after the class has concluded.

Facebook has been used as a social media tool although Twitter is used more frequently (Junco, 2012). Instructors can create groups in Facebook to serve as a structured discussion area. There are also social networks like NING. These tools require a fee and need to be created specifically for a purpose. This would make collaborating outside the course impossible.

Collaborative tools such as Google Apps and Quip are also an option for use in an online class. These tools are not always open to those outside the class, but they do allow users to collaborate and communicate in a dedicated workspace. One example of this using Google Docs to explicitly promote the use of student collaboration through working in small groups.

Instructor Control in Context of Discussion Forums

Costley (2017) investigated the effects of instructional design and the effects of instructor posts on student discussions in online threaded asynchronous forums. He further explored learner behavior in relation to instructor behavior and discovered that direct analysis of student discussions is needed to develop a comprehensive understanding of how instructor behavior can affect learner discussion. Critical to the analysis was to examine the instructor posts and to analyze and identify the degree to which the instructor interacts and guides the interactions and discourse in the learning environment.

The results showed that increasing the amount of control an instructor has over a learning environment increases the amount of cognitive presence but decreases the amount of social presence within the learners' posts. In general, these results are important because instructors must be aware of how their behavior may affect how learners interact (and therefore learn) online (p. 110).

Feedback

Whatever tool that is used for online discussions, the behavior and techniques used by the instructor during the discussions is also an important consideration. Consider setting some expectations for response time with all communication including and giving feedback in coursework and in discussion boards. Personalized feedback can also go a long way towards building social presence in a course and making students feel more welcome. It is important to consider what the students are seeing based on the frequency and quality of your posts. Students who see an instructor as more involved, tend to give more positive instructor reviews (Darby & Lang, 2019).

Table 1. Potential strategy for use with stage

Strategy	Stage
Icebreakers	Implementation
Introductions	Implementation
Netiquette Activities	Design and Implementation
Discussion Activities	Implementation

FUTURE RESEARCH DIRECTIONS

Icebreakers, introductions, netiquette activities, and discussion activities are just a sample of what online instructors and instructional designers can include in their online learning environment. The literature is replete with research-based and practitioner-based strategies that can increase engagement and interactivity in the online classroom. In particular, one strategy (category) worth investigating further is authentic learning strategies; those strategies that increase the students' interest by providing authentic learning activities and experiences. Britt (2015) has recommended authentic activities to help motivate the online learner and build connections.

Authentic learning has been of experimentation and trial and error exercises that require collaboration and communication among students seem to be impossible in the online classroom. With the emergence of [learning] management systems, students can be more engaged in authentic learning experiences (Britt, 2015, p. 88).

Britt (2015) specifically suggests the following research-based, authentic strategies which are adapted from Lombardi (2007, pp. 88-89):

1. Strategies that support real world relevance.
2. Challenged based learning that present an ill-defined problem to solve.
3. Sustained investigation through authentic activities comprising of complex tasks to be investigated by students over a sustained period of time, requiring intellectual resources.
4. Providing multiple sources from a variety of theoretical perspectives for assignments.
5. Offering activities that encourage collaboration as a team or community to increase authentic learning.
6. Introducing strategies that increase the opportunity for metacognition.
7. Interdisciplinary studies will increase the student's ability to make connections across domain or subject matter specializations.

8. Integrated assessments can vary the process and product for completion that go beyond summative style of assessments.
9. Projects and products produced that are connected to real-life are optimum.

CONCLUSION

There are strengths and weaknesses to online teaching. In many cases, potential issues can be countered and turned into strengths when instructors address these issues proactively and intentionally. One example is the perceived increase in miscommunications resulting from lack of body language and facial gestures. These missing interpersonal and emotional factors in online learning environments provide context cues in face-to-face interactions. Building a social presence in online learning environments helps build a feeling of belonging among class participants resulting in increased investment and in engagement with content, with the instructor, and with classmates. Categories of strategies that can help develop this sense of belonging and increase interactions include: Icebreakers, Introductions, Netiquette Activities, and Discussion Activities. Instructors can implement any of these strategies during the instructional design part of a course. However, some can also be embedded during the course of the opportunity presents itself. As mentioned in this chapter, the quality of feedback should be frequent and personalized. Instructors should also create expectations for response time for all class members including themselves. While the values and accomplishments of online learning have yet to be solidified, there are clear strategies and resources available to instructors to establish a clear social presence and create an effective online learning environment.

REFERENCES

Aloni, M., & Harrington, C. (2018). Research based practices for improving the effectiveness of asynchronous online discussion boards. *Scholarship of Teaching and Learning in Psychology*, *4*(4), 271. Retrieved from https://www.researchgate. net/publication/329828178_Research_based_practices_for_improving_the_ effectiveness_of_asynchronous_online_discussion_boards

Anderson, T., Rourke, L., Garrison, D., & Archer, W. (2001). Assessing teaching presence in a computer conferencing context. *Journal of Asynchronous Learning Networks*, *5*(2), 1–17.

Annand, D. (2011). Social presence within the Community of Inquiry framework. *International Review of Research in Open and Distance Learning*, *12*(5), 5. doi:10.19173/irrodl.v12i5.924

Armellini, A., & De Stefani, M. (2016). Social presence in the 21st century: An adjustment to the Community of Inquiry framework. *British Journal of Educational Technology*, *47*(6), 1202–1216. doi:10.1111/bjet.12302

Atif, Y. & Chou, C. (2018). Guest editorial: Digital citizenship: Innovations in education, practice, and pedagogy. *Journal of Educational Technology & Society*, *21*(1), 152-154. Retrieved from https://libdb.fairfield.edu/login?url=https://search.proquest.com/docview/2147873187?accountid=10796

Avery, T. L. (2017). Keep it Positive! Canadian Society for Studies in Education. Retrieved from https://www.researchgate.net/publication/327043525_Avery_T_Brett_C_Hewitt_J_2017_Keep_it_Positive_Paper_presented_at_the_Canadian_Society_for_Studies_in_Education_Ryerson_University_Toronto_ON_Canada

Berry, G. R. (2018). Learning from the learners: Student Perception of the Online Classroom. *Quarterly Review of Distance Education*, *19*(3), 39–56. Retrieved from http://search.ebscohost.com.contentproxy.phoenix.edu/login.aspx?direct=true&db=tfh&AN=134727270&site=eds-live

Braunschweig, D. (2014). *Graphic.* ADDIE Model, Creative Commons.

Britt, M., Goon, D., & Timmerman, M. (2015). How to better engage online students with online strategies. *College Student Journal*, *49*(3), 399–404.

Cavanaugh, J., & Jacquemin, S. (2015). A large sample comparison of grade-based student learning outcomes in online vs. face-to-face courses. *Online Learning*, *19*(2), 8. doi:10.24059/olj.v19i2.454

Chiasson, K., Terras, K., & Smart, K. (2015). Faculty perceptions of moving a face-to-face course to online instruction. *Journal of College Teaching and Learning*, *12*(3), 231–240. Retrieved from https://files.eric.ed.gov/fulltext/EJ1067275.pdf. doi:10.19030/tlc.v12i3.9315

Choi, M. (2016). A concept analysis of digital citizenship for democratic citizenship education in the internet age. *Theory and Research in Social Education*, *44*(4), 565–607. doi:10.1080/00933104.2016.1210549

Colwell, J., & Hutchison, A. C. (2018). Considering a Twitter-based professional learning network in literacy education. *Literacy Research and Instruction*, *57*(1), 5–25. doi:10.1080/19388071.2017.1370749

Costley, J. (2016). The effects of instructor control on critical thinking and social presence: Variations within three online asynchronous learning environments. *Journal of Educators Online*, *13*(1), 109–171. doi:10.9743/JEO.2016.1.3

Darby, F., & Lang, J. M. (2019). *Small Teaching Online: Applying Learning Science in Online Classes*. San Francisco, CA: Jossey-Bass.

Darling-Hammond, L., Hyler, M. E., & Gardner, M. (2017). Effective teacher professional development. Teacher Scholars. Retrieved from https://www.teacherscholars.org/wp-content/uploads/2017/09/Effective_Teacher_Professional_Development_REPORT.pdf

Haynes, F. (2016). Trust and the community of inquiry. *Educational Philosophy and Theory*, *50*(2), 1–8. doi:10.1080/00131857.2016.1144169

Horzum, M., & Uyanik, G. (2015). An item response theory analysis of the community of inquiry scale. *International Review of Research in Open and Distributed Learning*, *16*(2), 206–226. doi:10.19173/irrodl.v16i2.2052

Hwang, S., & Song, H. (2018). Effective Social Interaction in Online Learning. *National Teacher Education Journal, 11*(3).

Jaggars, S. S. (2014). Choosing between online and face-to-face courses: Community college student voices. *American Journal of Distance Education*, *28*(1), 27–38. doi:10.1080/08923647.2014.867697

Junco, R. (2012). The relationship between frequency of Facebook use, participation in Facebook activities, and student engagement. *Computers & Education*, *58*(1), 162–171. doi:10.1016/j.compedu.2011.08.004

Kent, M. (2016). Adding to the mix: Students use of Facebook groups and blackboard discussion forums in higher education. *Knowledge Management & E-Learning: An International Journal*, *8*(3), 444–463.

Lederman, D. (2018). Online education ascends. *Inside Higher Ed*. Retrieved from https://www.insidehighered.com/digital-learning/article/2018/11/07/new-data-online-enrollments-grow-and-share-overall-enrollment

Leong, P. (2011). Role of social presence and cognitive absorption in online learning environments. *Distance Education*, *32*(1), 5–28. doi:10.1080/01587919.2011.565495

Lombardi, M. M. (2007). Authentic learning for the 21st century: An overview. *Educause Learning Initiative, 1*, 1-12. Retrieved from http://net.educause.edu/ir/library/pdf/ELI3009.pdf

Mezirow, J. (2018). Transformative learning theory. In *Contemporary Theories of Learning* (pp. 114–128). Routledge. doi:10.4324/9781315147277-8

Molnar, A., Kearney, R., & Molnar, A. (2017). A comparison of cognitive presence in asynchronous and synchronous discussions in an online dental hygiene course. *Journal of Dental Hygiene*, *91*(3), 14–21. Retrieved from http://search.proquest.com/docview/1962427939/

Nguyen, T. (2015). The effectiveness of online learning: Beyond no significant difference and future horizons. *MERLOT Journal of Online Learning and Teaching*, *11*(2), 309–319.

Phirangee, K., & Malec, A. (2017). Othering in online learning: An examination of social presence, identity, and sense of community. *Distance Education*, *38*(2), 160–172. doi:10.1080/01587919.2017.1322457

Protopsaltis, S., & Baum, S. (2019). Does online education live up to its promise? A look at the evidence and implications for federal policy. Retrieved from https://mason.gmu.edu/~sprotops/OnlineEd.pdf

Taylor, B. (2016). The struggle is real: Student perceptions of quality in online courses using the Community of Inquiry (CoI) Framework. Retrieved from http://www.escholarship.org/uc/item/3qz4c14n

Thompson, P., Vogler, J. S., & Xiu, Y. (2017). Strategic tooling: Technology for constructing a community of inquiry. *Journal of Educators Online*, *14*(2), n2. doi:10.9743/jeo.2017.14.2.10

Wilson, A., Watson, C., Thompson, T. L., Drew, V., & Doyle, S. (2017). Learning analytics: Challenges and limitations. *Teaching in Higher Education*, *22*(8), 991–1007. doi:10.1080/13562517.2017.1332026

ADDITIONAL READING

Garrison, D. R. (2016). *Thinking collaboratively: Learning in a community of inquiry*. New York, NY: Routledge.

Garrison, D. R., & Anderson, T. (2003). *E-Learning in the 21st century: A framework for research and practice*. London. Falmer: Routledge. doi:10.4324/9780203166093

Garrison, D. R., Anderson, T., & Archer, W. (2000). Critical inquiry in a text-based environment: Computer conferencing in higher education. *The Internet and Higher Education*, *2*(2-3), 87–105. doi:10.1016/S1096-7516(00)00016-6

Garrison, D. R., Anderson, T., & Archer, W. (2001). Critical thinking, cognitive presence and computer conferencing in distance education. *American Journal of Distance Education, 15*(1), 7–23. doi:10.1080/08923640109527071

Garrison, D. R., & Arbaugh, J. B. (2007). Researching the community of inquiry framework: Review, issues, and future directions. *The Internet and Higher Education, 10*(3), 157–172. doi:10.1016/j.iheduc.2007.04.001

Garrison, D. R., Cleveland-Innes, M., & Fung, T. (2010). Exploring causal relationships among cognitive, social and teaching presence: Student perceptions of the community of inquiry framework. *The Internet and Higher Education, 13*(1–2), 31–36. doi:10.1016/j.iheduc.2009.10.002

Chapter 6

Using Learning Management Systems to Promote Online Instruction

Vaughn Malcolm Bradley

iD https://orcid.org/0000-0002-9724-4882
Montgomery County Public Schools, USA

ABSTRACT

Learning management systems (LMS) reinforce the learning process through online classroom environments. A standard LMS supports an inclusive learning environment for academic progress with interceding structures that promote online collaborative-groupings, professional training, discussions, and communication among other LMS users. Instructors should balance active learning with the use of LMS technological resources and the use of guidelines from the qualified curriculum. As Murcia stated regarding online environments in 2016, instructors can use an LMS to facilitate and model discussions, plan online activities, set learning expectations, provide learners with options, and assist in problem-solving and decision making, supporting learner engagement through their presence in the LMS; facilitators allow students to retain their autonomy, enthusiasm, and motivation. It is vital that stakeholders of the educational community find scientific studies to support their contributions in LMS platforms to assist scholars in learning mathematics and other academic subjects

DOI: 10.4018/978-1-7998-1622-5.ch006

INTRODUCTION

In online classroom environments, Learning Management Systems (LMS) reinforce teachers and students in the learning process. A standard LMS supports an inclusive learning environment for academic progress with interceding structures that promote online collaborative-groupings, professional training, discussions, and communication among other LMS users (Dias & Dinis, 2014; Jung & Huh, 2019; Oakes, 2002). Nasser, Cherif, and Romanowski (2011) state that LMS usage provides online learners with consistent information regarding their performance. LMS usage allows online learners to become independent (Blau & Hameiri, 2010; Nasser et al., 2011; Strayhorn, 2010; Wood et al., 2011). Learner engagement is sustainable as online users use an LMS to monitor their progress (Selwyn, Hadjithoma-Garstka S, & Clark, 2011).

Dating back to the 1950s, computer designers believed in the application of an LMS in education was conceivable and necessary (Watson & Watson, 2012). There were different strategies for using an LMS as an educational resource with multiple vocabulary words that relate to computer use (Kehrwald & Parker, 2019). Through time, the technology and tools which support online learning structures were progressing since the advent of online learning in the mid/late 1990s (Kehrwald & Parker, 2019). LMS compositions include a variety of media and communications tools and promote learner choice (Kehrwald & Parker, 2019)

HISTORY AND DEFINITION OF LMS

Watson and Watson (2012) list computer-based instruction (CBI), computer-assisted instruction (CAI), and computer-assisted learning (CAL), as general terms describing computer adoption throughout history. These apply to computer application programs, teaching, and design preparation. Other purposes include monitoring, giving approval, and disseminating materials.

An LMS describes multiple online operations and behaves as a framework to capture numerous layers of progressive learning (Jung & Huh, 2019; Kuosa et al., 2016; Oakes, 2002; Watson & Watson, 2012). An LMS acts as a platform to distribute and oversee pedagogical material (Watson & Watson, 2012). LMS functions include promoting specially designed information for capturing learner progress in meeting expectations (Oakes, 2002; Watson & Watson, 2012). An LMS platform cultivates an environment for engagement and learner achievement, allowing learners to register for classes, track their grades, and check updates and course announcements (Oakes, 2002; Watson & Watson, 2012).

Watson and Watson (2012) recommend that as school districts integrate the use of an LMS, they should make LMSs a functional requirement. They discuss LMS administrative management techniques, including enabling profile features, guidelines for following the curriculum, guidelines for managing assignments, discussion boards, resources for writing, and updates from the instructor. LMS users gain access to material and information disseminated by the instructor in synchronous or asynchronous settings (Jung & Huh, 2019; Kuosa et al., 2016; Watson & Watson, 2012).

An LMS provides users with a productive learning environment to assimilate multiple components of systematic applications (Jung & Huh, 2019; Watson & Watson, 2012). In an educational setting, computer users have access to operations with non-traditional terms, and many computer users in education could have access to applications with non-traditional terms and confusing acronyms to understand (Kuosa et al. 2016; Watson & Watson, 2012). Thus, users may not understand which interpretations are suitable to use; it is fundamental to differentiate an LMS from similar technologies (Watson & Watson, 2012).

Course Management Systems

A course management system (CMS) is an assembly of operation apparatuses that structure online interactions (Evolving Technologies Committee [ETC], 2003; Jung & Huh, 2019; Watson & Watson, 2012). It provides a process for governing information in a primary location (Jung & Huh, 2019; Watson & Watson, 2012). CMSs offer online and blended learning courses where users can access folders of course materials, along with tools and other materials that contain essential course information. Examples include checking progress, tracking grades, and communicative platforms for group discussions, chats, and posting information (Watson & Watson, 2012). While CMSs and LMSs have some features in common, a CMS specializes in managing and creating learning content, whereas an LMS provides a system training platform that holds e-Learning classes to track course completion and assessment scores (Jung & Huh, 2019; Watson & Watson, 2012).

Learning Content Management Systems

Learning content management systems (LCMS) are a modern version of LMSs (Watson & Watson, 2012). Both have different complementary applications, but as Watson and Watson (2012) point out, content is the term that separates an LMS from an LCMS (p. 36). An LCMS provides instructional designers with tools to create e-learning content more methodically (Jung & Huh, 2019; Watson & Watson, 2012). According to Oakes (2002), an LCMS arrangement is reused to "create, store, assemble and deliver personalized e-learning content in the form of learning objects" (p. 73). Watson and Watson (2012) state that an LCMS can integrate with an LMS to support the arrangement and presentation of learning objects (LO). An LMS serves as a base for providing guidelines for use, and it houses the LCMS content (Jung & Huh, 2019; Watson & Watson, 2012).

Learning Objects and Related Technologies

Learning objects or LOs are fundamental components in an LCMS or an LMS (Watson & Watson, 2012). An LO provides feasible options for users across different environments (Watson & Watson, 2012). The assimilation of LOs supports modern educational environments with tools that are adaptable to meet the specific needs of students, and operations to harbor conditions of larger and smaller audiences that could transform changes in disbursements (Kehrwald & Parker, 2019; Watson & Watson, 2012). An LO may contain digital correspondence that supports students with learning objectives (Kehrwald & Parker, 2019; Oakes, 2002; Watson & Watson, 2012). The LO may also follow standards that provide evidence to define the setting and material for enactment that attaches to a Shareable Content Object Reference Model or SCORM (Oakes, 2002; Watson & Watson, 2012). According to Oakes (2002) and Watson and Watson (2012), SCORM provides an assortment of stipulations for online technology use in education. There are multiple means for disaggregating how learners use LOs (Watson & Watson, 2012).

LCMSs, CMSs, and LOs can adjust and connect within an LMS to provide technologies that support a climate for learning (Watson & Watson, 2012). LOs act as meager types of material found within an LCMS to reinforce student attainment (Kehrwald & Parker, 2019; Watson & Watson, 2012). LOs that consist of recent work assignments and accomplishments to support defined instructional objectives are managed by an LMS (Watson & Watson, 2012). CMSs act as an academic structure to host pedagogical knowledge into classes that manage connections among other students and other professors (Jung & Huh, 2019: Watson & Watson, 2012).

ASYNCHRONOUS VS. SYNCHRONOUS STRUCTURES

An LMS provides a structure for asynchronous delivery methods that include emails, discussion groups, audio discussion presentations, and newspapers to foster positive interactions (Alzahrani, 2019). Asynchronous delivery methods allow learners to communicate with each other without the distraction of being separated through distance and time (Alzahrani, 2019). Asynchronous environments enable learners to work in conjunction with other commitments and responsibilities (Alzahrani,

2019). Additionally, in asynchronous structures, learners must navigate their way through an LMS to explore course materials, engage in effective communication, and manage the technologies of the course (Alzahrani, 2019).

Both asynchronous and synchronous methods use an LMS to provide learners with positive effects to facilitate their learning (Alzahrani, 2019). In comparing asynchronous learning with synchronous learning, Hrastinski and Keller (2007) state that in a distance learning environment, synchronous learning is essential for developing a student's critical reflection abilities. Asynchronous learning systems do not provide learners with instant feedback (Hrastinski & Keller, 2007). Asynchronous learning systems focus on expanding the use of asynchronous tools in an LMS. Alkhasawnh and Alqahtani (2019) believe asynchronous learning provides flexibility as learners can reflect and complete tasks.

Alzahrani (2019) implemented an experimental design with 49 students using the LMS Blackboard with both asynchronous and synchronous methods to take a physics course. Within the course, students were to use the synchronous videoconference method for lectures with their professor and course discussions for the first semester, and asynchronous video conferencing with Blackboard for the next seven weeks (Alzahrani, 2019). At the end of each of the seven weeks, the students took an exam (Alzahrani, 2019), then their grades were compared (Alzahrani, 2019). The results showed that 46.6% of the participants preferred the synchronous videoconferencing method, and 53.4% of the students preferred the asynchronous method with recorded video assets delivered through Blackboard (Alzahrani, 2019). The responses from the students indicate the students prefer to use the asynchronous video conferencing with Blackboard technology for their course (Alzahrani, 2019).

NUANCES TO LMS: PROPRIETARY VS. OPEN-SOURCES

A decision that school organizations face in selecting an LMS is whether to choose a proprietary system or open-source system (Kimmons, Hunsaker, Jones, & Stauffer, 2019). The decision depends mainly on the resources available and the knowledge or level of expertise of members within school organizations (Turnbull, Chugh, & Luck, 2019). A proprietary system uses an exclusive code where schools or school organizations purchase a license or subscription to access and use the LMS features (Kimmons et al., 2019). Some examples of proprietary systems include Blackboard, PowerSchool, SchoolWires, Edline, eSchoolView, and SchoolPointe (Kehrwald & Parker, 2019; Kimmons et al., 2019). Open-source systems use a free license at no cost where users have the freedom to access and use the system (Kimmons et al., 2019; Turnbull et al., 2019). Examples of open-source systems include Moodle, Wordpress, and Drupal (Kehrwald & Parker, 2019; Kimmons et al., 2019).

Most school organizations select proprietary systems that make-up 59.0% of the licenses held (Kimmons et al., 2019). In Cloud-based proprietary systems, most all vendors charge a service fee based on the number of LMS users (Turnbull et al., 2019). Turnbull, Chugh, and Luck (2019) state that school organizations who select proprietary systems receive advantages of working with a company that practices in the construction and distribution of online solutions to support learning. Clients who use proprietary systems also receive end-user training that does not require any configuration (Turnbull et al., 2019). The disadvantage of using a proprietary system is clients have limits and can only access designated LMS features from the school organization (Turnbull et al., 2019). School organizations with proprietary systems are starting to integrate Cloud-based LMS solutions where the LMS merchant maintains the client's data online (Turnbull et al., 2019). Cloud-based LMS solutions allow users to maintain the physical infrastructure for running an on-site LMS (Jung & Huh, 2019; Turnbull et al., 2019).

Some entrepreneur educators are promoting open-source systems to drive online learning environments that use a variety of media and communication tools and support learner choice in the selection and use of tools for online learning (Kehrwald & Parker, 2019). These open-source systems continue to evolve to accommodate the possibility of their system existing only in web-based settings (Turnbull et al., 2019). School organizations can use open source systems to suit their circumstances (Kehrwald & Parker, 2019). Turnbull et al., 2019). Open-source systems allow users to extend system functionality and use community source plugins (Kehrwald & Parker, 2019; Turnbull et al., 2019). College and University students are among the most abundant users of open source systems (Turnbull et al., 2019). IT expertise is available in most college settings to support the use of open-source systems (Turnbull et al., 2019).

This chapter explores several LMS topics and aspects of learning. Table 1 provides an overview of the LMS studies for review.

THE ROLE OF THE LMS IN EDUCATION

There is a purpose in differentiating other, similar technology resources from LMSs (Watson & Watson, 2012). These distinctions could impact the academic and learning needs of modern-day learners (Watson & Watson, 2012). There is a significant transformation among learners in society in going from a revolution of the industry to the 21st-century Age of Information (Kehrwald & Parker, 2019; Kimmons et al., 2019; Reigeluth, 1994; Toffler, 1984; Watson & Watson, 2012). In an LMS setting, teachers are facilitators, providing a learning environment where students can conduct research and engage with technological resources to

Table 1. Overview of studies

LMS Topic	Aspect of Learning
The role of LMS in education	• LMSs provide expectations for learners to monitor their learning progress continuously • Professors can prepare constructivist arrangements with adaptable pedagogical intentions
Toward an enhanced LMS to support student learning	• Najmul Islam (2016) Study • Dias and Dinis (2014) Study • You's (2016) Study
What current LMS(s) offer	• LMS Tools • Nasser, Cherif, and Romanowski (2011) Study • Selwyn, Hadjithoma-Garstka, and Clark (2011) Study
Using an LMS to foster an online learning environment	• Constructivists approaches to learning • Learner Engagement • Technology Infrastructure
How instructors use an LMS to support online student learning	• Wong's (2016) Study • Volitional functioning • Lerner Independence
LMS technological resource to support learners online	• Reynolds (2016) Study • Louwrens and Hartnett (2015) Study
How LMS resources impact teaching and learning	• Student Response Resources • LMS Technology Resource Implementation • LMS Use to Support Learner Outcomes • LMS Personalization

become Information Age professionals (Kehrwald & Parker, 2019; Reigeluth, 1994; Toffler, 1994; Watson & Watson, 2012). Student progress among learners using an LMS varies where low-achieving students may struggle in meeting deadlines with submitting assignments, and high-achieving students have limits in getting beyond meeting deadlines (Reigeluth, 1997; Watson & Watson, 2012). Watson and Watson (2012) believe a challenge for LMS instructors is to make managerial and pedagogical adjustments from a homogenous plane of deficiency to a classification of progress to support all learners.

Online professors can use LMSs for communicating precise expectations to learners (Kehrwald & Parker, 2019; Reigeluth, 1994; Watson & Watson, 2012). An LMS supports students by monitoring learning progress, continuously providing essential knowledge, and implementing assessments (Watson & Watson, 2012). Today, an LMS can evaluate a learners' current levels of accomplishment and attainment (Branch, 2015; Watson & Watson, 2012). Professors can also use a reserved record of achievement, sustain agreements, and produce descriptions to govern intelligence that magnifies the progressive attainment of learners in the online environment (Kehrwald & Parker, 2019; Watson & Watson, 2012).

LMSs allow online professors to prepare constructivist arrangements with adaptable pedagogical intentions (Branch, 2015; Kitchen & Berk, 2016; Reigeluth, 1994; Turnbull et al., 2019; Watson & Watson, 2012). An LMS allows online learners to participate in group-chats, monitor their grades and progress, participate in online discussions, and take assessments (Reigeluth, 1994; Turnbull et al., 2019; Watson & Watson, 2012). An LMS also allows online professors to cultivate an educational environment for learning and continuous improvement (Kitchen & Berk, 2016; Watson & Watson, 2012).

TOWARD AN ENHANCED LMS TO SUPPORT STUDENT LEARNING

As students learn to use LMS features, they become able to assess their learning progress better. Najmul Islam (2016) conducted a study in which LMS usage data collections from 179 university students using the Moodle LMS to collaborate in a blended-learning course. The study focused on learner outcomes, online application, and rapport. More specifically, the learner outcomes through online measures could develop with the use of pedagogical expectations, predictable academic means, and predictable support with association construction. Najmul Islam explored the use of partial least squares (PLS) to analyze the quantitative data. Qualitative measures were used to substantiate the analysis of the PLS data. The findings from the study showed that anticipated compatibility controlled the union among educational issues and e-learning system use and did not necessarily support learner outcomes (Najmul Islam, 2016).

As a strategy, learners can commit and use an LMS to work collaboratively on educational learning assignments. In a study conducted by Dias and Dinis (2014) focusing on learner profiles, instructors gave students comments on their performance through their learner profiles. The results indicate three types of learner profiles conformed to a reciprocal learning condition, Information and Communication Technologies (ICT) instructors' assurances, and learners' preparation (Dias & Dinis, 2014). As practitioners use an LMS within an online learning environment, consideration should go toward levels of interactions with students, supporting learners' ICT associates, and facilitating further professional development. Results from the study show that student profiles can correlate with online learning cultures, ICT Dias & Dinis, 2014).

Students who use LMS features will begin self-regulating their progress. You (2016) conducted a study using an LMS to find observable approaches, of course, learning attainment. Similar to Dias and Dinis (2014), You (2016) included Howell's (2001) endorsement for instructors to use LMS essential resources including assignments from the instructor. Howell's (2001) investigation showed that students would refer to the course website if they thought it was useful. Similar to the Dias and Dinis (2014) study, the You (2016) study collected data, including having students monitor and self-regulate their course learning. Students who kept track of their online assignments by continually logging into the online course and reading course materials frequently performed well (Dias & Dinis, 2014; You, 2016). Although data logged by an LMS could support a progression of indicators, there is no guarantee it could increase the probability of the student's achievement (You, 2016). Thus, professionals and leaders in education should continue to analyze LMS resources that could accurately capture online student engagement and strategies that support students in their ability to self-regulate (You, 2016).

Gašević, Dawson, Rogers, and Gasevic (2016) conducted a study that reviewed the influence of learning environments on learner success. In the study, nine blended learning courses offerings to 4,134 college undergraduate students. The study illustrates the difference in "predictive power and predictors between course-specific models such as mathematics and generalized predictive models" (p. 68). It showed broader implications for students who identify as being at risk of failing academically.

In future studies, analytics should consider learning conditions when constructing LMS resource models (Dias & Dinis, 2014; Gašević et al., 2016; You, 2016). Gašević et al. (2016) suggest reviewing instructional conditions before assigning the use of additional features.

WHAT CURRENT LMS(S) OFFER

According to Jung and Huh (2019) and Watson and Watson (2012), LMSs provide several tools such as a network webserver to support an interface between the learner and the LMS. An LMS also provides a database to store information relating to user's learning and an LMS video on demand (VoD) database for storing multimedia files, including voice and video files (Jung & Huh, 2019).

Nasser, Cherif, and Romanowski (2011) studied the use of an LMS known as Knowledge-Net or K-Net for instructor and student middle school achievements. They investigated variables that influence learner adoption of the LMSK-Net in Qatari independent institutions. The quantitative study included questionnaire survey data from 1,376 learners in 37 schools and qualitative semi-structured interviews to support findings from the quantitative portion by contributing supplemental understanding of learners' views about LMSs. The findings show that when instructors are reluctant to use an LMS, it impacts all students with communicating student progress. Student motivation and engagement increased when instructors provided rewards for using LMS resources. Nasser et al. (2011) recommended that professors and online instructors offer a system of rewards to help motivate learners. They could also model expectations in using an LMS to stimulate adoption.

Selwyn, Hadjithoma-Garstka, and Clark (2011) conducted a study to find how middle schools use an LMS to support online student engagement. The study included 12 schools and focused on using LMS resources to support teaching and learning, online student engagement, and management. The findings show that an LMS allows learners to submit assignments, view their grades and progress, post questions for social networking, and provides users with the possibility of using social media operations (Branch, 2015; Selwyn et al., 2011).

Selwyn et al., 2011 showed that an LMS can provide users with organizational assistance. Similar to Nasser et al. (2011), users also found that institutions could promote learner participation through premediating LMS features. School officials would share updates and information through announcements, online resources, and users could reciprocate by sharing information with other users. Unilateral distribution of resources and information proved to be a concern.

Learners can use an LMS to communicate, interact, and upload assignments. (Jung & Huh, 2019; Selwyn et al., 2011). Thus, LMS use appears to give learners a platform for updating and displaying their progress (Branch, 2015; Selwyn et al., 2011). School organizations can provide a culture with training to support learner and parental LMS engagement; Selwyn et al. (2011) suggest that trainers provide online users with LMS resources to use for discussions, communications, and continuous monitoring.

LMSs allow users to independently fill their emerging needs in communicating with others and checking their progress (Kehrwald & Parker, 2019; Kimmons et al., 2019; Turnbull et al., 2019). School organizations and institutions are expected to support LMS structures (Turnbull et al., 2019). Current trends for LMSs are to expand learner interactions with course content that allow users to use their mobile and electronic devices (Jung & Huh, 2019; Turnbull et al., 2019). The term *mobile learning* refers to a learning system with the use of a mobile device such as a mobile phone, personal media players, and tablet PCs (Jung & Huh, 2019; Turnbull et al., 2019). Mobile devices allow learners to access learning content from different locations at any time (Jung & Huh, 2019).

USING AN LMS TO FOSTER AN ONLINE LEARNING ENVIRONMENT

As central and constructivist online learning environments develop, students learn to manage their academics independently (Alkhasawnh & Alqahtani, 2019; Murcia, 2016). Constructivist approaches allow learners to construct awareness through active participation and assign value to the learners' autonomy (Murcia, 2016; Wang, 2011). In online environments, teachers facilitate and model discussions, plan online activities, set learning expectations, provide learners with choices and options, and assist learners in solving problems and making decisions (Jung & Huh, 2019; Murcia, 2016).

According to Murcia (2016), online facilitators provide learners with opportunities to ask questions and use their previous knowledge to create new concepts. Facilitators allow students to retain their autonomy, enthusiasm, and motivation. Online instructors support learner engagement through maintaining their presence in the LMS environment. Examples include responding to questions from participants, participating in the LMS course discussions, and giving students feedback on their performance.

LMS integration into different forms of activities promotes student learning and self-regulation (Alkhasawnh & Alqahtani, 2019). LMS use provides practitioners with modularity, customization, and flexibility (Kehrwald & Parker, 2019). Some enterprising online educators are supporting LMS use to promote user-driven online learning environments that utilize a variety of media and communications tools and promote learner choice in the selection and use of online learning tools (Kehrwald & Parker, 2019).

Similarly, the technology infrastructure evolves with faster internet connections, including the current National Broadband Network (Kehrwald & Parker, 2019). The technology infrastructure also creates new possibilities for the use of rich media in education and shifts the focus from the use of online text in combination with media packages toward more productive, integrated online learning materials with text, audio, imagery and interactive LOs (Kehrwald & Parker, 2019). As the access to technology improves for users, advances in computing adjust to provide LMS users with access to powerful computing devices, including affordable desktop and laptop computers, powerful yet mobile tablets, sophisticated mobile phones and, more recently, wearable technology (Kehrwald & Parker, 2019).

HOW INSTRUCTORS USE AN LMS TO SUPPORT ONLINE STUDENT LEARNING

Emphasis on science, technology, engineering, and mathematics (STEM) courses is growing (Wong, 2016). Thus, defining teacher's beliefs on how they integrate STEM areas into their online lessons are essential to know. In Wong's (2016) study, 21 U.S. middle school mathematics and science instructors participate in an Integrated Science Mathematics and Reflective Teaching program called iSMART. It was a two-year master's LMS online instructional program. Participants used an LMS to learn about pedagogies and theoretical perspectives of research-based mathematics and science methods of teaching. They could access and scaffold their assimilation of mathematical and scientific learning areas throughout the program. The participants would practice using the iSMART course strategies with their mathematics or science classes.

Wong (2016) concluded that mathematics instructors could integrate science strategies into their instruction to foster learner autonomy by expanding their student-centered ideas to support inquiry-based instruction. These findings also promote the sentiment that academic proficiency could influence instructor beliefs. Both mathematics and science instructors should grasp learner-centered beliefs that would align with inquiry-based instructional practices to support learners in creating concepts from existing prior knowledge (Murcia, 2016). Instructors can give learners their autonomy to investigate and develop their ideas of understanding (Murcia, 2016; Wong, 2016).

Advocacy of a course of action or volitional functioning is a belief to differentiate Deci and Ryan's self-determination theory (SDT; Deci & Ryan, 1985). The differentiation from new intentions to affiliate autonomy with advocating interdependence (Murcia, 2016). Volitional functioning accentuates the premonition of autonomy support of the self-determination model from new theories to affiliate autonomy and promotes independence (Murcia, 2016). Alkhasawnh and Alqahtani (2019) and Haerens, Vansteenkiste, Aelterman, and Van den Berghe (2016) found benefits through encouraging volitional functioning, which include a more in-depth level of learning, decisive influence, and observable and achievable perseverance. Instructors could advocate for voluntary operation through providing learners with the ability to make choices, giving students a rationale when an instructor says no to a learners' questions or inquiry, and using more connotative language that supports intrinsic motivation (Haerens et al., 2016).

Haerens et al. (2016) showed that instructors could set expectations for learners to monitor their progress independently. As instructors promote learner independence, students can autonomously complete assignments and tasks without influence from their instructor (Murcia, 2016; Shukla & Verma, April 2019). There is a different perspective from the viewpoint of SDT, where instructors emphasize answering and responding to learners' questions and interests (Murcia, 2016). Instructors can encourage learners to engage in collaborative strategies to research their interests (Murcia, 2016; Reynolds, 2016).

LMS TECHNOLOGICAL RESOURCE TO SUPPORT LEARNERS ONLINE

LMS resources can support learners in online environments. Reynolds (2016) conducted a synchronous game learning discovery-based guided study with U.S. middle school students. It included collaborative research information seeking and practices that support learners in gaining perspective and building their prior knowledge. Participants used a wiki as an LMS for providing curriculum, designing activities, accentuating aspects of social media, providing tutorials, and giving learners information-oriented assignments. Students participated in a constructivist online synchronous structure and work in collaborative groups. Measures for gathering data for the qualitative study include a video of six group cases of codes to categorize collaborative information seeking, problem-solving outcomes, and approaches to completing an assignment.

The findings from Reynolds (2016) support learners in assimilating knowledge acquisition with an entire cycle of cultural and fundamental suitable aspects to provide a framework for learning with gaming as the program's objective. The structure allows learners to collaborate in groups to seek information. The results show that LMS online educational environments should include social constructivism as a collaborative strategy to support knowledge construction. The approach can also apply in academic situations with inquiry learning.

Similar to Reynolds (2016), when seeking information collaboratively in synchronous online LMS settings, Haerens et al. (2016) found that premises to support behavior and cognition. Their information-seeking could intuitively rely on social factors that impact learners academically; for example, social influencers allowed learners to seek support autonomously. Potential influences include family members and peer groups (Haerens et al., 2016; Murcia, 2016). In online environments, instructors who support learner autonomy consider learners perspectives, feelings, thoughts, and encourage learners to develop self-regulatory practices that motivate and promote intrinsic motivation factors, provide learners with feedback, use instructional language, and present tolerance (Murcia, 2016; Shukla & Verma, April 2019).

Louwrens and Hartnett (2015) argue that LMS online learning environments are still in the developmental stage when it comes to establishing learner engagement among compulsory school settings. Seeing that many online engagement studies come from older students in tertiary education settings, Louwrens and Hartnett (2015) examined online student engagement among middle school learners in New Zealand. The analytical constructs of student engagement included behavioral cooperation, cognitive connections, and emotional engagement as part of the examination to look at how middle school learners engage in an online learning environment. Data sources included instructor and student interviews, online asynchronous discussion transcripts, and statistical LMS data sources.

Results indicate that learners engage behaviorally with all necessary activities. Similar to Jung & Huh (2019) and Reynolds (2016) regarding collaborative information seeking, Louwrens and Hartnett (2015) claim that cognitive engagement is more likely when learners receive and give their instructors feedback in addition to participating in learner engagement activities. Emotional attachments develop as learners interact and support the development of an online community of learners who feel safe to participate. The emotional attachments align with Reynolds' (2016) beliefs on how collaboration supports the increase with divulging assignment information that could also yield an increase with student learning.

In online distance education settings, learners can use an LMS to access knowledge with straightforward connections, and increasing academic competence also impacts self-esteem. Similar to Louwrens and Hartnett (2015) and Prior, Mazanov, Meacheam, Heaslip, and Hanson (2016) believe that face-to-face learning structures could positively impact self-efficacy. In distance online educational settings, instructors should provide learners with antecedents and digital literacy competency courses. Prior et al. (2016) showed that online learning environments could influence a learners' self-esteem in LMS collaboration, learner engagement, and course adoption. In their online study with 151 middle school learners, implementing digital literacy concepts and learner assurance approaches contributed to collaborative information seeking significantly — additionally, the ideas and strategies emotionally engaged learners with activities, promoting self-efficacy and peer engagement.

Increasing participation among middle school learners is necessary to develop an online environment where students feel safe to contribute their ideas and thoughts (Louwrens & Hartnett, 2015; Reynolds, 2016). Online instructors provide learners with the ability to choose and make decisions regarding their learning. The choices increase learners' ability to engage behaviorally and cognitively (Kimmons et al., 2019; Louwrens & Hartnett, 2015; Murcia, 2016; Prior et al., 2016). Online middle school instructors who include activities that promote interactions among learners along with scholarly information stemming from connections with learning sciences and information sciences can give learners new knowledge and understanding (Louwrens & Hartnett, 2015; Reynolds, 2016).

HOW LMS RESOURCES IMPACT TEACHING AND LEARNING

Studies on how LMS resources support student achievement are emerging steadily. Simplicio (2002) believes that instructors promote change in their teaching methodologies. Kehrwald and Parker (2019) and Pásztor, Molnár, and Csapó (2015) also believe creativity is essential when instructors use an LMS to support 21st-century learning. As part of an online instructors' role within the LMS, contemporary skills were fundamental to solving dilemmas, collaboration, metacognition, and literacy in ICT (Kimmons et al., 2019; Pásztor, Molnár, & Csapó, 2015).

Student Response Resources

A technological resource within an LMS to support online communication is a classroom response system. According to Barth-Cohen et al. (2016), during synchronous online classroom sessions, learners can use a response system in the form of clickers. In their study, they collected data from students taking a middle school online physical science course. The instructor gave students clicker questions to answer individually and set up online groups where students could discuss the issues collaboratively. Online instructors who allowed learners to use the instructional tool noticed that learners became willing to share questions with fellow students. Clicker use supported online discourse among learners.

Barth-Cohen et al. (2016) believe that instructors who foster online discussions among learners can allow learners to construct and adapt their interpretations of concepts. They also found the communications have both a positive and negative impact on student performance in the co-construction of collaborative knowledge. Instructors played essential roles in moderating clicker discussions in online academic settings to enhance the probability of learner engagement. As online automation makes it more cost-efficient to use LMS technological resources, more instructors can give learners access to technical systems in the online environment (Downes & Bishop, 2015).

In the 21st century, schools are providing learners with one-to-one laptops for access to LMS technological tools that are continuously in use to support online instruction (National Middle School Association [NMSA], 2010). Downes and Bishop (2015) conducted a qualitative case study that explored correlations between one-to-one system applications and successful middle schools. In the four-year investigation with 50 seventh- and eighth-grade students participating annually, instructors and learners received laptops for one-to-one wireless computing. Data sources included observations, structured interviews with instructors and learners, meeting transcripts, and student work samples. According to the results, three areas align with the most effective middle schools: (a) ability and society identifications; (b) instruction, curriculum, and testing characteristics; and (c) organization and leadership characteristics (Downes & Bishop, 2015; National Middle School Association, 2010).

According to Downes & Bishop (2015), during the first three years of their study, instructors would not distinguish community and environment distinctions that did not honor the goals or the expectations. Thus, learners became upset by the instructor's testimonies to provide learner engagement with technology-rich lessons never taught. In year four, the professors began to place more effort into promoting online student instruction. Toward the end of the study, both instructors and learners acknowledged receiving open online classroom settings.

Results from the study show that online structures need to incorporate LMS technology integration to build interdisciplinary culture and mutual support among instructors and learners (Downes & Bishop, 2015; Kimmons et al., 2019; Toffler, 1984). LMS technology resource use by groups of learners encourages online collaboration, and team activities also allow instructors to construct useful team environments (Downes & Bishop, 2015). Technology-intensive settings for learning environments could also help support inquiry-based learning (IBL) as an inductive approach to academic knowledge. The technology-intensive settings that enable learners to enhance their aptitude increase their interpretation skills and encourage academic enthusiasm and motivation (Avsec & Kocijancic, 2016).

Avsec and Kocijancic (2016) examined how different technologies impact student learning outcomes in IBL environments that emphasize individual aptitude, perspectives, and behavior, in 421 learners from 11 Slovenian middle schools. Measures of attainment included pre- and post-assessments along with IBL scenarios and interpretations to review. IBL had a specific impact on technology with literacy assessment accountability with a course design that highlights the effects of numerous. Findings from the study show that course content was most distinctive among factors and that prior knowledge and learning affect IBL with a decrease in psychologically important mechanisms (Avsec & Kocijancic, 2016; National Educational Technology Standards [NETS], 2015). Also, IBL has a positive impact on student learning with the use of technology and design, and IBL activities support metacognition and allow learners to make decisions (Avsec & Kocijancic, 2016; National Educational Technology Standards for Students [NETS-S], 2015).

LMS Technology Resource Implementation

According to Downes and Bishop (2015), continual LMS technology resource changes and refinement can impact the implementation of pedagogical changes to support students in online settings. Educational leaders can support the initiative by working with school instructional teams who support the effort. There is a balance that instructors should find with providing active learning with the use of LMS technological resources and using guidelines from the qualified curriculum (Kimmons et al., 2019). Opportunities for instructors to implement the official curriculum with the use of technical resources are diminishing (Downes & Bishop, 2015; Wenglinsky,

1998). Only recently have online instructors begun to use technological resources when implementing curriculum (Kimmons et al., 2019; Downes & Bishop, 2015).

Downes and Bishop (2015) conclude that one-to-one computing, along with guidelines of regular student training, can support the successful implementation of the curriculum with the use of LMS resources. Emphasis on pedagogy and content knowledge in education with the use of technology should match the instruction, teaming, and leadership practices that serve active learners in fulfilling their desire for responsive schools that use technology (Association for Middle Level Education [AMLE], 2013; Downes & Bishop, 2015; Mishra & Koehler, 2006).

Instructors can gain perspective as they examine the use of LMS technological resources through continuous professional development in online structures that support purposeful relationships (Bornstein, 2006; Downes & Bishop, 2015). Downes and Bishop (2015) recommend that attaching educational challenges with individual programs can increase support for learners with online learning. These examinations could combine to integrate technology acquisition, despite the demands, to face the expanding gap between in-school and out-of-school technology use among adolescents.

LMS Use to Support Learner Outcomes

One outcome for instructors is to design online lessons with the use of LMS technological resources that assess outcomes for learning with specific variables. Online instructors can encourage learners to make connections from the classroom to the real world (Kimmons et al., 2010; Downes & Bishop, 2015; Wenglinsky, 1998). In making connections, online instructors can begin to view themselves as part of an online instructional team with other online instructors, sharing ideas to support student learning (Dede, Honan, & Peters, 2005: Simplicio, 2002). Social and technological development requires innovative ideas and solutions (Pásztor et al., 2015). Examples set by professionals in the discipline of educational technology can inspire leaders to gather and analyze information that provides ideas into the effects of technology on student performance (Dede et al., 2005; Pásztor et al., 2015).

Technology resources for online teaching affect student learning and achievement positively (Eyyam & Yaratan, 2014; Kadosh & Dowker, 2015; O'Dwyer, Carey, & Kleinman, 2015). Eyyam and Yaratan (2014) conducted a quasi-experimental research design that examined learner attitudes towards technology use in a mathematics class and whether the use of technology, improves their academic achievement. The study included seventh-grade private school students with three experimental groups of 41 students and two control groups of 41 students. Each team completed a pretest and a posttest in which the experimental groups received online lesson designs using several LMS technological tools and the control groups used traditional teaching methods. At the end of the study, the experimental groups completed a scale to investigate student preferences and attitudes regarding technology-based instruction. Most students reported positive attitudes toward educational technology.

Similarly, Jung and Huh (2019) and Sung, Chang, and Liu (2016) found that mobile devices can enhance educational effects. Their study examined the usage of electronic devices, which included laptops, cell phones, and personal digital assistants that support possibilities for achieving a blended classroom learning environment. The study consists of synthesis and meta-research analysis that focuses on how integrating mobile devices impacts teaching and learning. It also contains 110 quasi and experimental periodical articles for coding and analysis. Results indicate mobile learning programs have enhanced impact with longer intervention durations, integrated technology and curriculum, and assessment of higher-level skills.

LMS technological resources are also useful in online mathematical environments. According to O'Dwyer et al. (2015), comparable achievement occurs with students taking an experimental online course and learners taking a face-to-face class. Their study compared 231 seventh and eighth-grade learners taking an online Algebra course with 232 seventh and eighth graders taking a face-to-face Algebra course. Research instruments included a formative assessment to address general ability in mathematics, a summative evaluation that was comparable to the state's Grade Level Expectations (GLE) in Algebra 1, and a survey to capture synchronous and asynchronous information regarding students' experiences from both types of courses. Students in the online preparatory courses outscored students in the control courses in 18 out of 25 components.

Students have a positive attitude toward LMS technology resources, but many learners do not know how to apply LMS tools in a mathematics classroom and online environment. O'Dwyer et al. (2015) showed how learners in their experimental courses aim to outperform other learners. Eyyam and Yaratan (2014) state that a significant number of seventh-grade students were indecisive about their preferences to use LMS technology they rarely use. They showed that people resist change, so in their study, participants received mathematical lessons that require the use of educational technology for the first time. They believe that after students become acquainted technology-based instruction in the mathematics classroom, the indecisive students and even students who report they do not like to use technology could recognize how technology can allow learners to self-regulate and monitor their progress.

LMS technology use also applies to online mathematical environments. Likewise, Kehrwald and Parker (2019) and O'Dwyer et al. (2015) found that when the experimental groups of online students compare to the face-to-face groups of learners, a significant percentage of learners in the innovative online organizations indicate that their experience was not progressive. Due to learners' unfamiliarity with the online classroom environment.

O'Dwyer et al. (2015) state that although the summative outcomes were similar to the comparison trial, fewer learners from the experimental online courses expressed enthusiasm for acquiring Algebra 1 knowledge after completing the online course. Similarly, a meta-analysis by Bernard et al. (2004), including 232 distance education studies and 688 independent-learning, behavioral, and retention-oriented outcomes, shows that many distance education students can outperform their face-to-face classroom counterparts. Participants in synchronous environments support classroom instruction, while participants in asynchronous settings support distance educational environments. O'Dwyer et al. (2015) also report that the online Algebra 1 model should require level changes on the relationships mathematics teachers establish with their online students.

LMS Personalization

O'Dwyer et al. (2015) also found that many students in experimental online classrooms feel they should have more interactions with their teachers. Studies on higher-level educational programs reveal that learners who enroll in online programs tend to isolate themselves as scholars. As studies in higher education show, online programs often separate students during learning (Bernard et al., 2004; O'Dwyer et al., 2015). O'Dwyer et al. (2015) found that students in experimental online classrooms reported more time interacting with other students using an LMS. However, learners' time allotted for social interactions, their ability to comprehend expectations with assignments, and their ability to collaborate with others was equivalent to face-to-face courses.

Over half a million learners enrolled in K–12 courses feel the impact of some form of online learning initiative (O'Dwyer et al., 2015). Høgheim and Reber (2015) examined the effect of context personalization and example choice on situational interest in adolescent-level mathematics. They studied 736 middle school students learning about probability calculus assigned to one of the several instructional conditions, including situational interest, value perception, and task effort. The results show that context personalization and example choice caught the attention of students with a low individual interest in mathematics and could support them in becoming more engaged in the software activity (Høgheim & Reber, 2015; Kehrwald & Parker, 2019).

O'Dwyer et al. (2015) found that 71.8% of students in an online Algebra 1 class identified that using technology was the aspect of the course they liked most. Teachers who adopted the use of technology had a progressive effect on learner achievement in specific academic areas such as mathematics or science. Students in the experimental group articulated aspects of the Algebra 1 online courses that supported student achievement. On the other hand, the Høgheim and Reber

(2015) study showed that online learning environments were associated with the opportunity for educators to adapt to education, which entailed tailoring education for every student. Context personalization and choice represented instructional formats suitable for implementation in a digitalized classroom where the content changed to students' interest.

Stakeholders of the educational community should find scientific studies to support their contributions in LMS platforms to assist scholars in learning mathematics and other academic subjects (Høgheim & Reber, 2015; Kehrwald & Parker, 2019; O'Dwyer et al., 2015). There is currently a shortage of studies to mitigate the effect on learner achievement and efficacy levels on results in elementary, middle, and high school online environments. (Bernard et al. 2004; O'Dwyer et al., 2015). Future studies could focus on the efficiency of LMS platforms in public school settings that highlight learner satisfaction and contentment (Jung & Huh, 2019: O'Dwyer et al., 2015).

SUMMARY

In online classroom environments, LMS reinforces teachers and students in the learning process. A standard LMS supports an inclusive learning environment for academic progress with interceding structures that promote online collaborative-groupings, professional training, discussions, and communication among other LMS users (Dias & Dinis, 2014; Jung & Huh, 2019: Oakes, 2002). Since the advent of online learning in the mid/late 1990s, the technology and tools which support online learning structures continue to progress (Kehrwald & Parker, 2019). LMS compositions include a variety of media and communications tools and promote learner choice (Kehrwald & Parker, 2019).

An LMS involves multiple online operations and behaves as a framework to capture several layers of progressive learning (Jung & Huh, 2019; Kuosa et al., 2016; Oakes, 2002; Watson & Watson, 2012). A course management system (CMS) is an assembly of apparatuses that structure online interactions (Evolving Technologies Committee [ETC], 2003; Watson & Watson, 2012). Learning Content Management Systems (LCMS) are current affiliates of an LMS, and both have assorted complimentary applications. Learning objects or LOs are fundamental components in LCMSs and LMSs, providing options for users across different environments (Jung & Huh, 2019Watson & Watson, 2012).

An LMS provides a structure for asynchronous delivery methods that include emails, discussion groups, audio discussion presentations, and newspapers to foster positive interactions (Alzahrani, 2019). Asynchronous delivery methods allow learners to communicate with each other without the distraction of being separated through distance and time (Alzahrani, 2019).

When selecting an LMS, school organizations can choose a proprietary system or open-source system (Kimmons, Hunsaker, Jones, & Stauffer, 2019). The decision depends on the resources available and the knowledge or level of expertise of members within school organizations (Turnbull et al., 2019). A proprietary system uses an exclusive code where schools purchase a license or subscription to access and use the LMS features (Kimmons et al., 2019). Open-source systems use a free license with no cost where users have the freedom to access and use the system (Kimmons et al., 2019; Turnbull et al., 2019).

Online professors and learners can use LMSs for characterizing precise expectations (Jung & Huh, 2019; Reigeluth, 1994; Watson & Watson, 2012). An LMS supports students in monitoring learning progress, continuously providing essential knowledge, and implementing assessments (Watson & Watson, 2012). LMSs allow online professors to prepare constructivist approaches with adaptable pedagogical intentions (Branch, 2015; Kitchen & Berk, 2016; Reigeluth, 1994; Turnbull et al., 2019; Watson & Watson, 2012).

As students learn to use LMS features, they can assess their learning progress better (Alkhasawnh & Alqahtani, 2019; Najmul Islam, 2016). As a strategy, learners can commit and use an LMS to work collaboratively on educational learning assignments (Dias & Dinis, 2014). As practitioners use an LMS within an online learning climate, consideration should go towards levels of interactions with students, supporting learners' ICT associates, and facilitating further professional development.

Teachers' beliefs can impact decisions made within an online environment (Jung & Huh, 2019; Wong, 2016). A teacher's ideas can influence decisions with curriculum processes of implementation to support online academic success (Jung & Huh, 2019: Wong, 2016). In online environments, instructors use LMSs to facilitate and model discussions, plan online activities, set learning expectations, provide learners with choices and options, and assist learners in solving problems and making decisions (Jung & Huh, 2019; Murcia, 2016). Facilitators allow students to retain autonomy, enthusiasm, and motivation (Murcia, 2016). Online instructors support learner engagement through maintaining their presence in the LMS environment (Murcia, 2016).

Studies on how LMS resources support student achievement are emerging steadily. Continual LMS technology resource changes and refinement can impact the implementation of pedagogical changes to assist students in online settings (Downes & Bishop, 2015; Jung & Huh, 2019). Educational leaders can support the initiative by working with school instructional teams who support the effort (Downes & Bishop, 2015). Opportunities for instructors to implement the official curriculum with the use of technical resources are diminishing (Downes & Bishop,

2015; Wenglinsky, 1998). Members of the educational community stakeholders must find scientific studies to support their contributions in LMS platforms to assist scholars in learning mathematics and other academic subjects (Høgheim & Reber, 2015; Kehrwald & Parker, 2019; O'Dwyer et al., 2015).

REFERENCES

Alkhasawnh, S., & Alqahtani, M. A. M. (2019). Fostering Students' Self-Regulated Learning Through using a Learning Management System to Enhance Academic Outcomes at the University of Bisha. *TEM Journal*, *8*(2), 662–669. doi:10.18421/TEM82-47

Alzahrani, A. A. (2019). The Effect of Distance Learning Delivery Methods on Student Performance and Perception. *International Journal for Research in Education*, *43*(1), 12. Retrieved from https://bit.ly/32bUuyq

Avsec, S., & Kocijancic, S. (2016). A path model of effective technology-intensive inquiry-based learning. *Journal of Educational Technology & Society*, *19*(1), 308–320. Retrieved from https://goo.gl/HN4ir3

Barth-Cohen, L. A., Smith, M. K., Capps, D. K., Lewin, J. D., Shemwell, J. T., & Stetzer, M. R. (2016). What are middle school students talking about during clicker questions? Characterizing small-group conversations mediated by classroom response systems. *Journal of Science Education and Technology*, *25*(1), 50–61. doi:10.100710956-015-9576-2

Bernard, M., Abami, C., Lou, Y., Borkhovski, E., Wade, A., Wozney, L., ... Huang, B. (2004). How does distance education compare to classroom instruction? A meta-analysis of the empirical literature. *Review of Educational Research*, *74*(3), 379–439. doi:10.3102/00346543074003379

Blau, I., & Hameiri, M. (2010). Implementing technological change at schools: The impact of online communication with families on teacher interactions through learning management system. *Interdisciplinary Journal of E-Learning & Learning Objects,* *6*(1), 245–257. Retrieved from https://goo.gl/hrHLia

Bornstein, H. (2006). Parenting science & practice. In W. Damon (Ed.), Renninger K., & Sigel, I. (Vol. Eds.), Handbook of child psychology (6th ed., Vol. 4, pp. 893–949). Academic Press. doi:10.1002/9780470147658.chpsy0422

Branch, L. (2015). The impact of project-based learning & technology on student achievement in mathematics. In W. Ma, A. Yuen, J. Park, W. Lau, & L. Den (Eds.), New media, knowledge practices & multiliteracies (pp. 259–268). Academic Press. doi:10.1007/978-981-287-209-8_24

Deci, L., & Ryan, M. (1985). *Intrinsic motivation & self-determination in human behavior*. New York: Plenum. doi:10.1007/978-1-4899-2271-7

Dede, C., Honan, P., & Peters, C. (2005). *Scaling up success: Lessons from technology-based educational improvement*. San Francisco: Jossey-Bass.

Dias, S. B., & Dinis, J. A. (2014). Towards an enhanced learning in higher education incorporating distinct learner's profiles. *Journal of Educational Technology & Society*, *17*(1), 307–319. Retrieved from https://bit.ly/2Wjo9H7

Downes, J., & Bishop, P. (2015). The intersection between 1:1 laptop implementation & characteristics of effective middle level schools. *Research in Middle Level Education*, *38*(7), 1–16. doi:10.1080/19404476.2015.11462120

Evolving Technologies Committee. (2003). Course Management Systems (CMS). Retrieved from http://www.educause.edu/ir/library/pdf/DEC0302.pdf

Eyyam, R., & Yaratan, H. S. (2014). Impact of use of technology in mathematics lessons on student achievement & attitudes. *Social Behavior and Personality*, *42*(1), S31–S42. doi:10.2224bp.2014.42.0.S31

Gašević, A., Dawson, S., Rogers, T., & Gasevic, D. (2016). Learning analytics should not promote one size fits all: The effects of instructional conditions in predicting academic success. *Internet & Higher Education*, *28*(1), 68–84. doi:10.1016/j.iheduc.2015.10.002

Haerens, L., Vansteenkiste, M., Aelterman, N., & Van den Berghe, L. (2016). Toward a systematic study of the dark side of student motivation: Antecedents & consequences of teachers' controlling behaviors. In Building autonomous learners (pp. 59–81). Academic Press. doi:10.1007/978-981-287-630-0_4

Høgheim, S., & Reber, R. (2015). Supporting interest of middle school students in mathematics through context personalization & example choice. *Contemporary Educational Psychology*, *42*, 17–25. doi:10.1016/j.cedpsych.2015.03.006

Howell, K. R. (n.d.). *Effective use of class Web sites* [Ph.D. thesis]. Vanderbilt University. Retrieved from https://www.learntechlib.org/p/126093/

Hrastinski, S., & Keller, C. (2007). Computer-mediated communication in education: A review of recent research. *Educational Media International*, *44*(1), 61–77. doi:10.1080/09523980600922746

Jung, S., & Huh, J. H. (2019). An Efficient LMS Platform and Its Test Bed. *Electronics (Basel)*, *8*(2), 154. doi:10.3390/electronics8020154

Kadosh, R., & Dowker, A. (2015). *The Oxford handbook of numerical cognition* (2nd ed.). New York, NY: Oxford University Press. Retrieved from https://goo.gl/sD5vku

Kehrwald, B. A., & Parker, B. (2019). Implementing online learning: Stories from the field. *Journal of University Teaching & Learning Practice*, *16*(1), 1. Retrieved from https://bit.ly/2BQ5fvq

Kimmons, R., Hunsaker, E. W., Jones, J. E., & Stauffer, M. (2019). The Nationwide Landscape of K–12 School Websites in the United States. *The International Review of Research in Open and Distributed Learning*, *20*(3). doi:10.19173/irrodl.v20i4.3794

Kitchen, R., & Berk, S. (2016). Educational technology: An equity challenge to the common core. *Journal for Research in Mathematics Education*, *47*(1), 3–16. doi:10.5951/jresematheduc.47.1.0003

Kuosa, K., Distante, D., Tervakari, A., Cerulo, L., Fernández, A., Koro, J., & Kailanto, M. (2016). Interactive visualization tools to improve learning & teaching in online learning environments. *International Journal of Distance Education Technologies*, *14*(1), 1–21. doi:10.4018/IJDET.2016010101

Louwrens, N., & Hartnett, M. (2015). Student & teacher perceptions of online student engagement in an online middle school. *Journal of Open, Flexible & Distance Learning*, *19*(1), 27–44. Retrieved from https://goo.gl/P2jzXD

Mishra, P., & Koehler, M. J. (2006). Technological pedagogical content knowledge: A new framework for teacher knowledge. *Teachers College Record*, *108*(6), 1017–1054. doi:10.1111/j.1467-9620.2006.00684.x

Murcia, J. A. M. (2016). Supported teaching autonomy support. *RICYDE. Revista Internacional de Ciencias del Deporte*, *12*(43), 2–4. doi:10.5232/ricyde2016.043ed

Najmul Islam, A. (2016). E-learning system use & its outcomes: Moderating role of perceived compatibility. *Telematics and Informatics*, *33*(1), 48–55. doi:10.1016/j.tele.2015.06.010

Nasser, R., Cherif, M., & Romanowski, M. (2011). Factors that impact the usage of the learning management system in Qatari schools. *International Review of Research in Open and Distance Learning*, *12*(6), 39–62. doi:10.19173/irrodl.v12i6.985

National Educational Technology Standards for Students. (2015). *ISTE National Educational Technology Standards adopted by the Oklahoma State Department of Education.* Retrieved from https://goo.gl/fZ4uFR

National Middle School Association. (2010). *This we believe: Keys to educating young adolescents.* Westerville, OH: Author.

O'Dwyer, L., Carey, R., & Kleiman, G. (2015). Learning theory & online learning in K-12 education: Instruction models & implications. In A. Kumi-Yeboah (Ed.), Curriculum design & classroom management: Concepts, methodologies, tools & applications (pp. 167–187). Academic Press. Retrieved from https://goo.gl/gsfV6H

Oakes, K. (2002). E-learning: LCMS, LMS—They're not just acronyms but powerful systems for learning. *Training & Development, 56*(3), 73–75. Retrieved from https://goo.gl/FrNSdp

Pásztor, A., Molnár, G., & Csapó, B. (2015). Technology-based assessment of creativity in educational context: The case of divergent thinking & its relation to mathematical achievement. *Thinking Skills and Creativity, 18*(1), 32–42. doi:10.1016/j.tsc.2015.05.004

Prior, D. D., Mazanov, J., Meacheam, D., Heaslip, G., & Hanson, J. (2016). Attitude, digital literacy & self-efficacy: Flow-on effects for online learning behavior. *The Internet & higher education, 29,* 91–97. doi:10.1016/j.iheduc.2016.01.001

Reigeluth, C. M. (1994). The imperative for systemic change. In C. M. Reigeluth & R. J. Garfinkle (Eds.), *Systemic change in education.* Englewood Cliffs, NJ: Educational Technology.

Reigeluth, C. M. (1997). Educational standards: To standardize or to customize learning? *Phi Delta Kappan, 79*(3), 202–206. Retrieved from https://goo.gl/56xLbS

Reynolds, R. B. (2016). Relationships among tasks, collaborative inquiry processes, inquiry resolutions, & knowledge outcomes in adolescents during guided discovery-based game design in school. *Journal of Information Science, 42*(1), 35–58. doi:10.1177/0165551515614537

Selwyn, N., Banaji, S., Hadjithoma-Garstka, S., & Clark, W. (2011). Providing a platform for parents? Exploring the nature of parental engagement with school learning platforms. *Journal of Computer Assisted Learning, 27*(4), 314–332. doi:10.1111/j.1365-2729.2011.00428.x

Shukla, V. K., & Verma, A. (2019, April). Enhancing LMS Experience through AIML Base and Retrieval Base Chatbot using R Language. In *Proceedings of the 2019 International Conference on Automation, Computational and Technology Management (ICACTM)* (pp. 561-567). IEEE Press. Retrieved from https://bit.ly/36pluhn

Simplicio, J. S. (2002). The technology hub: A cost effective & educationally sound method for the integration of technology into schools. *Education, 122*(4), 674–679. Retrieved from https://goo.gl/xy6ar7

Strayhorn, T. (2010). *The role of schools, families, & psychological variables on math achievement of black high school students.* The University of North Carolina Press. doi:10.2307/40865058

Sung, Y. T., Chang, K. E., & Liu, T. C. (2016). The effects of integrating mobile devices with teaching & learning on students' learning performance: A meta-analysis & research synthesis. *Computers & Education, 94*(1), 252–275. doi:10.1016/j.compedu.2015.11.008

Toffler, A. (1984). *The third wave.* New York, NY: Bantam Books.

Turnbull, D., Chugh, R. & Luck, J. (2019). Learning management systems: An overview. doi:10.1007/978-3-319-60013-0_248-1

Wang, P. (2011). Constructivism & learner autonomy in foreign language teaching & learning: To what extent does theory inform practice? *Theory and Practice in Language Studies, 1*(3), 273–277. doi:10.4304/tpls.1.3.273-277

Watson, R., & Watson, S. (2012). An argument for clarity: What are learning management systems, what are they not, & what should they become? *TechTrends, 51*(2), 28–34.

Wenglinsky, H. (1998). *Does it compute? The relationship between educational technology & student achievement in mathematics.* Princeton, NJ: Educational Testing Service.

Wong, S. S. (2016). Development of teacher beliefs through online instruction: A one-year study of middle school science & mathematics teachers' beliefs about teaching & learning. *Journal of Education in Science, Environmental Health, 2*(1), 21–32. doi:10.21891/jeseh.28470

Wood, D., Kurtz-Costes, B., & Copping K. (2011). Gender differences in motivational pathways to college for middle class African-American youths. *American Psychological Association, 47*(4), 961–968. doi:10.1037/a0023745

You, J. (2016). Identifying significant indicators using LMS data to predict course achievement in online learning. *Internet & Higher Education*, 29(1), 23–30. doi:10.1016/j.iheduc.2015.11.003

ADDITIONAL READING

De Lourdes Marta, M., Monteiro, V., & Peixoto, F. (2012). Attitudes towards mathematics: Effects of individual, motivational, & social support factors. *Child Development Research*, (1): 1–10. doi:10.1155/2012/876028

Demissie, D., & Rorissa, A. (2015). The effect of information quality & satisfaction of a parent's behavioral intention to use a learning community management system. *Libri: International Journal of Libraries & Information Services*, 65(2), 143–150. doi:10.1515/libri-2015-0019

Illustrative Mathematics (IM). (2015). Welcome to illustrative mathematics. Retrieved from https://goo.gl/ot784G

Liu, S., Cheng, Y., Chen, Y., & Wu, Y. (2009). Longitudinal effects of educational expectations & achievement attributions on adolescents' academic achievements. *Adolescence*, 44(176), 911–924. doi:10.1177/0143034312454361 PMID:20432607

Martin, A., & Dowson, M. (2009). Interpersonal relationships, motivation, engagement, & achievement: Yields for theory, current issues, & educational practice. *Review of Educational Research*, 79(1), 327–365. doi:10.3102/0034654308325583

McCallum, W. (2012). The U.S. common core state standards in mathematics. *Korea & World Affairs*, 12(July). Retrieved from http://goo.gl/H8bTQg

KEY TERMS AND DEFINITIONS

Asynchronous: Online learning communication that does not require time constraints.

Learner Autonomy: Refers to a student's ability at setting accurate learning objectives towards taking control of their learning.

LMS: A Learning management system is a technology tool that provides functionalities beyond the instructional contest such as management tracking, personalized instruction, and facilitative learning.

Online Instruction: Learning that is available through a computerized system.

Open-Source: Open-source systems use a free license at no cost where users have the freedom to access and use the system.

Proprietary: A proprietary system uses an exclusive code where schools or school organizations purchase a license or subscription to access and use the LMS features

Self-Efficacy: A belief or capability in self of accomplishing a task.

Student Motivation: A force that drives a learner to accomplish a goal.

Synchronous: Online learning communication that occurs at the same time.

Chapter 7
Instructional Design and Online Standards

Lesley S. J. Farmer
California State University, Long Beach, USA

ABSTRACT

Online education has a foundation so that beneficial practices can leverage online environments effectively. Besides generic instructional design principles, models of good online instructional design are emerging. These practices and models are codified into online instructional design standards that provide research-based criteria that can be used to measure the degree to which such instructional designs meet those standards and can serve as guidelines of factors to consider when designing online instruction. This chapter provides an overview of instructional design as it applies to online teaching and learning. It also discusses how standards can help improve such instructional design in order to optimize student learning and achievement.

INTRODUCTION

Increasingly, curriculum is being provided in online learning environments. Learners can access a broader range of resources, and can communicate in various media. Time and space seem to have "collapsed." These changes impact the educational experience – and how instruction is designed.

As models of online learning have changed over the decades, current instructors probably have not experienced these formats or have been trained in their design (Boettcher & Conrad, 2016). Furthermore, because of changing practice, online education has only now stabilized so that best practices and standards can be developed and employed.

DOI: 10.4018/978-1-7998-1622-5.ch007

To this end, this chapter provides an overview of instructional design as it applies to online teaching and learning and uses an autoethnographic case study to investigate how standards can help improve such instructional design in order to optimize student learning and achievement.

BACKGROUND

Instructional Design

Instructional design may be defined as a systematic process used to develop educational programs in a consistent, reliable manner. This reflective and iterative process generally involves aligned and congruent analysis, design, development, implementation, and evaluation (Reiser & Dempsey, 2014). More broadly, instructional design includes "a collection of activities to plan, implement, evaluate, and manage events and environments that are intended to facilitate learning and performance" (Spector & Ohrazda, 2004, p. 687).

Instructional design emerged from general systems theory, the intent of which was to apply the concept of interdependent system elements to efficiently train military and aerospace personnel. Education is conceptualized as a set of organized and regulated systems that need to deal with change: of students, academic disciplines, and contextual environments. To this construct, learners bring their past experiences, which reflect a complex network of concepts, and interact with the education system learner to process information that impacts their own existing networks. This instructional approach is now used in many higher education institutions and fits particularly well in online education. Using a systematic instructional design model has several benefits for instructors: it focuses on the learner, it supports effective instruction, it provides a systematic way to address learning problems, it fosters coordination among all the instructional components and stakeholders, and it facilitates diffusion and adaptation (Smith & Ragan, 2004).

Newer instruction design practices focus more on learner experiences to the point that learners co-construct knowledge. Reigeluth, Beatty, and Myers (2016) synthesized these practices into principles of learner-centered instructional design: attainment-based instruction rather than time-based, task-centered rather than content-centered, and personalized rather than standardized. These principles change the roles of learners, teachers and technology. Furthermore, it changes the nature of curriculum to focus more and relationships, critical thinking and action, and accomplishment.

Reigeluth and Dempsey (2018) asserted that almost all instructional design processes displayed the following characteristics: student-centered, goal-oriented, creative, focused on meaningful performance, assumed measurable outcomes that are reliable and valid, processes that are empirical and self-correcting iteratively, and collaborative.

Assessment

Assessment constitutes a core function of education. Instructors assess in order to get baseline information, diagnose needs, design and implement instruction, allocate resources, measure learning, determine success, and improve education. Assessment considers what is being assessed, who is assessing whom, and how assessment is conducted, analyzed, and acted upon. In general, practice, instructors typically look at learner performance relative to their ability and progress in comparison to others and to established criterion, such as performance indicators (Oosterhof, Conrad, & Ely, 2008). Ongoing assessment, not just at the pre-planning stage, but also during instructional implementation, enables instructors to make adjustments to the curriculum, resources, and delivery as well as provide feedback to learners so they can make adjustments to their own efforts (Richey, Klein, & Tracey, 2010).

More fundamentally, instructors should assess conditions throughout their instructional design and delivery. Since each step impacts the ultimate learning outcome, assessment needs to be planned and implemented carefully. An effective approach to assessment is a systems approach where each input and output factor is identified (Ozkan, Koseler, & Baykal, 2009). The following criteria can guide instructors' assessment of their efforts and the learning environment at benchmark points in the instructional design process: in pre-planning, the design stage, the implementation stage, and the reflective/debriefing stage.

- **Input**: Competences and dispositions, curriculum, resources, time, instructional strategies, institutional structures, stakeholders
- **Output:** Learning work, standardized tests, grades, courses, program exit
- **Technology Factors:** Speed, record-keeping, communication, dissemination options, assessments, statistics, equity of access and participation.

For example, even before any design begins, instructors should conduct a needs assessment to determine the curriculum:

- The discipline's needed knowledge and skills, both theoretical and applied
- The potential learners' characteristics and current knowledge and skills in light of the discipline
- The knowledge and skills that need to be learned in order to bridge the gap between the learners' current status and the desired learning outcome

- The learning environment's resources, support and infrastructure
- The context in which learning occurs.

At each step, instructors need to determine how to collect those data, and then analyze them. Only then can instructors draw valid conclusions and act upon their recommendations. For instance, instructors might examine the online course access patterns of students. Especially if those patterns are compared with students' assignment grades, instructors might observe that students who access the course at least twice a week perform better. Those findings could lead to instructors adding more engaging interactive elements such as peer discussions or mini quizzes. Instructors could also share the correlation with their students to motivate them to access and engage with the online course more often. Instructors can also use these data analyses to request resources or support from their institutions to improve the course and students' learning experiences, especially as institutional factors impact student success.

Standards

One way to analyze educational data is to compare it to a standard, that is, a level of quality or attainment used as a model by which to measure acceptable or desirable behavior or product. For instance, curriculum standards state what should occur in the learning environment. Similarly, standards are often used to determine whether an education program should be accredited.

Instructional design standards provide criteria and indicators to help instructors design instruction effectively. Furthermore, such standards can help institutions provide more consistent course structures and control the quality of instructional design. At first, the quality of an online course depended mainly on the isolated efforts of individual instructors; no other consistent factor accounted for effectiveness (Johnson, Mejia and Cook, 2015). With the expansion and stabilization of online instruction, underlying variables of best practices have been identified and systemized. While model actions have resulted in research-based standards being developed, few reflected those learning experiences that highlight the unique factors online teaching and learning (Jung & Latchem, 2016).

In her 2011 study of common quality indicators of distance education, Shelton identified six themes, which can then form the basis for standards:

- Teaching and learning effectiveness
- Student support
- Technology course development/instructional design
- Faculty support

- Evaluation and assessment
- Organizational/institutional impact.

The question remains: to what extent do instruction design standards, specifically for online education, address these themes?

Online Education

Increasingly, people are participating in online education for several reasons: geographical convenience, increased flexibility of timing and pacing, opportunity to improve technical skills, and possible greater equity for second language learners and learners with special needs. In the context of instructional design for online delivery, educators have to address the same set of elements as for face-to-face education: resources, instructor, method, time frame, sequence, location, grouping, individualization, affective, and social factors. However, some strategies have to change sometimes because people are not in the same place at the same time, and the experience has sensory and context limitations. Learners sometimes feel more self-directed and isolated (West, 2018). Online education increases instructor workload, but it can also enrich student learning and add to the body of academic knowledge (Blick, 2017).

In analyzing possible patterns in online course design, Lister (2014) identified four themes: course structure, content presentation, collaboration and integration, and timely feedback. In a similar vein, based on an extensive literature review, Mayes et al. (2011) recommended six practices in designing high-quality online courses: structuring courses, developing student-centered learning activities, using group projects to build collaboration, frequently assessing student progress, and providing detailed feedback and soliciting student feedback.

Salmon's model of web-based course development (201s) focuses on e-learning, and posits five phases, stepwise leading to increased learning. The model also recognizes the technical and instructional aspects of online course development, and folds those elements into each phase.

1. Student access requires setting up the system, as well as welcoming students.
2. Socialization requires telecommunications set-up as well as facilitating interpersonal relationships.
3. Information exchange requires orientation to the software as well as providing feedback.
4. Knowledge construction requires collaborative tools set-up as well as facilitating group dynamics.
5. Learning development requires links as well as monitoring.

MAIN FOCUS OF THE CHAPTER

Instructional Design Models for Online Education

In their analysis of twenty studies of instructional design models, Lee and Jan (2014) abstracted four dimensions across models: function (conceptual or procedural), origin (theory or practice driven), sources (literature, projects, experts), and analysis scheme. Several instructional design models predate online education so while their general principles still apply, elements that pertain strictly to virtual learning environments are not adequately addressed. Instructors can use these models to consider aspects of instructional design, but they will need to look to research-based online instructional design standards to make sure that their courses optimize online learning environments.

Early thinkers in instructional design were based in behavioral and cognitive psychology (Reiser & Dempsey, 2018). In the 1960s, Gagné posited nine events of instruction, the conditions of learning, which laid the foundation for instructional design models such as Kemp's instructional design model and Merrill's first principle of instruction, which identified the need to activate prior experience, demonstrate and apply skills. Gagné also believed in internal motivations and learn, which informed Reigeluth and Steins's Elaboration Theory and Keller's ARCS model of motivation and design. The latter model focuses on the learner: their attention, relevance to them, confidence of success, and satisfaction from the learning experience.

West (2107) identified over thirty instructional design models currently in use. He asserted that choosing an appropriate model depends on the objective or context of its use: its anticipated output, its instructional context, its scope, and its delivery format. For online contexts, West recommended ADDIE (Dick & Cariey, 2008), Bates 1995 model, ILDF (Dabbagh & Bannan-Ritland, 2004), and Kemp (1977).

The most popular instructional design model continues to be ADDIE, which was created by the U. S. Armed Forces (Branson & Rayner, 1975). Its five design steps apply to any delivery mode and may be repeated iteratively to optimize the final instructional design and delivery. The following italicized details demonstrate their application to online education.

1. **Analysis:** What do learners need to know, and what are their current skills? Are individuals ready to learn online?
2. **Design:** Can their needed knowledge and skills be designed and taught in an online environment? What online strategies will help students meet identified outcomes? How should content be organized online? What learning activities lend themselves to online access and engagement? How will an online environment impact assessment practices?

156

3. **Development:** How should strategies be packaged online? What online resources are needed, and how accessible are they? How will strategies be pilot-tested online?
4. **Implementation:** How will the course be mounted on a learning management system (LMS) and implemented? Who is responsible for each aspect?
5. **Evaluation:** What learning occurred that can be demonstrated online? How effective was the online instructional design planning and product?

Over the years, ADDIE has evolved. Management. prototyping and action mapping have been added, for instance.

An alternative to ADDIE's apparent linear model is the Successive Approximation Model (SAM), which emphasizes the more simultaneously iterative aspect of instructional design. Instructors gather information about the online course in the preparation stage, and then create and review their design in the iterative design and iterative development stages (Allen, 2012).

The ASSURE model was developed to support the incorporation of technology into classroom learning. While it was not specifically intended for online education, the model can be applied to online educational environments, as noted below (Smaldino et al., 2018).

- **Analyze** online learners. What are the learner's general characteristics? What specific competencies do they start with, including online experience? What are their online learning styles?
- **State objectives in terms of the target learner**. State the behavior to be demonstrated online, and conditions under which the behavior is demonstrated via technology.
- **Select and utilize online materials, technology, and strategies** based on the learners' existing status and the desired outcomes.
- **Require learner online participation**. Online learning activities should allow individuals to practice new knowledge and skills, and to receive online feedback on their efforts.
- **Evaluate** the online instruction design in terms of its impact on student learning, critiquing the instructional process and the resources used. Revise the design to address issues of concern.

Dick and Carey (2008) developed a systems approach for their instructional design model, which emphasized the interrelationship among its components of content, context, learning and teaching. Again, the model is modality-neutral; however, the creators would be quick to agree that the online context would impact the other components.

Increasingly, instructional design focuses on the learner as a co-creator of knowledge. To that end, instructional design focuses on providing a learning environment that facilities learner construction of meaning. Instructors provide a structure with a beginning choice of relevant resources that learners can investigate and integrate into their prior body of knowledge. Learners add to that body of knowledge from other sources and their own generation of knowledge. The emphasis of such instruction is student progress towards mastery of individual attainment (Reigeluth, Beatty, & Myers, 2016).

One of the few research-based instructional design models that specifically addresses online education is the aptly named instructional design for online learning (IDOL) model for higher education (Siragusa, 2006). It consists of three components, each of which can be identified along a dimension continuum.

- Analysis of the learner and instructor, the instructional goal and context, and teaching philosophy. For example, educational philosophy can range from behaviorist to constructivist.
- Strategy development of organization, materials, and instruction. In terms of a dimension continuum, organization can range from teacher-proof to easily modified.
- Evaluation that is formative and involve feedback, with the latter ranging from teacher to student control.

While the model's dimensions largely reflect the ADDIE model, the indicators address online considerations such as study flexibility, automated online learning activities and online learning management. Perhaps because the researcher publishes in Australia, this model has not been widely adopted. Nevertheless, not only is the idea of a continuum of approaches useful, but IDOL is one of the few instructional models that is not linear but rather uses a multistage approach supporting simultaneous development.

Czerkawski and Lyman (2016) developed an instructional design framework that focuses on student e-engagement, based on the National Survey of Student Engagement. The four phases include: instructional need, instructional objectives, learning environments, and summative assessment. While the researchers asserted that the framework was both linear and iterative, it too resembles ADDIE's model.

Online Education Standards

Choices

As online courses proliferate, the need for quality assurance grows. As Shelton (2011) summarized the need for quality evaluation, "Because of the changing landscape and increased call for accountability, higher education is now being challenged to reconceptualize methods and processes used to indicate quality and excellence, including those used for assessing and evaluating online education programs" (p. 2). Standards provide a way to ensure that online courses meet baseline expectations, and tend to encourage a consistent structure and organization of online courses across a campus. Institutions may create their own online course standards, but as the online education field has matured, professional groups have developed standards that have been adopted across the nation.

In a study of well-known distance education standards for higher education institutions, Southard and Mooney (2015) located twelve relevant sets of standards. The researchers then deconstructed these sets into 358 individual standards and indicators, which fit into six categories: online curriculum policies and infrastructure, faculty support, student support, course design, course delivery, and assessment. The first three categories focus on infrastructure and the next two focus on teaching and learning. Assessment crosses both domains. Out of the possible twelve sets of standards, the researchers mentioned two sets (both national proprietary sources) that focused mainly on instructional design: Quality Matters (QM), which focuses strictly on instructional design (not implementation), and the United States Distance Learning Association (USDLA), which has a majority of standards addressing instructional design.

USDLA (2018) includes 87 standards, which are classified into five areas (p. 2):

- Institutional prerequisites: infrastructure and resource capacity
- Administration, leadership and management: integrity, structure and organization, professional development, quality and fiscal management
- Learner affairs: recruitment and admissions, guidance, orientation, fees, records, grievances
- Teaching and learning: curriculum, course structure and instruction, learner and program assessment
- Infrastructure: distance learning advocacy and support, staff and learner support, contractor relations.

Professional association-based standards may be considered as valid and reputable. Shelton's study did not uncover such sourced standards that focused mainly on instructional design. In 2017 The Association of Educational Communications and Technology (AECT) helped fill that gap by developing instructional design standards specifically for distance learning (Pina, 2017). Their standards address online aspects of purpose, assumptions, sequencing, activities, resources, application, assessment, reflection, independent learning, and evaluation.

Esfijani's 2018 meta-synthesis of quality of online education included a comprehensive list of measurement criteria. Aspects of quality included input, resources, processes and outputs. Outputs were addressed less often than the first three aspects, and outcome standards were almost nonexistent. The Online Learning Consortium (OLC)'s course design standards were the most often used standards, according to Esfijani. OLC's standards assessed course information, technology tools and their use, LMS (learning management system) design and layout, content and activities, interaction, and assessment and feedback. The same standards and indicators could apply to face-to-face education; even LMS and technology indicators could apply to face-to-face and blended courses. OLC provides a separate scorecard for teaching and instructional practices; the interactive version was not yet available as of the time that this chapter was written. OLC also offers a standard that measures administrative support.

California Standards

California's higher education is the largest in the United States, and serves as an example of systematic and cost-effective incorporation of standards for instructional design. Institutions tend to use CVC-OEI, QLT or QM standards (Johnson, Mejia & Cook, 2015).

The California Virtual Campus-Online Education Initiative (CVC-OEI) developed a course design standards rubric that assesses course design, interaction, assessment, learning support, and accessibility. It has a Creative Commons license and is used mainly by the community college system. Professional development is offered online and in-person, typical at no or low cost.

Quality Learning and Teaching (QLT) is the California State University (CSU) Chancellor's Office 2015 rubric used to evaluate the quality of hybrid and online courses. This instrument was based on CSU Chico's rubric for online instruction, QM, community of inquiry model, and the National Survey of Student Engagement. QLT contains ten sections and 57 course objectives:

- Course overview and introduction
- Students learning assessment
- Instructional materials and resources utilized
- Student interaction and community

- Facilitation and instruction
- Technology for teaching and learning
- Learner support
- University design and accessibility
- Course summary and wrap-up
- Mobile platform readiness (optional)

One of the more popular national standards for hybrid and online instruction is QM. This product, developed through FIPSE grant funding, is a rubric of course design standards that guide the improvement of courses and certify the quality of hybrid and blended college courses. QM now includes quality assurance tools and professional development. QM's rubric consists of eight general standards, each of which have several indicators:

- Course overview and introduction: The course's design is made clear to learners at the course's start.
- Learning objectives: Objectives describe what learners will able to do upon the course's completion.
- Assessment and measurement: Central to instructional design, assessments evaluate learning project to meet learning objectives.
- Instructional materials: Resources enable learning to meet learning objectives.
- Learning activities and learner interaction: Learning activities facilitate and support learner engagement and interaction.
- Course technology: Technology help students met learning objectives.
- Learner support: The course helps learners access institutional support needed for learner success.
- Accessibility and usability: The course aims to be usable and accessible for all learners.

Method

To investigate how standards for online courses inform instructional design, the author used an autoethnographic case study approach to generate a defined set of rich data for research participant analysis. Specifically, the following case study traces the author's experience in determining how the use and application of QM's standards impacted the quality of her online course. The researcher also wanted to determine to what extent QM's standards aligned with online instructional design models.

When the author's university adopted an online learning management system (LMS), over twenty years ago, it also established a support group who consisted of instructional designers and early adopter instructors. Over the years, instructional design services have become more formalized and better financed so that now eight instructional designers make up the team. When the university's system adopted the QM quality assurance program in 2012, the local university team came on board. Since then over a hundred faculty have completed the "Independent Improving Your Online Course" training.

As an instructor who teaches face-to-face, hybrid and online courses in librarianship and educational technology, the author decided to take the course mainly to experience the training and inform her own instructional design so that she could in turn teach her students instructional design more effectively. Therefore, she took the three-week training using her Information and Digital Literacies course as the basis for improving that online course design.

The workshop was structured around the QM rubric and modeled instructional design. The workshop consisted of eight modules, each comprised of instructional material, a learning activity, and usually peer review. Participants could self-pace their work, but deadlines for each module were set.

1. Getting started, where the workshop facilitators gave an overview of the workshop and its navigation, and asked participants to introduce themselves and state their motivation for taking the workshop.
2. QM overview and principles, which included a quiz to check for understanding.
3. Workshop overview, which explain the QM rubric and started the participant's self-review
4. Course alignment, which asked participants to map their course
5. Learning objectives, basis for grading criteria
6. Learner support, accessibility and usability
7. Active learning and relationships, which included an active learning organizer with spaces to jot down examples of the participants' course components that showed evidence of addressing the standard and their own suggestions for improvements in meeting the standard
8. Synthesis, which included the participant's course self-review and improvement plan.

While the author's course was already well established and taught several times, upon working through the modules, the author found several specific items that merited inclusion or expansion in her course, such as an introductory video, a course map, technology requirements, module images, and a generic discussion rubric. Workshop standards, readings, learning activities, and peer examples provided inspiration for the author's improvement efforts. The workshop also confirmed the usefulness of standards and indicators for revealing instructional design blind spots and reinforcing the idea that all courses can be improved. For peers who did not have a background in instructional design or online instruction, this workshop provided very useful information and guidance. According to the workshop facilitator, ETEC 523 meet all the standards.

For the course to be QM certified, it had to be reviewed by the researcher's campus instructional designers who had QM training. The three reviewers explained that they would use the QM standards and list those standards that had not been met. The campus review took over a month because of other workload demands, and the reviewers had to write up and meet among themselves and then with the researcher with their finders. Not all the standards were met, according to the reviewers; the technology prerequisites and communications plan needed refinement, accessibility statements about all the technology tools had to be added, and a couple of module objectives needed to be reworded. The reviewers then stated that all of the QM standards had been met. Discussion with the reviews was informative, especially in terms of the rationale for the changes.

A final review of ETEC 523 my QM standards was conducted by three CSU Chancellor's Office QM-trained reviewers. By then, the researcher felt assured that the course met all the QM standards. Such as not the case. This level of reviewers was even more detailed and thorough than the prior two reviews, and took another three weeks; four of the 23 standards were not met, which was disheartening to the researcher. For each standard, the reviewers cited the evidence for their evaluation and gave suggestions for improvement. The researcher had to further refine the technology prerequisites and communications plan, add the specific SLOs alongside each module objective and in each module learning guide, add the required readings in the syllabus module guide, further clarify the relations between the use of instructional materials and completing learning activities. No other communication occurred between the researcher and the CSU reviewers, although the researcher asked one campus QM reviewer to look over the changes for possible further enhancement. Since a person has only one chance at the level to make changes without having to wait another six months, the stakes were high. Fortunately, the revised course then met all QM standards and earned a perfect score.

The entire process took seven months, and over forty hours of work for the researcher. The result was an improved course design. The interaction with the reviewers was uneven: too shallow at the first level and probably too granular at the final level. The verbal tone of the reviewers also impacted the researcher's own mental state; encouragement incentivized the researcher, and interrogation attitudes dis-incentivized her. The experience gave the researcher a new perspective about her own students' learning experiences, both in terms of caring interaction with the students and in constructive, encouraging timely feedback. The review process helped to flesh out the standards and to gain more insights about teacher-student relationships.

The QM standards review process also reinforced the iterative nature of instructional design, especially in assessing the design's quality and need for modification. The researcher's process aligned more with the SAM model than other instructional design models.

The question remained: would the QM certified course, now that it was improved, result in an improved learning experience for the students? The researcher was scheduled to teach the course in the fall, but at the last minute another instructor had to teach it. The researcher was designed the course such that other instructors could also use it as is. However, she thought that even with a QM certified course, its delivery was not guaranteed to be effective; whoever taught the course still needed to develop a trusting relationship with the learners, build a sense of a learning community, and give appropriate timely and specific feedback that encouraged learner progress. Fundamentally, the QM standards only assess the course as it is designed, but not as it is delivered.

This realization occurred throughout the review process. It was very evident to the researcher that the QM standards were input-oriented rather than outcomes-based. While the overall QM structure helps to clarify expectations for learners, the standards do not leave much room for co-created learning experiences. The underlying educational philosophy, even with constructivist learning activities, seems more in alignment with cognitivism with traces of behaviorist theory. At best, QM standards need to be complemented with standards that measure instructional effectiveness and impact on learner outcomes.

SOLUTIONS AND RECOMMENDATIONS

Utilizing research-based instructional design models and standards helps instructors design more effective online education that can facilitate student learning and achievement. While no perfect model or standard exists, instructors do have several satisfactory processes to choose from. However, instructors may want domain-specific examples of online designed courses that optimize student online engagement with relevant digital content materials, facilitate active learning online, and build an effective online learning community. At this point, standards for online instructional design are probably the most efficient way to jumpstart the development of online courses as their indicators provide specific criteria to consider.

For more specific guidance and exemplars, standards do not suffice. To supplement standards, educational institutions and systems should consider developing a cadre of experienced subject-online instructional developer specialists and online instructors to serve as mentors. Subject-specific videos that showcase representative online instructors' practices and sample exemplary online courses also inform and inspiring beginning online instructors.

A fundamental issue is teaching faculty in higher education to design online instruction systematically, following the above models and standards. Many higher education instructors do not have teaching credentials, nor have they taken education methods courses. Their expertise lies in their content knowledge, not their technological or instructional knowledge (Koehler & Mishra, 2009). Furthermore, even fewer higher education instructors have expertise in adult education, which applies to their primary learner population.

Ultimately, higher education institutions need to ensure that their students have high-quality learning experiences. Therefore, those institutions must conduct faculty needs assessments to determine the professional development needed by their instructors. In more centralized or smaller institutions, standardized training in online instructional design might be required; such is the case for the California community college system (2018). Similarly, higher education institutions that are completely online, such as the University of Phoenix and National University generally require all potential instructors to take and pass their instructional design training course before being hired. While some experienced faculty who have designed and instructed online might balk at such required training, they might be able to fast-track that training or show evidence of their quality work. As discussed above, even veteran instructors such as the author found areas for improvement, such as concept mapping and providing a communications plan, which can result in more effective teaching and learning.

Nor does one-time training suffice. Online instructors need to continuously review and update their curriculum, and should seek opportunities to keep current on educational technology and beneficial online instructional practices. Some professional organizations can provide such continuing education, such as the Online Learning Consortium, AECT and ISTE (International Society for Technology in Education). QM and other quality assurance programs also offer additional training for a fee. Websites such as https://www.elearninglearning.com/ and professional reading such as the *Journal of Online Learning and Teaching* provide valuable information that instructors can consult at their own convenience.

In the final analysis, instructors are accountable for their online courses. Therefore, their instructional designs should be assessed regularly as part of their professional review. Instructional design standards provide guidance and then a framework for evaluating online courses in a professional and equitable way. Instructors can draw upon such assessment to provide timely specific interventions as needed to insure high-quality online education.

FUTURE RESEARCH DIRECTIONS

At this point, many higher education institutions use some kind of standard to guide instructional design. As noted above, those standards measure different aspects of instructional design; some focus just on the design itself, others measure design implementation, and still others examine the broader picture of program and institutional factors. Researchers should employ factor analysis of these different areas to determine to what degree each area contributes to student success. Furthermore, researchers should consider qualitative methods such as think-alouds and textual tracking commentary to reveal the decision-making process used to design instruction. That way researchers can start to determine the critical thinking and information processing that underlies course design and the degree to which standards drive their decisions and actions.

In addition, higher education institutions increasingly employ instructional designers to help faculty develop their courses. In a few cases, academic librarians also join the team to provide expertise in locating relevant high-quality resources and incorporating information and communication technology (ICT) literacy (Farmer, 2018). As with standards in general, researchers should investigate the relevant contribution of each person's role in support teachers' design and implementation of online courses.

Learning analytics offer another way to determine the impact of standards. Learning analytics is a branch of data analytics that focuses on student learning. Long and Siemans (2011) defined learning analytics as "the measurement, collection, analysis and reporting of data about learners and their contexts, for purposes of understanding and optimising learning and the environments in which it occurs" (p. 31). Such analysis examines data about students and their learning environment, the latter of which may include the curriculum, instruction, resources, the physical and virtual learning environment, and other possible contextual factors.

Learning analytics not only looks at the individual factors but also their interaction and relationship; within a course, these factors can be clustered into the following categories: student-information (e.g., learning management system and its resources), student-student (sometimes referred to as social learning analytics), and student-teacher. Learning analytics typically draw from LMS data, which feature has expanded significantly over the last decade. At the course level, these detail data measure aspects of the course design and student engagement, which can be used to predict student success as well as signal the need for specific interventions to support student progress, be it advice to the student or course design modifications. Thus, learning analysis can be mapped onto standards to determine the impact of instructional design. LMS user statistics could also be used to assess course design over time within the term that the course is being offered, examining the impact of each intervention – and the decision-making process to make that change; the findings could again be linked to instructional design standards to address in-course improvements of instructional design.

Another area of research to expand upon is the impact that culture has upon instructional design. Few standards address language issues, let alone how resources and learning activities might need to be responsive to learners' different cultural backgrounds and experiences. Especially as online education has become more international in terms of student demographics, instructors need to consider these differences when designing instruction. Domer and Gorman (2006) identified several cultural factors that apply to instructional design for multicultural learners, and could be articulated in instructional design standards. At the least, exploratory research should be conducted to investigate the following culturally sensitive factors in light of instructional design.

- Student-teacher relations. Learners from high power-distance cultures expect formal, hierarchical relationships with their teachers. To ease their stress in more egalitarian or constructivist courses, instructors need to clearly and explicitly define their roles, and work with students to make clear decisions about learning expectations. Additionally, some cultures discourage student questions, so instructors need to build in optional ways to ask for assistance.
- Topics of discussion. Instructors should be aware of possible culture-specific taboo subjects. This issue might emerge in health issues where gendered practices might inhibit practice. Instructors can consult their peers in relevant countries to find out ahead of time what topics might be sensitive to their learners. Accommodations for alternative topics, resources, or ways of learning should be provided so as to not disadvantage affected learners.
- Choice of resources. Instructor choice of resources may reflect cultural bias – or ignore students' culture -- which might disadvantage some international students. At the least, instructors should enable students to choose from a wide spectrum of reading materials reflecting a variety of perspectives. Instructors might also consult counterparts in the relevant cultures as to appropriate local resources.
- Learner participation. The relative value of individual versus group work is culturally defined. If the student population includes a mix of cultures, then a corresponding combination of individual and collaborative activities would be appropriate. Likewise, a mix of cooperative and competitive activities allows learners from different backgrounds to excel at different points.
- Assessment issues. Culture impacts student performance in terms of valued expressions of competency, such as written versus oral traditions. In terms of language, even simple tasks such as following directions can disadvantage

some students. Some of the measures that can be taken to mitigate cultural discrepancies include: giving shorter tests and recall items rather than tasks that require language and literacy skills, providing bilingual glossaries and accurate translations in those cases where language ability is not the element being tested, and offering multiple ways for students to demonstrate their skill such as podcasts or videos.

Because technology continues to advance and expand, course delivery modality also needs to keep current with these changes. Already, some LMSs are structured to be mobile-compatible. However, individual courses are seldom structured to insure that all instructional materials and learning activities can be accessed and employed on mobile devices. QLT is one example of a standard that addresses mobile platform readiness, but even that standard is optional. As more learners depend on their mobile devices for course engagement, instructors will need to pay attention to this format issue. Furthermore, research needs to be conducted to ascertain the impact that mobile-based learning has on student achievement.

Pushing the envelope farther, augmented and virtual reality are intriguing formats for interactive learning. Second Life is an early example of virtual-based learning, which has had uneven success. Inman, Wright and Hartman (2011) reviewed the research since 2003 about Second Life's use in K-12 and higher education. They noted its potential use for role-playing, simulations, and student-centered learning activities, but also acknowledged its challenges: technology requirements, steep learning curve, and learner exposure to distractions and inappropriate content. The researchers pointed out the need to tie course objects to the need for this platform, as well as selecting the appropriate part of the virtual environment to carry out learning activities. Merchant et al. (2014) conducted a meta-analysis of virtual reality-based instruction on students learning outcomes in K-12 and higher education and found that virtual world negatively impacted student learning if assessments were repeatedly done on the students. The researchers emphasized the need to consider instructional design principles when incorporating virtual reality. As for the newer virtual reality immersive experiences that use specialized headgear and higher-end computer programs, their cost prohibits their incorporation except for institutions that that can supply a class set and real-time class interaction, thus cancelling out strictly online learning.

Augmented reality (AR) might be a more feasible platform than virtual reality as it is constructed for more individual use and is lower in cost than virtual reality environments. At the same time, AR enables learners to observe real world properties that would usually not be possible to see. Nevertheless, current use of AR tends to consist of class activities in local settings rather than as the platform base in online education. For example, a group of students can each explore a location through

AR apps, and then compare notes. One of the limitations of AR, therefore, is joint attention to a common interface since AR is most commonly viewed through a personal device; increasingly, though AR programs may be viewed on digital tablets, which enables a pair of joint viewers. Another challenge is the technology itself, which an online instructor cannot facilitate. Additionally, educational AR is still in its infancy, and AR programs tend to be activity-based rather than course-based. In that respect, AR programs may serve in the same capacity as other instructional materials to engage in and later share. In any case, little research has been conducted on its use and impact on learning in online education and its design (Akcayir & Akcayir, 2017).

CONCLUSION

Online instruction has expanded dramatically in recent years, and is likely to increase even more if for no other reason than today's population needs frequent updating and retooling of their knowledge base and skills. Online instruction offers convenient education that can span the globe. Particularly in very specific disciplines or areas of concentration, online instruction offers a cost-effective way to train – and retrain – adults.

Therefore, high-quality instructional design of online education is needed now more than ever before. Online education has stabilized its baseline foundation so that beneficial practices have been identified that leverage online environments effectively. Besides generic instructional design principles, models of good online instructional design are emerging. These practices and models are codified into online instructional design standards that provide research-based criteria that can be used to measure the degree to which such instructional designs meet those standards – and can serve as guidelines of factors to consider when designing online instruction.

As noted above, some standards focus specifically on instructional design. A few other standards address the implementation of those designs and their effectiveness in facilitating learning, but more rigorous and detailed standards are needed, especially in terms of measuring learning outcomes. Furthermore, more standards need to address the conditions for effective instructional design: instructor expertise, student online readiness, institutional resources and support, infrastructure, and evaluation. Especially when considering learner-centered online education, the notion of standards themselves may need deeper scrutiny.

The bottom line is not standards; it is learning -- and the ability to apply that learning to contribute to society, both in physical and online environments.

REFERENCES

Akçayır, M., & Akçayır, G. (2017). Advantages and challenges associated with augmented reality for education: A systematic review of the literature. *Educational Research Review*, *20*, 1–11. doi:10.1016/j.edurev.2016.11.002

Allen, M. (2012). *Leaving ADDIE for SAM: An agile model for developing the best learning experiences.* Alexandria, VA: American Society for Training and Development.

Bates, A. W. (1995). *Technology, open learning and distance education.* New York, NY: Routledge.

Boettcher, J. V., & Conrad, R. M. (2016). *The online teaching survival guide: Simple and practical pedagogical tips.* New York, NY: John Wiley & Sons.

Branson, R., & Rayner, G. (1975). *Interservice procedures for instructional systems development: Executive summary and model.* Tallahassee, FL: Center for Educational Technology, Florida State University. doi:10.21236/ADA023892

California State University. (2015). *Quality assurance for blended & online courses.* Long Beach, CA: California State University.

California Virtual Campus-Online Education Initiative. (2018). *Course design rubric.* Sacramento, CA: California Community Colleges.

Czerkawski, B., & Lyman, E. III. (2016). An instructional design framework for fostering student engagement in online learning environments. *TechTrends*, *60*(6), 532–539. doi:10.100711528-016-0110-z

Dabbagh, N., & Bannan-Ritland, B. (2004). *Online learning: Concepts, strategies, and application.* Upper Saddle River, NJ: Pearson.

Dick, W., & Carey, L. (2008). *The systematic design of instruction* (7th ed.). Glenview, IL: Scott, Foresman.

Domer, D., & Gorman, G. (2006). Information literacy education in Asian developing countries: Cultural factors affecting curriculum development and programme delivery. *IFLA Journal*, *32*(4), 281–293. doi:10.1177/0340035206074063

Esfijani, A. (2018). Measuring quality in online education: A meta-synthesis. *American Journal of Distance Education*, *32*(1), 57–73. doi:10.1080/08923647.2018.1417658

Farmer, L. (2011). *Instructional design for librarians and information professionals.* New York, NY: Neal-Schuman.

Farmer, L. (2018). The role of librarians in blended courses. In S. Keengwe (Ed.), *Handbook of research on blended learning and pedagogical professional development in higher education* (pp. 122–138). Hershey, PA: IGI Global.

Johnson, H., Mejia, M., & Cook, K. (2015). *Successful online courses in California's community colleges*. San Francisco, CA: Public Policy Institute of California.

Kemp, J. (1977). *Instructional design: A plan for unit and course development*. Belmont, CA: Fearon Publishers.

Koehler, M., & Mishra, P. (2009). What is technological pedagogical content knowledge (TPACK)? *Contemporary Issues in Technology & Teacher Education*, *9*(1), 60–70.

Lee, J., & Jang, S. (2014). A methodological framework for instructional design model development. *Educational Technology Research and Development*, *62*(6), 743–765. doi:10.100711423-014-9352-7

Lister, M. (2014). Trends in the design of e-learning and online learning. *Journal of Online Learning and Teaching / MERLOT*, *10*(4), 671–679.

Long, P., & Siemens, G. (2011). Penetrating the fog: Analytics in learning and education. *EDUCAUSE Review*, *46*(5), 31–40.

Mayes, R., Luebeck, J., Ku, H. Y., Akarasriworn, C., & Korkmaz, Ö. (2011). Themes and strategies for transformative online instruction: A review of literature and practice. *Quarterly Review of Distance Education*, *12*(3), 151–166.

Merchant, Z., Goetz, E., Cifuentes, L., Keeney-Kennicutt, W., & Davis, T. (2014). Effectiveness of virtual reality-based instruction on students' learning outcomes in K-12 and higher education: A meta-analysis. *Computers & Education*, *70*, 29–40. doi:10.1016/j.compedu.2013.07.033

Oosterhof, A., Conrad, R., & Ely, D. (2008). *Assessing learners online*. Upper Saddle River, NJ: Pearson.

Ozkan, S., Koseler, R., & Baykal, N. (2009). Evaluating learning management systems: Adoption of hexagonal e-learning assessment model in higher education. *Transforming Government: People. Process and Policy*, *3*(2), 111–130.

Pina, A. (Ed.). (2017). *Instructional design standards for distance learning*. Bloomington, IN: The Association of Educational Communications and Technology.

Quality Matters (QM). (2012). Why quality matters. Retrieved from https://www.qualitymatters.org/index.php/why-quality-matters/about-qm

Reigeluth, C. M., Beatty, B. J., & Myers, R. D. (Eds.). (2016). Instructional-design theories and models (Vol. 4). New York, NY: Routledge.

Reiser, R., & Dempsey, J. (2017). *Trends and issues in instructional design and technology* (4th ed.). Upper Saddle River, NJ: Pearson.

Richey, R., Klein, J., & Tracey, M. (2010). *The instructional design knowledge base: Theory, research, and practice.* New York, NY: Routledge. doi:10.4324/9780203840986

Salmon, G. (2013). *E-tivities: The key to active online learning.* New York, NY: Routledge. doi:10.4324/9780203074640

Shelton, K. (2011). A review of paradigms for evaluating the quality of online education programs. *Online Journal of Distance Learning Administration, 4*(1), 1–11.

Siragusa, L. (2006). Quality eLearning: An instructional design model for online learning in higher education. In *Western Australian Institute for Educational Research Forum.* Perth: Edith Cowan University.

Smaldino, S., Lowther, D., Mims, C., & Russell, J. (2018). *Instructional technology and media for learning* (12th ed.). Upper Saddle River, NJ: Pearson.

Smith, P., & Ragan, T. (2004). *Instructional design* (3rd ed.). New York: John Wiley & Sons.

Southard, S., & Mooney, M. (2015). A comparative analysis of distance education quality assurance standards. *Quarterly Review of Distance Education, 16*(1), 55–76.

Spector, J., & Ohrazda, C. (2004). Automating instructional design: Approaches and limitations. In D. Jonassen (Ed.), *Handbook for research for educational communications and technology* (2nd ed., pp. 685–699). Mahwah, NJ: Lawrence Erlbaum.

United States Distance Learning Association (USDLA). (2018). *Quality standards certification.* Washington, DC: United States Distance Learning Association.

West, R. (2018). *Foundations of learning and instructional design technology.* Montreal, Quebec: Pressbooks. Retrieved from http://lidtfoundations.pressbooks.com

ADDITIONAL READING

Arshavskiy, M. (2018). *Instructional design for eLearning: Essential guide for designing successful eLearning courses* (2nd ed.). Scotts Valley, CA: CreateSpace.

Horton, W. (2012). *E-learning by design*. San Francisco, CA: Pfeiffer.

Inman, C., Wright, V. H., & Hartman, J. A. (2010). Use of Second Life in K-12 and higher education: A review of research. *Journal of Interactive Online Learning*, *9*(1), 44–63.

Jolliffe, A., Ritter, J., & Stevens, D. (2012). *The online learning handbook: Developing and using web-based learning*. New York, NY: Routledge.

Jung, L., & Latchem, C. (Eds.). (2016). *Quality assurance and accreditation in distance education and e-learning: Models, policies and research*. New York, NY: Routledge.

Kats, Y. (Ed.). (2013). *Learning management systems and instructional design: Best practices in online education*. Hershey, PA: IGI Global. doi:10.4018/978-1-4666-3930-0

Keengwe, J., & Agama, J. (Eds.). (2015). *Models for improving and optimizing online and blended learning in higher education*. Hershey, PA: IGI Global. doi:10.4018/978-1-4666-6280-3

Moore, M., & Diehl, W. (Eds.). (2018). *Handbook of distance education* (4th ed.). New York, NY: Routledge. doi:10.4324/9781315296135

Nelson, B. C., & Erlandson, B. E. (2012). *Design for learning in virtual worlds*. New York, NY: Routledge. doi:10.4324/9780203836378

Rothwell, W. J., & Kazanas, H. C. (2011). *Mastering the instructional design process: A systematic approach*. New York, NY: John Wiley & Sons.

Vai, M., & Sosulski, K. (2015). *Essentials of online course design: A standards-based guide* (2nd ed.). New York, NY: Routledge. doi:10.4324/9781315770901

KEY TERMS AND DEFINITIONS

Accessibility: The extent to which a product or service is available to all people.

ADDIE: A conceptual and iterative application model for instructional systems design; the components include analysis, design, development, implementation, and evaluation.

Alignment: Critical course elements working together to ensure that learners achieve the desired outcomes.

Hybrid (course): Description of courses in which some face-to-face "seat time" is replaced by online learning activities.

Indicator: Measurable specific criteria that demonstrate that one has met a standard or satisfied an outcome.

Instructional Design: The name given to the process of creating instruction in order to close a performance gap that is due to a lack of knowledge and skills.

Learning Management System (LMS): A software (web) application used to plan, implement, and assess learning processes. An LMS provides instructors with a way to create and deliver content, monitor learner participation, and assess performance. An LMS provide interactive features such as threaded discussions, video conferencing, and discussion forums, etc.

Needs Assessment: A tool used to identify "the gap" between what is already known and what needs to be learned in order to address particular organizational or personal needs. Needs assessment uses questionnaires, surveys, interviews, observation, etc. to collect data.

Online Learning: A term used to describe distance learning conducted via the Internet.

Outcome: The desired and measurable goal, specifying what student should accomplish.

Standard: A level of quality or attainment used as a model by which to measure acceptable or desirable behavior or product.

APPENDIX

Table 1. Course learning outcomes and supporting modules

1. Use technological resources fluently and critically.
M4 Create a database of information literacy learning objects
M5 Represent information visually in an infographic
M7 Produce a digital citizenship podcast
M8 Develop a content management system
M9 Design a lesson that incorporates technology in instruction and learning
M10 Create a spreadsheet
Create a PD screencast
Create an eportfolio
2. Use available technology to assess, plan, and deliver instruction so all students can learn.
M1 Self-assess current knowledge about course student learning outcomes (SLOs)
M2 Analyze how people seek information, and relate it to information behavior theories
M7 Suggest ways to incorporate digital literacy and digital citizenship into your practice in a blog
M7 Produce a digital citizenship podcast
M9 Explain the impact of technology in education in a blog
M9 Design a lesson that incorporates technology in instruction and learning
Create a PD screencast
3. Enable students to use technology to advance their learning.
   M4 Evaluate and select information literacy learning objects
   M4 Create a database of information literacy learning objects
   M6 Suggest ways to incorporate and teach media literacy and trans literacy in a blog
   M9 Identify factors leading to the successful incorporation of technology in information and digital literacy education in a blog
   M9 Explain ways to provide learning opportunities to solve problems with technology in a blog
   M9 Design a lesson that incorporates technology in instruction and learning
   M10 Critique and select learning resources that align learning objectives, curriculum, and learner populations in a spreadsheet, Create a PD screencast
4. Communicate and collaborate with students, colleagues, resource personnel, and families to provide learners equitable access to state-adopted academic content standards.
   M3 Explain ways to make information more accessible in a blog
   M4 Evaluate and select information literacy learning objects
   M5 Represent information visually in an infographic
   M5 Suggest ways to incorporate and teach visual literacy in a blog
   M7 Identify digital literacy standards in a blog
   M8 Provide information service
   M8 Develop a content management system
   M9 Design a lesson that incorporates technology in instruction and learning
   M10 Create a spreadsheet
   M10 Critique and select learning resources that align learning objectives, curriculum, and learner populations in a spreadsheet
Create a PD screencast
5. Follow technology policies to maximize students' learning and awareness around privacy, security, and safety issues.
M7 Identify digital literacy standards in a blog
M7 Explain digital citizenship
M7 Produce a digital citizenship podcast
M7 Suggest ways to incorporate digital literacy and digital citizenship into your practice in a blog
   M9 Explain the impact of technology in education in a blog
   M9 Identify factors leading to the successful incorporation of technology in information and digital literacy education in a blog
6. Explain theories about information and digital literacy, including the nature, architecture, and cycle of information, technology resources and tools.
   M1 Differentiate among data, information, knowledge, and wisdom in a blog
   M1 Explain at least three information theories
   M2 Explain how information is created and disseminated in a blog
   M2 Explain how people access, value, and use information in an observation
   M3 Identify what architecture is the most effective way to structure and communicate information
   M7 Explain digital literacy in a blog
Create a PD screencast
7. Model information literacy: how to access, evaluate, process, use, integrate, generate, and communicate information.
   M2 Analyze how people seek information, and relate it to information behavior theories
   M4 Link information seeking behaviors to an information literacy model in a blog
   M4 Evaluate and select information literacy learning objects
   M4 Create a database of information literacy learning objects
   M6 Explain media literacy in a blog
M8 Provide information service
   M8 Explain how to curate information
   M8 Develop a personal content management system
   M9 Design a lesson that incorporates technology in instruction and learning
Blog
8. Practice trans-literacy
   M5 Represent information visually
   M6 Explain trans literacy in a blog
   M9 Design a lesson that incorporates technology in instruction and learning
Create a PD screencast
9. Articulate how formats and communication channels impact information, and how information and ideas are processed and transformed using digital tools.
   M3 Interpret information in light of its communication channel
   M3 Identify what architecture is the most effective way to structure and communicate information
   M3 Explain ways to make information more accessible in a blog
   M5 Explain visual literacy in a blog
   M6 Explain media literacy in a blog
   M9 Explain the impact of technology in education in a blog

Table 2. Assessment assignments

Module	Assessment Assignment / Student Learning Outcome	1	2	3	4	5	6	7	8	9
I	Information theories comparison	x					xx			
II	Information behavior observation	x	xx		x		x	x		x
III	Format analysis	x					x	x	xx	xx
IV	Information literacy learning objects database	x	x	xx	x			x		x
V	Common Core infographic	x	x	x	xx			x	x	x
VI	Digital citizenship podcast	x	x	x		xx		x	x	x
VII	Pathfinder	x	x		x			xx		
VIII	WebQuest	xx	xx	x	x			x		x
IX	Assistive technology resources spreadsheet	x		xx	x			x		x
X	Screencast	x	xx	x			x	x	x	x
XI	Eportfolio	x	x	x	x	x	x	x	x	x
XII	WebQuest Fake news perspectives	x				x	xx	x		x
XIII	WebQuest Fake news literacies	x					x	x	x	xx
XIV	WebQuest fact-checking	x		x				xx		

Table 3. Learner support scavenger hunt

Item	Does my institution provide this item?	Does my course include this item?
Specific Review Standard 7.1 **The course instructions articulate or link to a clear description of the technical support offered and how to obtain it.**		
Clear description of the institution's technical support services	Yes: http://web.csulb.edu/divisions/ aa/academic_technology/thd/	Yes
Link to a technical support website	Yes: http://web.csulb.edu/divisions/ aa/academic_technology/thd/	Yes
Email link to the technical support center or help desk	Yes: helpdesk@csulb.edu	Yes
Phone number for the technical support center or help desk	Yes: 562.985.4959 http://web.csulb.edu/divisions/ aa/academic_technology/thd/	Yes
Links to tutorials or other resources on how to use course technologies	Yes: http://web.csulb.edu/divisions/ aa/academic_technology/thd/	Yes
Link to "frequently asked questions"	Yes: http://www.csulb.edu/academic-technology-services/instructional-design/ student-support/frequently-asked-beachboard	Yes
Directions for obtaining technical support for any external resources not supported by the institution's internal technical support	No	Yes, for tools we use
Specific Review Standard 7.2 **Course instructions articulate or link to the institution's accessibility policies and services.**		
Link to the institution's accessibility policy	Yes, http://www.csulb.edu/information-technology/accessible-technology AND http://www.csulb.edu/academic-technology-services/instructional-design/ student-support/frequently-asked-beachboard	Yes, in content area
Statement informing learners how to obtain disability support services	Yes, http://www.csulb.edu/dss	Yes, in syllabus
Phone number for the disability services office	Yes, **562-985-5401**	Yes, in syllabus
Link to the disability services office website	Yes, http://www.csulb.edu/dss	Yes, in syllabus
Specific Review Standard 7.3 **Course instructions articulate or link to the institution's academic support services and resources that can help learners succeed in the course.**		
An online orientation or demo course	Yes: http://www.csulb.edu/academic-technology-services/instructional-design/ student-support/getting-started-beachboard%E2%80%AF	Yes, in video
Link to library resources, info on how to access them, how to contact a librarian	Yes: http://www.csulb.edu/university-library	Yes, in content
A readiness assessment or survey	No	Yes, in content
Testing services	Yes: http://web.csulb.edu/divisions/students/testing/	Yes, in content
Tutoring	Yes: http://web.csulb.edu/divisions/students/ student_resources/tutoring.html	Yes, in content
Non-native language services	Yes: https://www.cpie.csulb.edu/international/	Yes, in content
Writing and/or math centers	Yes: http://www.cla.csulb.edu/ departments/english/wrl/	Yes, in syllabus (via disabilities)
Tutorials or other guidance for conducting research, writing papers, citing sources, using an online writing lab, and using course-specific technology	Yes: http://www.csulb.edu/ university-library (not course-specific tech)	Yes, in content
Supplemental instruction programs	Yes: https://www.csulb.edu/academic-technology-services/faculty-resources; Lynda.com	Yes, in content
Teaching assistants	http://www.csulb.edu/academic-senate/policy-statement-17-18-employment-of-graduate-students-as-student-assistants	N/A

Chapter 8

Process Considerations for the Development and Assessment of Virtual Education Doctorates

Erika Prager
Northcentral University, USA

Barbara M. Hall
iD https://orcid.org/0000-0002-6732-2616
Northcentral University, USA

Laurie Wellner
Northcentral University, USA

B. Andrew Riggle
iD https://orcid.org/0000-0003-3897-5236
Northcentral University, USA

Robin Throne
iD https://orcid.org/0000-0002-3015-9587
Northcentral University, USA

ABSTRACT

This chapter focuses on the use of a customized backward instructional design process used to re-engineer a virtual university's integration of institutional learning outcomes within a practice-based online dissertation process for a doctorate in education (EdD). The EdD will incorporate specialization areas in instructional design, learning analytics, and e-learning and through a lens of best assessment practices

DOI: 10.4018/978-1-7998-1622-5.ch008

for doctoral education. This program will highlight the unique considerations for virtual environments especially those that incorporate asynchronous instructional elements in program and course design. The education doctorate is leadership-based and practitioner-focused to prepare candidates as scholar practitioners who utilize the learning outcomes for research-based decision making and problem solutions within their scope of practice. A new three chapter dissertation allows candidates to solve a practice-based problem as a culminating doctoral learning activity which will be assessed across institutional outcomes and expectations.

INTRODUCTION

The education doctorate or Doctor of Education (Ed.D.) is a leadership-based/practitioner-focused terminal degree developed for the purpose of preparing candidates as scholars who utilize best-practice research for decision-making, effective real-world leadership, and outcome-based applied problem-solving within the individual practitioner's scope of practice. The practice-based dissertation, now a component of the redesigned Ed.D. program of study presented in this case, allows candidates to address a field-based problem as a culminating doctoral learning activity. The revised Ed.D. program is assessed across institutional outcomes and expectations with the intent of the Ed.D. dissertation research study to serve as a rigorous culminating activity related to the practitioner's field of study. Topolka-Jorissen and Wang (2015) stressed the importance of program redesign for Ed.D. degrees due to the significant implications for practice, ensuring carefully selected learning outcomes and structures support the development of effective applied leaders. Further emphasis on the integration of institutional and program learning assessment within the redesign was added as a further enhancement and measurement for program effectiveness.

The original Ed.D. program was first revised in 2012 to align with the Guiding Principles of the Carnegie Project on the Education Doctorate (CPED). The establishment of complex practice-based problems serving as the focus of Ed.D. research has been well documented within the literature (Hawkes & Yerrabati, 2018; Perry, 2015). The relevant literature has also expanded in recent years with reports of re-engineered Ed.D. programs and improved practice-based initiatives within practitioner doctorates driven by an advising framework specifically to facilitate the improved Ed.D. (Buss et al., 2017). Further, the preparation of scholar practitioners engaged within an online doctoral community of practice through the inquiry-as-practice model and the use of high-mentoring, technology-rich resources led to improved Ed.D. persistence and completion (Throne, Shaw, Fore, Duffy, & Clowes, 2015).

In 2016, the Ed.D. degree program underwent a five-year academic program review focused on improving student persistence, scholar-practitioner preparation, and dissertation completion in practitioner doctoral programs (Throne & Duffy, 2016). The following year, Northcentral University conducted an annual program review resulting in further changes and substantive enhancements targeting improved program entry foundational skill development, sequence and scaffolding of graduate-level research skill development, and innovation in practice-based research for a dissertation-in-practice (DIP). Finally, a task force was created in 2017 comprised of administrators, faculty, and other stakeholders called upon to again to make extensive revisions to the existing Ed.D. based on the analysis and results of these previous reviews. This updated Ed.D. program successfully launched in early 2019.

Based on student perceptions noted through informal communication between faculty and students and through ongoing student satisfaction and graduation surveys, University leaders identified a need to develop clear and distinguishable differences between the Ed.D. as a practitioner-based doctorate compared to the more traditional theoretical-based PhD degree program. As both degree programs are delivered similarly via the online teaching and learning platform employing an asynchronous, one-to-one learning model, a clear delineation was necessary to ensure that students and advisors could recognize the distinctions between the two programs and choose the program best aligning with the personal learning goals and objectives of the students. Starting with the end in mind, the culminating learning experiences in each of these two programs could demonstrate these distinct differences in the program expectations and student preparation as well as the outcome of the program components. Thus, the Ed.D. degree program was re-aligned to ensure the dissertation research was focused on the complex problems of real-world application.

The changes made to the Ed.D. program were geared toward the principles and tenets of practice-based research. Similarly, the remastered Ed.D. degree program illustrated the necessary distinctions between research contributions to theory and contributions to field-based practice often called for by past researchers as a further assurance for program distinction among doctoral programs (Kochhar-Bryant, 2016). This critical distinction in the culminating research experience for the revised Ed.D. then allowed for the redesign of the curriculum from the beginning to prepare students for this new experience.

The concept of the Backward Design (BWD) Model is often credited to Tyler (1949), though use of the term "backward design" specific to curriculum design is more often attributed to Wiggins and McTighe (2005). While the BWD model may not be new, its general application within higher education curricular development is less evident. Though there are many models of instructional design and curriculum development, BWD was chosen for the redesign of the EDD because BWD focuses more on the learning than on the teaching. That is, BWD is more concerned with the output of instruction than the input. Focusing on the output of learning provides organization of the learning experience and decreases the chances that learning activities and resources will be selected based on personal preferences of individual instructors more than efficacy of the materials in achieving the learning goal.

In this case, the intentional application of BWD in redesigning a practitioner-based doctoral program is particularly disruptive. Instead of simply revising the existing courses, the entire Ed.D. program was redesigned using the BWD. Buss et al. (2017) noted the importance of the incorporation of considerations from the growing segment of research into Ed.D. program redesigns and highlighted the value of use of this research for design considerations, which the authors adopted. In addition, research into the processes of operational assessment and assessment integration served to further inform the intentionality of the integration of institutional and program-learning assessment measures throughout the course of the redesign process (Riggle, Wellner, Prager, & Hall, 2019). Finally, considerations of a revamped DIP as the culminating learning demonstration for the Ed.D. degree program offered a customized research study to better prepare scholar practitioners to focus their dissertation journey on problems from practice and foster the dissemination of this practice-based research.

BACKGROUND

Current trends in the development of an education doctorate involve disruptive innovations to the traditional dissertation processes to ensure Ed.D. candidates are prepared to solve the complex problems of practice (Buss et al., 2017). In this chapter, the authors explore the current research and innovation of online doctoral learning assessment within the virtual settings. We explore best practices and innovation for direct and indirect assessment data, continuous improvement feedback loop, collaborative elements for the online doctoral learning community; faculty-designed assessment rubrics; faculty training, development, and buy-in; and doctoral student expectations as specific to a re-engineered education doctorate within one School of Education (Riggle et al., 2019).

With more than a decade of national dialogue to articulate differences between research and practitioner-based doctoral programs in education and parallel efforts to distinguish doctorate in practice degrees such as the Ed.D. from more traditional PhD degrees (Perry, 2015; Riggle et al., 2019; Throne, 2012; Throne & Walters, 2019), many schools of education clearly convey overarching distinctions between Ed.D. and PhD degree programs. However, beyond these overarching differences, the practical distinctions between the PhD and practitioner doctorates are subtler yet must be considered (Hawkes & Yerrabati, 2018; Robinson, Morgan, & Reed, 2016).

As a result, the authors purport the instructional design considerations must be direct and intentional for the integration of institutional and program learning assessment within the instructional design and BWD process (Wiggins & McTighe, 2005).

This deliberate approach to program design, including the incorporation of asynchronous and synchronous instructional methods and learning design, must be maintained to ensure, not only the dissertation research proposal and final dissertation manuscript meet the rigor and quality expectations of the University and accrediting bodies, it is also being supported by a doctoral learning community with external evaluators (Lehan, Hussey, & Mika, 2016). The intention in this process for a global redesign is to best prepare Ed.D. candidates to present research appropriate to disciplinary expectations, address the complex problems within educational professional practice, and foster dissemination of practice-based research and acquire research-based decision-making skills as outcomes of Ed.D. completion. The practice-based nature of the dissertation in practice allows for doctoral scholars to develop leadership skills within an empirical research study to seek solutions to the educational problems within the field. These outcomes are subsequently assessed for continuous quality improvement and continued innovation to guide practitioner researchers through an empirical research study with implications for practice and contributions to the discipline.

The critical process of institutional assessment allows measurements of the program to be aligned with the institutional mission, vision, and values coupled with program outcomes to ensure effective doctoral candidate preparation (Perry, 2015; Salter-Dvorak, 2014). Robertson and Larkin (2019) noted the necessity of outcomes assessments to ensure applicability to specific disciplines. For example, a dissertation in practice for nurse educators and the solutions offered may differ from a PK12 educator seeking solutions within an elementary school classroom. In the current case study, considerations for the assessment of the institutional and program learning outcomes integrated within a BWD model for the revised Ed.D. have allowed for a valid substantive revision and continuous improvement of the Ed.D. program. Further, asynchronous elements were considered incrementally within the course development process and refined upon deployment.

BACKWARD INSTRUCTIONAL DESIGN

The virtual course content and the asynchronous learning system of this re-engineered Ed.D. program were designed with a focus on the practitioner-based versus research-oriented learning goals for scholar practitioners to include the requisite leadership skills needed to improve practice. While the more traditional dissertation supervision is intended to guide students to conduct research via a specific lens (e.g., applied problem solving vs. theoretical-based research contributing to the field of knowledge), a more contemporary approach incorporated into the redesign of this program was to reexamine the merits of the traditional five-chapter dissertation versus a three-chapter dissertation. Intending to address these challenges, the Ed.D. was comprehensively redesigned, including the development of new curriculum and a customized DIP experience. The DIP culminates in a three-chapter dissertation focused on solving a complex application-based problem from educational practice. This redesigned dissertation model is applicable to other practitioner-based doctoral programs and intentionally disrupts traditional notions of dissertation research for the purpose of ensuring Ed.D. graduates complete the program as innovative and research-based leaders able to solve problems within their own area of educational practice (Riggle et al., 2019; Robinson et al., 2016).

The backward design model can be simplified to the three stages illustrated in Figure 1. While this high-level overview seems simple, the decisions made at each stage are certainly more complex.

Figure 1. Three stages of backward design

The first stage of the BWD model is to identify the desired results (Wiggins & McTighe, 2005) as to what a learner should know (understand), do (skills), or feel (affective) at the end of a learning experience. These understandings, skills, and emotions are the desired results of the student learning experience. While many educators believe that they have considered the desired results by writing learning outcomes, many educators would correspondingly have to admit such outcomes were written later in the curriculum planning process, not necessarily at the beginning. Perhaps an even greater fault, educators or instructional design experts may abdicate their responsibility to frame learning outcomes and simply use the laundry list of objectives provided by textbooks or other content providers who offer similar resources. Individual courses and programs thus are not designed so much as collated from a collection of publisher-provided resources. This approach to focus first on content, while recognized as one of the doorways to the design process discussed by Wiggins and McTighe (2005), reflects an older educational paradigm focusing on the teaching (an input) and not the learning (an output). By first considering the desired results, the focus shifts to learner output in terms of the results identified.

The Dean of the associated School of Education assembled a task force of full-time and part-time professors, professional advisory council members, and other University stakeholders to consider the goals, values, hallmarks, and qualities of an applied doctoral degree while maintaining the rigor expected in the traditional dissertation. The group sought guidance from relevant literature, specifically the work of the CPED, environmental scans, and program review data. This dedicated task force articulated the goal of the applied education doctorate as the development of educational leaders who are to focus on the improvement of practice through evidence-based solutions to complex educational problems. Furthermore, the foundational values of the program graduates included knowledgeable and empathetic leaders who support the betterment of all students and faculty, independent thinkers and informed decision-makers who function as leaders within the discipline rather than technicians, facilitators of effective positive change in varied educational environments, and individuals who conduct and implement actionable, job-relevant research to improve policy, programs, and practice. The task force was then able to consider desired results in terms of alignment between these goals and values and the institutional learning outcomes (ILOs) related to oral communication, written communication, quantitative reasoning, critical thinking, information literacy, and research skills. The group drafted revised program learning outcomes (PLOs) reflecting the group's response to the question about desired results for the applied doctoral program while also aligning to the ILOs. In the case of this revised Ed.D. program, five new PLOs focused on the following themes: (1) advancing equity and social justice, (2) making ethical decisions, (3) developing leadership skills, (4) creating strategic and tactical plans for improving organizations, and (5) solving complex problems in practice. By articulating the desired results in terms of the PLOs, the work group was then able to consider how students would demonstrate proficiency in each of those outcomes. In terms of this case, the desired results prompted thoughtful discussions as to what an educational scholar practitioner must be able to understand, evaluate, and apply at the conclusion of an Ed.D. degree program.

While considerations for the integration of institutional and learning assessment is also the focus of this chapter, it is beneficial to further explore the provisions of BWD for assessment generally prior to exploring assessment in the context of the specific case example. The second stage of the BWD model is to determine acceptable evidence (Wiggins & McTighe, 2005). The second stage builds on the identification of results in the first stage by asking how learners can demonstrate evidence they achieved the desired results. The disruption of the BWD model is particularly evident in this stage. In traditional models of program planning, assessments often are considered at the end of the design process, after lectures have been delivered or a set number of consecutive chapters in a textbook have been assigned. A particularly acute problem at the level of higher education is settling for evidence the professor can easily gather (e.g., automated multiple choice exam) rather than striving for other forms of authentic assessments providing more authentic representations of what the desired results look like in practice. Wiggins and McTighe (2005) offer the comparison of an activity designer and an assessor, with the goal being to think like an assessor in determining acceptable evidence. This second BWD stage anchors the program design to the desired results developed in the first stage while also offering a map to the choices needing to be made in the third stage.

In the example of the university in this chapter, the question became what type of academic experience allows students to demonstrate proficiency of all or nearly all of the desired results, which were framed as program learning outcomes? There is no big surprise in a chapter about doctoral assessment, with one of the defining assessments of learner proficiency being a dissertation, though it is still worth exploring just what type of dissertation provides acceptable evidence for an applied doctoral degree. As mentioned previously, the differences in the traditional five-chapter dissertation manuscript and three-chapter dissertation document are explored later in this chapter. On the doctoral journey to the three-chapter dissertation, students are assessed three times on their progress toward demonstrating proficiency of the program learning outcomes. Using the course learning outcomes as the guiding objectives, the Director of Assessment identified three specific assessment points within the curriculum map and corresponding assignments as acceptable evidence of proficiency across the applied doctoral program to serve as measurement points for each of the program and institutional learning outcomes. These assessment points were rated as introduced, reinforced, and mastered to indicate the level at which the learner was expected to perform on the associated learning outcome.

Certainly, both formative and summative assessment of learning should be embedded within any well-designed learning experience and an applied doctoral program would be no different. Because the BWD model calls for a collection of evidence across time rather than a single assessment at a particular point in time, there is value in exploring the course level for evidence beyond the culminating dissertation. For example, Wiggins and McTighe (2005) offered a continuum of assessment options for gathering evidence: informal checks for understanding, observations and dialogues, tests and quizzes, academic prompts, and performance tasks. In a similar potentially useful approach for a virtual learning environment, Scalise and Gifford (2006) proposed a framework for computer-based assessments in e-learning. After reviewing 44 articles and book chapters on assessment item types and designs, a taxonomy of questions and tasks for assessment in e-learning were developed. The taxonomy categorized 28 different question types by the amount of constraint and complexity offered by each of the questions. The level of constraint or construction is used in directing the learner's thinking. Along the top (horizontal) axis, this taxonomy considers the level of the constraint of a question, meaning how constrained the learner is in forming a response (Scalise & Gifford, 2006).

The response can be fully selected, meaning the responses are provided for the learner. An example is a multiple-choice question. Conversely, the response can be fully constructed, in which the learner completely generates his or her own responses, such as with a presentation or portfolio project. The range from most constrained and fully selected to least constrained and fully constructed spreads across seven types of questions: multiple choice, selection and identification, reordering or rearrangement, substitution or correction, completion, construction, and presentation or portfolio. On the left (vertical) axis lies the complexity of the question in each type, from less complex questions to more complex questions. So, the simplest type of question would be a true/false question, while the most complicated task would be diagnosing a problem or teaching a concept.

The third stage of the BWD model is where many universities start rather than end in planning degree programs, specifically to plan learning experiences and instruction (Wiggins & McTighe, 2005). Many educators have proclivities for content aligning with personal preference or creativity over learning engagement or learning events with specific activities or preferred resources. While these preferred learning activities might indeed be incorporated into the final design, further consideration must be given to the alignment of the activities and resources within the broader structure of the desired results and acceptable evidence. Thus, considerations for content rather than desired results opens the programmatic design to a bias toward content coverage and an ensuing tendency toward a disjointed collection of courses more than a unified program of learning, differentiated within and among individual courses and programs as well as scaffolded with an increasing progression of rigor. This is a particularly poignant point when considering the literature, possibly suggesting poor differentiation among doctoral degree programs, especially for practitioner doctorates versus research doctorates (Perry, 2015; Riggle et al., 2019; Throne, 2012; Throne & Walters, 2019). Without first focusing on desired results, graduate students, doctoral faculty, administrators, employers, accreditors, and other key stakeholders may not detect essential differences between a practitioner doctorate focused on educational practice and a more theoretical degree focused on broader contributions to the field or theory. Only after the desired results and evidence of the achievement of those goals are envisioned during the program planning process, did the program designers and development team consider specific content intentions. This process prevented content decisions made without the benefit of a guiding framework and in a void of evidence-based decisions.

In the case reviewed throughout this chapter, the task force considered the sequence of the applied doctoral program. In terms of desired results, understandings, skills, attitudes, and dispositions were prioritized over other understandings, skills, attitudes, and dispositions. The development team sought means and alignment to sequence course work to ensure an appropriate instructional scaffolding of the necessary outcomes while also continuously engaging each learner with high-quality, authentic learning activities in which students could immediately apply their learning within their existing work environments or otherwise relate their learning to their personal and professional contexts. Institutional and program learning assessment discussions were embedded within these considerations to ensure these were not relegated to add-ons, but fully integrated within curricular and outcomes discussions.

The courses within the program are categorized as follows: foundations courses, content specialization courses, research courses, a comprehensive research prospectus, and dissertation research courses. Particularly in this open access University, the task force faculty recommended the need to forge tighter linkages from foundations to specialization courses, as the specialization courses can continue to help candidates refine leadership skills and culminating project structure and opportunities. By having students take their specialization courses immediately following the foundation courses, students develop deeper knowledge about their study area prior to beginning the research course sequence. With regard to the research block, courses were reorganized and a new course was designed in the area of qualitative data analysis. In the new course sequence, students choose a qualitative or quantitative research track and develop necessary research skills to successfully progress through the program. The considerations given to the content and progression of courses resulted in improved scaffolding which was needed to ensure a logical research methods course sequence for skill development and to ensure the selection of a research problem from educational practice well-aligned with methods of inquiry appropriate for the Ed.D. candidate's aspirational goals of leadership development within and beyond the practitioner doctoral program. Thus, the final course sequence was followed: two foundations courses, four content specialization courses, five research courses, one comprehensive research prospectus course, and four dissertation research courses (with supplemental courses as needed by doctoral candidates requiring extended time within their dissertation research) (see Figure 2).

Figure 2. Ed.D. institutional and learning assessment integration within a scaffolded BWD

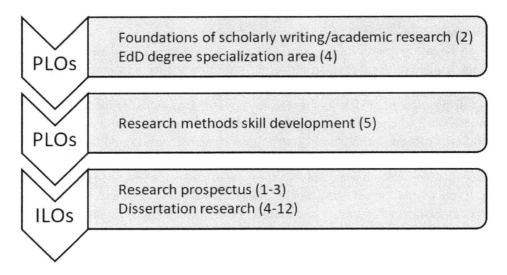

Needless to say, the implementation of the BWD model within any graduate degree program is a far more extensive process than what can be discussed here. However, this section offers key points for the alignment between the BWD approach, the revision of the applied education doctorate, and process considerations for integration of institutional and learning assessment measures as described in the following section.

To summarize, a cross-level task force accepted the charge to re-envision the Ed.D. program of study by starting first with the desired results and then moving to a determination of what evidence would reflect those results as the BWD emphasizes a collection of evidence, so there was some consideration of evidence at both the program and course levels. The task force also considered the sequence of the individual courses comprising the Ed.D. program to ensure appropriate alignment, scaffolding of the desired results, and student preparation to demonstrate proficiency throughout the evidence gathered. Finally, the plan for institutional and program learning assessment was incorporated directly into the Ed.D. redesign to ensure integration and applicability of the assessment process and shared understanding.

BACKWARD DESIGN FOR INSTITUTIONAL AND LEARNING ASSESSMENT CONSIDERATION

Institutions should give careful consideration to assessment during program revision and development of programs using the BWD model (Moore, 2018). When used effectively within instructional design, BWD can lead to the development of high-quality assessments and by employing the BWD, integration, scaffolding, and appropriate sequencing can ensure institutional and program outcomes are well integrated and aligned with course learning outcomes and linked successfully to specific learning activities in each virtual course. Assessment data can then be used to not only measure the particular course learning outcome, but inform learning attained at the program level, thus allowing institutions to develop rich and valuable data to determine student performance of critical skills and abilities linked to program goals (Russell & Markle, 2017). In the case of this practitioner-based education doctorate, the authors focused on three important aspects of assessment: (1) the development of processes resulting in evidence to determine student acquisition and attainment of critical knowledge, skills, and abilities central to the scholar-practitioner focus of the remastered Ed.D. degree; (2) a school-level desire to create space for ongoing faculty dialogue about student performance in an online, asynchronous learning environment; and (3) the need to develop cost effective assessment processes sustainable over time.

Assessment processes for the revised Ed.D. must result in evidence to determine student acquisition and attainment of the critical knowledge, skills, and abilities related to the scholar-practitioner focus of the degree. To ensure Ed.D. degrees are leadership-based and practitioner focused, assessment considerations must be well-planned and intentional, and the BWD must incorporate assessment at the start of the program revision to ensure students meet the program outcomes and the assessment data collected aligns with program goals (Braskamp & Engberg, 2014). Here, requisite learning elements include the development of critical thinking, problem-solving, and leadership skills in the context of real-world educational problems experienced by scholar practitioners in the contemporary workplace (Buss et al., 2017; Rueda, Sundt, & Picus, 2013), all embedded within the program learning outcomes established for the remastered Ed.D. program. As such, good assessment practices should incorporate multiple measures of learning yielding quantitative and qualitative data to assure learning outcomes are met at key measurement points identified throughout the progression of coursework, the dissertation journey, and after students complete their program (Braskamp & Engberg, 2014).

In the case of the Ed.D. program, these measurement points would occur at the beginning, middle and end of the program to align with rating learner skills and abilities at three different levels of expected performance: performance after outcomes were introduced; performance after outcomes were reinforced; and performance after outcomes were mastered (see Figure 3). These efforts of periodic assessment at key intervals of the program support the alignment of assessment standards within the instructional design of virtual courses whereby interaction involves multimodal communication, both synchronous and asynchronous (Nyysti & Walters, 2018) and align with WASC standards for assessment and program differentiation (WASC Senior Colleges and University Commission, 2013, 2014).

Figure 3. Ed.D. institutional and learning assessment collaborative and scaffolded integration

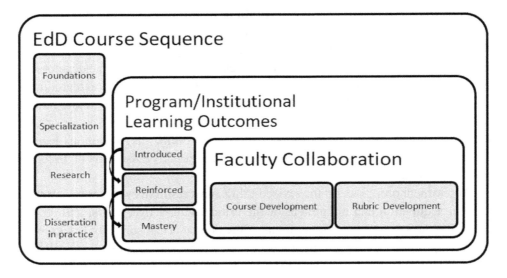

The focus of doctoral level educational assessment for traditional PhD programs frequently emphasizes culminating experiences such as the dissertation manuscript, dissertation defense, and qualifying or comprehensive exams. While these are valid assessments of doctoral learning at the mastery level, they must be reimagined so assessment criteria focus on the intersection of theory and practice to inform decision-making and problem solving as reflected in the revised DIP experience. Any rubrics or other dissertation committee member evaluation tools used to assess the DIP must be revised to emphasize the importance of the application of theory in real world scenarios, analysis and evaluation of research. Information, and the ability to communicate regarding complex problems of practice and solutions within diverse settings (Perry, 2015), all of which align with the revised PLOs for the Ed.D. while departing ways from the goals of the institution's traditional PhD of training students to conduct original research through the lens of one or more theoretical frameworks (Buss et al., 2017; Rueda et al., 2013).

In addition to assessment practices at the mastery level, other useful assessment practices include formative and summative assessment using direct measures of learning at the introductory and developing levels to align with WSCUC standards (WASC Senior Colleges and University Commission, 2013, 2014) and to ensure quality scaffolding of courses and learning experiences throughout the virtual course work to reach mastery for the culminating event. The WSCUC standards also aided the program designers and faculty to further distinguish the Ed.D. from the traditional PhD research doctorate, which was aided by CPED Guiding Principles and Framework providing an external disciplinary context to do so. While faculty input and oversight of assessment is an essential part of good practice, an often-overlooked stakeholder group is the learners themselves who should recognize assessment as an integrated part of the learning process (Braskamp & Engberg, 2014; Russel & Markle, 2017). In the case of the Ed.D., learner knowledge of and participation in assessment is critical if institutions want learners to fully understand the intended differences between this scholar practitioner degree and the more traditional PhD degree (Riggle et al., 2019). For this practitioner-based Ed.D. degree, deliberate efforts were made to develop authentic assignments in core courses to emulate real world scenarios or problems, allowing learners to develop their critical thinking, problem-solving, leadership skills, and communication skills (Riggle et al., 2019). Example assignments include but are not limited to written and oral responses to scenarios, case studies, plan and project development, and proposal development and revisions.

For culminating assignments within each course, referred to as Signature Assignments, faculty are now developing dual purpose rubrics with clearly defined criteria and performance levels to be used for both grading and assessment for all non-dissertation courses. These four-point rubrics, aligned to the recently adopted School rubric style and format, are being added to courses in the new Ed.D. sequence, eventually providing additional assessment data for learner performance beginning in the foundation courses and continuing up to the prospectus course. In addition to these new signature assignment rubrics, the school continues to use PLO and ILO rubrics developed in compliance with the University format used across programs. Assignments are selected within courses where students demonstrate their attainment of one or more PLOs and ILOs and faculty use these rubrics to assess student performance at the three levels (introduced, reinforced, and mastery). In the case of doctoral degrees at the University, the PLOs and ILOs are assessed in the prospectus course and/or in one or more of the courses within the dissertation sequence. This course-embedded assessment approach allows faculty to determine student performance of critical skills and abilities as mapped to the program learning outcomes while maintaining efficiencies for single-channel learning assessment and grading purposes across multiple course sections, an important component of the University's unique one-on-one teaching model supported by distributed resources among an online doctoral learning community (Babcock, Lehan, & Hussey, 2019; Kumar et al., 2005). Likewise, through the incorporation of course-embedded assessment, learners will become more aware of their own educational attainment in the context of program learning outcomes and can use the results for self-reflection during their educational journey. Finally, this iterative and sequenced feedback aids instructional designers and curriculum developers to recognize potential curricular gaps, outdated or ineffective learning events, and the ongoing need for curricular revisions and potential degree program enhancement. As this chapter highlights the experiences of one university case of a recently revised program, institutional data are limited to the elements of curricular design and assessment methods used.

Other learning and institutional assessment considerations, not entirely confined to the virtual environment, but certainly magnified by it, include the need to create collaborative spaces within the online doctoral learning community for faculty and research supervisors to garner buy-in and facilitate the use of assessment data for decision-making and improvement. While a single-channel learning assessment process is necessary for efficiency given the number of students and faculty in the Ed.D. program as well as the virtual nature of the program (Babcock, Lehan, & Hussey, 2019; Kumar et al., 2005), institutional assessment within a virtual environment cannot simply be left to individual faculty operating in isolation to use online synchronous and asynchronous tools (Klein, Endfinger, & Crumley, 2018). At a minimum, institutions must train faculty on the use of any rubrics employed for assessment. However, merely understanding the mechanics of using assessment rubrics is not enough. Further efforts are essential to provide opportunities for faculty to engage in ongoing dialogue about learning and performance, especially for the culminating research experience, in this case the DIP. It is in these virtual spaces where faculty, through shared experiences and constructive dialogue, build a shared understanding of what constitutes different levels of learning performance and dissertation research quality (Russel & Markle, 2017).

For the University in this case study, faculty members meet with School leadership at an annual university symposium, which is part of the University's graduation week. Plans are underway to work within the School on these aspects of institutional and program learning assessment to continue with consensus building and increase buy-in to assessment processes, and more importantly, to discuss current assessment findings with the goal of drawing conclusions from the results and developing subsequent action plans for improvement (Braskamp & Engberg, 2014) on an annual basis. Other ongoing collaborations include the creation of a school-wide assessment committee that meets regularly to discuss assessment-related matters.

These assessments related activities will inform annual and longer term program review processes for the Ed.D. program.

Other ideas not yet operationalized, but in the planning stages, include analyzing assessment results soon to be yielded from the use of course-embedded rubrics. In particular, the School will focus on analyzing assessment results in the context of the rubric-generated quantitative results for all learners, but also supplementing this evaluation with faculty observations from examining a random selection of learner artifacts and work products to identify thematic areas for improvement based on additional qualitative data contributions. Through the implementation of comprehensive assessment processes at the department or school-level, faculty employ discipline-specific preferences to assessment practices and undergo a "deeper dive" to ensure Ed.D. scholar practitioners demonstrate the expected institutional and program outcomes. Thus, faculty become more vested in these vital assessment processes than they may otherwise be if such processes were conducted at the institutional level. This then can result in an ongoing collaborative approach between faculty and instructional designers for the collective responsibility of curricular improvement and overall doctoral learning engagement (Klein et al., 2018; Nyysti & Walters, 2018; Riggle et al., 2019; Young, DeMarco, Nyysti, Harpool, & Mendez, 2019).

Finally, institutional and learning assessment processes for the remastered Ed.D. must be cost-effective and sustainable over time, an assessment challenge continuing to be highlighted over the past decade as needing reconsideration by regional accreditors and assessment experts (Gannon-Slater, Ikenberry, Jankowski, & Kuh, 2014). Likewise, Lehan et al. (2016) noted the specific challenges for dissertation quality from these doctoral programs, which may also have accreditation implications. More recently, Suskie (2019) articulated revised rules for what is considered good assessment, which included this idea of cost-effectiveness, something often discussed on campuses but noted less frequently in the assessment literature. With limited time to conduct quality assessments, institutions must ask initial questions about the ease and sustainability of potential assessment processes during program development, recognizing assessment always requires more time than planned for in best-case scenarios. In a virtual environment, the University recognizes most assessments will be conducted by faculty in an asynchronous, solo environment. Therefore, faculty-training needs must be considered from the onset and budgeted for accordingly. In the case of this University, the authors rely on the Center for Teaching and Learning to develop online training courses required of all faculty. In addition, two faculty coaches are available to assist faculty members with curriculum and assessment related questions as well as using ongoing collaborative tools to foster the online doctoral learning community (Young et al., 2019). Subsequent discussions about assessment occur at faculty team meetings and through the School assessment committee. With a rather large number of part-time faculty, careful attention must be given to including part-time faculty to ensure their understanding of program expectation and accompanying assessment processes and participation in the doctoral learning community (Young et al., 2019).

Lehan, Hussey, and Shriner (2018) have also noted the challenges of assessment within the University's distributed online learning community amidst diverse academic support resources available apart from course work as all aspects of the online learning community impact program quality and outcomes mastery. Rubrics for the Ed.D. at the University are constructed via the learning management system (LMS) and with this University's customized one-on-one teaching model and careful consideration was given to pilot assessments before full implementation to ensure effectiveness, as changes to hundreds of unique course sections can be unwieldy. The authors played critical roles in collaboration with doctoral faculty for the development, testing, implementation, and revision the assessment rubrics within the LMS. Because of the complex nature of building assessments within a virtual one-on-one learning environment, it was essential for thoughtful planning of data collection points from carefully selected learning experiences to ensure institutional assessment processes remain sustainable over time.

Like many higher education institutions with terminal degree programs, institutional and program learning outcomes assessment continues to be a work-in-progress due to its innate process orientation and necessary iterative measures (Russell & Markle, 2017). One area of significant improvement with the Ed.D. is planning assessment at the beginning with the end in mind to mirror the BWD approach used for instructional design. Through this integration of institutional and program learning outcomes assessment rubrics into courses at the onset of course development under BWD, assessment plays a more central role and is fully integrated within the curriculum as opposed to afterthought or subsequent add-on of the curriculum. In this case, the University identified the core skills and abilities desired of doctoral graduates and only then created curriculum and assessments around those central student learning outcomes and program goals. This represented a significant improvement over former layered assessment processes, which functioned as add-ons after the fact rather than part of a well-thought process. In addition, the University expanded the avenues for faculty involvement in these assessment processes and carefully considered the design, development, and deployment of quality assessment and instructional design training materials for all faculty. By using a course-embedded assessment model, and through pilot testing and rubric revision prior to implementation in all course sections, the University is optimistic these revised assessment processes will produce valuable data for decision-making and be sustainable over time as continuous improvement measures aligning with WASC required program review and assessment practices (WASC Senior Colleges and University Commission, 2013, 2014).

SOLUTIONS AND RECOMMENDATIONS

Instructional designers, whether they are teaching faculty, administrative faculty, or collaborative design teams, might consider the BWD model as a means to improve not only individual course design but also overall program design to ensure coherent integration of program-level learning outcomes and consideration of individual course level appropriate scaffolding within and among the individual courses representing a cohesive degree (Hall & Summerville, 2018). These specialized strategies coupled with the larger context and requirements of institutional assessment allow for instructional design with "the end" in mind. This is particularly important for practitioner degree programs, such as the Ed.D., as assessment of institutional and program learning outcomes be measured by appropriate and valid assessment methods aligned with a three-chapter dissertation addressing a field-based problem as a culminating doctoral learning activity. The revised Ed.D. program is assessed across institutional outcomes and expectations and data will be used for continuous quality improvement for the recently implemented dissertation in practice.

The authors of this chapter agree accepting the current state of higher education, specifically the changes and demands for quality and rigor, must drive the ongoing improvement process of programs at this level. In this case, the redesign of the EDD program was specially aligned to the Carnegie Project, thus allowing for substantive discussions and multi-disciplinary collaboration in the process of professional doctoral preparation. The authors recommend teams who seek to engage in the same or similar process as described in this chapter engage in six specific and foundational actions:

1. The national expectations in the field of higher education in the development or revision of doctoral programs are constantly in flux; teams must ensure they are meeting the needs of their clientele at the local level.
2. Those committed to the conscious redesign of the scholarly practitioner-focused Ed.D. must be collectively engaged not only in continuous improvement strategies which, when conducted with transparency and collaboration with key stakeholders, lead to continuous innovational outcomes.
3. The identification of the necessary knowledge, skills, and dispositions for a scholarly practitioner-focused Ed.D. program design must be deliberately examined in the areas of equity, ethics, and social justice to solve the complex problems arising in various fields of practice while linking practical and research knowledge.
4. Good design and assessment practices are essential for all aspects of program alignment; therefore, careful attention is needed beginning from the creation of program learning outcomes to course development and assessment design.

5. Program design teams would benefit by ensuring sufficient scaffolding both within and across the individual courses that collectively represent the degree program. Consistent with the BWD model, such scaffolding begins with adequately planning progressive rigor of the desired results and acceptable evidence at the course level in addition to the program level.

6. Consider additional ways to measure the relationships and potential influences of the BWD model and other factors at the higher education level, such as student achievement at course and program levels, student, and instructor satisfaction at course level, and project team satisfaction at conclusion of design experience.

Hawkes and Yerrabati (2018) reported the need to move beyond single case study analysis and instead, apply findings from Ed.D. research to other applicable practitioner doctoral programs such as the Doctor of Business Administration or the Doctor of Clinical Psychology. Throne and Walters (2019) echoed these recommendations and noted the importance of considering the unique aspect of research supervision for the research phase of practitioner doctorates in general and interdisciplinary insights potentially be developed across practice-based doctoral programs. The authors of this chapter agree with this and as a result, institutional sharing across programs and schools is underway for the current case study as the University offers practitioner doctoral programs across the various schools.

FUTURE RESEARCH DIRECTIONS

Additional research to further explore collaborative uses of BWD and integrated assessment processes within higher education contexts would be useful. Such research might include additional case studies, such as the Ed.D. case presented in this chapter, or comparisons between practice-based research courses versus research-based doctoral courses with similar focus but unique designs incorporating BWD and other approaches. This research, conducted over-time, could further enhance the quality of practitioner-based doctorates as well as further differentiate them from more traditional research-based doctoral programs. Current trends reflect preferences to incorporate synchronous elements within instructional design for online degree programs due to the advancements in instant messaging, evolution to 5G wireless technology, and other factors that offer real-time communication in addition to asynchronous elements of traditional online education.

Hawkes and Yerrabati (2018) noted two gaps in research into the research phase of Ed.D. programs and called for ongoing research into further aspects of Ed.D. programs beyond coursework as well as further exploration into the post-doc aspects of the

Ed.D. and the wider implications of terminally degreed professionals as they return to practice. In addition, Throne and Walters (2019) called for ongoing development of a standard nomenclature for what constitutes doctoral research supervisor agency specific to non-hierarchical research supervision with a high mentoring ethos for practitioner doctoral programs. Buss et al. (2017) noted past and future research conclusions of the Ed.D. should inform educational leadership to continually re-envision or redesign the Ed.D. for maximum program effectiveness. The chapter authors call for further research into the balance of synchronous versus asynchronous instructional methods to consider whether doctoral students' communication needs are met especially when they arrive at the Ed.D. dissertation research phase.

CONCLUSION

This chapter offered a case application of BWD for an online redesigned practitioner doctorate and use of the three stages as articulated by Wiggins and McTighe (2005) as well as incorporation of a three-chapter dissertation in practice as the culminating doctoral experience. Further, process considerations for the integration of PLOs and ILOs directly embedded within the instructional design process demonstrated collaboration among faculty, assessment experts, instructional design experts, and School leadership. Assessment considerations included the piloting of rubrics before the full-scale implementation and development of training,which is believed to be critical for faculty understanding of the assessment methods developed for the remastered Ed.D. program. The new Ed.D. degree program is expected to prepare scholar practitioners to commence primary ethical research culminating in a DIP founded upon a scholarly practice-based inquiry into a specific and complex problem.

Further, the Ed.D. program was redesigned to support the transformation of the doctoral candidate to the scholar practitioner within their chosen field of practice. The purpose of this approach was intended to foster innovation, collaboration, professional knowledge, research and evidence-based decision-making, and ultimately bringing quality improvement across educational settings. The program components have been intentionally redesigned to ensure the candidate is prepared to solve the complex problems arising in their selected field of study while linking their practical and research knowledge. The embedded learning assessment measures presented in this chapter are expected to bear this out and inform further quality improvements needed as the program continues.

Future research directions involve deliberate follow-up to post-implementation measures for the Ed.D. institutional and program learning assessment to ensure the data produced by theses assessments are yielding useful information about the attainment of outcomes by leaners and the quality of the program. Additional assessment methods will be added as needed to clarify ambiguities around learning, maintaining careful attention to the scaffolded learning experiences leading to the DIP as a culminating learning experience and are customized to engage doctoral faculty, scholar practitioners, and School leadership as ongoing inquiry to inform future program revision.

REFERENCES

Babcock, A., Lehan, T., & Hussey, H. D. (2019). Mind the gaps: An online learning center's needs assessment. *Learning Assistance Review (TLAR), 24*(1).

Braskamp, L. A., & Engberg, M. E. (2014). *Guidelines for judging the effectiveness of assessing student learning*. Chicago, IL: Loyola University Chicago.

Buss, R. R., Zambo, R., Zambo, D., Perry, J. A., & Williams, T. R. (2017). Faculty members' responses to implementing re-envisioned Ed.D. programs. *Studies in Higher Education, 42*(9), 1624–1640. doi:10.1080/03075079.2015.1113951

Gannon-Slater, N., Ikenberry, S., Jankowski, N., & Kuh, G. (2014). Institutional assessment practices across accreditation regions. Learning Outcome Assessment. Retrieved from http://www.learningoutcomeassessment.org/documents/Accreditation%20report.pdf

Hawkes, D., & Yerrabati, S. (2018). A systematic review of research on professional doctorates. *London Review of Education, 16*(1), 10–27. doi:10.18546/LRE.16.1.03

Klein, J., Endfinger, B., & Crumley, C. (2018, April 26). Leveraging instructional design effectively. In *Proceedings of the WSCUC Academic Resource Conference*. Academic Press.

Kochhar-Bryant, C. A. (2016). Identity, commitment, and change agency: Bedrock for bridging theory and practice in doctoral education. In V. Storey, & K. Hesbol (Eds.), *Contemporary Approaches to Dissertation Development and Research Methods* (pp. 29-42). Hershey, PA: IGI Global. doi:10.4018/978-1-5225-0445-0.ch003

Kumar, R., Myers, J., Aytug, Z. G., & Presider-Houy, L. (2018). Purposeful assessment design: Aligning course-embedded assessment with program-level learning goals. *Business Education Innovation Journal, 10*(1), 6-15. Retrieved from http://www.beijournal.com/

Lehan, T., Hussey, H., & Mika, E. (2016). Reviewing the review: An assessment of dissertation reviewer feedback quality. *Journal of University Teaching & Learning Practice, 13*(1), 4.

Lehan, T. J., Hussey, H. D., & Shriner, M. (2018). The influence of academic coaching on persistence in online graduate students. *Mentoring & Tutoring, 26*(3), 289–304. doi:10.1080/13611267.2018.1511949

Moore, D. E. Jr. (2018). Assessment of learning and program evaluation in health professions education programs. *New Directions for Adult and Continuing Education, 2018*(157), 51–64. doi:10.1002/ace.20268

Nyysti, K., & Walters, K. (2018). Out of isolation: Building online higher education engagement. In A. Scheg & M. Shaw (Eds.), *Fostering effective student communication in online graduate courses* (pp. 179–192). Hershey, PA: IGI Global. doi:10.4018/978-1-5225-2682-7.ch010

Perry, J. A. (2015). The Carnegie Project on the Education Doctorate. *Change: The Magazine of Higher Learning, 47*(3), 56–61. doi:10.1080/00091383.2015.1040712

Riggle, B. A., Wellner, L., Prager, E., & Hall, B. (2019, April). Professional practice doctorates: Rethinking the dissertation experience. In *Proceedings of the WSCUC Academic Resource Conference*. Academic Press.

Robertson, R. L., & Larkin, M. J. (2019). Developing an instrument to observe and evaluate assessment system maturity. *Journal of Educational Research and Practice, 9*(1), 55–80. doi:10.5590/JERAP.2019.09.1.05

Robinson, G., Morgan, J., & Reed, W. (2016). Disruptive innovation in higher education: The professional doctorate. *International Journal of Information and Education Technology (IJIET), 6*(1), 85–89. doi:10.7763/IJIET.2016.V6.664

Rueda, R., Sundt, M., & Picus, L. O. (2013). Developing scholarly practitioners: Lessons from a decade-long experiment. *Planning and Changing, 44*(3), 252–265. Retrieved from https://eric.ed.gov/?q=Developing+Scholarly+Practitioners%3a+Lessons+from+a+Decade-Long+Experiment.&id=EJ1145925

Russell, J., & Markle, R. (2017). Continuing a culture of evidence: Assessment for improvement. Princeton, NJ: Educational Testing Service. doi:10.1002/ets2.12136

Salter-Dvorak, H. (2014). 'I've never done a dissertation before please help me': Accommodating L2 students through course design. *Teaching in Higher Education, 19*(8), 847-859. doi:10.1080/13562517.2014.934344

Scalise, K., & Gifford, B. (2006). Computer-based assessment in e-learning: A framework for constructing "intermediate constraint" questions and tasks for technology platforms. *The Journal of Technology, Learning, and Assessment, 4*(6).

Suskie, L. (2019, April 17). What is good assessment, revisited. Retrieved from: https://www.lindasuskie.com/apps/blog/

Throne, R. (2012). *Practitioner research in doctoral education*. Dubuque, IA: Kendall Hunt.

Throne, R., & Duffy, J. (2016, April 7). Situated Ed.D. dissertation advising in an online doctoral community of practice. In *Proceedings of the WSCUC Academic Resource Conference*. Academic Press.

Throne, R., Shaw, M., Fore, C., Duffy, J., & Clowes, M. (2015, November 2). Doctoral candidate milestone achievement: A philosophy for situated dissertation advising. In *Proceedings of the Eighth International Conference on e-Learning and Innovative Pedagogies*. Academic Press.

Throne, R., & Walters, K. (2019, May 18). Doctoral research supervisor agency: Fostering engagement in guiding U.S. online practitioner doctorates. In *Proceedings of the 15th Annual International Congress of Qualitative Inquiry*. Academic Press.

Topolka-Jorissen, K., & Wang, Y. (2015). Focus and delivery of doctoral programs in Educational Leadership. *International Journal of Educational Reform*, *24*(3), 212–232. doi:10.1177/105678791502400302

Tyler, R. A. (1949). *Basic principles of curriculum and instruction*. Chicago, IL: University of Chicago Press.

WASC Senior Colleges and University Commission. (2013). *2013 Handbook of accreditation*. Retrieved from Western Association of Schools and Colleges.

WASC Senior Colleges and University Commission. (2014). *Meaning, quality, and integrity of degrees FAQ*. Retrieved from Western Association of Colleges and Schools.

Wiggins, G., & McTighe, J. (2005). *Understanding by design* (2nd ed.). Alexandria, VA: Association for Supervision and Curriculum Development.

Young, C., DeMarco, C., Nyysti, K., Harpool, A., & Mendez, T. (2019). The role of faculty development in online universities. In K. Walters & P. Henry (Eds.), *Fostering Multiple Levels of Engagement in Higher Education Environments* (pp. 260–275). Hershey, PA: IGI Global. doi:10.4018/978-1-5225-7470-5.ch012

ADDITIONAL READING

Berg, G. (2019). Alternatives to the traditional doctoral dissertation: A research literature and policy review. In A. Raman & M. Rathakrishnan (Eds.), *Redesigning higher education initiatives for industry 4.0* (pp. 221-231). Hershey, PA: IGI Global.

Costley, C., & Fulton, J. (Eds.). (2018). *Methodologies for practice research: Approaches for professional doctorates.* London: SAGE.

MacGregor, C. J., & Fellabaum, J. (2016). Dissertation redesign for scholarly practitioners in Educational Leadership: Increasing impact through dissemination-ready sections. In V.A. Storey & K. A. Hesbol (Eds.), *Contemporary approaches to dissertation development and research methods* (pp. 53-69). Hershey, PA: IGI Global.

Perry, J. A. (2012). To Ed.D. or not to Ed.D.? Universities are working intentionally to refashion Ed.D. and transform it into a degree that truly serves professional practitioners. *Kappan, 94*(1), 41–44. doi:10.1177/003172171209400108

Perry, J. A. (2016). The Ed.D. and the scholarly practitioner. Charlotte, NC: IAP.

Perry, J. A. (2017). The Carnegie Project on the Education Doctorate: Transforming education practice in multiple contexts. In D. E. Neubauer, K. H, Mok, & J. Jiang (Eds.), The sustainability of higher education in an era of post-massification. New York: Routledge.

Ravitch, S. M., & Lytle, S. L. (2017). Becoming practitioner-scholars: The role of practice-based inquiry dissertations in the development of educational leaders. In *Educational Leadership and Administration: Concepts, Methodologies, Tools, and Applications* (pp. 1914–1929). Hershey, PA: IGI Global. doi:10.4018/978-1-5225-1624-8.ch088

Storey, V. A. (Ed.). (2016). International perspectives on designing professional practice doctorates: Applying the critical friends approach to the Ed.D. and beyond. New York: Palgrave Macmillan.

Storey, V. A. (2017). *Exploring the impact of the dissertation in practice.* Charlotte, NC: IAP.

Throne, R., & Oddi, B. (2019). Dissertation research supervisor agency for U.S. online doctoral research supervision. In A. Elçi, L. L. Beith, & A. Elçi (Eds.), *Faculty development for digital teaching and learning.* Hershey, PA: IGI Global.

Wiggins, G. P., & McTighe, J. (2011). *The understanding by design guide to creating high-quality units.* Alexandria, VA: ASCD.

Chapter 9

Precision Education:
Engineering Learning, Relevancy, Mindset, and Motivation in Online Environments

Huda A. Makhluf
National University, USA

ABSTRACT

Higher education is a pathway to social equality and mobility. Unfortunately, a great number of students who enter Higher Education are not ready to succeed in rigorous college-level courses and fail as a result or drop out. Our nation has entered a transformative period in higher education brought about by the demands of an evidence-based approach that uses rigorous scientific methodologies designed to capture valid and reliable data to drive student success and improve outcomes. Math literacy especially remains a significant challenge for student success in college, in particular for STEM students. Herein, the author describes an innovative solution that leverages technology and data analytics to expand student success, with a special emphasis on engineering an environment for effective learning, mindset, and motivation.

DOI: 10.4018/978-1-7998-1622-5.ch009

INTRODUCTION

Setting the Stage: The Challenge, the Solution, and the Process

To set the stage, higher education is grappling with several issues: equity gaps, defining the meaning and value of a degree, and leveraging innovative technology to ensure student access, success, and affordability in an ethical and unbiased manner. National University (NU), headquartered in La Jolla, California, is a nonprofit institution founded in 1971 by retired U.S. Navy Captain David Chigos. NU is the largest private nonprofit university in San Diego and is a pioneer in the digital space. To meet the evolving demands for education in the 21st century, NU has been offering online education for the past two decades.

BACKGROUND OF NATIONAL UNIVERSITY

National University (NU) was founded in 1971 with the mission and vision to deliver an exceptional student experience with relevant, current and meaningful transformational education. NU continues to build a robust infrastructure to increase its capacity to collect meaningful and actionable data on all its students. NU serves adult learners with an average age of 32 and boasts an open-enrollment policy that welcomes students at any time of the year; this open access and non-selective admission model, however, creates a challenge for accommodating the wide array of academic needs enrollees bring.

NU is embarking on an ambitious goal to create a comprehensive ecosystem that leverages technologies, such as machine learning, data analytics, and artificial intelligence, to serve all students, to help them reach their full potential and ensure that no learner is left behind. How might the institution handle the challenge of extreme diversity among its student population in a traditional system not currently flexible enough to adapt to the needs of every learner? The solution may be to provide an academic "Global Positioning System" (GPS) that navigates all learners from their academic locations and skill levels towards their goals by using specific guidance and pathways that are uniquely personalized and dynamic. The process may be to implement this solution so that it entails developing assessments tools and systems, as well as best practices sufficiently rich to assist students in achieving their goals through effective guidance in a custom-tailored adaptive learning environment. Having multiple tools is paramount to the success of the NU initiative. Equally important is to engineer a flexible learning environment, ecosystem to provide motivation and attend to the social and emotional learning components of the student experience;

this includes reduction of anxiety, offering content that is relevant, valued, and increases student self-efficacy, eliminates attribution errors, and provides the learner with opportunity for developing a positive, and growth mindset. This chapter will broadly describe the different parts of this adaptive learning ecosystem and present two sample pilots as case studies that model an in-depth Precision Education initiative to engineer a supportive learning environment at both the cognitive and non-cognitive level with the overall goal to enhance student learning.

BACKGROUND

It is important to note that none of these innovations would have been explored or realized without the presence of online teaching and learning as a pedagogical and technological backbone. Quality Matters (QM), a leading quality assurance organization for online learning, in collaboration with Eduventures Research an advisory company, believe that distance learning is becoming a fundamental component of higher education (EVOLLUTION). Together they deployed a survey to track the "Changing Landscape of Online Education" with the CHLOE Survey, (Garrett, Legon, & Fredericksen, 2018). They found that online learning is an integral and vital endeavor at the heart of many institutions, their missions, and their strategic plans. Looking closely at the basic building blocks of online learning in the online course, these organizations reported that institutions that established instructional design teams and relied on their design acumen, saw significant student engagement with faculty and students. Remarkably, institutional course design practices and faculty professional development has shaped the student experience and engagement with content, peers, and faculty. Innovation in the online space such as Artificial Intelligence (AI) with all its risks and rewards is keeping online learning at the forefront of a major transformation that is revolutionizing the educational landscape.

Value of a Degree

At a time when parents, students, unemployed graduates, legislators, accreditors, and employers are questioning the value of a degree in higher education, coupled with escalating student debt and a lack of competency in the workforce, the emergence of career dashboards, electronic portfolios of student assessment and badging have been hailed as attractive solutions to address outcomes and graduate preparedness for the workforce. A staggering 80% of employers acknowledge that it would be expedient to see an electronic portfolio of student work which demonstrates a candidate's competencies in key knowledge and skills areas (Hart & Associates, 2015). Unfortunately, and despite the benefits of career dashboards and ePortfolios, many students still do not have ePortfolios that showcase their accomplishments and display hard-earned badges and investment in degree-awarding programs.

In 2014, the Association of American Colleges and Universities (AAC&U) and Hart Research Associates administered an online survey to 400 employers as well as to more than 600 college students, which reviewed 17 essential learning outcomes. In their report, entitled: "Falling Short? College Learning and Career Success," the majority of employers felt that college graduates were neither well-equipped to achieve the learning outcomes that employers deemed critical nor were they well-prepared to achieve long-term career success (Hart & Associates, 2015). From working effectively in teams to assist students in their quest for proficiency in a language other than English, employers universally agreed that in order to be successful at their companies, graduates ought to demonstrate certain critical capacities:

The ability to effectively communicate orally (85%)
The ability to work effectively with others in teams (83%)
The ability to effectively communicate in writing (82%)
Ethical judgment and decision-making (81%)
Critical thinking and analytical reasoning skills (81%)
The ability to apply knowledge and skills to real-world settings (80%)

The percentage points indicate the proportion of employers who rated each outcome an 8, 9, or 10 on a 0-to-10 scale (Hart & Associates, 2015, p. 4-8).

Additionally, the Hart & Associates' study found that employers valued and endorsed an emphasis on applied learning as a means of preparing students for successful careers. These employers were more likely to hire graduates who have engaged in collaborative research projects, internships, senior projects, or field-projects in diverse settings. The majority of employers also believed that improvement was required at the university and college levels in order to ensure the success of graduates in the workforce. Indeed, 64% think that curricular enhancements were required to guarantee that graduates have the skills and knowledge needed to progress within their company. Interestingly, Hart & Associates, in another comparative perspective survey among college students (Hart & Associates, 2015, pp. 8-9), found a clear gap between employer impressions and student optimistic views on career readiness.

Looking at Employer Impressions

For entry-level positions, 42% of employers believed that students were doing a good job, with 58% articulating a need though for improvement. In contrast, 74% of surveyed students felt that they were doing a good job and only 26% felt the need to improve. Notably, in advanced positions, an even smaller percentage of employees (36%) felt that students were doing a good job, with a significant 64% thinking that improvements were needed. Ironically, 64% of students felt good about their preparedness levels in these advanced positions and only 36% felt the need to improve.

Given such discrepancies between student perception of preparedness and employer assessment and observation of graduate skills, there is a clear need to help students showcase their academic work, evolution and maturity to prospective employers in both a professional and transparent fashion. Building such an ecosystem that prepares competent students and provides them with a mechanism to showcase their skills, e.g., ePortfolios, thus allowing employers to spot a potential employee with the perfect set of competencies best suited for a specific position. In fact, 80% of employers thought it very (36%) or fairly (44%) useful to see an electronic portfolio of student work prior to hiring (Hart & Associates, 2015, p.13).

A CASE FOR EPORTFOLIOS

The benefits of ePortfolios are numerous. Building them provides students with a structured opportunity to collect artifacts throughout their academic life cycle at a university while creating a professional web presence and personal branding (Brooks, 2011). Furthermore, ePortfolios can afford students the opportunity to purposefully select artifacts along with self- reflections to showcase their learning and competencies to prospective employers. Likewise, employers could screen these ePortfolios to discover market-ready students with the ideal competencies needed for the job.

ePortfolios could also prove to be a very valuable tool for universities, colleges and other educational institutions. They could help track student development in academic programs through precise documentation of acquired skills, abilities, broad, integrative and specialized knowledge while capturing key milestones as evidence along the way. ePortfolios could also be shared with various stakeholders (academic advisors, mentors, faculty, and academic program directors) or to show student growth and continuous improvement. More importantly, harvesting student artifacts for assessment endeavors would empower program leads to provide evidence of achieving program outcomes. Finally, institutions of higher education, in turn, would be able to validate student learning and institutional outcomes in their reaffirmation reports to accreditors. For students, the perceived ease of handling an ePortfolio could influence their attitudes towards the usage and perceived usefulness of that technology tool (Shroff & Deneen, 2011). As such, selecting an ePortfolio system with valuable features and flexible approaches would increase student motivation and "buy in". Fortunately, the Precision Institute in collaboration with the Center for Innovation and Learning (CIL) at NU adopted a portfolio system (Portfolium by Infrastructure) that provides learners with visually friendly and intuitive means for managing projects, as well as learned skills and competencies. These systems are "cutting edge" and use cloud-hosted platforms with accessibility to social networks. Unlike LinkedIn and Facebook, these systems house actual works created by the student and are much more than professional connections or a work history. Digital badges may also be added to ePortfolios, as well as resumes, providing more students with more opportunities to leverage their skillsets. These portfolios are for perpetual lifelong learning and can plug students into an open ecosystem of employers, mentors, educators, and peers.

Another forward-thinking piece of the precision ecosystem, in addition to providing ePortfolios, is a digital badging platform for all of its students. Such features allow students to be recognized, engaged and potentially hired, priceless qualities in this day and age of connectivity. Both the Mozilla Foundation and McArthur Foundation are still leading the way in establishing a badging ecosystem where badges are issued for validated and assessed competencies based on student artifacts. Badging stipulates flexibility to support learning innovation as it recognizes precise skills and competencies at various stages, and creates taxonomies of achievements with more granularity, hence allowing students to expand the value of their learning journey and unlock new opportunities and learning paths. The ability to keep an ePortfolio for life, coupled with the ability to display badges as lifelong achievement, would prove beneficial for all students.

ePortfolios could substantiate the learning-hiring operation at all of its different levels by supporting the student's learning process in all its outcomes and competencies, the employer's process of screening and hiring, and the academic institution's process of continuous improvement to learning and teaching, thus coming full circle. The focus, of course, is not the technology or the tool itself, but owning one's learning journey through reflective thinking and the accumulation of artifacts as evidence of transformative learning. Six different programs are coupling assessment and badging with ePortfolios through formal or informal learning channels, thus providing students with the brilliant opportunity of broader connections to a fast-evolving learning ecosystem, and for leveraging their comprehensive skillsets with higher impact, with various stakeholders and prospective employers. One such example is the Scholars Program, an educational and scholarship program fashioned to reward students who demonstrate exceptional leadership, service, scholarship, and academic excellence at National University.

Precision Learning

Another component of the Precision Learning ecosystem is that it can help navigate students through career exploration and future goal setting with powerful dashboards aligned to the programmatic level. The premise is that students who engage early on in their programs in setting specific goals tend to persist and graduate on time. These dashboards empower advisors, faculty, and students alike to track the student's academic journey or pathway throughout the life cycle of each student. The same concept of deconstructing courses to micro-competencies applies here, wherein programs are mapped out as modules and domains of competencies, knowledge, skills, and abilities. "Stackable" competencies can lead to credentials and can be transferable to a different academic pathway if need be, thus providing the student with varied choices and navigation control. The role of the faculty is key in providing students with a framework for navigation, one that clearly articulates the precise knowledge type, be it factual, conceptual, procedural, broad & integrative, or specialized, as well as applied skills and abilities essential to the specific credential and degree. This is accomplished through a backward design, starting with the end in mind and reverse engineering the pathways for all students. The social, emotional, motivational components, as well as the level of proficiency are clearly articulated and delineated too. Data collection and real time tracking and communication with the student would allow the university to create a truly customized learning experience for all users. Even though this system is still in the early stages of its implementation, with a large number (N) of students, and through machine-learning and powerful predictive analytics, the system may well provide a streamlined access to all integrated information applicable to diverse learners and will surface valuable insights to ensure academic success for all learners, one student at a time. Thus far, these parts of the ecosystem occur at the meta-level, but moreover are student-centered, and grounded in the classroom learning experiences.

At the Classroom Level

The assessment piece of such a comprehensive ecosystem is an integral component and crucial for its overall success. Many in higher education advocate the complete integration of the assessment component into the instruction process, making it the endoskeleton (the internal level of support) rather than an "exoskeleton" of teaching (Ewell & Schneider, 2013, p. 8). Across institutions, faculty and staff strive to ensure that student assessments remain an ongoing operation, capturing the continuum of student performance.

The body of students, at NU especially in General Education, is diverse in terms of ethnicity and college readiness. National University is a Hispanic Serving Institution.

In fiscal year 2018, 36.1% of the active student body was white, 26% was Hispanic, 9% was African American, 7.7% Asian, 1.7% international, 1.1% native Hawaiian/ Pacific Islanders, and 0.4% Native Indian, while 4.7% claimed two or more races, and 13% had an unknown ethnicity. Students also enter with a variety of academic skills and backgrounds. Regardless of student readiness, the onus is on the faculty and staff to support students along their curricular journey from the beginning of their academic journey to the finish line, graduation. Rather than adopting an existing platform or courseware, the Precision Institute embarked on an ambitious goal to build its own adaptive platform, named National University Navigator (NuNav), to navigate students at their own pace, and to identify their unique areas of strengths and weaknesses in multiple disciplines. It is incumbent upon the academician to determine the most effective path for each individual student and to engineer an environment that provides the proper instruction at the proper time and dosage.

The primary focus is on what students need to know and what they should be able to do at the completion of the course. As such, a backward design was deployed, going systematically, with the end in mind, through the learning objectives of courses in math, science, and the humanities deconstructing each learning outcome into competencies and micro-competencies, in an effort to precisely map deficiencies or strengths in students' knowledge.

The process starts with the deconstruction of the course learning outcome into competencies and micro-competencies and determining which competencies scaffold up to the course learning outcomes. Next, follows the curation of valid and reliable formative assessments against each of the identified micro-competencies. These formative assessment questions are validated by a psychometrician who specializes in micro-assessments. On the navigation platform (NuNav), students are instructed to 1) complete a knowledge check (KC) also labeled as KC1, 2) use open educational resources effectively and engage earnestly before moving to KC2 or the next micro competencies (MCs), and 3) avoid excessive cramming by completing the assigned competencies and micro competencies on regular basis.

According to the NU website, the NuNav platform is based upon an Adaptive Machine Learning Instruction. The re-designing of courses into units of learning that can be tested online to measure progressive subject mastery provides optimum achievement possibilities for students. On NuNav, at the micro competency level, students would be presented with a KC, a set of five questions, prior to their lessons. If students score 80% or more, the system would then navigate students to the next micro-competency. If on the other hand, students score below 80%, the system would offer them a curated learning object to remedy that deficiency. Following their interaction with that resource, students would subsequently engage with a second KC. The system records the lift, or score change between KC1 and KC2, and based on the new score, either navigate the student to a new micro-competency or offer the student another learning object to remedy the deficiency. After three unsuccessful attempts to demonstrate proficiency, the system would unlock all the learning resources for this specific micro-competency and alert the instructor through a live dashboard to initiate and interact substantially with the student by deploying a successful intervention strategy.

The rationale behind pitching these learning objects one at a time and recording lift between the Knowledge Checks (KCs is to gather data on the effectiveness of the learning objects to remedy the deficiency and determine the intervention potency. The system also captures the students' perception of the value of the object by asking them to rate the resource. This trains the algorithms to better serve the learner. Earnest engagement is monitored by tracking time spent on the assessments, as well as the time devoted to the learning resources. That data, combined with the pre- and post-KC scores, presents an exceptional view into the progress of students. Understanding the areas where students seem to struggle, will guide the prioritization of real-time interventions by the faculty teaching the course. Unique and novel to NuNav is the employment of a varied and diverse content model, based on curated Open Educational Resources (OERs), as well as created and crafted faculty content. The NuNav system is adaptable and allows for quick modification and flexibility. The NuNav is a microscope for the learning process, allowing faculty and staff to continually fine tune the courses in order to provide the best and most effective learning experience for our students.

MATH I AND II AS AN EARLY PROTOTYPE PRECISION COURSE

This engineered math environment identifies student strengths and areas for development, and provides various pathways for targeted assistance and is capable of the following:

- Assessing students at the competency and micro-competency levels,
- Testing their math anxiety levels,
- Addressing their mindsets and intellectual predispositions, and
- Designing content that focuses on quantitative reasoning and on the relevancy of math in everyday living, i.e., why it matters to learn math, thus highlighting the meaning and value of these courses.

In Math I and Math II, there are 182 micro-competencies covered, grouped into more than 30 Competency areas. Each micro-competency has one pre and two post assessments (Knowledge Checks) for a total of three attempts, and a diversity and variance of learning object resources aligned to each one. They range from Podcasts and YouTube videos to e-texts, animation, and voice-over tablets, to name a few.

The following are the competencies that have been deconstructed and presented on NuNav:

- Perform Operations with Integers and Rational Numbers
- Identify and Use the Properties of Real Numbers
- Evaluate Exponential Expressions and Use the Order of Operations
- Identify, Evaluate and Simplify Variable Expressions
- Solve Linear Equations in One Variable
- Solve Linear Inequalities in One Variable
- Translate Sentences into Equations
- Solve Geometry Problems
- Solve Applications of Inequalities
- Use the Rectangular Coordinate System: Find Slope of Lines
- Write Linear Equations in Two Variables
- Graph Linear Equations in Two Variables
- Graph Linear Inequalities in Two Variables
- Solve Systems of Linear Equations in Two Variables by Graphing
- Solve Systems of Linear Equations in Two Variables by the Substitution Method
- Solve Systems of Linear Equations in Two Variables by the Elimination (or Addition) Method
- Solve Simple Problems that can be Reduced to a System of Two Linear Equations in Two Variables
- Add and Subtract Polynomials
- Multiply Polynomials and Simplify the Result
- Evaluate and Simplify Integer Exponents
- Divide Polynomials
- Factor Polynomials and Simplify the Result
- Simplify Rational Expressions
- Multiply and Divide Rational Expressions and Simplify the Result
- Add and Subtract Rational Expressions and Simplify the Result
- Solve Equations Containing Rational Expressions
- Define and Evaluate Roots and Radicals
- Simplify Radical Expressions
- Solve Operations with Radicals
- Solve Operations with Radicals and Rational Exponents
- Solve Quadratic Equations

Table 1. Summative assessment scores on NuNav versus business as usual (course not using PL)

T-Test Condition	NuNav (n)	BAU (n)	T-Test Results	p-value
Math I Midterm	88% (34)	84% (82)	t = 1.67, df = 66.0	0.100
Math I Final	82% (34)	76% (85)	t = 2.01, df = 82.4	0.005**
Math I Midterm & Final	85% (34)	80% (82)	t = 2.34, df = 79.8	0.021*
Math II Midterm	89% (14)	79% (17)	t = 1.80, df = 28.7	0.082
Math II Final	75% (14)	75% (17)	t = -0.05, df = 28.9	0.959
Math II Midterm & Final	82% (14)	77% (17)	t = 1.35, df = 27.1	0.186

Note: * denotes p<.05 and ** denotes p<.01

Following this comprehensive mapping, authentic formative assessments (KCs) were created and vetted by a psychometrician to gauge the students' math knowledge in each micro-competency and to precisely map their cognitive location in the course. To further test the effectiveness of this platform in developmental math at NU, a randomized controlled trial was deployed in developmental math classes. Students enrolled in MTH12A and 12B (Developmental Math I and II), were randomly assigned to either the NU MATH (NU Navigator platform) experimental group or the business as usual (BAU) control (or standard) group. At week 2 (midterm) and week 4 (final), all students in both the experimental and control groups received the exact set of summative assessments. Students on the NU MATH (phase I) system scored an average of 85.5% on these summative assessments, whereas students in the control class scored an average of 79.86%. Changes in student outcomes were attributed with a high level of confidence to the impact of NU MATH (t = 2.34, df = 79.8, p-value = 0.021). Results were particularly striking in showing that the NU MATH (phase I) system outperformed a solid vendor's platform used in the business as usual classes (Table 1). Students on the NU MATH (phase II) system scored an average of 82.4% on summative assessments whereas students in the control class scored an average of 79.77%. The percent of students who failed the developmental math (scored below 60%) was 2.9% and 11.6% for NU MATH and BAU, respectively (Table 2).

Table 2. Success rates on NuNav versus business as usual (course not using PL)

	Fail	Pass	Total	Percent Failed
BAU/ Control	10	76	86	11.6
NuNav	1	33	34	2.9

Chi-squared test: X-squared = 1.2882, df = 1, p-value = 0.2564

Additional experiments and data collection are underway, aimed at determining statistical significance with a larger sample size; however, this proof of concept experiment surfaced four key areas of insight. Firstly, mastery-based learning with criteria-referenced assessments that depart from the traditional norm-referenced assessments with low, average, and high performers is achievable. Thus, the notion of "moving the needle" with fewer Ds, Fs, and Ws at the class level, one student at a time and at scale, is attainable through a paradigm shift in faculty teaching philosophy, where norm-referenced criteria with a target grade point average (GPA) isn't front and center in the classroom.

Secondly, the intentional design of summative and formative assessments is critical as well. Increasing rigor in both the formative and summative assessments is paramount in ensuring that students don't acquire a false sense of security about the material presented in the course, especially when the summative assessments are extremely rigorous and don't correlate with the formative ones. This is also critical to address any negative notion or the perception of diluting standards or inflating the grades. Thirdly, the creation of a test bank of questions with clear tagging of the difficulty level of each question and the alignment to the MCs by design is critical to surface up academic collusion and dishonesty. Performance should be highly correlated. Fourthly, and finally, faculty can initiate substantive interaction with students based on the live NuNav dashboard that clearly displays areas of weakness allowing them, i.e., the faculty, to send nudging interventions and ensure student success. These targeted interventions would help move the needle on retention rates by helping non-persisters complete the course.

The role of the faculty in ensuring student success is paramount in this engineered ecosystem. The faculty responsibilities are diverse and may vary wildly per faculty forte and inclination, ranging from 1) instruction, to 2) competency and micro- competency definition and alignment to learning resources, to 3) course content development or curation of open educational resources, to 4) assessment development and/ or 5) scoring, to 6) academic advising, 7) career advising and 8) coaching. Having an open and innovative faculty mindset to imagine the possibilities in redefining the role of the faculty is key in building a shared vision and mission to transform student lives through efficient and impactful learning.

ENGINEERING A MINDSET AND POSITIVE EMOTIONS

Many students fail or drop out of college for non-cognitive reasons particularly those affective, emotional, and motivational in nature. Yet research shows that little attention is given to support these non-cognitive elements in a student's academic journey (Clark & Saxberg, 2018). As such, addressing motivational challenges facing students may prove beneficial in navigating them successfully through their academic career at any institution. The focus of the faculty should not be primarily on self-driven, highly ambitious and intrinsically motivated students who have effectively mastered self-regulation and efficacy, but rather on learners who might still be missing foundational building blocks for learning and academic tenacity. Many students who fail or drop out could need further development and improvement of their social-emotional and cognitive skills, as well as the acquisition of growth mindsets, in order to engage in learning before they can truly thrive.

Similar to their remedial needs in Math and English, such students may only have remedial cognitive, motivational, and social-emotional skills (Stafford-Brizard, 2018). This is different from addressing learning problems caused by either inefficient teaching methods or insufficient faculty guidance, or even the students' lack of readiness or prerequisite knowledge to support new learning. This approach is about tackling the absence of motivation, by defining the underlying mechanisms for motivational problems (Clark & Saxberg, 2018). Clark and Saxberg articulate clearly what they believe goes wrong with motivation by pointing to four main factors: value, self-efficacy, emotions, & attribution errors, all recognized as impacting students' expectancies and beliefs about the control they have over their academic goals.

A myriad of reasons can cause students to stop persisting and avoid putting in the needed mental effort and commitment to succeed. Invariably, most students value academic tasks that give them a sense of accomplishment, effectiveness, and control over their lives. Eccles and Wigfield (2002) describe three types of values: interest, importance, and utility values.

Students will choose to persist and persevere in tasks that interest them the most and are willing to put in the needed mental effort to succeed. Additionally, despite a lack of interest in and perceived value for a particular task, the utility value of completing a certain task becomes the students' drive to accomplish goals, such as fulfilling a certain requirement in order to earn a degree. The utility value could also be the driver of hard work and effort by simply avoiding a bad outcome that would deter students from achieving their ultimate personal goal. Knowing how to appeal to the students' interests, faculty can masterfully craft relevance and value and surface key connections between a learning task and the students' interests. For instance, in a dreaded math course that could trigger anxiety and fear of failure in some students, for those who may value it simply as a need for graduation (but have little interest in the subject itself), faculty in NuNav could purposefully and intentionally create relevancy videos to showcase the value of learning math in students' daily lives, i.e., why it matters to learn math. Students are being surveyed on the effect of these videos on their perception of the value of math.

Typically, students end up procrastinating and some may resort to academic collusion and cheating given the high value of any college level course and the high mental effort required for them. Many students feel that this effort is commensurate to their brain climbing Mount Everest. Subsequently, this leads to a discussion of self-efficacy and confidence, a second factor well worthy of the faculty's attention. Perceived self-efficacy, defined as the students' beliefs in their success, expectations and capabilities, could be a predictor of procrastination and of insufficient mental effort. Indeed, on a confidence scale of 0 to 100 percent, the most desirable zone for self-efficacy is between 40% and 70%. Students who have a high self-efficacy score tend to be overconfident and also avoid both high mental effort and industriousness, in contrast to students with low scores who tend to underrate their efficacy, refusing to invest work and effort and tend to procrastinate (Bandura, 2006).

Faculty can craft deliberate feedback to overconfident students and propose a more successful outcome by changing their strategies. On the other hand, faculty ought also to investigate the underlying mechanisms of students with low self-efficacy. This could be due to three reasons: firstly, a stereotype threat; secondly, a lack of foundational skills and the need for remedial instruction; and finally, a lack of self-confidence despite having the needed skills. Accordingly, faculty could deploy targeted interventions, for instance, communicating to students their belief in them that they can do the required task and that they have the skills needed to succeed and that they are capable of successfully completing this task with extra effort and hard work.

Strong emotions have a huge influence on student cognitive load and processing (Sweller, 1988). Fear and anxiety could shrink student thinking space and cognitive ability, whereas positivism and optimism could result in increased mental effort and achievement. A domino effect could ensue with negative thinking leading to procrastination, disengagement and withdrawal; students quit persevering and stop working hard. Positive students tend to persist and endure in the face of setbacks, with success begetting more success. Faculty can assess and solve emotional problems by encouraging positive self-talk and by having the will to listen attentively and discuss solutions and strategies in a non-judgmental fashion. One must keep in mind that for an adult student, the attempt to balance life, family and school is upset by disruptive and negative emotions not just in an academic setting, but from non-academic day to day challenges at work or at home, all resulting in interference with academic work alike. Caring, positive, and compassionate faculty could deploy their own emotional intelligence to support and help their students to emotionally self-regulate and manage the demanding workload despite disruptive emotions or refer them to special and professional services. This is key in helping students achieve their academic dreams and goals in the face of setbacks and adversity.

Another tripping point for students is attribution errors or the underlying causes of failures, which often cause students to lose motivation and quit, especially if they believe that they don't have control over their situation. These attribution errors could be categorized as controllable or uncontrollable and could be grouped into two classifications internal and external. For example, teacher bias is defined as both uncontrollable and external. The lack of adequate effort meanwhile is considered controllable and is internal. Inaccurate beliefs about uncontrollable causes of academic failure lead students to quit. It is crucial for faculty to identify precisely the motivation problem by discerning them from learning problems and by designing the precise intervention to combat student procrastination and encourage hard work and focus.

The mindset of the faculty is equally important to the student mindset in any learning environment. From believing in the power of implementing a novel learning technological tool to boosting positive emotions and motivation, faculty who express genuinely and authentically their belief in student capabilities can inspire students to engage earnestly and put in the needed effort. For example, telling students about neurogenesis, neuroplasticity, and the detrimental effects of anxiety and stress on the brain will explicitly help the students connect the dots between emotions, mindset, motivation, mental effort and academic learning and help them comprehend why holding on to a fixed mindset could indeed be detrimental to their own success (Blackwell & Trzesniewski, 2007; Maguire et al., 2000).

Case in point, in a recent study conducted in Britain that looked at the MRIs of the brains of licensed taxi drivers subjected to stringent driving examination, compared to control drivers, the posterior hippocampus, responsible for cognitive functions, of a taxi driver was shown to be larger than that of the control subject. In response to environmental demands, a healthy adult brain has the capacity to undergo local plastic changes in its structure as evidenced in brain scans of taxi drivers who had to acquire a significant amount of spatial information in comparison to a control group of drivers who lacked a comparable navigation exposure and mastery (Maguire et al., 2000). Additionally, studies exploring the role of theories of intelligence indicated that believing that intelligence is malleable predicted an upward trajectory in grades. In contrast, a belief that intelligence is fixed predicted a flat trajectory. Teaching a growth mindset promoted a positive change in classroom motivation and performance compared with a control group (Blackwell & Trzesniewski, 2007). Remarkably, Claro et al showed that a growth mindset tempers even the effects of poverty and socioeconomic disadvantage on academic achievement (Claro, Paunesku, & Dweck, 2016) suggesting that student mindset might improve the consequences of socioeconomic disadvantages by stressing hard work and consistent effort in growing one's intelligence.

Remarkably, physical activity and enriched environment are inducers of neurogenesis in contrast to sedentary aging and stress which are notorious negative regulators of neurogenesis (Zhao, Deng, & Gage, 2008). The genesis of new cells and their survival in the adult human brain and the vast networks of neurons firing and wiring together in learner's brain is a good indication of a growth mindset. Articulating this scientific message about neuroplasticity to students, how the brain can grow and change and stressing that intelligence and talent are developed through hard work and neuronal wiring is a powerful catalyst for a growth mindset.

Student beliefs about their abilities and expectations of success are predictors of academic performance. Hence, engineering a learning environment that addresses anxiety and fixed mindsets, and that systematically tackles attribution errors whether external, internal, controllable or uncontrollable, is key to increasing student engagement and success.

Preliminary Results on Baseline Anxiety and Math Mindset

Since there is little to no data on math anxiety, mindset, and motivation from surveys of adult learners in developmental math courses at NU, a comprehensive survey to determine the baseline levels of students' anxiety, math mindset, academic locus of control, math confidence and self-efficacy, coping mechanisms, and value of studying math was deployed.

In this study, a total of 253 students were surveyed, of which 68 (27%) completed the survey. Over half of these students (n= 44; 64.7%) stated that they feel nervous when they do math problems. Of those, nine students stated that they feel tense and have trouble breathing when they get confused about something in math. 67% reported 1) having a growth mindset and agreed that 2) those who struggle in math can do better by putting in more effort or trying new strategies, while 72% agreed that mistakes made in math are a good opportunity to learn math. When surveyed for academic locus of control, 46% of the students agreed that there are some subjects in which they could never do well, but 61% of students still agreed that there is always something they can do to improve their situation. As for student perception of the value of studying math, 44% of students did not like math at all and found it boring, while 51% agreed that math is useful even after graduation.

Analysis of adult student responses to open-ended questions on expected performance in class revealed three emerging themes, centered around 1) pace, 2) struggle, and 3) retrieval. One student particularly liked the self-paced navigation. Three others indicated a commitment to success in this fast-paced course, while the rest acknowledged an initial phase of struggle given a lack of application of math concepts in the preceding 5-10 years.

Quoting students verbatim:

- "Before starting this class, I was nervous because I haven't done this type of math since High School. So, it has been at least 10 years. In the beginning, it was hard, but then once I started going, it all came back to me. I love that this is self-paced".
- "I feel like this class gives you the needed information and materials to be successful."
- "I expected to gain an understanding of basic algebra in this class, and I am started to slowly grasp the concepts. I am still not good, and I forget fast, but the amount I have learned in a short period of time makes me very happy."
- "I expected I would do better than I currently am. I was always in advanced math classes in high school, but that was 10+ years ago. So, some of the problems took me awhile to catch on again."
- "Starting this week, I have not used Algebra to solve problems in five years. After going through some of the lessons I started remembering how to work through problems more and more."
- "I was not aware that there was so much to learn in Algebra. Adding to that, the class is only one month; therefore, it is coming at me faster than I am able to process it, without stressful effort."
- "I knew going into the class I was going to struggle. I can do regular math pretty easily and do fine when it's used on a repetitive basis, but I am finding it a struggle re-learning outside a classroom setting. I try to learn the things I need to via the internet and some things come back to me fairly easily."
- "I knew that starting in math again is something that would be a little bit of a struggle but I'm getting it back."
- "I hope that this course will be very beneficial to me learning math. I hope that the professor can help make math easier for me to learn."

This initial survey was successful at capturing baseline anxiety level, motivation, and mindset, with some results being particularly striking: 1) The mindset data obtained from our adult learners indicated a growth mindset, and 2) The ability to mark and identify students at high risk of a fixed mindset and anxiety in math is promising for targeted interventions.

Such a Mindset EduMarker and Anxiety EduMarker will help in future studies to investigate whether learners with these EduMarkers could benefit from well-designed interventions to ensure their success in this course. This proof of concept experiment is paving the way to a yet larger one with a larger sample size (given that the response rate was 27%), one with a survey by experts in behavioral psychology (Rosenzweig et al., 2019).

FUTURE RESEARCH DIRECTIONS

Why Math Matters, a Broader Impact

Based on a recent survey by the National Assessment of Educational Progress, minority students have a performance gap in math and the sciences as early as elementary school, with more students struggling to complete a high school degree and enroll in college as they progress. Additionally, a growing body of evidence indicates that these students are even less likely to major in STEM fields. According to the U.S. Department of Education, only 35.1% of students who enrolled in STEM fields graduated with a STEM degree. Moreover, the nation's demographics are changing, California's in particular, becoming more and more a diverse nation and a diverse state. Given, the academic achievement lag in minority, low income and first-generation students, a true crisis may be developing.

For a vision to close the gap, tremendous effort is required to shepherd these students from the start line to the finish line. This is both a call and an opportunity to positively impact people's lives, to improve local economies and that of the nation's, its global competitiveness at large as well. Results from the Program for International Student Assessment (nced.ed.gov) on collaborative problem-solving skills of 15-year-olds indicated a U.S. average score of 520 which was higher than the Organization for Economic Cooperation and Development (OECD) average of 500 with average scores ranging from 382 in Tunisia to 561 in Singapore. Students in the U.S. had lower average scores than students from Singapore, Japan, Hong Kong, Korea, Canada, Estonia, Finland, Macau, New Zealand, Australia, Chinese Taipei, and Germany. Among the 35 members of OECD, U.S. 15-year-olds ranked 30th in math and 19th in science (Pew Research Center, 2017). Building an environment that helps tackle the M in STEM, which, for that matter, could easily stand for both Mathematics and Mindset, by constructing personalized pathways for students to help alleviate math fear and math anxiety and build math proficiency is ideal for students with diverse math backgrounds.

Training the Next Generation of Teachers

Given that the Sanford College of Education (SCOE) at National University offers over fifty certificates, credentials, and degree programs ranging from education administration to teacher education, school counseling and psychology and has recommended more candidates for teaching credentials in California than any other Institution in California, SCOE, using the Precision Learning platform, is poised to drive innovation and train the next generation teachers in the classroom.

The same motivational theory applies to faculty who embrace a growth mindset and aren't afraid to fail forward while imagining the possibilities of experimenting with a new tool (Yeager et al., 2019) without fear of failure or fear of lowering their evaluations or student satisfaction. Sally Hoskins, a retired college biology professor, wrote in a recent article in Science Magazine (Hoskins, 2019), that she will miss the creativity of teaching and highlighted how she helped her students tap into their own creativity and imagination and how she helped them think critically and deeply about relevant research processes (Hoskins, 2019). Faculty are lifelong learners too and tapping into their curious and creative selves to improve their craft is a win-win for themselves and their students alike.

The Precision Institute is training a next generation of teachers to use this innovative engineered platform for learning and motivation, to educate and train at a competency and mastery level on teaching methods, pedagogy, and practices. Students navigate through an innovative environment and witness firsthand the value of precision education; the system matches diverse resources to diverse states of intellectual readiness and mind. Through engagement in this content, these future teachers have begun to reflect on their own learning journey, mindset, emotions, values, and attributional errors. It is the belief that these students as future teachers will be poised to deploy a growth and innovative mindset in their future classrooms, thus, inspiring the next generation of STEM students and leaders.

Additionally, math literacy, i.e., thinking procedurally and conceptually in math, is an essential skill for students wishing to embark on undergraduate research particularly in the STEM fields. Strong evidence points out to the importance of mathematics as a gateway course that will afford students entry to higher order thinking and undergraduate research to create new knowledge, the epitome of the Bloom's taxonomy pyramid. The return on this kind of investment in frontloading math skills is crucial in enhancing the role of undergraduate research which in turn is decidedly influential in college degree completion and preparation of a highly skilled STEM workforce (Altman et al., 2019). Creative minds researching the new frontiers of how the human brain learns, paves the way to discovering the neuroscience pathways in neurogenesis by applying an interdisciplinary approach to their investigation - be it focusing on the neurogenesis of the posterior hippocampal area in learning and memory or the equally important anterior area for affective behavior (Fenslow & Dong, 2011), or the myriad of mental health issues that campuses face these days.

No one can better describe the impact of such work than a stellar report by the National Academy of Sciences, Engineering, and Mathematics entitled: "Rising Above the Gathering Storm"

We owe our current prosperity, security, and good health to the investments of past generations, and we are obliged to renew those commitments in education, research, and innovation policies to ensure that the American people continue to benefit from the remarkable opportunities provided by the rapid development of the global economy and its not inconsiderable underpinning in science and technology. (National Research Council, 2007, p. 13)

This report represents a true call for action and a noble mission for all involved stakeholders.

CONCLUSION

Embarking on a Precision Education initiative is no easy feat. It requires a grand vision and a growth mindset to push the creative thinking outside the box. One piece of this Ecosystem is National University's experimentation with its general education courses on NuNav. It is boosting math literacy and confidence by personalizing the student-learning journey and providing adaptive pathways to students who hit a roadblock, redirecting them to resources that can better assist them in grasping and comprehending math concepts. On the other hand, it is also fast-tracking successful students capable of grasping complex concepts based on their specific competencies. The hope is that piloting and adopting precision courses across the general education curriculum will improve student engagement and task completion. Not only is this system affordable and able to provide access to inclusive excellence, but it also aligns to core competencies in critical thinking, quantitative reasoning, digital literacy, and writing skills. This is an ongoing process of continuous improvements both at the cognitive and non-cognitive levels. While the regular monitoring of the designed, delivered and received learning objects and item analysis of all the corresponding assessments and student motivation is no easy task, the role of the faculty is key in providing students with a framework for navigation and for higher order thinking. By leveraging innovative technology through personalized learning and navigation, NU is identifying novel educational models to empower faculty to reach proactively to students and impact both completion and student success. Successful transdisciplinary collaboration between pediatricians for K-12, neuroscientists, geneticists, cognitive & behavioral psychologists, and educators can overcome the devastating effects of leaving human talent behind and wasting unfulfilled student potential.

REFERENCES

Altman, J. D., Chiang, T., Hamann, C. S., Makhluf, H., Peterson, V., & Orel, S. E. (2019). Undergraduate Research: A Road Map for Meeting Future National Needs and Competing in a World of Change. Retrieved from www.cur.org

Association of American Colleges & Universities. (2015). Falling Short? College Learning and Career Success. Retrieved from https://www.aacu.org/leap/public-opinion-research/2015-survey-falling-short

Bandura, A. (2006). Guide for constructing self-efficacy scales. In F. Pajares & T. Urdan (Eds.), *Self-efficacy beliefs of adolescents* (pp. 307–337). Charlotte, NC: Information Age Publishing.

Blackwell, L. S., Trzesniewski, K. H., & Dweck, C. S. (2007). Implicit Theories of Intelligence Predict Achievement across an Adolescent Transition: A Longitudinal Study and an Intervention. *Child Development, 78*(1), 246–263. doi:10.1111/j.1467-8624.2007.00995.x PMID:17328703

Brooks, D. (2011). Should Graduate Students Create EPortfolios? Retrieved from https://www.chronicle.com/article/Should-Graduate-Students/129813

Clark, R. E., & Saxberg, B. (2018). Engineering Motivation Using the Belief-Expectancy-Control Framework. *Interdisciplinary Education and Psychology, 2*(1), 1–26. doi:10.31532/InterdiscipEducPsychol.2.1.004

Claro, S., Paunesku, D., & Dweck, C. S. (2016). Growth mindset tempers the effects of poverty on academic achievement. *Proceedings of the National Academy of Sciences of the United States of America, 113*(31), 8664–8668. doi:10.1073/pnas.1608207113 PMID:27432947

Eccles, J. S., & Wigfield, A. (2002). Motivational beliefs, values and goals. *Annual Review of Psychology, 53*(1), 109–132. doi:10.1146/annurev.psych.53.100901.135153 PMID:11752481

Ewell, P. T., & Schneider, C. G. (2013). National Institute for Learning Outcomes Assessment. The Lumina Degree Qualifications Profile (DQP): Implications for Assessment. *Learning Outcome Assessment*. Retrieved from http://www.learningoutcomesassessment.org/documents/EwellDQPop1.pdf

Fenslow, M., & Dong, H. (2011). Are The Dorsal and Ventral Hippocampus functionally distinct structures? *Neuron, 65*(1), 1–25. PMID:20152109

Garrett, R., Legon, R. & Fredericksen, E. E., (2019). CHLOE 3 Behind the Numbers: The Changing Landscape of Online Education 2019. *Quality Matters*. Retrieved from qualitymatters.org/qa-resources/resource-center/articles-resources/CHLOE-3-report-2019

Hoskins, S. G. (2019). Teaching ingenuity. *Science, 364*(6445), 1102. doi:10.1126cience.364.6445.1102 PMID:31197016

Maguire, E. A., Gadian, D. G., Johnsrude, I. S., Good, C. D., Ashburner, J., Frackowiak, R. S. J., & Frith, C. D. (2000). Navigation-related structural change in the hippocampi of taxi drivers. *Proceedings of the National Academy of Sciences of the United States of America, 97*(8), 4398–4403. doi:10.1073/pnas.070039597 PMID:10716738

National Research Council. (2007). Rising Above the Gathering Storm: Energizing and Employing America for a Brighter Economic Future. Committee on Prospering in the Global Economy of the 21st Century: An Agenda for American Science and Technology. Committee on Science, Engineering, and Pub. Retrieved from https://s3.wp.wsu.edu/uploads/sites/618/2015/11/Rising-Above-the-Gathering-Storm.pdf

Pew Research Center. (2017). U.S. students' academic achievement still lags that of their peers in many other countries. Retrieved from https://www.pewresearch.org/fact-tank/2017/02/15/u-s-students-internationally-math-science/

Rosenzweig, E. Q., Hulleman, C. S., Barron, K. E., Kosovich, J. J., Priniski, S. J., & Wigfield, A. (2019). Promises and Pitfalls of Adapting Utility Value Interventions for Online Math Courses. *Journal of Experimental Education, 87*(2), 332–352. doi:10.1080/00220973.2018.1496059

Shroff, R. H., Deneen, C. C., & Ng, E. M. (2011). Analysis of the technology acceptance model in examining students' behavioral intention to use an ePortfolio system. *Australasian Journal of Educational Technology, 27*(4), 600–618. doi:10.14742/ajet.940

Stafford-Brizard, K. B. (2016). Building Blocks for Learning. Retrieved from https://www.turnaroundusa.org/wp-content/uploads/2016/03/Turnaround-for-Children-Building-Blocks-for-Learningx-2.pdf

Sweller, J. (1988). Cognitive load during problem solving: Effects on learning. *Cognitive Science, 12*(2), 257–285. doi:10.120715516709cog1202_4

U.S. Department of Education NCES. (2017). Collaborative Problem-Solving Skills of 15-Year-Olds: Results from PISA 2015. Retrieved from https://nces.ed.gov/pubs2017/2017249.pdf

Yeager, D. S., Hanselman, P., & Dweck, C. S. (2019). A national study reveals where a growth mindset improves achievement. *Nature, 573*(7774), 364–369. doi:10.103841586-019-1466-y

Zhao, C., Deng, W., & Gage, F. H. (2008). Mechanisms and Functional Implications of Adult Neurogenesis. *Cell, 132*(4), 645–660. doi:10.1016/j.cell.2008.01.033 PMID:18295581

KEY TERMS AND DEFINITIONS

Badging: A digital badge is a type of micro credentialing that indicates accomplishment or mastery of a skill. The badge can be displayed, accessed, and verified online. Badges can be associated with a specific skill or competency that is recognized in a particular industry.

Cloud-hosted platforms: The hardware and operating environment of a server in an Internet-based datacenter.

Engineering a Mindset: The intention that mindset, attitudes, or beliefs along with emotional self-efficacy and success can drive an individual to successfully accomplish academic tasks.

ePortfolio: A digital portfolio (one that is hosted on a website) allows the end user to upload artifacts: documents, project examples, resumés, and show evidence of skills connected to workforce competencies.

Fundamental Attribution: According to the field of social psychology, fundamental attribution error, also known as correspondence bias or over attribution effect, is the tendency for people to under-emphasize personal characteristics and ignore situational factors in judging the behavior of others.

Growth Mindset: Coined by researcher Carol Dweck in 2015, growth mindset it the belief that a person's most basic abilities can be developed through dedication and hard work and is not determined by intellect or IQ.

Micro-Competencies: Knowledge, skills, abilities and content specific outcomes divided into small units or micro-measures, typically identified for assessment.

Mindset: A believed set of assumptions, attitudes, and schema.

Precision Education Model or Precision Learning: According to the Precision Institute at National University, Precision Education is organized in the same navigational framework used to create Google Maps. The system uses artificial intelligence to select learning units that have been deconstructed into micro-competencies and are assessed through frequent knowledge checks. These pathways customize and personalize the content "as just in time."

Chapter 10
The Transition of a School Counseling Program:
The Shift From Traditional to Synchronous to Asynchronous Learning

Sladjana Sandy Rakich
National University, USA

Sonia Rodriguez
National University, USA

Ronald Morgan
National University, USA

ABSTRACT

This chapter outlines the evolution of a Master of School Counseling Program from a traditional in-person model to an asynchronous online program with an integrated field experience component. It utilizes a case study approach to how this transition occurred with an overview of the process and strategies used for the program course redesign presented. The primary goal of the redesign efforts was to sustain efficient student instructor engagement in an online setting while training aspiring school counselors for the complex 21st century educational settings. This chapter also includes a brief literature review of best practices, rubrics used for program development, progress monitoring, and program assessment. Additionally, descriptive data that is presented illustrates the perspectives of adjunct faculty and students in regard to teaching effectiveness, student engagement and satisfaction in an asynchronous fast paced online program.

DOI: 10.4018/978-1-7998-1622-5.ch010

INTRODUCTION

Online learning is the fastest growing sector of higher education (Means, Toyama, Murphy, Bakia, & Jones, 2010). To meet growing student demands for web-based instruction, many higher education programs are either redesigning their traditional degree programs to include online coursework or moving certain degree programs entirely online. Emerging principles and practices of effective online instruction rely on various pedagogical best practices documented in the research literature and the experiences of individuals with differing roles in these new learning environments (Bobok & Koc, 2019). Therefore, a body of powerful relevant examples is required to carry this line of research and to illustrate how online teaching and learning can become sustainable in an era of increasing demand for web-based instruction and effective in the era of increasing accountability. This descriptive case study addresses the parameters, principles of design, implementation, and evaluation of an effective Web-based asynchronous instructional setting. This research aims to inform educators in colleges and universities of relevant factors influencing web-based educational quality and to provide strategies for continuous improvement of online teaching and learning.

Asynchronous learning (AL) is not confined to a specific time or place. Consequently, asynchronous learning environments commonly provide all learning materials and tools at the outset of a course for students to access at their convenience. Other common features of asynchronous learning environments are spaces for shared discussion and communication and multimodal learning options (audio lectures, videos and graphics, text notes of lectures) that allow students greater control of the environment through choice of materials in their preferred learning modality (University of Michigan, n.d.).

Transitioning from a traditional face-to-face model of learning to an online format often requires students to accept more responsibility for their learning (Glenn, 2018). Exploring various ways to help both students and instructors "bridge the gap" between traditional and online learning is essential to the success of this venture. Having all the stakeholders invested in this change process is essential to its success.

BACKGROUND

This chapter details how a master's program in counseling transitioned from a traditional learning model to an asynchronous learning model in response to a university-wide asynchronous initiative. The rationale for the initiative is that it would provide students with greater flexibility, increased accessibility, and more choices regarding content, materials, and resources. The asynchronous initiative provided a common design model with general guidelines and parameters, but as part of the pre-design process, the school counseling department reviewed several theoretical frameworks to determine which recommendations and features were essential to the program's learning outcomes. The department reviewed recent research literature on effective online instruction and evaluation, asynchronous learning, precision learning, competency-based instruction, inquiry-based instruction, and learner control to determine the pedagogical approach to the content and web-based instruction.

During the literature review, several questions emerged apposite to a school counseling program: 1) How do students in an asynchronous environment know the instructor is there for them? 2) How can the instructor replicate the sense of a physical presence in an asynchronous learning environment? 3) What role does course structure play in effectively establishing an instructor's presence? (Ekmekei, 2013).

Reviews of research examining learner control in adult web-based instruction produced mixed findings with many confounding variables (Landers & Reddock, 2017). However, a number of studies over the past five years have provided greater insight into the importance of learner-controlled instruction in achieving positive academic outcomes (Landers & Reddock, 2017).

Four of the most significant issues to emerge are: 1) student engagement, 2) student satisfaction, 3) the role of the instructor, and 4) keeping the "human touch" in AL (Glenn, 2018). In reviewing the literature for this chapter, these four areas will be examined more extensively, especially as they pertain to the creation of an AL master's program in school counseling.

STUDENT ENGAGEMENT

In exploring ways to enhance student engagement in asynchronous learning, there were several critical factors. The first was maintaining a student-centered approach. Student-centered learning is associated with overall depth of learning, making it a crucial component of any school counseling program, in any format. In an asynchronous learning environment, students' ability to self-select learning opportunities and construct an interactive learning space is a key component in student engagement (Northey, Bucic, Chylinski, & Govind, 2015). Further, Northey, Bucic, Chylinski, and Govind (2015) found that enabling a strong learning ecosystem, with self-directed learning interactions via asynchronous communication tools and platforms, is a student-centered approach that shifts "the locus of responsibility for learning from educator to student, as an empowered cocreator." Additionally, they found "that students who participated in both face-to-face on-campus classes and asynchronous online learning opportunities were more engaged than students who only attended face-to-face classes." Further findings in this study report that active student participation in AL was a contributing factor to a student's final grade being a positive one versus a negative one (Northey, Bucic, Chylinski & Govind, 2015).

While asynchronous communication tools provide opportunities for students to engage, interact, and cocreate, AL counseling programs can also enhance student engagement in other ways. In a study by Peterson, Beymer, and Putman, (2018), the researchers cite the importance of cooperative learning in online learning environments and examine the effects of synchronous learning versus asynchronous learning in small-group discussions. Their findings support prior AL research, indicating that asynchronous discussions can interfere with cooperation and student involvement in the learning process if student engagement isn't an essential consideration in the program's design. Peterson, Beymer, and Putman, (2018) further stated that "asynchronous cooperative learning may not work as designed because the presence of cooperative goals did not predict cooperative outcomes." Hence, if AL is going to be effective in cooperative learning, then student engagement must be a key component of the learning process.

STUDENT SATISFACTION

In the area of student satisfaction with AL, several factors, must be considered. These include but are not limited to student interest, participation and overall level of involvement in their courses. As stated by Larbi-Siaw aned Owusu-Agyeman (2017) investigated student satisfaction with AL by utilizing seven key considerations. These considerations included: 1) The e-learning environment, 2) Student-content interaction, 3) Student-to-student interaction, 4) Student-to-teacher interaction, 5) Group cohesion, 6) Timely participation and, 7) Knowledge of Internet usage. The study found that all seven of these considerations were essential components for student satisfaction in AL (Larbi-Siaw & Owusu-Agyeman, 2017). And while the students who participated in this study were not in a counseling program the findings can nonetheless be applied to students across a plethora of educational programs.

Students also express satisfaction about the AL process more often when they participate in a cohort. According to Dziuban, Moskal, Brophy, and Shea (2007), there are four underlying factors related to student satisfaction with online learning, which are: 1) Student-faculty interaction, 2) Active learning, 3) Time on task, and 4) Cooperation among students. When students are part of a cohort, they are more likely to have some if not all of these factors. Additionally, student satisfaction tends to increase when they are part of a strong learning community that is embedded in a "social presence construct" (Dziuban, Moskal, Brophy, & Shea, 2007). This supports the notion that student satisfaction often comes from them valuing interaction and welcoming opportunities that will help them communication more with their fellow students as well as the instructor. Thus, ensuring student satisfaction is an important component of AL just as it is in the traditional face-to-face counseling programs.

ROLE OF THE INSTRUCTOR

The role of the instructor is a key component for any learning environment and AL is no exception. A study by Gomez-Rey, Barbera, and Fernandez-Navarro (2017) explored which instructional roles are important in the 21st century to students who were specifically in AL environments. A new role has emerged for instructors who are primarily utilizing AL. This new role essentially involves the instructor in becoming more of a "pedagogue," where they design, manage and effectively ensure that quality instruction is occurring (Gomez-Rey, Barbera, & Fernandez-Navarro, 2017). Further they reported that the managerial role of the online instructor has declined in its importance due to more intuitive and transparent pedagogy emerging.

Additional roles for the online instructor in an AL environment include being available to their students in larger chunks of time. This availability ranges from checking for student emails more often to scheduling phone appointments when students have questions that are difficult to respond to electronically. Ekmekci (2013) explored the following question regarding online learning: "Do students really know that their instructors are there for them?" One of the answers to this question lies in examining course structure and the role it plays in improving "teaching presence." This method of improving teaching presence is most often accomplished by AL instructors, when they utilize case-based and problem-based learning methods (Ekmekci, 2013).

The notion of teaching presence includes social, emotional, and cognitive processes for personal and meaningful learning outcomes. The focus is on course design, facilitation, direct instruction which are a significant in helping students know that their instructors were indeed there for them. Hence one of the main goals for AL instructors should be to consistently work at strengthening their teaching presence.

Human Touch

The human touch component of learning is important across all learning environments and also true with AL. In the virtual setting, the interaction and engagement among instructor, student, and classmates which is viewed as the human touch differs from a brick and mortar setting in the Glenn (2018) reviewed specific methods for bridging AL with traditional brick and mortar learning. The challenge for motivating meaningful student contact in the AL setting is the process of creating a collaborative, engaging, and respectful learning environments. This is especially true in counseling programs where the human factor is an essential part of the training.

The findings showed that, in order for students to effectively learn in an AL environment, they must be willing to accept responsibility for being in a virtual classroom. Similar, to traditional types of courses, students in AL need to be an integral part of the learning process and not place the sole responsibility on the instructor. Key to this shared learning experience is extending the "human touch" to AL, which will then help the instructors better understand the learning preferences of their students (Glenn, 2018). By utilizing the human touch, instructors can more effectively bridge the gap of student involvement that have been a part of traditional courses and those taught in an AL environment. The question then, is how does human touch become a significant part of AL? While Glenn (2018) reiterated that the human factor needs to be part of AL, how can this be accomplished pragmatically? According to Choi (2016), "peer learning" was instrumental in helping online learning be more effective. Other contributing factors to improving human touch in AL learning were learning circles, more video assignments and other interactive tools where all students are part of the learning process.

Method

Case study research is preferred for studying contemporary events (Yin, 2014). Case studies are appropriate to investigate new phenomenon, develop theories, and establish a foundation for future research studies. In this case study, full-time faculty examine the process of designing and developing new graduate level courses in school counseling for an asynchronous learning environment. Additional perception data was obtained through an online survey of adjunct program faculty and student end of course feedback. The following research questions were used to guide this study:

1. What was the overall impetus in the decision to shift from a traditional learning model to an asynchronous format?
2. What factors affecting the quality of online instruction and course outcomes were considered?
3. How were these factors then incorporated into the course design and overall evaluation process?
4. What lessons can be garnered from this case study that may be useful to other online design or redesign efforts?
5. What recommendations arose from this process and can be utilized for continuous improvement?

ASYNCHRONOUS INITIATIVE OBJECTIVES
AND DEVELOPMENT MODEL

During the 2017-18 school year, our university launched a new initiative to convert our online courses from a synchronous learning format to an asynchronous learning format. This new initiative established the following operational definition to guide departments with the redesign process.

1. Students are not required to log in to the class at a specific time to access required course materials.
2. Students are not required to participate in live sessions. To maintain student engagement, optional live learning activities should be incorporated in the course content, such as review sessions in chats, discussion, and collaborative session. Equivalent learning activities are provided for students who cannot attend or participate.
3. Students are given at least 24 hours from when the assignment is made available to them to complete any required assignment.

The university acknowledged that implementing the asynchronous initiative would be a significant undertaking and took steps to ensure that all stakeholders were fully invested in the process (Hall & Hord, 2006). To support and manage the change process, the faculty senate and provost formed a joint taskforce to cooperatively govern the asynchronous initiative. The taskforce and the provost agreed on 1) the initiative's objectives, and 2) a common development model with guidelines.

The objectives of the Asynchronous Initiative are to:

1. Guarantee the availability of a course in a program in an asynchronous format for each term to facilitate degree progression and completion;
2. Reduce the number of independent studies with increased availability of courses;
3. Upgrade courses as needed within a program to an internal standard with an externally validated level of quality online content delivery;
4. Ensure each course comply with federal regulations (e.g., ADA and Title IV);
5. Identify and address student services that are salient to the Asynchronous format; and
6. Add a modality of choice to students that will increase geographic scope.

The common development model, which includes research-based best practices, is a set of general guidelines for enhancing the quality of all online courses, not just those in the school counseling program. Its features are presented below.

Course Overview and Introduction

- Course includes Welcome and Getting Started content.
- Contact information for the instructor is easy to find and includes multiple forms of communication.
- Course Instructions provide clear how to get started and where to find various course components.
- Learners are introduced to the purpose and structure of the courses, suggestion
    - introductory video to provide relevance beyond course description, discuss value of course outcome, and program purpose.
- Course syllabus outlining,
    - Learning outcomes, assignments, student expectations, time requirements, required materials, grading policy, teacher-student contact policies, the intended audience, and the content scope and sequence. Etiquette expectations are clearly stated for online discussions, email, and other forms of communication.

Learning Objectives
(aligned to course learning outcomes and program learning outcomes)

- Course objectives are clearly defined, measurable, and aligned to student learning activities and assessments.
- Weekly learning objectives that are easily located.
- Suggest 3 to 5 weekly learning objectives per week.
- Learning objectives written in Operational Language (e.g. Students will be able to…).

Assessment and Measurement

- It is clear how the instructional strategies will enable students to reach course goals and objectives.
    - Activities promote achievement of learning objectives.
    - Assignments/assessments measure the stated learning outcomes and align to the course learning goals and objectives.
    - Assignments and assessments are created to measure the appropriate course rigor.
    - Lecture and other course content contribute to the achievement of the stated course learning outcomes and weekly learning objectives.

- Course includes frequent and appropriate methods to assess students' mastery of content (formative versus summative, graded versus non-graded, direct versus indirect measures for understanding).
- Criteria for the assessment of a graded assignment are clearly articulated (rubrics, exemplary work).
- Discussion Board and assignment rubrics are integrated and linked.

Instructional Materials

- Content is made available and/or chunked into manageable segments as appropriate.
- A variety of delivery media are incorporated into the course.
- Course provides activities that emulate real world applications of the discipline, such as experiential learning, case studies, and problem-based activities as appropriate and aligned to course learning outcomes.
- Students have opportunities to review their performance and assess their own learning throughout the course (pre-tests, automated self-tests, reflective assignments, rough drafts, etc.).
- All course content is available asynchronously, any new or required instructional material is not provided during and optional synchronous session.

Course Activities and Learner Interaction

- Course offers access to a variety of engaging resources to promote student engagement, communication and collaboration, and supports student learning.
- Student-to-student interactions are embedded in the course.
- There are plentiful opportunities for asynchronous interaction such as open-ended discussion questions.
- Students are encouraged to share resources and inject knowledge from diverse sources of information in their course interactions.

Course Technology

- Requisite skills for using technology tools (websites, software, and hardware) are clearly stated and supported with resources
- Frequently used technology tools are easily accessed
- Course includes links to privacy policies for technology tools
- Any technology tools meet accessibility standards
- Course provides clear instruction on technology set-up

- The tools available for use support the learning outcomes and competencies
- Course technologies are up to date and current

Learner Support

- Course provides access to student success resources (technical help, orientation, tutoring).
- Course instructions articulate or link to an explanation of how the institution's academic support and student services and resources can help learners succeed in the course and how leaners can obtain them.
- Each course has the following student support resource links included as a standard:
  - Blackboard Support Portal
  - University Support
  - Library Resources
  - Math and Writing Centers
- Link to standard course syllabus including the institution's policies and services regarding plagiarism, ethics, technology use, diversity, civility, student grievance policy and information on the University Library and Student Accessibility Services. Ensure Syllabus is printable and available to learners.

Accessibility and Usability

- Text content and multimedia are available in an easily accessed format, preferably HTML. All text content is readable by assistive technology, including a PDF or any text contained in an image. When possible, information is displayed in a linear format instead of as a table.
- A text equivalent for every non-text element is provided ("alt" tags, captions, transcripts, etc.).
- The course provides alternative means of access to course materials in formats that meet the needs of diverse learners (audio, video, lecture scripts, etc.).
- Supportive mechanisms allow learners with disabilities to participate fully in the online community.
- Course design facilitates readability and usability (responsive design – responds to user's behavior based on screen size, platform, orientation and accessibility, contrast between text and background is easily viewed, flashing and blinking text are avoided).

The Counseling Program Design Process

After a reviewing the asynchronous literature apposite to the school counseling program and conducting a needs assessment, the faculty met to determine the objectives of redesign process, the vision for the new asynchronous courses, to identify challenges, and create an action plan. The shared vision was to create courses that would leverage current technology to present a flexible, student-centered learning environment that provides all students with the knowledge, skills, and dispositions required to become effective future school counselors.

When designing web-based educational programs special considerations must be given to pedagogy, organization and presentation of content, technology, institutional and ethical issues (Khan, 1997), as well as, individual student needs, and accountability mandates. Additionally, having a high degree of learner control in the web-based learning environment is desired (Landers & Reddock, 2017). Each of these factors were evaluated collaboratively with department faculty members during an initial need's assessment using a rubric.

The creation of the new courses was a collaborative effort with various departments, including the technology team and instructional design department. The transition process included meetings between the academic program director (APD), program faculty, and instructional designers to discuss programmatic expectations. The APD identified a subject matter expert (SME) to serve as content expert for each course. SMEs were typically faculty who had taught a course several times in the past and would be responsible for supporting any other instructors who might teach the new, asynchronous version. The APD also implemented programmatic expectations and other improvements needed for each course. The SMEs developed course content with support from the instructional designer, including the course overview and introduction, learning objectives, assessment and measurement, instructional materials, resources, and content, and course activities centered around learner interaction. The technical team was responsible for developing interactive student-centered course design and supporting faculty with creating engaging and what the authors see as "revolutionary" on-line course content, while the instructional designer determined the best manner to deploy that content in the course with final approval from the academic program director.

Backwards design was used to tackle the development of course content and structure by using the Exemplary Course Program Rubric as a guide (Blackboard Inc., 2017). Key principles for quality instructional structure, delivery, and content were derived and used to create a course evaluation rubric with 8 general standards for quality delivery of online instruction that align with 8 areas in the common development model.

BEST PRACTICES IN THE COUNSELING PROGRAM

The faculty of the master's in science in educational counseling program are committed to training candidates to provide best practices counseling services in educational settings. The curriculum provides foundational knowledge and experience in the areas of human development and learning, contemporary and multicultural issues, comprehensive guidance programs, individual and group counseling, leadership and consultation, academic and career guidance programs, psycho-educational assessment, legal and ethical issues, and action research.

Clinical experiences including practicum are embedded in the program. These is a central component to training school counseling candidates and allowing the student to apply acquired knowledge and professional skills in field-based settings. Each asynchronous course has an embedded assignment where students conduct monthly practicum (observational) hours. These practicum hours are mandated by the State credential agency for accreditation purposes. Students in the Educational Counseling program shadow current school counselors throughout their 16 months in the program and gain insight on the varying roles and expectations of school counselors. These practicum hours are conducted at a PK-12 school setting and the end of the year review data reveals that this type of engagement has overall benefits for student success

The mission of the program is to prepare aspiring school counselors for effective and satisfying careers as professional and ethical counselors working with individuals, families, and other groups in educational settings. It places an emphasis on the counselor's role as a leader and advocate for positive transformation to improve student achievement.

Instructional Shifts for Asynchronous Learning

The asynchronous task force determined that each Academic Program Director would have autonomy in determining whether their programs or courses would be taught synchronously or asynchronously. The designing of asynchronous learning for the counseling program was influenced by the arrival of three new faculty over three years, and with the recruitment of a new academic program director to be part of the initial plan for this innovative transition. Their commitment to this transition to asynchronous learning was instrumental in assuring it occurred, not only in a timely manner but with a high degree of quality for best instructional practices and ensuring effective student learning outcomes.

The course design allows individual instructors to host optional, ungraded synchronous sessions for office hours, for discussion and review of course material, and for many other purposes. However, synchronous sessions are not the primary source of material essential for student success in each course. Subject to APD approval, individual instructors are free to bring their own content and pedagogical expertise to a course. Nonetheless, a course designated as "asynchronous" must be taught asynchronously.

Instructor Satisfaction

The data from instructor surveys revealed that their perceptions of effective instructional delivery, did not differ from synchronous to asynchronous learning, however the APD reported that it took some training and planning to ensure the shift infused collegial learning for a more effective change process for all members of the program (Hall & Hord, 2006).

Question 1 in the instructor survey asked instructors to describe how their teaching shifted or changed for online/asynchronous courses (compared to hybrid or synchronous)? The major theme that emerged from this question was the emphasis on communication with students. While communication with students has always been an important consideration for instructional effectiveness and course design, in an asynchronous course, the instructor has to be very intentional with all communication with students. They must ensure that they are providing clear and consistent communication throughout the course. One instructor wrote: "I increased my communication with online courses through course announcements, Blackboard Collaborate sessions, and one-on-one office hour Zoom meetings."

Another instructor noted: "I also make sure that I am clear with my expectations in writing, so that information presented throughout the course experience (within each week, within the course outline/syllabus, and within Collaborate) all match up."

In addition to providing clear and consistent communication about course expectations, assignments, and content, intentional communication with students to foster student engagement was another theme instructor highlighted. One instructor stated: "I feel more of a need to make a presence within the discussion board. While some students may choose to attend the Collaborate sessions, others may not, so I want to be very specific about having interactions with every student."

Another instructor shared similar sentiments stating: "I facilitated weekly sessions, quick turn around on grading, virtual office, discussion board conversation, and other components that create a positive, innovative, effective learning environment."

The importance of meeting with and engaging students through weekly, live Collaborate sessions was discussed by all the instructors. While, in an asynchronous course these live meetings are not required, many students are choosing to attend these meeting versus the option of an alternative learning assignment or viewing the recording of the meeting at a later time. All instructors stated that conducting online live collaborative meetings through Blackboard was a key component in their instructional design and practices. One change in teaching behaviors with collaborative sessions was noted by an instructor in the following statement:

I am more aware of providing material in such a way a student that cannot attend our chat sessions, will still be able to get the gist of what was covered with students that do attend each session. Interesting enough there are very few students that do not attend the live sessions. Of those that cannot, the alternative assignments plus communication with their classmates helps keep them informed. Thus, my assignments, lectures, attachments, announcements are consistently to all in an organized manner. (Counseling Instructor, 2018)

Instructors Identified Best Practices for Online Teaching

Question 2 of the instructor survey asked instructors to provide examples of best practices and recommendations that foster effective teaching and learning. Similar to the responses from question 1, themes of communication and student engagement were prominent. The following list of instructional best practices for online courses was extrapolated from the responses to Question 2:

- Grade promptly and provide student feedback.
- Provide a "course overview" outlining assignments and due dates in a welcome email prior to the start of the course.
- Ensure all live sessions are recorded so that students can review the meeting at any time.
- Respond to emails and student questions promptly.
- Provide two options (neither obligatory) for a weekly live session.
- Provide tech-related job aides.
- Be flexible regarding due dates but still hold them accountable.
- Send out welcome email prior to the start of a course.
- Provide virtual office hours in addition to blackboard collaborate sessions (i.e. one-on-one Zoom or Collaborate meetings)
- Be accessible and provide constant communication via emails, virtual announcements, and phone calls.
- Be student-centered and passionate about student achievement.
- Engage students in group work and discussion board responses.
- Provide individualized instruction or interaction in writing via email or posted discussions/chats.
- Remind students regularly in multiple ways (email, course announcements, Collaborate sessions, and listings in the course outline) about assignments, due dates, chat sessions, etc.

- Audio record weekly announcements in addition to the written post for auditory learners.
- Provide real work samples/examples that tie into the lessons and assignments.
- Create interactive activities and discussions (such as www.kahoot.com, "what would you do" scenarios, weekly highlights, etc.).
- Create open Collaborate sessions for groups to utilize throughout the course (without an end date or time). That way, if a group wants to get a head start on an assignment, it is available for them without having to wait on me to set up a session.
- Ensure students demonstrate learning and application of course content through video tape demonstrations.

IMPORTANT CONSIDERATIONS FOR EFFECTIVE ASYNCHRONOUS TEACHING AND LEARNING

According to Glenn (2018), instructors teaching in an asynchronous online course should consider student engagement, student satisfaction, the role of the instructor, and personalized interactions (i.e. "keeping the human touch"). Question 3 asked instructors to reflect on these areas and describe how they address each factor.

Human Touch

With the limitation of physical interaction in an on-line setting, creating a collaborative and engaging environment and motivating students to accept responsibility of their own learning requires some innovative reflection from the instructor One instructor listed the following actions and activities that students indicated was helpful to provide the "human touch."

- "I offer the opportunity for students to shadow me at my school site (I have had around 20 students take up my offer!"
- "I have created field trips for local students to accompany me to places like Cal State San Marcos Career Center, Casa De Amparo, Mission Hills High School, Community meetings at the District Office, etc."
- "I offer internship placement assistance (at my site and at my colleagues' sites; I have had 3 NU interns!"
- "I have allowed my students to create questions for my interns to answer through Google Drive."

- "I have done mock interviews with students applying and interviewing for internships and entry level counseling jobs. (I have served on interview panels for SMUSD.)"
- "I share additional resources they may use for the University or outside of school (Praxis tips from interns, career resources like resume and cover letter samples, etc.)"

Student Engagement in the Asynchronous Learning

Our annual program review and conclusions from student responses indicates student satisfaction with student-to-student engagement remains high.

Student Question 1. Describe your learning experience with the Blackboard Collaborate session or the Learning Activity. Reflect on what you learned.

Getting to know my classmates and Professor...will provide a stronger base for our cohort, than had we not been able to meet face to face despite distance. I got a clearer view of what the course and program will be and expect of me, making me feel much more secure in the asynchronous environment. One of my biggest fears coming into this course was not interpreting expectations correctly. My previous experiences with online courses made me feel that each time I sent an email to a classmate or professor, I was a bother.

I'm glad that even though this course is all online, we get to be able to get into groups and collaborate with other students. Exchanging different ideas and collaborating will only help us become better advocates to students.

This being my first online class I was a little nervous and expected some hiccups. Of course, there were some difficulties finding where I needed to long in and figuring out the camera but after that I really enjoyed all of our discussions... It was nice to get some questions answered and some ideas affirmed. The last weeks' class was very helpful for reviewing and relieving some of the anxiety of the final week.

I am extremely grateful that I attended the collaborative session this week for many reasons, but the main takeaways I felt were a tremendous sense of relief and company. Having taken courses online before (through a different university), I never interacted with my classmates or professor beyond discussion posts and grade feedback. I was glad that I wasn't alone in confusion on several items, as I saw classmates pose the exact questions I faced! I had pre-written several questions down before the session, and found myself scratching many off as we went and others asked. (I also think the virtual office is a really fantastic resource, as it can function the way the session did, 24/7.)

I really like the fact that our instructor takes the time to know us, even though it's over the video, it provides some kind of normalcy and gives me a sense of who my fellow classmates are. It is paced very appropriately so it fits into my busy life -work, motherhood etc..... I learn different perspectives through chat and discussion board is very new and helpful at the same time. I always look forward to reading replies and look forward to responding like we would if we were in a real classroom.

I was not able to be part of the collaborative activity this week. I had a doctor's appointment. I did get a chance to complete the learning activity. It was a great activity. It shows the type of problems one will faced as a counselor. I learned that becoming a school counselor comes with a great deal of training.

Findings

Student enrollment was impacted with the evolution from brick and mortar, hybrid, synchronous to the final launching of an asynchronous learning program. There were notable increases in student enrollment with significant changes in student demographics over a 7-year span; see figure 1 and 2.

Figure 1.

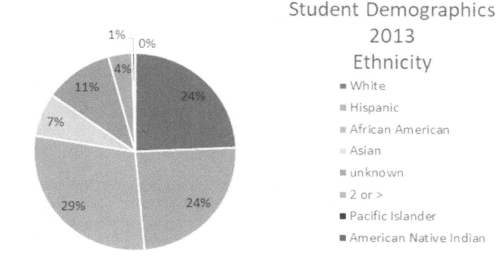

Figure 2.

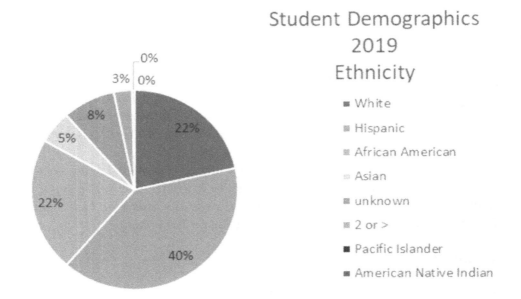

Student Demographics 2019 Ethnicity

- White
- Hispanic
- African American
- Asian
- unknown
- 2 or >
- Pacific Islander
- American Native Indian

Additional findings demonstrated how the changing role of the instructor is essential in this transition to an online learning platform. If instructors do not change their beliefs, thoughts and even possible biases on how online learning can be an effective modality, then chances for its overall success are diminished.

SOLUTIONS AND RECOMMENDATIONS

The central commitment for the asynchronous model is the ability to offer an online format that allows for flexible accessibility and a variety of creative and innovative course material and resources for student choice. The format ensures student progression and completion, by increasing the availability of courses, with a quality online delivery model, and ensures that each course complies with federal regulations and increases geographic scope, so students can attend at any place, any time, and any term.

Students remain engaged in this setting. The use of videos, live chat sessions, virtual chat sessions, discussion posts proved to be an effective strategy for enhancing student learning particularly in the asynchronous courses. Since several of the following themes emerged from a review of the literature on asynchronous learning, they are reviewed in detail as they relate to this specific case study.

ROLE OF INSTRUCTOR

Ekmekci (2013) posited that "teaching presence" is emerging as a key role of an instructor in an asynchronous learning environment. Similarly, all adjunct faculty surveyed echoed the importance of ongoing clear and effective communication to ensure students feel that teaching presence. Instructors shared strategies to ensure they engage with each student at multiple points throughout the course, such as a personal response to each student's introduction, individual feedback in threaded discussions, frequent posting of course announcements with reminders/hints/ resources, and detailed feedback on assignments. However, teaching presence should include more than visibility and communication; it also incorporates effective pedagogy for online instruction. Students in this school counseling program complete practicum observations with corresponding culminating assignments that are tailored to course learning outcomes. This project provides instructors the opportunity to mentor students and share their knowledge, skill, and experience. Creating these structured learning and growth opportunities where the instructor can be a mentor, coach, and facilitator is an important role that each instructor must actively embrace.

STUDENT SATISFACTION

As previously mentioned, student satisfaction was one of the major topics that emerged from a review of the literature on asynchronous learning. Since measuring student satisfaction, especially with online courses, can be difficult, it's helpful to use some type of structured approach to improve efficacy. There are many structured approaches available to help gauge student satisfaction but most include such areas as: 1) The frequency and depth of instructor/student interaction; 2) The strength of the overall learning community; 3) Effective communication between the student and instructor; and 4) How engaged the student is with the instructor in active learning.

The following comments were given by NU Instructors regarding student satisfaction.

Comment 1: "I do review the course evaluations and collaborate with other NU adjunct instructors to ensure I continue to grow and improve."
Comment 2: "Students who have finished the program or no longer are my students still reach out to me for guidance and navigating the job market."

FUTURE RESEARCH DIRECTIONS

Future research regarding asynchronous learning could involve both the overall role of the instructor in this online learning modality and how that role differs from traditional face to face learning. By focusing more in-depth research on the instructor's role could possibly help further explain such labels as "facilitator," "manager," and "pedagogue," that are often given to online instructors. Further research might help prove or disprove these labels, as well as provide more insight into how the instructor's role in online learning is similar or dissimilar to traditional face to face learning.

CONCLUSION

The case study in this chapter on transitioning a master's degree program in counseling to asynchronous learning illustrates several important findings. First, strategic planning at both the university and department level worked well to facilitate a smooth transition to asynchronous courses for the counseling program. As part of this strategic planning process, rubrics and resources were identified and then allocated to assist with course development. While adjunct instructors and students were asked to provide feedback after the asynchronous courses were launched, their feedback could have been utilized to strengthen the strategic plan, had they been included in the initial planning process.

Additionally, findings from the faculty survey, showed that while most instructors modified their instructional practices somewhat, continued professional development would be beneficial to support continuous learning of instructional best practices for an asynchronous environment. Many of the instructors surveyed, reported the importance of continuous communication with students as an important shift in their practices. However, it isn't entirely clear how instructors facilitate student learning aside from feedback on course assignments. Future training on how to interact more effectively with the content, in order to foster increased student engagement, emerged as a theme that would help instructors as they transition from traditional face to face learning to asynchronous learning. This case study provided findings that reinforced the importance of all stakeholders being part of the transition from the initial discussions to implementation of the changes.

REFERENCES

Bobok, M., & Koc, S. (Eds.). (2019). Student-centered virtual learning environments in higher education. Hershey, PA: IGI Global. doi:10.4018/978-1-5225-5769-2

Choi, B. (2016). How People Learn in an Asynchronous Online Environment: The Relationship between Graduate Students' Learning Strategies and Learning Satisfaction. *Canadian Journal of Learning and Technology, 42*(1).

Dziuban, C. Moskal, P., Brophy, J., & Shea, P. (2007). Student Satisfaction with Asynchronous Learning. *Journal of Asynchronous Networks, 11*(1).

Ekmekci, O. (2013). Being There: Establishing Instructor Presence in an Online Learning Environment. *Higher Education Studies, 3*(1).

Glenn, C. (2018). Adding Human Touch to Asynchronous Online Learning. *Journal of College Student Retention: Theory & Practice, 19*(4).

Gomez-Rey, P., Barbera, E., & Fernandez-Navarro, F. (2017). Student Voices on the Roles of Instructors in Asynchronous Learning Environments in the 21st Century. *International Review of Research in Open and Distributed Learning, 18*(2).

Hall, G. E., & Hord, S. M. (2006). *Implementing Change, Patterns, Principles, and Potholes.* Pearson Publishing Inc.

Khan, B. H. (1997). *Web-based instruction.* Englewood Cliffs, NJ: Educational Technology Publications Inc.

Landers, R. N., & Reddock, C. M. (2017). A meta-analytic investigation of objective learner control in web-based instruction. *Journal of Business and Psychology, 32*(4), 455–478. doi:10.100710869-016-9452-y

Larbi-Siaw, O. & Owusu-Agyeman, Y. (2017). Miscellany of Students' Satisfaction in an Asynchronous Learning Environment. *Journal of Educational Technology Systems, 45*(4).

Means, B., Toyama, Y., Murphy, R., Bakia, M., & Jones, K. (2009). *Evaluation of evidence-based practices in online learning: A meta-analysis and review of online learning studies.* US Department of Education.

Northey, G., Bucic, T., Chylinski, M., & Govind, R. (2015). Increasing Student Engagement Using Asynchronous Learning. *Journal of Marketing Education, 37*(3).

Peterson, A., Beymer, P., & Putman, R. (2018). Synchronous and Asynchronous Discussions: Effects on Cooperation, Belonging, and Affect. *Paper presented at the annual meeting of the American Educational Research Association.* Academic Press. 10.24059/olj.v22i4.1517

University of Michigan. (n.d.). Asynchronous Learning. Retrieved from http://umich.edu/~elements/asyLearn/learning.htm

Yin, R. K. (2014). *Case study research: Design and methods.* Thousand Oaks, CA: Sage Publishing.

Chapter 11

A Study on the Effectiveness of College English Blended Learning Under MOOCs Philosophy in China

Zhaohui Dai

https://orcid.org/0000-0002-0161-2530

Shanghai University, China & University of Wisconsin, Madison, USA

ABSTRACT

This study investigated the effectiveness of college English blended education under a MOOCs philosophy in China. The findings suggest that many features of MOOCs philosophy are evident in college English blended education and eight factors influence effectiveness. Relationships of the influencing factors demonstrate that interactions and evaluations are highly influencing factors in autonomous learning and motivations exert high influences on autonomous learning. However, students have low motivation in interaction and evaluation, for they are more extrinsically than intrinsically motivated. And also, collaborative learning is the least influencing factor in the study. To motivate the students, great emphasis should be laid on interactions and evaluation in student's autonomous learning. Moreover, students' negative attitude towards autonomous learning hampers their adaptability to college English blended learning, and, as attitude and motivation are highly related, this deserves equal attention.

DOI: 10.4018/978-1-7998-1622-5.ch011

INTRODUCTION

China's rapid economic development and increasing trades with the world, particularly the recent implementation of "The Belt and Road Initiative" policy, has made English learning unprecedentedly important in the country. The Chinese government has made it clear in the newly-launched the *"Medium and long-term National Education Reforms and Development Plan (2010-2020)"* that promoting educational reform and equality has become core tasks in English education and that great efforts should be made to the effective cohesion of information technology into curriculum in higher education.

College English is a compulsory course for non-English majors in China, undergraduate and graduate. Its objective is to foster students' English language competence in an all-round way. It also aims to provide them with effective means for communications and lifelong learning strategies so that they can learn independently, collaboratively and creatively to continuously cultivate themselves key competencies for the 21st century even after graduation.

In the year 2004 and 2007, the national Ministry of Education issued *"College English Curriculum Requirements"* ("Requirements" hereafter), a guideline for English education, particularly for non-English majors. And in the year 2015, with the assistance of a pool of top educational experts nationwide, the national Ministry of Education issued another *"Guidelines for College English Education"* ("Guidelines" hereafter). It encourages deeper innovations in college English education, in particular, the adoption of blended learning and further application of Micro lecture and Massive Open Online Courses (MOOC hereafter). Ever since the Requirements was issued in 2004, great changes in college English education have been made in curriculum design, teaching models, evaluation and teacher development (Zhao et al., 2014; Xu, 2015).

However, innovations of college English education in China is by no means easy. It meets with challenges, and the learning environment is perhaps the biggest one. It is generally accepted that English is a foreign language instead of a second language in China. Compared with their counterparts in L2 countries, such as Canada and Singapore, Chinese college English learners have comparatively limited language input outside the classroom. Surprisingly, a lot of key universities in China have been deducting the course credits of college English, mainly because, as surveys show, students are becoming increasingly discontented with what they have learned from the course (Cai, 2011; Wang, 2009; Fen, 2010; He et al., 2012). And the rise of MOOCs constitutes another challenge for college English education. By giving college English learners brand new online and offline blended learning experiences and interactions with peers and instructors in virtual learning communities, as well as giving them access to high quality learning resources from prestigious universities,

MOOCs has paved a new way for language learning and pressed for re-innovation and further cohesion of information technology into the curriculum.

The educational effectiveness and improvement research develop rapidly in recent decades. It has three research areas, and the school effectiveness research centers upon describing factors that affect the learning outcomes of the students (Chapman et al., 2015). Different kinds of e-learning as MOOCs, crowdsourcing and social networks have made it necessary the identification and isolation of critical factors for educational effectiveness. College English blended learning, with combination of both online and offline education, seeks to improve the educational effectiveness and tackles the challenges facing e-learning effectiveness, i.e. students' motivation, sense of isolation and impersonal (Montebello, 2018).

This paper aims to shed lights on the effectiveness of college English blended learning under MOOCs philosophy through empirical study.

BACKGROUND

College English blended learning in China

The requirements issued in 2004 and 2007 by National Education Ministry signifies the nationwide implementation of college English blended learning in China. A new model comprising online, and traditional classroom learning was widely adopted, and has gained recognition from both instructors and students (Jiang & Ma, 2013).

Definitions of blended learning still vary, with the emphasis on the combination of online and face-to-face (F2F for short) instruction (Graham & Bonk, 2006; Rovai & Jordan, 2004), replacement of F2F with the online instruction (Picciano, 2009) and the quality of blended learning (Garrison & Kanuka, 2004; Bliuc, Goodyear & Ellis, 2007; Singh & Reed, 2001). These definitions clearly manifest itself that blended learning requires careful curriculum design instead of the mere mixture of online and offline components. Researchers in China, however, lay much emphasis on its functions and outcomes. They argue that blended learning is the combination of F2F and online learning to improve learning efficiency while deducting the labor costs (Li, 2004). It brings into full play the advantages of both e-learning and traditional classroom learning, which are believed to be complementary (He, 2005). Thus, the linchpin of blended learning is, so to speak, to yield better outcome than the traditional way of learning.

However, problems still have been widely rehearsed. To begin with, information technology has been underused or abused, generating useless information to distract student's attention in blended learning. And secondly, functions of learning management systems (LMS for short) needs improving. For instance, quite a few online learning resources are the digital copies of the paper textbooks with little interactive function (Cha & Wu, 2010), forcing students' preference to the traditional textbooks. Moreover, online learning data are not open to language tutors and most management functions are absent, either because of the design of LMS or of their instructors, who disregard the supreme importance of online learning (Wang, 2012). In this way, students' motivations may gradually die out, and they may even go to extreme as to reject college English blended learning. Besides, the effective ratio of online and offline components in blended learning is still unsettled. It is changeable and makes blended learning seemingly dubious.

Such problems arise from various reasons. The most prominent setback is the unclear goal setting of the curriculum. Su (2013) argues that college English education is at the crossroads, quite at a loss of what to do and where to go next. Cai (2010) put the blame on Chinese examination-oriented educational system, which fosters students who can get high scores in exams but are low in competence. Others (Zhang, 2014) believe the low effectiveness of college English education should find its way to the belief that looks upon English as only a tool for communication and cultivate the students as such.

Another possible reason goes to the ways of instruction in English classes. Most students in China are prone to take passively what they are taught from their instructors rather than to learn independently and think critically, due to years of practices before tertiary education. And likewise instructors are not competent in course design and look upon imparting knowledge from the textbooks as most important activity in the classroom (Wang, et al. 2012; Zhou, & Zhu, 2016). All these hinder the innovation and improvement of college English education.

In order to overcome these setbacks and to improve the effectiveness of college English education, scholars in China have done a lot of research so far. Some study into the components of effective classroom teaching (Zhu, 2013; Wang, 2014), some design the measurement scale for the effectiveness of classroom education (Ren, 2013), while others probe into the possibilities of adopting information technology to improve the effectiveness of English education (An, 2004).

However, current studies focus a lot on the effectiveness of classroom instruction rather than blended learning as a whole.

MOOCs and bMOOC/hMOOC

The term MOOC was first coined in 2008 by Dave Cormier of the University of Prince Edward Island in response to a course called Connectivism and Connective Knowledge (also known as CCK08). CCK08 was led by George Siemens of Athabasca University and Stephen Downes of the National Research Council. As MOOCs evolved, there appeared to be two distinct types: those that emphasized the connectivist philosophy, and those that resembled more traditional courses. To distinguish the two, Stephen Downes proposed the terms "cMOOC" and "xMOOC", in which the 'C' stands for 'connectivist', while the 'x' stands for extended (as in TEDx, edX) and represents that the MOOC is designed to be additional to university courses. Different from cMOOCs, which are based on principles from connectivist pedagogy, indicating that materials should be aggregated, remixable, re-purposable, and feeding forward (Kop, 2011) and instructional design approaches attempt to connect learners collaboratively on joint projects, xMOOCs have a much more traditional course structure typically with a clearly specified syllabus of recorded lectures and self-test problems. With dynamic evolution of MOOCs, different postMOOCs concepts constantly appear, such as sMOOCs and tMOOCs, in which the initial "s" stands for social and seamless while "t" stands for transfer (Osuna-Acedo, et al., 2018).

However, MOOCs also have major concerns related to attrition rates and course dropouts. Some scholars even point out that MOOCs lack effective means to motivate the students and make them actively involved in online learning community, which is somewhat impersonal compared with F2F communications (Tan, 2013).

MOOCs has evolved from the open Educational Resource Movement (OER movement for short), and it endows with important philosophical features. MOOCs provide numerous high-quality education resources with characteristics of collaboration, sharing and big data. Hybrid MOOC (hMOOC for short) or blended MOOC (bMOOC for short) mixes MOOCs with traditional F2F learning, comprising both features of xMOOC and cMOOC, i.e. not only structured knowledge imparting but also non-structured network and social learning, as well as the benefits of traditional personal F2F interactions with instructors and peers. hMOOC or bMOOC is regarded as the milestone and signified the comprehensive cohesion of traditional learning with information technology. It is entitled MOOC 3.0 and is widely accepted as the most effective forms of MOOCs (Sandeen, 2013).

Scholars have conducted research into the effectiveness of blended learning with MOOCs. Hung (2018) studies the flipped mathematics classroom in 7th- and 8th-grade Taiwanese junior high school students, integrated with MOOCs and game-based learning. Tan (2013) studies MOOCs game, and Zhang & Ma (2015) has researched the blended education of modern educational technology courses.

It is believed that college English blended learning under MOOCs philosophy will become much more effective than the mere blended or MOOCs components in English learning. However, still little has been done for the effectiveness of college English blended learning under MOOCs philosophy, especially its influencing factors and how they influence the educational effectiveness.

MAIN FOCUS OF THE CHAPTER

This study aims to explore the effectiveness of college English blended learning under MOOCs philosophy, including its influencing factors and their relationships in how they influence the educational effectiveness. In this study, the research questions are as follows:

1. What is the status quo of college English blended learning under MOOCs philosophy? Is it effective?
2. What are the factors that affect the effectiveness of college English blended learning under MOOCs philosophy?
3. How do these factors affect the effectiveness of college English blended learning under MOOCs philosophy?
4. In what ways can these factors facilitate the effectiveness of college English blended learning under MOOCs philosophy?

Research Methodology

This study will be mostly mixed methods research in nature. Creswell (2008) defines four main types of mixed methods design, i.e. embedded design, convergent parallel design, explanatory sequential design and exploratory sequential design. The convergent parallel design simultaneously collects both qualitative and quantitative data, merges them and uses the result to understand the research problem. An explanatory sequential mixed method design first collects the quantitative data and then the qualitative data to help explain or elaborate the quantitative data, while an exploratory sequential mixed method design first collects the qualitative data and then collect quantitative data to explain the relationships found in qualitative data. The embedded design is to have one form of data play a supportive role to the other form of data. In this study, the explanatory sequential mixed method design is adopted with quantitative data being collected first from questionnaire and then quantitative data from open questions and interviews.

Participants

Participants in this study were students from four different colleges and universities nationwide, and they were selected by means of purposive sampling in an effort to get the reliable data. In these colleges and universities, college English blended learning is a common practice. To be more specific, university A is a national key comprehensive university in Beijing and is listed among the first batch of model units for college English educational reform. It has the partnership with world famous

MOOCs as Edx and Coursera; university B is a key provincial normal university in the south and is listed among the second batch of model units for college English educational reform. This normal university has built up its own LMS for English education; university C is a national key university of science and engineering in the west and is listed among the third batch of model units for college English educational reform. The university has built up its own MOOCs platform; while university D is a provincial key medical university in the south and has not been listed as a model unit for college English educational reform. LMS provided by textbook publishers is used in this university.

Research Methods

The study was mainly carried out in a two-year study based on the previous pilot study. Specifically, the following methods and techniques were used:

- The objective questions in the questionnaire were employed to collect quantitative data.
- The open questions in the questionnaire and in-depth semi-structured interview were employed to collect qualitative data and to complement quantitative results for augmented interpretations.

Questionnaire

The questionnaire in this study has only students' version. All the questionnaires begin from the respondents' demographic information and end with open questions. It collects students' responses about belief, attitudes, motivation, learning behaviors, learning environment and engagement.

After finishing the draft of the questionnaire, self-evaluation was employed to look into the content validity and overall evaluation of each part, particularly the correctness of the title, the indent of each line and font sizes as well as the spelling and expression of each item. There were originally sixty items in the draft version. In view of the revision suggestions from college English instructors and experts, explanations of key terms in the questionnaire were added and reverse question items were also designed. A trial test was then followed, collecting forty students' responses. The Cronbach alpha reliability for the questionnaire was 0.853, indicating the high reliability. In consideration of the procedures for the questionnaire design, the questionnaire is believed to have high content validity.

The questionnaire was then sent to these four universities in the year 2015, in which altogether 600 students' responses were collected. In order to sift valid questionnaire, invalid criteria for the questionnaire were set up. Any responses from the questionnaire are invalid if:

- One-third of all the items are unanswered;
- The polygraph test in the questionnaire proves positive (Qin, 2009).
- The same value is assigned to almost all the question items.

As a result, a total of 24 student responses were judged as invalid and were deleted from the questionnaire bank, and the valid responses from students were 524 at the end of the procedure.

Interview

Semi-structured interviews were conducted, together with the open questions in the questionnaire to get a clearer picture of the research variables. The interviews were all carried out face-to-face, and the student interviewees were those that expressed their willingness to be interviewed in the questionnaire.

The interviews began with students' general impressions of the course and then survey deeply into the present problems and future suggestions for the improvement of college English blended learning.

The interviews went on smoothly and were recorded after getting clear consent from the interviewees. The researcher followed the outline of the interview but would continue to ask the interviewees when they brought up topics not included in the outline but apparently valuable to the research. After the interview, transcription was immediately followed to reproduce the interview to its fullest extent.

Preparing Data for Analysis

The quantitative data were put into SPSS 22.0 and went through the following analytic procedures to prepare the data:

Step 1: Using average mean of the column to replace the missing value in that column.
Step 2: Assigning reverse values to the fourteen reverse questions items.
Step 3: Running independent t-test to verify the validity of the questionnaire.
Step 4: Deleting any items with insignificant value of the test.

As a result of these procedures, four items were deleted as they failed to meet the significant value of the test. The qualitative data were then imported into NVivo 12 and case classification attributes were assigned to each interviewee for subsequent case analysis for the data.

Data Analysis Procedures

After the preparation of the data, qualitative and quantitative data were analyzed with the following procedures:

Step 1: Descriptive analysis of each close-ended item in questionnaire.
Step 2: Factor and descriptive analysis and reliability test of quantitative data.
Step 3: SEM modelling of retrieved factors to analyze their relationships.
Step 4: Qualitative text analysis for open-ended questions.

RESULTS AND DISCUSSIONS

Status Quo of College English Blended Learning

The questionnaire demonstrates that students can search for the appropriate learning resources and supplements them into English learning (M=3.9), however, students still rely mostly on the written texts to learn language knowledge instead of multimodality resources, the reasons are probably because of insufficient variety and poor networks infrastructure, draining students' enthusiasm of using the multimedia resources. Students can monitor and improve their learning with the help of information provided by MOOCs platform (M=3.34), which further manifests the MOOCs philosophy of instant feedback. As for the learning community, the first preferential means of communications for the students are F2F interactions, followed by communications via software or apps, while online posting is their least favorite means of communications.

Students agree that their college English language competency has improved as a result of PBL and collaborative learning (M=3.33). However, problems still arise. Some students found the evaluation rubrics of collaborative learning were not fair and reasonable enough. Some failed to learn much from collaborative learning only because they were unfamiliar with each other due to the course selection practice. Moreover, some instructors liked to dominate the class with knowledge imparting, greatly shrinking the time for the students' activities.

Peer assessment was adopted in two of the colleges and universities, but in the other two universities, it was solely instructor's responsibilities to evaluate the performances of the students, because they were unable to collect necessary information online and peer assessing in the conventional ways would be too complex for instructors to handle.

The students don't review the lessons immediately after class unless the examination is right at hand (M=2.89). Further investigations proved that they were heavily burdened with assignments of other courses and some students were either over-confident of their English competence or lack of self-discipline.

In a word, though many features of MOOCs philosophy are evident in college English blended learning, some still needs improving. This includes the variety of learning resources, the improvement for the network infrastructure, effective ubiquitous means of communications out of class, and the changing of educational philosophy among some instructors, etc.

Analysis of Influencing Factors

In order to find the influencing factors, factors analysis is used in this research. The results of KMO & Bartlett test are 0.985 and 15638.528 (p=.000) respectively, signifying that it is very suitable for the factor analysis.

With the use of principle component analysis and Kaiser normalization, eight factors with eigenvalue over one are retrieved, accounting for 58.82% of all the variance. After looking into the questionnaire items that made up each factor, each factor is thus named.

The first factor consists of thirteen items, which involves student's motivation, thus the first factor is named as motivation factor.

The second factor consists of ten items, which center around the questions about the interactions between students and instructors, posting questions in the online forum, peer assessment and review and assessing after class. Thus, it is named as interaction and evaluation factor.

The third factor consists of six items, which center around collaborative learning, completing the group tasks and problem-based learning, etc. Therefore, the third factor is named collaborative learning factor.

The fourth factor has five items, which center around autonomous learning, self-selecting the learning resources, readjusting the learning with the help of the system, and autonomously setup learning plans. Therefore, the fourth factor is named as autonomous learning factor.

The fifth factor has seven items, all items are about learning contents in the classroom, video learning resources, peer help learning environment, etc. Thus, the fifth factor is named as learning resources and environment factor.

The sixth factor has eight items. These items are about instructor's timely feedback in the classroom, instructor's explanation in the classroom, instructor's task setting before the class, instructor-student relations and instructor's information literary and learning competence. Thus, the sixth factor is named as role of instructor factor.

The seventh factor has six items. They are about students' attitudes about the instructor's role, the course and the influence on English learning, etc. Hence, it is named as learning attitude factor.

The last factor has four items, which are about the students' adaptivity on the learning environment, posting questions online, student-centered learning and revision after class, as well as adaptivity on the school learning environment and the traditional classes. Thus, it is named as adaptability factor.

After the naming process, descriptive analysis and reliability test of each factor are conducted. The Cronbach alpha of seven factors exceeds the limit of 0.70, hence, they are all reliable. The possible reason for the factor of learning attitude (0.657) being slightly below the limit is that it is an emotional factor, and, as such, lower reliability value is also acceptable (Qin, 2009).

We notice in the descriptive analysis of the factors that both interaction and evaluation factor and adaptability factor have the lowest mean value among the eight, which are 2.96 and 3.00 respectively. It hypothesizes that the interactions and evaluation is not adequate in the college English blended learning and the students still find it hard to adapt to this new model. Interestingly, results also show that the role of instructor factor has the highest mean value, which means that the role of instructor is still important in this kind of learning.

Relationships of the Influencing Factors

Path analysis is adopted primarily to examine the comparative strength of direct and indirect relationships of variables. AMOS is used in this study to draw path diagram to find the relationships between influencing factors. The following table shows the model fit summary.

Table 1. Model fit summary

Model	NPAR	CMIN	DF	P	CMIN/DF	GFI	AGFI	NFI	RMSEA
Default model	27	20.982	9	0.013	2.331	0.990	0.960	0.947	0.050
Saturated Model	36	.000	0			1		1	
Independence Model	8	395.955	28	0	14.141	0.811	0.757	0	0.159

Table 1 shows that CMIN/DF yields a value of 2.331, which is below the cut-off value of three, while GFI, AGFI, NFI are all above the cut-off value of 0.9. RMSEA is a measure of fit first introduced by Steiger and Lind (1980). In this study, it reaches 0.05, a cut-off value for accepting the model fit, which suggests a close fit of the model in relation to the degrees of freedom. All these show that the model matches the observed data well and therefore the null hypothesis is rejected.

Figure 1. Path diagram of influencing factors

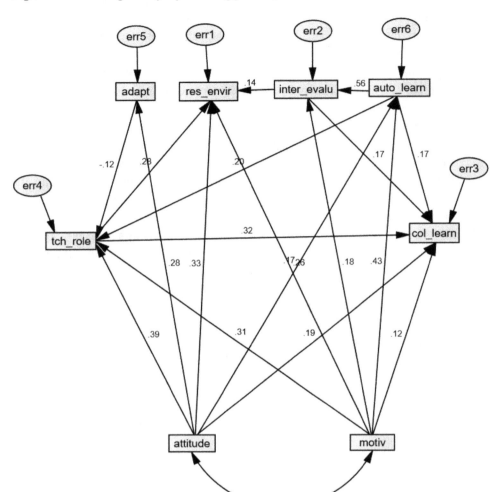

Figure 1 demonstrates that there are two exogenous variables, which are attitude and motive (motivation), and six endogenous variables, i.e. tch_role (instructor's role), adapt (adaptability), inter_evalu (interaction and evaluation), auto_learn (autonomous learning), res_envir (resources and environment), col_learn (collaborative learning). All these eighteen relationships are significant, ranging from sixteen relationship as extremely significant to one relationship as very significant and one relationship as significant.

Table 2. Regression weights: (group number 1 - default model)

			Estimate	S.E.	C.R.	P	Label
adapt	<---	attitude	.360	.055	6.560	***	par_2
auto_learn	<---	attitude	.179	.059	3.056	.002	par_8
auto_learn	<---	motiv	.266	.035	7.683	***	par_19
tch_role	<---	adapt	-.133	.033	-4.000	***	par_1
tch_role	<---	motiv	.272	.040	6.859	***	par_3
tch_role	<---	attitude	.573	.065	8.821	***	par_4
inter_evalu	<---	motiv	.130	.028	4.601	***	par_14
tch_role	<---	auto_learn	.279	.048	5.833	***	par_16
inter_evalu	<---	auto_learn	.649	.046	14.184	***	par_18
res_envir	<---	motiv	.225	.032	7.018	***	par_5
res_envir	<---	attitude	.475	.052	9.089	***	par_6
res_envir	<---	tch_role	.277	.033	8.410	***	par_7
col_learn	<---	motiv	.081	.033	2.446	.014	par_9
col_learn	<---	attitude	.228	.054	4.240	***	par_10
col_learn	<---	tch_role	.257	.034	7.496	***	par_11
col_learn	<---	auto_learn	.187	.045	4.174	***	par_12
col_learn	<---	inter_evalu	.166	.036	4.587	***	par_13
res_envir	<---	inter_evalu	.170	.030	5.617	***	par_17

It can be seen from table 2 that the relationships between autonomous learning to interaction and evaluation has the highest standardized weight (0.559), while relationship between motivation to autonomous learning ranked the second (0.431).

High Influence Between Autonomous Learning with Interaction and Evaluation

Autonomous learning is highly related with interaction and evaluation. Autonomous learning is by no means learning alone, but rather, through strengthening collaborative engagement. Language learning, from constructivist point of view, is getting knowledge generated from experience, which entails collaborative epistemologies (Hafner & Miller, 2011). That is to say, students learn through the interactions with their peers and instructors through questions and problems solving process. And most importantly, students need to constantly self-reflect their autonomous learning and make necessary adjustments, and self-reflections rely heavily on evaluation.

In this sense, the cultivation of autonomous learning competence of the students will lead to the effective implementation of interactions between instructors and peers and evaluation in the learning process. In the blended learning environment, this is even more convenient when taking into account the integration of online to offline learning environment as well as the application of ubiquitous learning devices.

High Influence from Motivation to Learning Autonomy and Other Factors

Besides, learning autonomy is closely related with motivation (Ryan, et al., 2011). The successful autonomous learning depends on the learner's motivation for embracing the technique and persist in the agreed direction. They monitor, plan and readjust their own learning process. The ability to schedule, evaluate and implement are all the basics for a successful autonomous learner. It is rare that without high motivation, students can learn well autonomously.

Moreover, the path diagram and standardized regression weights also show that motivation factor has positive influence on two other factors. They are learning resources and environment factors and the role of instructor factors. Undoubtedly, the increase of student's motivation will not only facilitate students' autonomous learning in view of searching for and using appropriate learning resources and put themselves in learning out of their own initiatives, but will also, in return, help the instructor to teach effectively.

To sum up, it has been found out that interactions and evaluation are highly influencing factors in autonomous learning and motivation exerts high influences on autonomous learning, and two other factors.

Low Influence from Motivation to Interaction and Evaluation with Collaborative Learning

However, it is also a little astonishing to find that six relationships have low standardized weights in the path diagram, particularly that the motivation factor has comparatively little influence on interaction and evaluation factor (0.18), and still less on the factor of collaborative learning (0.11), indicating that students have low motivation in interaction and evaluation as well as collaborative learning.

And besides, after careful calculation from the decomposition of path effects, it was found that the direct effect from motivation factor to interaction and evaluation factor is 0.18, while its indirect effect through autonomous learning factor is 0.24 (=0.431*0.559). Hence, the direct effect is lower than the indirect effect. This also indicates that autonomous learning is the key mediator variable, which means greater emphasis should be given to the interactions and evaluation process in students' autonomous learning to motivate the students in their college English blended learning.

It is widely accepted that motivation can be categorized into intrinsic and extrinsic motivation. People who have intrinsic motivation do things because of their inherently interests and enjoyment, while those who have extrinsic motivation cater for a separable outcome (Benabou & Tirole, 2003). In this sense, students out of intrinsic motivation will learn actively rather than getting the satisfaction from imparting the knowledge from the textbooks and passing the examination, while those with the extrinsic motivation are content with external factors, such as getting high scores and other material benefits. In the follow-up interviews, students express their concerns on their motivation:

I think we should be motivated by the scores of course, which, I believe, is very meaningful. On the whole, final outcomes such as scores are really important. Otherwise, talking about the improvement of various competence is nothing but a castle in the air. (C-S2-L)

From the above interview, it is quite clear that students are more extrinsically motivated than intrinsically. While it is true that collaborative learning may help students improve their scores, it is not necessarily true that posting questions online and assessing peer's assignment will have such a direct effect. These are to be evaluated in a more complex way, from quality rather than quantity and besides, there doesn't seem to be, up to now, an effective means to relate them with the scores that the students can get in the course. It is true that functions of some of systems are limited, and instructors and students prefer to interact via social software or apps. However, such means of communications, as they are unembedded into LMS, make systematic tracking of student's learning difficult. It is, therefore, necessary to upgrade the systems so that easy and proper surveillance is procured.

What's more, it is evident from the path diagram that collaborative learning is the least influencing factor. Instructors were reluctant to give students collaborative work, not because it is comparatively difficult to be evaluated without the assistance of information technology, but because some students look upon it in a negative light. As the following interview except indicates:

Some students did dislike collaborating with others. They may have a good writing competence of English, but when talking about collaborating and learn with others, they tried to ignore it or even sneered at it, thinking it is of no avail for them to get high scores in English examinations. (C-T1-L0)

Low Influence from Attitude to Adaptability

The same is true of learning attitude factor. It is an important factor for adaptability. In other words, what the students perceive of college English blended learning will influence how they adapt to the course. However, although learning attitude factor has positive influence on learning resources and environment, as well as the role of instructor, it has little influence on adaptability. It is later found out that some students are not engaged in English learning fervently or out of their own interests and take negative attitudes toward it.

Students' negative attitude may relate to their adaptation of autonomous learning. As Hiemastra and Burns (1997) point out learning attitudes are also closely related to autonomous learning. But for the underlying cultural differences, Chinese students, unlike their western counterparts, are accustomed to the passive taking methods of learning before entering the colleges and universities, and it would become extremely difficult for them to change their roles and take most of their responsibilities of learning overnight. College English blended learning under MOOCs philosophy is so different from their former traditional learning that some of the students fail to adapt to or even accept it, which, in turn, drains their enthusiasm from English learning.

As a matter of fact, attitudes and motivation are highly related (0.77), if students find it hard to adapt to the education, that will render negative influence on the effectiveness of education. Therefore, it is of utmost importance to improve the students' intrinsic motivation by creatively designing the courses, awakening the students' interests in learning and guiding them gradually to adapt to the education.

SOLUTIONS AND RECOMMENDATIONS

It is suggested in the above discussions that many features of MOOCs philosophy are evident in college English blended learning, but some still needs improving. And though motivation exerts high influence on students' autonomous learning, which also highly influences interactions and evaluation, students nevertheless have low motivation in interaction and evaluation, for they are more extrinsically than intrinsically motivated. And also, collaborative learning is the least influencing factor in the study. To motivate the students, great emphasis should be laid on interactions and evaluation process in student's autonomous learning. Moreover, students' negative attitudes towards autonomous learning hampers their adaptability to college English blended learning. And, as attitude and motivation are highly related, this deserves equal attention

Motivating the Students Intrinsically

In the era of globalization and cultural diversity, there is an increasing demand in the society for college graduates with high competencies. These competencies include not only language, but autonomous and life-long learning. Most importantly, in the information era, 4Cs competencies are necessary for the learners in the 21st century. They are critical thinking, communication, collaboration and creativity. In view of this, college English education is again at another crossroads for self-innovation. In order to motivate the students intrinsically and foster qualified students rather than students with high scores but low qualities, college English administrators and instructors need to change radically its course design as well as the contents. Course designers should give first priority to arousing students' curiosity and make them interested in learning. For instance, the learning contents are to be closely related to their needs and experiences. In order for the students to get confidence and satisfaction from learning, tasks are designed to be challenging, through which students can make improvements after some struggles of learning. Sharing their products of learning and get compliments or even criticisms will make them feel a sense of achievement or even critical and reflective.

As for the change of learning contents, there are disputes now as to the positioning of the college English education. It is acknowledged that college English education should be content-based and multiple-content. The aims of college English education are not only to provide a communicative tool for the students in their future work, as General English does, but to cultivate their sense of humanity and make them fully prepared for their specialization study. Thus, the learning contents are to be divided into English for general purpose (EGP), English for specific purpose (ESP) and English for general education (EGE) (Wang, 2012), which separates the once one-for-all college English into several different courses to cater to the diversified needs of students and society.

Improving Functions of the MOOCs Systems

Though MOOCs, as its name indicates, evolves from OER movements and has its own open features, they are really controversial. Most world-famous MOOCs are open only to its registered members and onlookers have only limited access to the resources and functions of MOOCs. Besides, to be a partner of these famous MOOCs are far from easy for most universities in Mainland China. As for the domesticated MOOCs systems in China, they are low in satisfaction, especially in terms of instructors' support, content design and technical assistance (Liu & Li, 2014). It is also important to note that these MOOCs have relatively little means of interactions, as most of the interactions occur only in online forum or via emails.

Therefore, there are ways to improve interactions and collaboration in learning. To begin with, the online education systems, such as Moodle, BB, etc. can serve as a complement. These systems are developed rather early and are mature in technology with a better support for interactions and collaboration than MOOCs systems. Students and instructors can embed the MOOCs into the online education system and wrap the learning resources into the online courses while doing other interactions and collaboration activities on online system (Dai, 2015). With the blended use of MOOCs and online educational systems, instructors and educational administrators are able to strengthen the functions of the systems. All they should do is to add the functional module, upload the learning resources, posting resources links of famous MOOCs, retrieve and analyze the learning analytical data.

As is found in the study, students and instructors favor using social communication apps to interact. Therefore, the second way is to bring these apps into full play, making them another online system. There are some applications which can turn these apps instantly into educational platform. Instant data of learning will easily be collected and there are multiple ways of interactions favored by young students.

Promoting Peer Evaluation

Stephen Bostock believed that peer assessment will increase student's motivation, encourage the students to be responsible for their own learning and promote their autonomous learning (Schmid, et al., 2000). The process of peer assessment will also promote the learner for self-evaluation and evoke deeper learning. However, controversies still exist, suggesting that not all evaluators are capable for peer evaluation. Some have neither the necessary qualification, nor the appropriate attitudes, making the accuracy, fairness and correctness of feedback on a shaky ground (Grieves, et al., 2006).

In this study, interaction and evaluation factors have the lowest mean value, suggesting that students fail to find a sense of belonging in the virtual learning community and were not willing to participate in the online interaction. Besides, collaborative learning is the least influencing factor. Therefore, peer evaluation is a good way to increase the student's motivation and make them actively involved in online interaction and evaluation.

However, assessments in MOOCs system in China are, to a greater extent, objective questions and are evaluated instantly by the system. There are some peer assessments in college English blended learning, but are carried out mostly in the classroom, either written or orally. In fact, it is online peer evaluation that is especially valuable, with features of anonymity and independence.

As the major influences for peer evaluation are knowledge, background and attitudes of the peers (Topping, 1998), the effective implementation of peer evaluation depends on the principle of dynamic. Through accessing big data of learning, the system has a pool of students' personal information through their learning process, including knowledge level and motivation, and matches them to an appropriate evaluator according to a predesigned algorithm. The students evaluate others' work anonymously, and by comparing the results of the two evaluators, the system then assigns it to another evaluator for further assessing. Through the process, the evaluators are changing with features matched, and the role of the evaluators may change as well, from the ordinary evaluator, to the leader or even to the assistant of the instructor, in accordance with their performances in the peer assessment. In this way, peer evaluation is implemented, and student's motivation may be improved.

CONCLUSION

This study investigated the effectiveness of college English blended learning under MOOCs philosophy. It looks into its influencing factors and their relationships in how they influence the educational effectiveness.

The findings suggest that though many features of MOOCs philosophy are evident in the quantitative research, some still needs improving, including the variety of learning resources, the improvement for the functions of the MOOCs platform, effective ubiquitous means of communications out of class, and the changing of educational philosophy among instructors, etc. The results also indicate that eight factors influencing educational effectiveness, namely motivation factor, interaction and evaluation factor, collaborative learning factor, autonomous learning factor, learning resources and environment factor, role of instructor factor, learning attitude factor and adaptability factor. It also hypothesizes that the interactions and evaluation is not brought into full play in the college English blended learning and the students find it hard to adapt to this news model, while the role of instructor is still important in the education.

Relationships of the influencing factors demonstrate that interactions and evaluation are highly influencing factors in autonomous learning and motivation exerts high influences on autonomous learning.

However, the findings also suggest that students have low motivation in interaction and evaluation, for they are more extrinsically than intrinsically motivated. And also, collaborative learning is the least influencing factor in the study. To motivate the students, great emphasis should be laid on interactions and evaluation process in student's autonomous learning. Moreover, students' negative attitude towards autonomous learning hampers their adaptability to college English blended learning, and great attention should also be made to students' motivation, as attitude and motivation are highly related.

Hence, course design and learning contents of college English should undergo substantive changes, arousing student curiosity and separating it into several different courses to cater to the diversified needs of students and society. This study also suggests the merging of online education systems with MOOCs systems to improve interaction and collaboration in learning, together with mobile applications. Effective implementation of online peer evaluation should also be promoted in college English blended learning to motivate the students, which is carried out on the principle of dynamic, matching evaluators and constantly evaluating them.

LIMITATIONS AND AREAS OF FUTURE RESEARCH

At the time when this study was conducted, not many colleges and universities nationwide had adopted this kind of college English blended learning. Therefore, only four colleges and universities in China were selected. It is anticipated that any results and findings in the study might not be generalized to other larger samples. Besides, as educational practices continue, theories and concepts will develop as well, making the philosophical features of MOOCs discussed in this study diachronic and needs constantly updating.

This study attempts to identify the influencing factors for effectiveness of college English blended learning under MOOCs philosophy. Future researchers can analyze these factors from a larger sample, covering most parts in the country, especially the developed eastern part of China. The findings of this study show that collaborative learning is the least influencing factor and students have low motivations in interaction and evaluation in online learning. Future researchers can probe deep into these research areas and come up with plausible ways to enhance these features so as to improve the effectiveness in college English blended learning.

REFERENCES

An, J. (2004). A study on the effectiveness of promoting English learning and pragmatic competence under CALL. *Computer-Assisted Foreign Language Education*, (4), 63-66.

Benabou, R., & Tirole, J. (2003). Intrinsic and extrinsic motivation. *The Review of Economic Studies*, *70*(3), 489–520. doi:10.1111/1467-937X.00253

Bliuc, A. M., Goodyear, P., & Ellis, R. A. (2007). Research focus and methodological choices in studies into students' experiences of blended learning in higher education. *The Internet and Higher Education*, *10*(4), 231–244. doi:10.1016/j.iheduc.2007.08.001

Cai, J. (2010). Reflections on repositioning of college English education in China. *Foreign Language Teaching and Research, 42*(04), 306–308.

Chapman, C., Muijs, D., Reynolds, D., Sammons, P., & Teddlie, C. (Eds.). (2015). *The Routledge international handbook of educational effectiveness and improvement: Research, policy, and practice.* Routledge. doi:10.4324/9781315679488

Chen, Y. & Wu, J. (2010). Status quo of current College Online Education. *Education Exploration,* (8), 72-73.

Creswell, J. W. (2008). *Educational research: planning, conducting, and evaluating quantitative and qualitative research* (3rd ed.). Upper Saddle River, NJ: Pearson/ Merrill Prentice Hall.

Dai, Z. (2015). An Analysis of the Current Research Foci of MOOC---Implications of the First National Symposium on Foreign languages education of tertiary level in the era of MOOCs. *Computer-Assisted Foreign Language Education,* (1), 73-78.

Garrison, D. R., & Kanuka, H. (2004). Blended learning: Uncovering its transformative potential in higher education. *The Internet and Higher Education, 7*(2), 95–105. doi:10.1016/j.iheduc.2004.02.001

Graham, C. R. (2006). Blended learning systems. In C. J. Bonk & C. R. Graham (Eds.), *The handbook of blended learning* (pp. 3–21). San Francisco, CA: Pfeiffer Publishing.

Grieves, J., McMillan, J., & Wilding, P. (2006). Barriers to learning: Conflicts that occur between and within organisational systems. *International Journal of Learning & Intellectual Capital, 3*(1), 86–103. doi:10.1504/IJLIC.2006.009212

Hafner, C. A., & Miller, L. (2011). Fostering learner autonomy in English for science: A collaborative digital video project in a technological learning environment. *Language Learning & Technology, 15*(3), 68–86.

He, K. (2005). New development of educational technological theories from blended learning. *Journal of National Academy of Education Administration,* (9), 37-48+79.

He, X. & Jianshi, W. (2012). Reflections on the improvements of College English Education. *Journal of North-Eastern University: social philosophy edition,* (1), 92-94.

Jiang, Y. & Ma, W. (2013). Research on continuous course design of new century college English-students' needs analysis (part two). *Computer-Assisted Foreign Language Education,* (4), 64-69, 75.

Kop, R. (2011). The challenges to connectivist learning on open online networks: Learning experiences during a massive open online course. *The International Review of Research in Open and Distributed Learning*, *12*(3), 19–38. doi:10.19173/irrodl. v12i3.882

Li, K., & Zhao, J. (2004). Principles and application models of blended learning. *E-education Research*, (7), 1-6.

Liu, H., & Li, Q. (2014). Concepts exploration of Chinese MOOC and strategies for optimizing platform---A survey on Chinese MOOC platform. *Modern Educational Technology*, *24*(05), 81–87.

Montebello, M. (2018). *AI Injected e-Learning*. Cham: Springer. doi:10.1007/978-3-319-67928-0

Osuna-Acedo, C., Marta-Lazo, C., & Frau-Meigs, D. (2018). From SMOOC to TMOOC, learning towards professional transference: ECO European project. *Comunicar*, *26*(55), 105–114. doi:10.3916/C55-2018-10

Picciano, A. G. (2009). Blending with purpose: The multimodal model. *Journal of Asynchronous Learning Networks*, *13*(1), 7–18.

Ren, Q. (2013). Theoretical framework for establishing and evaluating effective college English classroom environment. *Foreign Language Teaching and Research*, *45*(05), 732–743.

Rovai, A. P., & Jordan, H. (2004). Blended learning and sense of community: A comparative analysis with traditional and fully online graduate courses. *The International Review of Research in Open and Distributed Learning*, *5*(2). doi:10.19173/irrodl.v5i2.192

Ryan, R. M., Lynch, M. F., Vansteenkiste, M., & Deci, E. L. (2011). Motivation and autonomy in counseling, psychotherapy, and behavior change: A look at theory and practice. *The Counseling Psychologist*, *39*(2), 193–260. doi:10.1177/0011000009359313

Sandeen, C. C. E. (2013). Integrating MOOCS into Traditional Higher Education: The Emerging "MOOC 3.0" Era. *Change*, *45*(6), 34–39. doi:10.1080/00091383.2 013.842103

Schmid, B., Miao, S. L., & Bazzaz, F. A. (2000). Student peer assessment. *Journal of Community & Applied Social Psychology*, *114*(5), 9–15.

Singh, H., & Reed, C. (2001). A white paper: Achieving success with blended learning. *Centra Software, 12*, 1–11.

Steiger, J. H. (1980). Statistically based tests for the number of common factors. *Paper presented in the annual meeting of the Psychometric Society*. Academic Press.

Su, D. (2013). Reorienting College English to Serve National Development Strategies and Cultivate Talents with International Visions. *Foreign Language Research*, (6), 90-96.

Tan, C. T. (2013, September). Towards a MOOC game. *Paper presented at the 9th Australasian Conference on Interactive Entertainment: Matters of Life and Death*. Academic Press. 10.1145/2513002.2513040

Topping, K. (1998). Peer assessment between students in colleges and universities. *Review of Educational Research*, *68*(3), 249–276. doi:10.3102/00346543068003249

Wang, H. (2009). Investigations on the teaching and teachers of College English. *Foreign Language World*, (4), 6-13.

Wang, P., Li, M., & Huang, H. Y. (2012). Promoting educational quality: challenges and way out for college English teachers take college English classroom education as an example. *Chinese College Education*, (10), 81-84.

Wang, S. (2012). Teacher development in the construction of college English course system. *Foreign Language World*, (4), 2-5.

Wang, Z. (2014). On effective teaching in the foreign English classroom: from a constructivist learning perspective. *Foreign Language World*, (4), 71-79.

Xu, J. (2015). Research on foreign language classroom: In retrospect and into the future. *Contemporay Foreign Language Studies*, (9), 1-6+76.

Zhang, H., & Ma, J. (2015). The design and practice of flipped classroom under MOOCs—taking modern educational technology course as an example. *Modern Educational Technology*, *25*(2), 53–60.

Zhang, Q., & Yan, J. (2014). Phenomena of college English education going away from goals and strategies for correcting. *Modern College Education*, (6), 101-108.

Zhou, X., & Zhu, X. (2016). Criteria driven college English curriculum implementation and evaluation. *Foreign Language Learning Theory and Practice*, (3), 32-36.

Zhu, Y. (2013). Effectiveness of foreign language classroom teaching: A case study of an outstanding teaching episode in the third SFLEP national foreign language teaching contest. *Foreign Language World*, (2), 50-58.

ADDITIONAL READING

Bonk, C. J., & Graham, C. R. (2012). *The Handbook of Blended Learning: Global Perspectives, Local Designs*. John Wiley & Sons.

Bruff, D. O., Fisher, D. H., McEwen, K. E., & Smith, B. E. (2013). Wrapping a MOOC: Student perceptions of an experiment in blended learning. *Journal of Online Learning and Teaching / MERLOT*, 9(2), 187–200.

Chapman, C., Muijs, D., Reynolds, D., Sammons, P., & Teddlie, C. (Eds.). (2015). *The Routledge international handbook of educational effectiveness and improvement: Research, policy, and practice*. Routledge. doi:10.4324/9781315679488

Holotescu, C., Grosseck, G., Creţu, V., & Naaji, A. (2014). Integrating MOOCs in blended courses. *Elearning & Software for Education*, (1).

Krause, S. D., & Lowe, C. (2014). *Invasion of the MOOCs: The Promise and Perils of Massive Open Online Courses*. Anderson, South Carolina: Parlor Press.

Zhang, X. (2012). *Research on Effective Education of College English*. Chengdu: Southwestern University of Finance and Economics Press.

KEY TERMS AND DEFINITIONS

AMOS: A statistical software and an added SPSS module, used for structural equation modeling, path analysis, and confirmatory factor analysis.

College English Education: English education for non-English majors at tertiary level in China, also labeled as College English Teaching (CET).

Endogenous Variables: A factor whose value is dependent on other variables in the system.

Exogenous Variables: A factor whose value is wholly independent from other variables in the system.

SEM Modelling: Abbreviation for structural equation modeling, which includes confirmatory factor analysis, confirmatory composite analysis, path analysis, etc. It is used in the social sciences because it can impute relationships between latent variables from observable variables.

Semi-Structured Interviews: A method of research often used in the social sciences, in which the interviewer has a general framework to be explored and is open to allow new ideas to be brought up during the interview.

Ubiquitous Learning: (Also u-Learning) Learning anytime, anywhere with the help of mobile devices and wireless networks.

Chapter 12

A Holistic Approach to Integrating ePortfolios as Instructional Methods in Online Programs

Barbara Miller Hall

iD https://orcid.org/0000-0002-6732-2616
Northcentral University, USA

Miranda R. Regnitz
Northcentral University, USA

ABSTRACT

The purpose of this chapter is to review a holistic approach to the integration of digital portfolios ("ePortfolios") as an instructional method in online degree programs. The chapter reviews the evidence-based best practices that support four phases to the integration of ePortfolios as an instructional method in online degree programs: scaffolding, tutorials, course integration, and student engagement. Each phase offers a different way to make a lasting impact on students. The innovative instructional method is not the portfolio itself, the supporting tutorials, or any one piece of the ePortfolio project. Rather, the true innovation is the project as a whole, taking a holistic look at how portfolios fit into the program and how to support the development and evaluation of the portfolio for both students and faculty.

DOI: 10.4018/978-1-7998-1622-5.ch012

BACKGROUND

A portfolio is a collection of artifacts collated by an individual or group, usually including reflections on those artifacts, which serve to illustrate knowledge, skills, dispositions, and growth. An ePortfolio is a digital version of a traditional portfolio. The use of ePortfolios has been growing for some time. The number of campuses using ePortfolios for program review and assessment of General Education ("GenEd") those courses required of all students regardless of major area of study tripled between 2009 and 2013 (Eynon, Gambino, & Török, 2014). More than half of college students in the United States reported using an ePortfolio at some time in their collegiate studies (Eynon & Gambino, 2017), and as of a few years ago, 57% of U.S. colleges and universities offered some form of ePortfolio experience (Dahlstrom, 2015). In 2016, based on a decade of accumulated evidence, the Association of American Colleges and Universities named ePortfolios the eleventh high-impact practice (Watson, Kuh, Rhodes, Light, & Chen, 2016).

The literature describes an ePortfolio in several ways. In brief terms, an ePortfolio is "a pedagogical method for connected and integrated learning" (Matthews-DeNatale, 2013, p. 42) and "more of a process, a way of teaching and learning" (Eynon, et al., p. 108). A useful definition from Barrett (2005), who adds that an ePortfolio includes authentic, diverse, and reflective evidence that is representative of a larger body of work created over a period of time and intended "for presentation to one or more audiences for a particular rhetorical purpose" (p. 5). A more extensive definition emerges from Duncan-Pitt and Sutherland (2006) who described an ePortfolio with these contrasts (p. 70):

- A system that belongs to the learner, not the institution
- Populated by the learner not their examiner
- Primarily concerned with supporting learning not assessment
- For life-long and life-wide learning not a single episode or a single course
- That allows learners to present multiple stories of learning rather than just a simple aggregation of competencies; and, importantly
- Where access to them is controlled by the learner who is able to invite feedback to support personal growth and understanding

Despite this poetic definition reflective of a high-impact practice, some educators, students, and employers think of ePortfolios simply as collections of artifacts used mostly for assessment. Eynon et al. (2014) suggested that it was the increasing pressure for accountability that led to so many campuses using ePortfolios for program review and assessment. This myopic view as portfolio-for-assessment persists despite decades of arguments to the contrary, such as those of Barrett (2005) who argued that ePortfolios had escaped their confines as evidence repositories and provided features that enabled not only the presentation of artifacts, but even more so the development of advanced learning skills through effective scaffolding. Roberts, Maor, and Herrington (2016) found a middle ground by recognizing that assessment is an important part of the learning process while also recognizing that an emphasis on assessment limits the utility of an ePortfolio to its end product without fully exploring the potential of the ePortfolio as a learning tool. Stefani, Mason, and Pegler (2007) suggested that this full potential of ePortfolios included six key learning requirements: assessment, presentation, learning, personal development, collaboration, and ongoing working documents. Rather than any one typology, Matthews-DeNatale (2013) suggested three "genres" that reflect the purposes of ePortfolios: directed portfolios, developmental portfolios, and showcase portfolios. The ePortfolio integrated into the online master's degree that serves as the case example for this chapter can be described as a directed and developmental portfolio. While students do use professional standards and program outcomes (directed portfolio), students also work iteratively on several artifacts across courses (developmental portfolio).

MAIN FOCUS OF THE CHAPTER

Issues, Controversies, Problems

As noted above, the main problem with ePortfolios is that they often lack proper scaffolding and are used more for assessment than their broader potential as a learning tool (Barrett, 2005; Eynon et al., 2014; Roberts et al., 2016; Stefani, et al, 2007). This chapter examines a potential solution by adopting four phases to integrating the ePortfolio as an instructional method within an online master's degree program. These four phases are scaffolding, tutorials, course integration, and student engagement. Each phase offers a different way to make a lasting impact on students. The innovative instructional method is not the ePortfolio itself, the supporting tutorials, or any one piece of the ePortfolio project. Rather, the true innovation is the project as a whole; that is, the innovation is taking a holistic look at how ePortfolios fit into the program and how to support the development and evaluation of the ePortfolio for both students and faculty.

Scaffolding

The first phase of the ePortfolio project is labeled "scaffolding." Scaffolding was first introduced by Ausubel and Fitzgerald (1962) in their discussion of advance organizers. Scaffolding refers to the process of building new information and skills on those previously introduced or acquired. Scaffolded learning designs are incremental, and both add complexity while also reducing explicit support. Related to Vygotsky's (1986) zone of proximal development, scaffolding would be the intervention or support necessary to bridge that gap between what the learner can do alone and what the learner can do with guidance.

In mathematics, for example, students initially practice with the same concepts and formulas demonstrated in a fully worked example. As student skills progresses, the practice extends beyond identical problems to include novel applications of the concepts based on only partially completed examples. Word problems illustrate this technique because students practice a specific calculation such multiplying two numbers and then progress to word problems in which the specific calculation is undefined and must be identified by the student and then calculated.

There is little debate about the need to differentiate among degree programs and appropriately scaffold both individual courses and entire programs; how to design differentiation and scaffolding is a tougher challenge. At the programmatic level, how does the design of each course represent a necessary progression of cognitive rigor, such that students are gaining advancing skills at each level rather than repeating tasks with the same cognitive requirements, thereby reiterating a skill level rather than advancing it?

Scaffolds can be categorized as soft or hard (Saye & Brush, 2002). Soft scaffolds are more dynamic, as they are offered by students and course facilitators. Hard scaffolds are more static because they are planned in advance as part of the course design. Scaffolding can also be categorized as macro or micro (Engin, 2014). Similar to a soft scaffold, micro-scaffolding occurs at the level of interaction with others; macro-scaffolding occurs at the structural level and includes the broader curriculum within a specific educational context. Sequencing, then, can be seen as hard scaffolding, because it is part of the course design, and macro-scaffolding, because it involves the sequence of courses within a curriculum. Strategies for sequencing curriculum, instruction, and training have been considered at two levels (Hammond & Gibbons, 2005; Lim, 2016): macro level sequencing, which refers to the course or curriculum level sequencing, and micro level sequencing, which refers to the sequencing of individual learning activities within a course. These two sequencing levels, illustrated in Figure 1, are consistent with the categories of scaffolding.

In this phase of the case example, a task analysis was completed to identify the knowledge and skills necessary for a student to graduate from the program with an effective ePortfolio. For the purposes of this program, an effective ePortfolio was one which met the definition of Duncan-Pitt and Sutherland (2006) provided in the introduction. A task analysis is the process of analyzing and communicating the kind of learning that the students should know how to perform. Jonassen, Tessmer,

Figure 1. Graphical representation of sequencing and scaffolding across a degree program

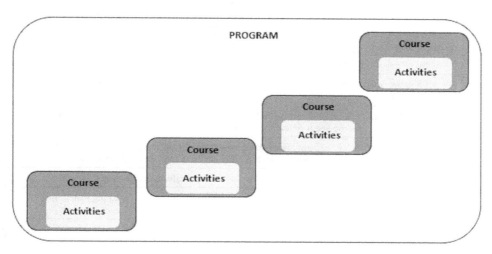

and Hannum (1999) suggested five functions of the task analysis: inventorying tasks, describing tasks, selecting tasks, sequencing tasks and task components, and analyzing tasks and content level. For more thorough explanations of task analyses and their procedures, consult Dick, Carey, and Carey (2011), Morrison et al. (2006), and Smith and Ragan (2004). The component tasks were then scaffolded throughout the online MSID program, as illustrated in Table 1. To be effective, the scaffolding required a dual focus on both the process of building an ePortfolio as well as the end product of the ePortfolio itself; this dual focus helps to keep learners focus on current objectives while also building a curated demonstration of learning for themselves, their colleagues, and their potential clients or employers (Hanbidge, McMillan, & Scholz, 2018).

This scaffolding has a positive, lasting impact on students because the students are able to articulate the value of an ePortfolio and learn the navigation and organization of a specific platform's ePortfolio features before ever trying to load an artifact into the ePortfolio. This approach reduces the potential for frustration, prepares students for a positive ePortfolio experience, allows students to focus on the artifacts over the technology challenges, and models for students how to integrate ePortfolio design into their current or future workplace projects. The next phase is to prepare tutorials for both students and faculty.

Table 1. Scaffolding of ePortfolio-related tasks by course across master's level degree program

Course	Portfolio-Related Task
1	No ePortfolio-related tasks
2	No ePortfolio-related tasks
3	From the perspectives of both learners and organizations, students review the value of ePortfolios and their use in demonstrating specific competencies.
4	Students learn about the technical affordances of the LMS portfolio and customize features to accommodate specific needs of learners and organizations.
5	Students consider how ePortfolios illustrate assessment for, of, and as learning by correlating some of their own learning artifacts with professional standards and competencies.
6	Students create a multimedia learning asset and then re-evaluate that asset in Course 7.
7	Students assemble in their ePortfolios evidence of the effectiveness of learning materials for specific needs, contexts, and learners.
8	Students demonstrate their proficiency with authoring tools through the development of multimedia learning assets.
9	Students evaluate the artifacts they have curated in their ePortfolios.
10	Students curate reflections on the ethical, legal, and political influences most commonly found in the instructional design field.
11	Students consider how the development of an ePortfolio reflects project management skills.
12	Students appraise the value of their ePortfolios in comparison with not only the program learning outcomes, but also with professional competencies and standards recognized across the industry.

Tutorials

The second phase of the ePortfolio was the creation of tutorials. These print and video (with transcript) resources combined general information about the ePortfolio features with information specific to items the students would need to curate their artifacts. Figure 2 shows the landing page of the ePortfolio platform used in the context of this chapter.

The authors created an ePortfolio Resources learning artifact that included four distinct tutorial resource folders, one for each process connected with the ePortfolio tool:

- Logging into ePortfolio
- Uploading Artifacts into ePortfolio
- Creating Collections in ePortfolio
- Creating Presentations in ePortfolio

Figure 2. ePortfolio landing page

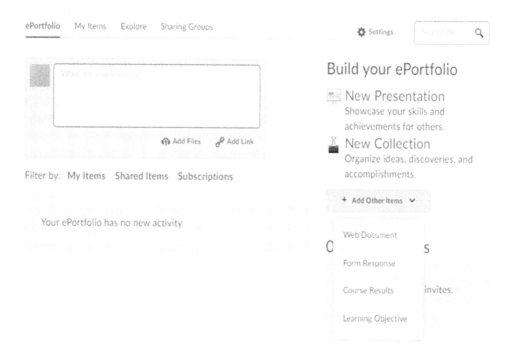

Each folder provided written, step-by-step tutorials, video tutorials, and video transcripts. These resources have a positive, lasting impact on students in several ways. One way is that these resources were shared with other schools across the university and with the university's external instructional design and educational technology colleagues to be used or modified for other programs. Another way these resources have a lasting, positive impact is by offering the technical training prior to the student's need to load anything into the ePortfolio; similar to the first phase, this approach reduces frustration and prepares students for a more positive experience in which they can focus on artifacts in future courses. Yet another way these resources have a lasting, positive impact on students is through their "chunking"; the bite-sized tutorials offer a just-in-time approach to performance support when students need a refresher later in their programs, in both text-based and media-based formats.

Tutorials can be developed in many forms, including bulleted or numbered lists of instructions, videos or interactive walk-throughs, static pictures or screenshots of an interface, and more. Especially in a wholly online learning environment, utilizing more than one tutorial type is beneficial for several reasons:

- Video and written tutorials can accommodate varied learning styles and abilities of their students.
- Video and written tutorials showcase best practices to future educators, trainers, and designers.
- Written transcripts for video tutorials are utilizing ADA-best practices.
- Written transcripts and/or written tutorials may better serve students who are unable or prefer not to watch or listen to videos due to necessary accommodations or lifestyle circumstances such as working, traveling, present in quiet areas, etc.).

Intentionally providing multiple methods for tutorial delivery is highly recommended. Regardless of the output, many educators rely on tutorials to help explain or describe a process which students may need to follow. In the case of learning about and using an online ePortfolio tool, the need for tutorials was identified early in the program planning process in order to reduce confusion around a potentially new process for students and to promote a focus on the learning evidence through the artifacts and reflections.

Providing well-developed, consistently clear tutorials throughout a training program in any organization, including an individual course or entire program within a school, can reinforce for future educators the usefulness and importance of effective practices for creating and using tutorials. For example, Farrugia and Al-Jumeily (2012) suggested four distinct areas to address when considering ePortfolio technology: usefulness, ease-of-use, ease-of-learning, and satisfaction. Providing tutorials that appear professional and free from unnecessary clutter will be appreciated by students who are increasingly eager to add more tools to their educator toolbox (Clark & Mayer, 2016). Additionally, the tutorials serve as examples and provide templates for students to modify and replicate for their own contexts. Indeed, as noted elsewhere, one of the purposes of the holistic approach to ePortfolio integration is to model for students the integration of ePortfolios in the students' future contexts.

For online learners specifically, many researchers have concluded that the availability of resources, including documentation, is critical to a student's intention to effectively use technological tools in the classroom (e.g., Sivo, Ku, & Acharya, 2018). It can be surmised that by providing adequate resources and documentation, students are less concerned about technology challenges and might be more willing and able to engage in the important learning processes, including knowledge acquisition, skill development, and disposition development.

Creating Branded, Context-Specific Tutorials

Traditionally, when software is developed and adopted by customers, there are video and/or written tutorials available to showcase features that might need more detailed explanation. A quick Internet search will also produce publicly accessible tutorials from other users of the same software, likely created for the same reasons the authors elected for the ePortfolio Resources collection: the need for branded, context-specific tutorials for their end-users. In this case, the end users are students (primary) and faculty (secondary). One of the challenges in using pre-existing tutorials is that often the software (in this case, an ePortfolio platform) is tailored to each customer, so the interface shown in a pre-existing tutorial is not identical to the interface in the designer's specific context. In some cases, the differences are subtle, such as color or organizational logo; in many cases, though, the navigation tabs and available options are different, which can be confusing to new users.

Searching for pre-existing tutorials can be very worthwhile, especially when there is an obligation to create a tutorial or set of tutorials for a program or tool never used before. Reviewing available materials from the software developer is a great place to start; in addition to the actual tutorials, there is usually a Frequently Asked Questions (FAQ) database or troubleshooting support system available online. By using these available resources, it becomes easier to fully understand the ePortfolio tool, all of its available features, and any potential shortcuts available for completing tasks.

Tutorial Challenges

Once the program was approved and the course development process began, the authors began reviewing ePortfolio materials from the software developer and other schools. They quickly realized the need for branded, context-specific tutorials for their school, and began requesting more information from partner departments. While initially it was not considered within the scope of either author's current role to create branded tutorials, it became apparent after several months there was not a designated resource or department available to produce the tutorials needed.

After researching the ePortfolio tool for several weeks and comparing the functionality to the original vision of the program, the authors were able to narrow down requirements for the specific tutorials needed to support students navigating the course material. Initially, the scope of the ePortfolio Resources project included written tutorials only, and so the authors began developing the materials themselves between other projects and responsibilities.

Once the written tutorials were created and reviewed, the authors wanted to create something more interactive and engaging. With the written tutorials in hand, it was very easy to produce a screencast following the steps already captured. During the screen casting process, however, the authors discovered student information protected by the Family Education Rights and Privacy Act (FERPA) was visible. With a quick review of tools available in the screen casting software, though, the authors were able to adequately blur the protected information and finalize the videos. Another way to work around this challenge is to load pseudonyms and other fictitious data in the system and create a tutorial using the fictitious context.

Hidden Tech Support

In many ways, effective tutorials are great assets to make available to users who may struggle with a new or complex process. While reviewing trends in tech support requests, one might discover a high number of instances related to users unable to understand or complete a task within certain software. A great example would be employees responsible for entering purchase orders into an accounting system, especially if doing so is an uncommon occurrence. Purchase order system tutorials would be a great solution as they can outline all steps in a somewhat uncommon, unfamiliar, or complex process.

As more employees access the tutorial, tech support calls and manager support should reduce. In the case of students in an online course, tutorials can help reduce the load on tech support, faculty members, advisors, etc. As the organization or school becomes used to providing tutorials, it may be determined that all future software rollouts, or introduction of new technology/process will include written and video tutorials linked in a centralized, easy-to-find location.

Course Integration

The third phase is integrating everything into the actual course design. For each course, this integration includes the scaffolding of the knowledge and skills planned for that course level, identifying appropriate places within the courses for the ePortfolio-related tasks, composing instructions, adding relevant tutorials, and including other resources as may be needed. Supporting guidance is also offered in the teaching guide for each course. This course integration phase involves the way in which students will be introduced first to the overall concept of the ePortfolio as well as the different tasks assigned to the students in each course. Scaffolding and tutorials have been included separately in this chapter. Effectively integrating the ePortfolio-related tasks into each course builds on the existing value of the first two phases. A strong integration within each course ensures low frustration for both students and faculty.

From the onset of developing the master's degree program, the authors and were intentional about providing one set of ePortfolio resources that it would be accessible to all students. In addition to ensuring consistency for their students, one set of resources is much easier to manage and maintain long-term. It was also necessary to ensure the responsibility for ongoing maintenance of the resources was communicated to all necessary stakeholders. In the event of potential LMS revisions, ePortfolio platform changes, user feedback, or change in academic program requirements, having a single point-of-contact identified as the ePortfolio Resources "owner" would allow information to be collected and acted upon while ensuring the original requirements were still being met.

While many LMSs offer native ePortfolio options, there is value in exploring third-party options in order to identify a resource to meet specific programmatic and student needs. There are many considerations for selecting the right tool, one of which is whether or not students will have access to their ePortfolio after they complete an individual course and/or program. It is important to understand these types of limitations or constraints of the tool, as well as the limitations or constraints of the school's information technology (IT)-related student policies. The authors worked with their organization's internal IT department to ensure the native ePortfolio tool within their LMS would allow students to access their ePortfolio outside of the normal LMS login for purposes of sharing their work with others unaffiliated with the university, such as potential future employers, clients, and colleagues.

As mentioned in the section about tutorials, the authors created an ePortfolio Resources learning artifact that included four distinct tutorial resource folders, one for each process connected with the ePortfolio tool: logging into ePortfolio, uploading artifacts to ePortfolio, creating Collections in ePortfolio, and creating Presentations in ePortfolio. Each folder provided written, step-by-step tutorials, video tutorials, and video transcripts. Additional introductory materials were provided to outline the concept of ePortfolios within the context of the student's degree program and to describe long-term benefits, such as retaining lessons learned, recalling past achievements, integrating peer and professor feedback, and illustrating knowledge, skills, and dispositions). A glossary of terms was also included within the ePortfolio Resources learning artifact.

The authors had previously adopted the process of "chunking" material throughout their years of curriculum development and instructional design experience and felt it would be beneficial for the set of tutorials included within the ePortfolio Resources. Chunking material allows a user/student to learn new content over a series of clearly defined segments, or chunks. When it comes time to recall important information, including detailed steps in a previously "chunked" process, often students need to see only the topic or label within the call-to-action to remember the material they previously learned (Thalmann, Souza, & Oberauer, 2019).

Once the video tutorials were completed, reviewed, and approved, transcripts were generated and all materials were loaded into a Learning Object Repository

(LOR). While partnering with the information technology and instructional design and development departments, it was recommended that we use the LOR to "house" everything in order to reduce the chance of having outdated material linked somewhere, particularly in a student-facing context like a course. Similar to an intranet site or asset management system, the LOR allowed the collection of ePortfolio Resources to appear linked across many courses and alternate locations.

Student Engagement

The final phase is when the students engage their individual ePortfolios. The lasting impact to the student is a collection of multimedia artifacts that not only demonstrates the acquired knowledge and skills but also offer an introspective look into the student's interests and goals through the organization of the ePortfolio and associated reflections. Portfolios are a necessity in the instructional design field, which is the domain of the master's level course in which this innovation was implemented. The lasting impact to the student is not only in the development of the ePortfolios themselves, but also in the learning that has occurred about ePortfolios and modeling how to design and integrate ePortfolios in current or future organizations at which the learners will work.

Starting at the beginning is the best place for both this section of the chapter as well as for the students themselves. As explained in the previous sections, the ePortfolio tasks were integrated into the program from the third course. In addition, the students practiced navigating the ePortfolio platform prior to the requirement to post a particular artifact. Integrating such practice from early in the program is consistent with the recommendations of Roberts (2016) and Hallum, Harper, McAllister, Hauville, and Creagh (2010), who noted the need to introduce electronic learning platforms, such as ePortfolios, from the beginning of student studies. Starting at the beginning of the program also supports the student's ability to make connections between ideas and be more aware of their growth and development as a learner, as reported by 70% and 66%, respectively, of Connect to Learning (C2L) students reported (Enyon & Gambino, 2016). If the ePortfolio is introduced later in the program, and especially if done so in the very last course, students are denied the opportunity to make such connections, growth, and development.

Students demonstrated engagement in other ways. In the C2L project, students reported that building their ePortfolios helped them to think more deeply about content (62%) and to synthesize information and experiences in new ways (78%) (Enyon, et al., 2014). Students who built ePortfolios also demonstrated higher grade-point averages, credit accumulation, and retention rates than students who did not create ePortfolios (Hakel & Smith, 2009). In the current case example, there is insufficient data to ensure anonymity in publishing student outcomes. Anecdotally, the holistic approach has received positive praise from students and faculty alike.

Even with the extensive preparation, there are some challenges to student engagement. One challenge noted in the section on scaffolding was using the task analysis to identify, place, and design individual ePortfolio assignments within the greater structures of the overall degree program completion sequence as well as the overall ePortfolio preparation and completion needs. This challenge relates to student engagement through another challenge: the portfolio-related tasks were sometimes difficult to integrate into the flow of the course. Especially in the earlier courses in the program, tasks like learning the ePortfolio navigation stood out from other tasks which were focused more acutely on instructional design content. Fortunately, there are ways to connect instructional design with navigation through discussions of user experience design. While technology should not drive pedagogy, technology certainly provides boundaries for what is possible. Nonetheless, some students might see distinct tasks related to ePortfolio preparation as disruptive to the course flow and, thus, disruptive to the student's engagement, as well.

Another challenge to student engagement was helping students in the initial courses within the program to see the value of the preparatory work, such as exploring the general utility of ePortfolios and the navigation of the specific LMS ePortfolio tool, in particular. A focus on alignment with the learning outcomes at the course, program, and institutional levels as well as alignment with competencies and standards of professional practice in the instructional design field helped to ameliorate this challenge to engagement. The instructional design content of the master's program was aligned to the competencies and standards of the International Board of Standards for Training, Performance and Instruction (IBSTPI), the Association for Educational Communications and Technology (AECT), and the Association for Training Development (ATD). Such explicit alignment illustrated the authentic nature of the ePortfolio tasks and offered motivation for students to engage wholly in completing the tasks.

A final challenge to student engagement is actually faculty engagement. After all, a well-designed course experience must also be well-facilitated to fully engage learners. The university in this case example uses a standardized curriculum, which means that all students are exposed to the same learning outcomes, content, and assessments. Even within a standardized curriculum, faculty still have the opportunity to "make the magic happen" through their facilitation. To ensure a similar experience consistent with a standardized approach, the design team creates faculty teaching guides. These guides offer additional information about the design thinking, justification of choices, potential student challenges, and suggestions for overcoming those challenges. Clearly, these guides need to consider the ePortfolio tasks as much as the other learning activities and assessments. In addition, the culminating signature assignment for each course has a standardized rubric for grading and feedback.

SOLUTIONS AND RECOMMENDATIONS

Solutions have been offered throughout this chapter to the challenges identified in a holistic approach to the integration of ePortfolios in online degree programs. Perhaps the greatest recommendation is to consider the institutional values and how an ePortfolio project does or does not support these values. At the institution of the case example, the ePortfolio supports several values espoused by many educational institutions.

Innovation

Effectively integrating ePortfolios in a way that is supportive of both students and faculty continues to be a challenge, particularly in online education, and this holistic approach offers a solution to this challenge and improves the overall quality of online degree programs

Diversity

The holistic approach to ePortfolio integration exemplifies the value of diversity by recognizing the value of each student's unique characteristics and experiences. Portfolios support students in presenting their true version of themselves not only in the content of their curated artifacts, but also in the reflections that tell their stories.

Continuous Improvement

By scaffolding the ePortfolio throughout the program, students engage in a continuous improvement cycle of their work; they return to previous artifacts to improve upon their work based on additional learning and reflection.

Outcomes

Portfolios offer evidence of learning outcomes at the course, program, and institutional level.

Accountability

This holistic approach to ePortfolio integration represents the value of accountability by offering a medium to portray such work.

After examining the alignment between a desired ePortfolio project and institutional values, the next recommendation is to identify how the ePortfolio project aligns with learning outcomes at the institutional, program, and course level and any competencies and standards of relevant professional organizations. As these recommendations suggest, the greatest recommendation in implementing an ePortfolio project is to begin the process early so as to allow sufficient time for a holistic approach that supports the design team as well as the eventual users - students and faculty.

FUTURE RESEARCH DIRECTIONS

The broad concept of portfolios has been the topic of research for quite some time, including the development of the digital or ePortfolio. As the nature of learning and learners themselves continues to change at an unprecedented pace, there are still emerging opportunities to explore how ePortfolios are evolving to meet these changes.

For example, what do potential employers think of the utility in assessing candidates with the different types of ePortfolios? Typically, do employers prefer a portfolio that focuses on an illustration of growth and development, or would employers prefer to see illustrate the end results of developing the knowledge, skills, and dispositions?

Based on the challenges discussed in this chapter and elsewhere in the literature, how might developers of learning management systems - or whatever the LMS develops into - overcome these challenges in their ePortfolio platforms? How might the successes and challenges of ePortfolio platforms outside of an LMS inform improvements of both integrated and independent platforms?

What faculty insight can be gleaned from their experiences with learners and their ePortfolios? Future research might identify more effective scaffolding for faculty development of ePortfolio proficiencies as well as scaffolding for students. How might faculty needs differ based the type of portfolio or specific LMS? How do faculty integrate ePortfolios in their self-designed courses versus such integration within a standardized curriculum? In programs where the ePortfolio was built into a capstone course, what might be the most effective way to revise the program to draw out the ePortfolio tasks throughout the program?

Of course, there are the students themselves. As their learning preferences and enrollment patterns change, how might ePortfolios need to change in terms of their scaffolding, integration, and engagement? How are ePortfolios integrated effectively into shorter credentials than a full degree program, such as micro-credentials, certificates, and nanodegrees?

While there is much research about portfolios and their digital counterparts, there is still much to learn. And there will always be more to learn as needs change among occupations, employers, and learners.

CONCLUSION

In summary, the innovative instructional method is not the ePortfolio itself, the supporting tutorials, or any one piece of the ePortfolio project. Rather, the true innovation is the project as a whole - taking a holistic look at how ePortfolios fit into the program and how to support the development and evaluation of the ePortfolio for both students and faculty. Such a holistic approach needs to start with extensive planning of how an ePortfolio project aligns with values, learning outcomes, and existing technologies; extensive analyses of specific ePortfolio tasks required; then scaffolding and tutorials to support course integration and student engagement.

ACKNOWLEDGMENT

While this project received no specific grant from any funding agency in the public, commercial, or not-for-profit sectors, the authors acknowledge that their work was conducted within the context of a university and its support services. The authors wish to thank specifically Dr. Brian Endfinger, Associate Director for Instructional Design Technologies at Northcentral University, for his expertise in the specific learning management system aforementioned in this chapter.

REFERENCES

Ausubel, D. P., & Fitzgerald, D. (1962). Organizer, general background, and antecedent learning variables in sequential verbal learning. *Journal of Educational Psychology, 53*(6), 243–249. Retrieved from http://www.apa.org/pubs/journals/edu/. doi:10.1037/h0040210

Barrett, H. C. (2005). Researching electronic portfolios and learner engagement (White Paper). The Reflect Initiative. Retrieved from http://www.citeulike.org/group/2518/article/800018

Clark, R. C., & Mayer, R. E. (2016). e-Learning and the science of instruction: Proven guidelines for consumers and designers of multimedia learning (4th ed.). Hoboken, NJ: Wiley.

Dahlstrom, E., Brooks, D. C., Grajek, S., & Reeves, J. (2015). *ECAR study of undergraduate students and information technology.* EDUCAUSE Center for Analysis and Research. Retrieved from https://library.educause.edu/resources/2015/8/~/med ia/24ddc1aa35a5490389baf28b6ddb3693.ashx

Dick, W., Carey, L., & Carey, J. O. (2011). *The systematic design of instruction* (7th ed.). Columbus, OH: Allyn & Bacon.

Duncan-Pitt, L., & Sutherland, S. (2006). An Introduction to the use of ePortfolios in professional practice. *Journal of Radiotherapy in Practice, 5*(02), 69–75. doi:10.1017/S1460396906000100

Engin, M. (2014). Macro-scaffolding: Contextual support for teacher learning. *Australian Journal of Teacher Education, 39*(5). doi:10.14221/ajte.2014v39n5.6

Enyon, B., & Gambino, L. M. (2016). Professional development for high impact eportfolio practice. *Peer Review: Emerging Trends and Key Debates in Undergraduate Education, 18*(3), 4–8.

Eynon, B., & Gambino, L. M. (2017). High-impact ePortfolio practice: A catalyst for student, faculty, and institutional learning (reprint ed.). Sterling, VA: Stylus.

Eynon, B., Gambino, L. M., & Török, J. (2014). What difference can ePortfolio make? A field report from the Connect to Learning Project. *International Journal of ePortfolio, 4*(1), 95-114.

Farrugia, A., & Al-Jumeily, D. (2012). The design, implementation and evaluation of a web-based student teachers' ePortfolio (STeP). In *Proceedings of the International Conference on Education and E-Learning Innovations, Education and e-Learning Innovations (ICEELI)* (pp. 1-7). Academic Press. 10.1109/ICEELI.2012.6360612

Hakel, M., & Smith, E. (2009). Documenting the outcomes of learning. In D. Cambridge, B. Cambridge, & K. Yancey (Eds.), *Electronic portfolios 2.0: Emergent research on implementation and impact* (pp. 133–136). Sterling, VA: Stylus.

Hammond, J., & Gibbons, P. (2005). Putting scaffolding to work: The contribution of scaffolding in articulating ESL education. *Prospect, 20*, 6–30.

Hanbidge, A. S., McMillan, C., & Scholz, K. W. (2018). Engaging with ePortfolios: Teaching social work competencies through a program-wide curriculum. *The Canadian Journal for the Scholarship of Teaching and Learning, 9*(3). doi:10.5206/cjsotl-rcacea.2018.3.3

Jonassen, D. H., Tessmer, M., & Hannum, W. H. (1999). *Task analysis methods for instructional design*. Mahwah, NJ: Lawrence Erlbaum Associates.

Lim, J. (2016). The relationship between successful completion and sequential movement in self-paced distance courses. *International Review of Research in Open and Distributed Learning, 17*(1). doi:10.19173/irrodl.v17i1.2167

Matthews-DeNatale, G. (2013). Are we who we think we are? ePortfolios as a tool for curriculum redesign. *Journal of Asynchronous Learning Networks, 17*(4), 41–55. doi:10.24059/olj.v17i4.395

Roberts, P., Maor, D., & Herrington, J. (2016). ePortfolio-based learning environments: Recommendations for effective scaffolding of reflective thinking in higher education. *Journal of Educational Technology & Society, 19*(4), 22–33.

Saye, J. W., & Brush, T. (2002). Scaffolding critical reasoning about history and social issues in multimedia-supported learning environment. *Educational Technology Research and Development, 50*(3), 77–96. doi:10.1007/BF02505026

Sivo, S. A., Ku, C.-H., & Acharya, P. (2018). Understanding how university student perceptions of resources affect technology acceptance in online learning courses. *Australasian Journal of Educational Technology, 34*(4), 72–91. doi:10.14742/ajet.2806

Smith, P. L., & Ragan, T. J. (2004). *Instructional design* (2nd ed.). Hoboken, NJ: Wiley & Sons.

Stefani, L., Mason, R., & Pegler, C. (2007). *The Educational potential of e-portfolios: Supporting personal development and reflective learning*. New York, NY: Routledge. doi:10.4324/9780203961292

Thalmann, M., Souza, A. S., & Oberauer, K. (2019). How does chunking help working memory? *Journal of Experimental Psychology. Learning, Memory, and Cognition, 45*(1), 37–55. doi:10.1037/xlm0000578 PMID:29698045

Vygotsky, L. S. (1986). *Thought and Language*. Cambridge, MA: MIT Press.

Watson, C. E., Kuh, G. D., Rhodes, T., Light, T. P., & Chen, S. (2016). ePortfolios - The eleventh high impact practice (editorial). *International Journal of ePortfolio, 6*(2), 65-69.

ADDITIONAL READING

Light, T. P., Chen, H. L., & Ittelson, J. C. (2011). *Documenting learning with ePortfolios: A guide for college instructors.* San Francisco, CA: Wiley & Sons.

Reynolds, C., & Patton, J. (2014). *Leveraging the ePortfolio for integrative learning: A faculty guide to classroom practices for transforming student learning.* Sterling, VA: Stylus.

Tse, C. T., Scholz, K. W., & Lithgow, K. (2018). Beliefs or intentionality? Instructor approaches to ePortfolio pedagogy. *The Canadian Journal for the Scholarship of Teaching and Learning*, *9*(3).

Yancey, K. B. (Ed.). (2019). ePortfolio as curriculum: Models and practices for developing students' ePortfolio literacy. Sterling, VA: Stylus.

KEY TERMS AND DEFINITIONS

Chunking: The process of dividing content into brief, focused pieces of text or video often used to provide just-in-time support at the moment of learning need.

ePortfolio: Digital version of a portfolio.

LMS: Abbreviation for learning management system, which is usually a collection of software used for the delivery of educational and training modules.

Portfolio: Collection of artifacts collated by an individual or group, usually including reflections on those artifacts, that serve to illustrate knowledge, skills, dispositions, and growth.

Scaffolding: Support provided before or during a learning endeavor to increase acquisition of knowledge, skills, and dispositions.

Task Analysis: Analysis of an activity that results in a linear, detailed description of how to perform a task and what knowledge, skills, or dispositions are needed before or during performance of the activity.

Tutorial: A video or text document that illustrates the steps necessary to complete a specific task.

Compilation of References

Akçayır, M., & Akçayır, G. (2017). Advantages and challenges associated with augmented reality for education: A systematic review of the literature. *Educational Research Review*, *20*, 1–11. doi:10.1016/j.edurev.2016.11.002

Albrecht, J. R., & Karabenick, S. A. (2017). Relevance for learning and motivation in education. *Journal of Experimental Education*, *86*(1), 1–10. doi:10.1080/00220973.2017.1380593

Alkhasawnh, S., & Alqahtani, M. A. M. (2019). Fostering Students' Self-Regulated Learning Through using a Learning Management System to Enhance Academic Outcomes at the University of Bisha. *TEM Journal*, *8*(2), 662–669. doi:10.18421/TEM82-47

Allen, I. E., & Seaman, J. (2017). Digital Compass Learning: Distance Education Enrollment Report 2017. *Babson survey research group*.

Allen, M. (2012). *Leaving ADDIE for SAM: An agile model for developing the best learning experiences*. Alexandria, VA: American Society for Training and Development.

Aloni, M., & Harrington, C. (2018). Research based practices for improving the effectiveness of asynchronous online discussion boards. *Scholarship of Teaching and Learning in Psychology*, *4*(4), 271. Retrieved from https://www.researchgate.net/publication/329828178_Research_based_practices_for_improving_the_effectiveness_of_asynchronous_online_discussion_boards

Althaus, S. L. (1997). Computer-mediated communication in a university classroom: An experiment with on-line discussions. *Communication Education*, *46*(3), 158–174. doi:10.1080/03634529709379088

Altman, J. D., Chiang, T., Hamann, C. S., Makhluf, H., Peterson, V., & Orel, S. E. (2019). Undergraduate Research: A Road Map for Meeting Future National Needs and Competing in a World of Change. Retrieved from www.cur.org

Alzahrani, A. A. (2019). The Effect of Distance Learning Delivery Methods on Student Performance and Perception. *International Journal for Research in Education*, *43*(1), 12. Retrieved from https://bit.ly/32bUuyq

An, J. (2004). A study on the effectiveness of promoting English learning and pragmatic competence under CALL. *Computer-Assisted Foreign Language Education*, (4), 63-66.

Anderson, T., Rourke, L., Garrison, D., & Archer, W. (2001). Assessing teaching presence in a computer conferencing context. *Journal of Asynchronous Learning Networks, 5*(2), 1–17.

Annand, D. (2011). Social presence within the Community of Inquiry framework. *International Review of Research in Open and Distance Learning, 12*(5), 5. doi:10.19173/irrodl.v12i5.924

Arbaugh, J. B. (2001). How instructor immediacy behaviors affect student satisfaction and learning in web-based courses. *Business Communication Quarterly, 64*(4), 42–54. doi:10.1177/108056990106400405

Arbaugh, J. B. (2007). An empirical verification of the community of inquiry framework. *Journal of Asynchronous Learning Networks, 11*(1), 73–85.

Arensdorf, J., & Naylor-Tincknell, J. (2016). Beyond the Traditional Retention Data: A Qualitative Study of the Social Benefits of Living Learning Communities. *Learning Communities: Research & Practice, 4*(1), 4.

Armellini, A., & De Stefani, M. (2016). Social presence in the 21st century: An adjustment to the Community of Inquiry framework. *British Journal of Educational Technology, 47*(6), 1202–1216. doi:10.1111/bjet.12302

Asfaranjan, Y., Shirzad, F., Baradari, M., Salimi, M., & Salehi, M. (2013). Alleviating the Senses of Isolation and Alienation in the Virtual World: Socialization in Distance Education. *Procedia: Social and Behavioral Sciences, 93*(October), 332–337.

Association of American Colleges & Universities. (2015). Falling Short? College Learning and Career Success. Retrieved from https://www.aacu.org/leap/public-opinion-research/2015-survey-falling-short

Atif, Y. & Chou, C. (2018). Guest editorial: Digital citizenship: Innovations in education, practice, and pedagogy. *Journal of Educational Technology & Society, 21*(1), 152-154. Retrieved from https://libdb.fairfield.edu/login?url=https://search.proquest.com/docview/2147873187?accoun tid=10796

Ausubel, D. P., & Fitzgerald, D. (1962). Organizer, general background, and antecedent learning variables in sequential verbal learning. *Journal of Educational Psychology, 53*(6), 243–249. Retrieved from http://www.apa.org/pubs/journals/edu/. doi:10.1037/h0040210

Avery, T. L. (2017). Keep it Positive! Canadian Society for Studies in Education. Retrieved from https://www.researchgate.net/publication/327043525_Avery_T_Brett_C_Hewitt_J_2017_Keep_it_Positive_Paper_presented_at_the_Canadian_Society_for_Studies_in_Education_Ryerson_University_Toronto_ON_Canada

Avsec, S., & Kocijancic, S. (2016). A path model of effective technology-intensive inquiry-based learning. *Journal of Educational Technology & Society, 19*(1), 308–320. Retrieved from https://goo.gl/HN4ir3

AZ Quotes. (2019). Bill Gates. *Wise Old Sayings*. Retrieved from https://www.azquotes.com/author/5382-Bill_Gates/tag/vision

Babcock, A., Lehan, T., & Hussey, H. D. (2019). Mind the gaps: An online learning center's needs assessment. *Learning Assistance Review (TLAR), 24*(1).

Baker, K. (2016). Peer review as a strategy for improving students' writing process. *Active Learning in Higher Education, 17*(3), 179–192. doi:10.1177/1469787416654794

Bali, M. (2014). Bringing out the human in synchronous and asynchronous media for learning. Pressbooks. Retrieved from https://humanmooc.pressbooks.com/chapter/bringing-out-the-human-in-synchronous-and-asynchronous-media-for-learning/

Bandura, A. (1977). *Social learning theory*. Englewood Cliffs, NJ: Prentice Hall.

Bandura, A. (2006). Guide for constructing self-efficacy scales. In F. Pajares & T. Urdan (Eds.), *Self-efficacy beliefs of adolescents* (pp. 307–337). Charlotte, NC: Information Age Publishing.

Barrett, H. C. (2005). Researching electronic portfolios and learner engagement (White Paper). The Reflect Initiative. Retrieved from http://www.citeulike.org/group/2518/article/800018

Barth-Cohen, L. A., Smith, M. K., Capps, D. K., Lewin, J. D., Shemwell, J. T., & Stetzer, M. R. (2016). What are middle school students talking about during clicker questions? Characterizing small-group conversations mediated by classroom response systems. *Journal of Science Education and Technology, 25*(1), 50–61. doi:10.100710956-015-9576-2

Bary, R., & Rees, M. (2006, March). Is (self-directed) learning the key sill for tomorrow's engineers? *European Journal of Engineering Education, 31*(1), 73–81. doi:10.1080/03043790500429021

Bates, T. (2016). *Online learning for beginners*: 1. What is online learning? Online Learning and Distance Education Resources. Retrieved from https://www.tonybates.ca/2016/07/15/online-learning-for-beginners-1-what-is-online-learning/

Bates, A. W. (1995). *Technology, open learning and distance education*. New York, NY: Routledge.

Beaudoin, M. F. (1990). The instructor's changing role in distance education. *American Journal of Distance Education, 4*(2), 21–29. doi:10.1080/08923649009526701

Benabou, R., & Tirole, J. (2003). Intrinsic and extrinsic motivation. *The Review of Economic Studies, 70*(3), 489–520. doi:10.1111/1467-937X.00253

Berge, Z. (2009). Changing instructor's roles in virtual worlds. *Quarterly Review of Distance Education, 9*(4), 407–415.

Bernard, M., Abami, C., Lou, Y., Borkhovski, E., Wade, A., Wozney, L., ... Huang, B. (2004). How does distance education compare to classroom instruction? A meta-analysis of the empirical literature. *Review of Educational Research, 74*(3), 379–439. doi:10.3102/00346543074003379

Bernard, R. M., Abrami, P. C., Borokhovski, E., Wade, A., Tamim, R., Surkes, M. A., & Bethel, E. C. (2009). A meta-analysis of three interaction treatments in distance education. *Review of Educational Research, 79*(3), 1243–1289. doi:10.3102/0034654309333844

Berry, G. R. (2018). Learning from the learners: Student Perception of the Online Classroom. *Quarterly Review of Distance Education, 19*(3), 39–56. Retrieved from http://search.ebscohost.com.contentproxy.phoenix.edu/login.aspx?direct=true&db=tfh&AN=134727270&site=eds-live

Blackwell, L. S., Trzesniewski, K. H., & Dweck, C. S. (2007). Implicit Theories of Intelligence Predict Achievement across an Adolescent Transition: A Longitudinal Study and an Intervention. *Child Development, 78*(1), 246–263. doi:10.1111/j.1467-8624.2007.00995.x PMID:17328703

Blau, I., & Hameiri, M. (2010). Implementing technological change at schools: The impact of online communication with families on teacher interactions through learning management system. *Interdisciplinary Journal of E-Learning & Learning Objects, 6*(1), 245–257. Retrieved from https://goo.gl/hrHLia

Blau, I., & Shamir-Inbal, T. (2018). Digital technologies for promoting student voice and co-creating learning experience in an academic course. *Instructional Science, 46*(2), 315–336. doi:10.100711251-017-9436-y

Bliuc, A. M., Goodyear, P., & Ellis, R. A. (2007). Research focus and methodological choices in studies into students' experiences of blended learning in higher education. *The Internet and Higher Education, 10*(4), 231–244. doi:10.1016/j.iheduc.2007.08.001

Bobok, M., & Koc, S. (Eds.). (2019). Student-centered virtual learning environments in higher education. Hershey, PA: IGI Global. doi:10.4018/978-1-5225-5769-2

Bocchi, J., Eastman, J., & Swift, C. (2004). Retaining the online learner: Profile of students in an online MBA program and implications for teaching them. *Journal of Education for Business, 79*(4), 245–253. doi:10.3200/JOEB.79.4.245-253

Boettcher, J. V., & Conrad, R. M. (2016). *The online teaching survival guide: Simple and practical pedagogical tips*. New York, NY: John Wiley & Sons.

Boling, E., Hough, M., Krinsky, H., Saleem, H., & Stevens, M. (2012, March). Cutting the distance in distance education: Perspectives on what promotes positive, online learning experiences. *The Internet and Higher Education, 15*(2), 118–126. doi:10.1016/j.iheduc.2011.11.006

Bork, R. H., & Rucks-Ahidiana, Z. (2013, October). *Role ambiguity in online courses: An analysis of student and instructor expectations*. Teachers College, Columbia University.

Bornstein, H. (2006). Parenting science & practice. In W. Damon (Ed.), Renninger K., & Sigel, I. (Vol. Eds.), Handbook of child psychology (6th ed., Vol. 4, pp. 893–949). Academic Press. doi:10.1002/9780470147658.chpsy0422

Bower, B. L., & Hardy, K. P. (2004). From correspondence to cyberspace: Changes and challenges in distance education. *New Directions for Community Colleges, 128*(128), 5–12. doi:10.1002/cc.169

Branch, L. (2015). The impact of project-based learning & technology on student achievement in mathematics. In W. Ma, A. Yuen, J. Park, W. Lau, & L. Den (Eds.), New media, knowledge practices & multiliteracies (pp. 259–268). Academic Press. doi:10.1007/978-981-287-209-8_24

Branson, R., & Rayner, G. (1975). *Interservice procedures for instructional systems development: Executive summary and model.* Tallahassee, FL: Center for Educational Technology, Florida State University. doi:10.21236/ADA023892

Braskamp, L. A., & Engberg, M. E. (2014). *Guidelines for judging the effectiveness of assessing student learning.* Chicago, IL: Loyola University Chicago.

Braunschweig, D. (2014). *Graphic.* ADDIE Model, Creative Commons.

Britt, M., Goon, D., & Timmerman, M. (2015). How to better engage online students with online strategies. *College Student Journal, 49*(3), 399–404.

Brookhart, S. (2008). *How to give effective feedback to your students.* Alexandria, VA: Association for Supervision and Curriculum Development.

Brooks, D. (2011). Should Graduate Students Create EPortfolios? Retrieved from https://www.chronicle.com/article/Should-Graduate-Students/129813

Bruce, C. (2002, July). Information literacy as a catalyst for educational change: A background paper. In P. Danaher (Ed.). *Lifelong Learning: Whose responsibility and what is your contribution? Proceedings of the 3rd International Lifelong Learning Conference* (pp. 8-19). Australia: Yeppoon, Queensland.

Buffo, S. (2015, January 9). The power of storytelling in the college classroom. Faculty Focus. Retrieved from https://www.facultyfocus.com/articles/effective-teaching-strategies/power-storytelling-college-classroom/

Business-Software Site. (2019). Advantages and disadvantages of online synchronous learning. Retrieved from https://www.business-software.com/advantagesand-and-disadvantages-of-online-synchronous-learning

Buss, R. R., Zambo, R., Zambo, D., Perry, J. A., & Williams, T. R. (2017). Faculty members' responses to implementing re-envisioned Ed.D. programs. *Studies in Higher Education, 42*(9), 1624–1640. doi:10.1080/03075079.2015.1113951

Cai, J. (2010). Reflections on repositioning of college English education in China. *Foreign Language Teaching and Research, 42*(04), 306–308.

California State University. (2015). *Quality assurance for blended & online courses.* Long Beach, CA: California State University.

California Virtual Campus-Online Education Initiative. (2018). *Course design rubric.* Sacramento, CA: California Community Colleges.

Carroll-Barefield, A., Smith, S., Prince, L., & Campbell, C. (2005, January 1). *Transitioning from brick and mortar to online: A faculty perspective.* Retrieved from library.educause.edu/resources/2005/1/transitioning-from-brick-and-mortar-to-online-a-faculty-perspective

Cavanaugh, J., & Jacquemin, S. (2015). A large sample comparison of grade-based student learning outcomes in online vs. face-to-face courses. *Online Learning, 19*(2), 8. doi:10.24059/olj.v19i2.454

Caverly, D. C., & MacDonald, L. (2002). Online learning communities. *Journal of Developmental Education, 25*(3), 36–37.

Cerezo, R., Esteban, M., Sánchez-Santillán, M, & Núñez, J. (2017). Procrastinating Behavior in Computer-Based Learning Environments to Predict Performance: A Case Study in Moodle.

Cerezo, R., Esteban, M., Sánchez-Santillán, M., & Núñez, J. C. (2017). Procrastinating Behavior in Computer-Based Learning Environments to Predict Performance: A Case Study in Moodle. *Frontiers in Psychology, 8*, 1403. doi:10.3389/fpsyg.2017.01403

Chapman, C., Muijs, D., Reynolds, D., Sammons, P., & Teddlie, C. (Eds.). (2015). *The Routledge international handbook of educational effectiveness and improvement: Research, policy, and practice.* Routledge. doi:10.4324/9781315679488

Chauhan, V. (2017) Synchronous and Asynchronous Learning. *Imperial Journal of Interdisciplinary Research* (IJIR) 3(2), 1345-1348. Retrieved from https://www.stitcher.com/podcast/citr-synchronicity

Chen, W., & You, M. (2007). The Differences Between the Influences of Synchronous and Asynchronous Modes on Collaborative Learning Project of Industrial Design. In *Online Communities and Social Computing: Second International Conference, OCSC 2007* (pp. 275-283). Academic Press. 10.1007/978-3-540-73257-0_31

Chen, Y. & Wu, J. (2010). Status quo of current College Online Education. *Education Exploration,* (8), 72-73.

Chiasson, K., Terras, K., & Smart, K. (2015). Faculty perceptions of moving a face-to-face course to online instruction. *Journal of College Teaching and Learning, 12*(3), 231–240. Retrieved from https://files.eric.ed.gov/fulltext/EJ1067275.pdf. doi:10.19030/tlc.v12i3.9315

Chickering, A. W., & Gamson, Z. F. (1991). *Applying the seven principles for good practice in undergraduate education. In New Directions for Teaching and Learning.* San Francisco, CA: Jossey Bass.

Choi, B. (2016). How People Learn in an Asynchronous Online Environment: The Relationship between Graduate Students' Learning Strategies and Learning Satisfaction. *Canadian Journal of Learning and Technology, 42*(1).

Choi, H., & Johnson, S. D. (2005). The effect of context-based video instruction on learning and motivation in online courses. *American Journal of Distance Education, 19*(4), 215–227. doi:10.120715389286ajde1904_3

Choi, M. (2016). A concept analysis of digital citizenship for democratic citizenship education in the internet age. *Theory and Research in Social Education, 44*(4), 565–607. doi:10.1080/00933104.2016.1210549

Chorianopoulos, K. (2018). A taxonomy of asynchronous instructional video styles. *International Review of Research in Open and Distributed Learning, 19*(1), 294–311. doi:10.19173/irrodl.v19i1.2920

Christensen, C., & Eyring, H. (2011). *The innovative university: Changing the DNA of higher education from the inside out.* San Francisco, CA: Jossey-Bass.

Cilliers, L. (2017). Wiki acceptance by university students to improve collaboration in higher education. *Innovations in Education and Teaching International, 54*(5), 485–493. doi:10.1080/14703297.2016.1180255

Clark, R. C., & Mayer, R. E. (2016). e-Learning and the science of instruction: Proven guidelines for consumers and designers of multimedia learning (4th ed.). Hoboken, NJ: Wiley.

Clark, R. E., & Saxberg, B. (2018). Engineering Motivation Using the Belief-Expectancy-Control Framework. *Interdisciplinary Education and Psychology, 2*(1), 1–26. doi:10.31532/InterdiscipEducPsychol.2.1.004

Claro, S., Paunesku, D., & Dweck, C. S. (2016). Growth mindset tempers the effects of poverty on academic achievement. *Proceedings of the National Academy of Sciences of the United States of America, 113*(31), 8664–8668. doi:10.1073/pnas.1608207113 PMID:27432947

Coates, H. B. (2008). *Attracting, engaging and retaining: a new conversation about learning.* Australian Council for Educational Research.

Cole, M., Shelley, D., & Swartz, L. (2014). Online instruction, e-learning, and student satisfaction: A three-year study. *The International Review of Research in Open and Distributed Learning, 15*(6). doi:10.19173/irrodl.v15i6.1748

Colwell, J., & Hutchison, A. C. (2018). Considering a Twitter-based professional learning network in literacy education. *Literacy Research and Instruction, 57*(1), 5–25. doi:10.1080/19388071.2017.1370749

Comprehensive Data on Demands and Preferences. (2017, June 24). *The Learning House, Inc. and Aslanian Market Research.* Retrieved from https://www.learninghouse.com/knowledge-center/research-reports/ocs2017/?utm_source=pressrelease&medium=PR&utm_campaign=OCS2017

Conrad, R.-M., & Donaldson, J. A. (2011). *Engaging the online learner: Activities and resources for creative instruction* (2nd ed.). San Francisco, CA: Jossey-Bass.

Cook, C., Kilgus, S., & Burns, M. (2018). Advancing the science and practice of precision education to enhance student outcomes. *Journal of School Psychology, 66*, 4–10. doi:10.1016/j.jsp.2017.11.004

Costley, J. (2016). The effects of instructor control on critical thinking and social presence: Variations within three online asynchronous learning environments. *Journal of Educators Online, 13*(1), 109–171. doi:10.9743/JEO.2016.1.3

Crawford, S. (2019, March 20). Busting multimedia myths: An evidence-based approach to quality instructional media [webinar]. Quality Matters. Retrieved from https://www.qualitymatters.org/professional-development/free-webinars

Creswell, J. W. (2008). *Educational research: planning, conducting, and evaluating quantitative and qualitative research* (3rd ed.). Upper Saddle River, NJ: Pearson/Merrill Prentice Hall.

Crews, T. B., Wilkinson, K., & Neill, J. K. (2015). Principles of good practice in undergraduate education: Effective online course design to assist student success. *MERLOT Journal of Online Learning and Teaching, 11*(1), 87–103.

Czerkawski, B., & Lyman, E. III. (2016). An instructional design framework for fostering student engagement in online learning environments. *TechTrends, 60*(6), 532–539. doi:10.100711528-016-0110-z

Dabbagh, N., & Bannan-Ritland, B. (2004). *Online learning: Concepts, strategies, and application.* Upper Saddle River, NJ: Pearson.

Daccord, T., & Reich, J. (2015). How to transform teaching with tablets. *Educational Leadership, 72*(8), 18–23.

Dahlstrom, E., Brooks, D. C., Grajek, S., & Reeves, J. (2015). *ECAR study of undergraduate students and information technology.* EDUCAUSE Center for Analysis and Research. Retrieved from https://library.educause.edu/resources/2015/8/~/media/24ddc1aa35a5490389baf28b6ddb3693.ashx

Dai, Z. (2015). An Analysis of the Current Research Foci of MOOC---Implications of the First National Symposium on Foreign languages education of tertiary level in the era of MOOCs. *Computer-Assisted Foreign Language Education, (1),* 73-78.

Darby, F., & Lang, J. M. (2019). *Small Teaching Online: Applying Learning Science in Online Classes.* San Francisco, CA: Jossey-Bass.

Darling-Hammond, L., Hyler, M. E., & Gardner, M. (2017). Effective teacher professional development. Teacher Scholars. Retrieved from https://www.teacherscholars.org/wp-content/uploads/2017/09/Effective_Teacher_Professional_Development_REPORT.pdf

Darsih, E. (2018). Learner-centered teaching: What makes it effective. *Indonesian EFL Journal, 4*(1), 33–42. doi:10.25134/ieflj.v4i1.796

Dawley, L. (2007). *The tools for successful online teaching.* Hershey, PA: IGI Global. doi:10.4018/978-1-59140-956-4

Deci, L., & Ryan, M. (1985). *Intrinsic motivation & self-determination in human behavior.* New York: Plenum. doi:10.1007/978-1-4899-2271-7

Dede, C., Honan, P., & Peters, C. (2005). *Scaling up success: Lessons from technology-based educational improvement.* San Francisco: Jossey-Bass.

Dennen, V., Darabi, A. A., & Smith, L. J. (2007). Instructor-learner interaction in online courses: The relative perceived importance of particular instructor actions on performance and satisfaction. *Distance Education*, *28*(1), 65–79. doi:10.1080/01587910701305319

Dewey, J. (1916). *Democracy and education: An introduction to the philosophy of education.* New York: Macmillan.

Dias, S. B., & Dinis, J. A. (2014). Towards an enhanced learning in higher education incorporating distinct learner's profiles. *Journal of Educational Technology & Society*, *17*(1), 307–319. Retrieved from https://bit.ly/2Wjo9H7

Dick, W., & Carey, L. (2008). *The systematic design of instruction* (7th ed.). Glenview, IL: Scott, Foresman.

Dixson, M. D. (2010). Creating effective student engagement in online courses: What do students find engaging? *The Journal of Scholarship of Teaching and Learning*, *10*(2), 1–13.

Domer, D., & Gorman, G. (2006). Information literacy education in Asian developing countries: Cultural factors affecting curriculum development and programme delivery. *IFLA Journal*, *32*(4), 281–293. doi:10.1177/0340035206074063

Downes, J., & Bishop, P. (2015). The intersection between 1:1 laptop implementation & characteristics of effective middle level schools. *Research in Middle Level Education*, *38*(7), 1–16. doi:10.1080/19404476.2015.11462120

Duncan-Pitt, L., & Sutherland, S. (2006). An Introduction to the use of ePortfolios in professional practice. *Journal of Radiotherapy in Practice*, *5*(02), 69–75. doi:10.1017/S1460396906000100

Durrington, V., Swafford, J., & Berryhill, A. (2006). Strategies for enhancing student interactivity in an online environment. *College Teaching*, *54*(1), 190–193. doi:10.3200/CTCH.54.1.190-193

Dyar, A. (2016). Designing an online classroom. Retrieved from https://edtech.sesp

Dziuban, C. Moskal, P., Brophy, J., & Shea, P. (2007). Student Satisfaction with Asynchronous Learning. *Journal of Asynchronous Networks*, *11*(1).

Dziuban, C., Graham, C., Moskal, P., Norberg, A., & Sicilia, N. (2018). Blended learning: The new normal and emerging technologies. *International Journal of Educational Technology in Higher Education*, *15*(1), 3. doi:10.118641239-017-0087-5

Dziuban, C., & Moskal, P. (2011). A course is a course is a course: Factor invariance in student evaluation of online, blended and face-to-face learning environments. *The Internet and Higher Education*, *14*(4), 236–241. doi:10.1016/j.iheduc.2011.05.003

Eccles, J. S., & Wigfield, A. (2002). Motivational beliefs, values and goals. *Annual Review of Psychology*, *53*(1), 109–132. doi:10.1146/annurev.psych.53.100901.135153 PMID:11752481

Ekmekci, O. (2013). Being There: Establishing Instructor Presence in an Online Learning Environment. *Higher Education Studies*, *3*(1).

Endo, J. J., & Harpel, R. L. (1982). The effect of student-faculty interaction on student educational outcomes. *Research in Higher Education, 16*(2), 115–138. doi:10.1007/BF00973505

Engin, M. (2014). Macro-scaffolding: Contextual support for teacher learning. *Australian Journal of Teacher Education, 39*(5). doi:10.14221/ajte.2014v39n5.6

Enyon, B., & Gambino, L. M. (2016). Professional development for high impact eportfolio practice. *Peer Review: Emerging Trends and Key Debates in Undergraduate Education, 18*(3), 4–8.

Eom, S. B., Wen, H. J., & Ashil, N. (2006, July). The determinants of students' perceived learning outcomes and satisfaction in university online education: An empirical investigation. *Decision Sciences Journal of Innovative Education, 4*(2), 215–235. doi:10.1111/j.1540-4609.2006.00114.x

Esfijani, A. (2018). Measuring quality in online education: A meta-synthesis. *American Journal of Distance Education, 32*(1), 57–73. doi:10.1080/08923647.2018.1417658

Evans, J. (2015). A vision for more mobile learning: More verbs, fewer nouns. *Educational Leadership, 72*(8), 10–16.

Everett, D. R. (2015). Adding value: Online student engagement. *Information Systems Education Journal, 13*(6), 68–76.

Evering, L., & Moorman, G. (2012, September). Rethinking Plagiarism in the Digital Age. *JAAL, 56*(1), 35–44. doi:10.1002/JAAL.00100

Evolving Technologies Committee. (2003). Course Management Systems (CMS). Retrieved from http://www.educause.edu/ir/library/pdf/DEC0302.pdf

Ewell, P. T., & Schneider, C. G. (2013). National Institute for Learning Outcomes Assessment. The Lumina Degree Qualifications Profile (DQP): Implications for Assessment. *Learning Outcome Assessment*. Retrieved from http://www.learningoutcomesassessment.org/documents/EwellDQPop1.pdf

Eynon, B., & Gambino, L. M. (2017). High-impact ePortfolio practice: A catalyst for student, faculty, and institutional learning (reprint ed.). Sterling, VA: Stylus.

Eynon, B., Gambino, L. M., & Török, J. (2014). What difference can ePortfolio make? A field report from the Connect to Learning Project. *International Journal of ePortfolio, 4*(1), 95-114.

Eyyam, R., & Yaratan, H. S. (2014). Impact of use of technology in mathematics lessons on student achievement & attitudes. *Social Behavior and Personality, 42*(1), S31–S42. doi:10.2224bp.2014.42.0.S31

Fadde, P., & Vu, P. (2014). Blended Online Learning: Benefits, Challenges, and Misconceptions. In P. Lowenthal, C. S. York, & J. C. Richardson (Eds.), *Online Learning: Common Misconceptions, Benefits and Challenges* (pp. 33–48). New York: Nova.

Farmer, L. (2011). *Instructional design for librarians and information professionals*. New York, NY: Neal-Schuman.

Farmer, L. (2018). The role of librarians in blended courses. In S. Keengwe (Ed.), *Handbook of research on blended learning and pedagogical professional development in higher education* (pp. 122–138). Hershey, PA: IGI Global.

Farrugia, A., & Al-Jumeily, D. (2012). The design, implementation and evaluation of a web-based student teachers' ePortfolio (STeP). In *Proceedings of the International Conference on Education and E-Learning Innovations, Education and e-Learning Innovations (ICEELI)* (pp. 1-7). Academic Press. 10.1109/ICEELI.2012.6360612

Fenslow, M., & Dong, H. (2011). Are The Dorsal and Ventral Hippocampus functionally distinct structures? *Neuron, 65*(1), 1–25. PMID:20152109

Ferriter, W. M. (2010, May). Preparing to teach digitally. *Educational Leadership, 67*(8), 88–89.

Freeman, S., Eddy, S. L., McDonough, M., Smith, M. K., Okoroafor, H. J., & Wenderoth, M. P. (2014). Active learning increases student performance in science, engineering, and mathematics. *Proceedings of the National Academy of Sciences of the United States of America, 111*(23), 8410–8415. doi:10.1073/pnas.1319030111 PMID:24821756

Friedman, J. (2017). 10 facts about student interaction in online programs. US News. Retrieved from https://www.usnews.com/topics/author/jordan-friedman

Friend, C. (2017, June 21). Humanizing the online course experience. Retrieved from https://uslti.bbcollab.com/collab/ui/session/playback/load/1B0DF06FE78A11AA56A842F9953224D3

Gannon-Slater, N., Ikenberry, S., Jankowski, N., & Kuh, G. (2014). Institutional assessment practices across accreditation regions. Learning Outcome Assessment. Retrieved from http://www.learningoutcomeassessment.org/documents/Accreditation%20report.pdf

Garrett, R., Legon, R. & Fredericksen, E. E., (2019). CHLOE 3 Behind the Numbers: The Changing Landscape of Online Education 2019. *Quality Matters*. Retrieved from qualitymatters.org/qa-resources/resource-center/articles-resources/CHLOE-3-report-2019

Garrison, D. R., & Kanuka, H. (2004). Blended learning: Uncovering its transformative potential in higher education. *The Internet and Higher Education, 7*(2), 95–105. doi:10.1016/j.iheduc.2004.02.001

Garrison, D., Anderson, T., & Archer, W. (2000). Critical inquiry in a text-based environment: Computer conferencing in higher education. *The Internet and Higher Education, 2*(2-3), 87–105. doi:10.1016/S1096-7516(00)00016-6

Garrison, R., & Cleveland-Innes, M. (2005). Facilitating cognitive presence in online learning: interaction is not enough. *American Journal of Distance Education, 19*(3), 133-148. doi:0.120715389286ajde1903_2

Gašević, A., Dawson, S., Rogers, T., & Gasevic, D. (2016). Learning analytics should not promote one size fits all: The effects of instructional conditions in predicting academic success. *Internet & Higher Education, 28*(1), 68–84. doi:10.1016/j.iheduc.2015.10.002

Gast, N. (2018/19). Introducing live group meetings in an online class: Tips and techniques. *Internet Learning Journal, 7*(1), 49–64.

Gaytan, J. (2013). Factors affecting student retention in online courses: Overcoming this critical problem. *Career and Technical Education Research, 38*(2), 145–155. doi:10.5328/cter38.2.147

Giesbers, B., Rienties, B., Tempelaar, D., & Gijselaers, W. (2013). A Dynamic Analysis of the Interplay between Asynchronous and Synchronous Communication in Online Learning: The Impact of Motivation. *Journal of Computer Assisted Learning.* doi:10.1111/jcal.12020

Glenn, C. (2018). Adding Human Touch to Asynchronous Online Learning. *Journal of College Student Retention: Theory & Practice, 19*(4).

Glossary of Education Reform. (2016). Student engagement. Retrieved from https://www.edglossary.org/student-engagement/

Goik, A. (2018, September 6). How Convenience and Comfort Caused the Downfall of Personal Responsibility. *The Accent.* Retrieved from https://theascent.pub/how-convenience-and-comfort-caused-the-downfall-of-personal-responsibility-feebbd6dabed

Gomez-Rey, P., Barbera, E., & Fernandez-Navarro, F. (2017). Student Voices on the Roles of Instructors in Asynchronous Learning Environments in the 21st Century. *International Review of Research in Open and Distributed Learning, 18*(2).

Graham, C. (2006). Blended learning systems: Definition, current trends, and future directions. In C.J. Bonk & C.R. Graham (Eds.), The Handbook of Blended Learning: Global Perspectives, Local Designs. San Francisco, CA: John Wiley and Sons.

Graham, C. (2013). Emerging practice and research in blended learning. In M. Moore (Ed.), *Handbook of Distance Education* (3rd ed.). New York: Routledge. doi:10.4324/9780203803738.ch21

Graham, C. R. (2006). Blended learning systems. In C. J. Bonk & C. R. Graham (Eds.), *The handbook of blended learning* (pp. 3–21). San Francisco, CA: Pfeiffer Publishing.

Grieves, J., McMillan, J., & Wilding, P. (2006). Barriers to learning: Conflicts that occur between and within organisational systems. *International Journal of Learning & Intellectual Capital, 3*(1), 86–103. doi:10.1504/IJLIC.2006.009212

Gunter, G. A. (2007). The effects of the impact of instructional immediacy on cognition and learning in online classes. *International Journal of Social, Behavioral, Educational, Economic, Business and Industrial Engineering, 1*(11), 729–735.

Haerens, L., Vansteenkiste, M., Aelterman, N., & Van den Berghe, L. (2016). Toward a systematic study of the dark side of student motivation: Antecedents & consequences of teachers' controlling behaviors. In Building autonomous learners (pp. 59–81). Academic Press. doi:10.1007/978-981-287-630-0_4

Hafner, C. A., & Miller, L. (2011). Fostering learner autonomy in English for science: A collaborative digital video project in a technological learning environment. *Language Learning & Technology*, *15*(3), 68–86.

Hakel, M., & Smith, E. (2009). Documenting the outcomes of learning. In D. Cambridge, B. Cambridge, & K. Yancey (Eds.), *Electronic portfolios 2.0: Emergent research on implementation and impact* (pp. 133–136). Sterling, VA: Stylus.

Hall, C. (2012). Teaching and learning in a virtual environment. *The Journal of Education, Community, and Values*, *12*(1).

Hall, G. E., & Hord, S. M. (2006). *Implementing Change, Patterns, Principles, and Potholes.* Pearson Publishing Inc.

Hammond, J., & Gibbons, P. (2005). Putting scaffolding to work: The contribution of scaffolding in articulating ESL education. *Prospect*, *20*, 6–30.

Hanbidge, A. S., McMillan, C., & Scholz, K. W. (2018). Engaging with ePortfolios: Teaching social work competencies through a program-wide curriculum. *The Canadian Journal for the Scholarship of Teaching and Learning, 9*(3). doi:10.5206/cjsotl-rcacea.2018.3.3

Harackiewicz, J. M., Smith, J. L., & Priniski, S. J. (2016). Interest matters: The importance of promoting interest in education. *Policy Insights from the Behavioral and Brain Sciences*, *3*(2), 220–227. doi:10.1177/2372732216655542 PMID:29520371

Hargis, J. (2005). Collaboration, community and project-based learning—does it still work online? *International Journal of Instructional Media*, *32*(2), 157–162.

Harris, J., Mishra, P., & Koehler, M. (2009). Teachers' technological pedagogical content knowledge and learning activity types: Curriculum-based technology integration reframed. *Journal of Research on Technology in Education*, *41*(4), 393–416. doi:10.1080/15391523.2009.10782536

Hattie, J., & Timperley, H. (2007). The power of feedback. *Review of Educational Research*, *77*(1), 81–112. doi:10.3102/003465430298487

Hawkes, D., & Yerrabati, S. (2018). A systematic review of research on professional doctorates. *London Review of Education*, *16*(1), 10–27. doi:10.18546/LRE.16.1.03

Haynes, F. (2016). Trust and the community of inquiry. *Educational Philosophy and Theory*, *50*(2), 1–8. doi:10.1080/00131857.2016.1144169

He, K. (2005). New development of educational technological theories from blended learning. *Journal of National Academy of Education Administration*, (9), 37-48+79.

He, X. & Jianshi, W. (2012). Reflections on the improvements of College English Education. *Journal of North-Eastern University: social philosophy edition*, (1), 92-94.

Herndon, K. (1996). Analyzing mentoring practices through teachers' journals. *Teacher Education Quarterly*, *23*(4), 27–44.

Herold, B. (2017, June 23). Online classes for K-12 students: An overview. *Education Week.* Retrieved from https://www.edweek.org/ew/issues/online-classes/index.html

Hidi, S., & Harackiewicz, J. M. (2000). Motivating the academically unmotivated: A critical issue for the 21st century. *Review of Educational Research, 70*(2), 151–179. doi:10.3102/00346543070002151

Hill, R., & Serdyukov, P. (2010). Setting the example: Role modeling in an online class. In *Proceedings of 21st International Conference of the Society for Information Technology and Teacher Education. (SITE).* Academic Press.

Hills, J. (1979). *Teaching and learning as a communication process.* Hoboken, NJ: Wiley & Sons.

Hiltz, S. R., Shea, P., & Eunhee, K. (2004). Using focus groups to study ALN faculty motivation. *Journal of Asynchronous Learning Networks, 11*(1), 107–124.

Hiltz, S. R., Turoff, M., & Harasim, L. (2007). Development and philosophy of the field of asynchronous learning networks. In R. Andrews & C. Haythornthwaite (Eds.), *The Sage handbook of E-learning research* (pp. 55–72). Los Angeles, CA: Sage. doi:10.4135/9781848607859.n2

Hiltz, S. R., & Wellman, B. (1997). Asynchronous learning networks as a virtual classroom. *Communications of the ACM, 40*(9), 44–48. doi:10.1145/260750.260764

History of the LMS. (2020) Learning Management Retrieved from https://learning-management.financeonline.com/history-learning-mamagement-system/

Høgheim, S., & Reber, R. (2015). Supporting interest of middle school students in mathematics through context personalization & example choice. *Contemporary Educational Psychology, 42,* 17–25. doi:10.1016/j.cedpsych.2015.03.006

Hoidn, S. (2017). *Student-centered learning environments in higher education classrooms.* New York, NY: Springer. doi:10.1057/978-1-349-94941-0

Horzum, M., & Uyanik, G. (2015). An item response theory analysis of the community of inquiry scale. *International Review of Research in Open and Distributed Learning, 16*(2), 206–226. doi:10.19173/irrodl.v16i2.2052

Hoskins, S. G. (2019). Teaching ingenuity. *Science, 364*(6445), 1102. doi:10.1126cience.364.6445.1102 PMID:31197016

Howell, K. R. (n.d.). *Effective use of class Web sites* [Ph.D. thesis]. Vanderbilt University. Retrieved from https://www.learntechlib.org/p/126093/

Hrastinski, S. (2008). Asynchronous & Synchronous E-Learning. *EDUCAUSE Quarterly, 4,* 51–55. http://sigproject.pbworks.com/f/sychronous+and+asychrouns+tools.pdf

Hrastinski, S. (2010). The informal and formal dimensions of computer-mediated communication: A model. *International Journal of Networking and Virtual Organizations, 7*(1), 23–38. doi:10.1504/IJNVO.2010.029869

Hrastinski, S., & Keller, C. (2007). Computer-mediated communication in education: A review of recent research. *Educational Media International, 44*(1), 61–77. doi:10.1080/09523980600922746

Hulett, K. H. (2019, March 27). Community from a distance: Building a sense of belonging in an online classroom. Scholarly Teacher. Retrieved from https://www.scholarlyteacher.com/blog/community-from-a-distance-building-a-sense-of-belonging-in-an-online-classroom

Hwang, S., & Song, H. (2018). Effective Social Interaction in Online Learning. *National Teacher Education Journal, 11*(3).

Inkelaar, T., & Simpson, O. (2015). Challenging the 'distance education deficit' through 'motivational emails.' *Open Learning: The Journal of Open, Distance and e-Learning, 30*(2), 152-163.

Jackson, L. C., Jones, S. J., & Rodriguez, R. C. (2010). Faculty actions that result in student satisfaction in online courses. *Journal of Asynchronous Learning Networks, 14*(4), 78–96.

Jacobs, H. H. (2010). *Curriculum 21 Essential education for a changing world.* Alexandria, VA: ASCD.

Jaggars, S. S. (2014). Choosing between online and face-to-face courses: Community college student voices. *American Journal of Distance Education, 28*(1), 27–38. doi:10.1080/08923647.2014.867697

Jiang, Y. & Ma, W. (2013). Research on continuous course design of new century college English-students' needs analysis (part two). *Computer-Assisted Foreign Language Education,* (4), 64-69, 75.

Johnson, D., & Johnson, R. (2002). Learning together and alone: Overview and meta-analysis. *Asia Pacific Journal of Education, 22*(1), 95–105. doi:10.1080/0218879020220110

Johnson, H., Mejia, M., & Cook, K. (2015). *Successful online courses in California's community colleges.* San Francisco, CA: Public Policy Institute of California.

Jonassen, D. H., Tessmer, M., & Hannum, W. H. (1999). *Task analysis methods for instructional design.* Mahwah, NJ: Lawrence Erlbaum Associates.

Junco, R. (2012). The relationship between frequency of Facebook use, participation in Facebook activities, and student engagement. *Computers & Education, 58*(1), 162–171. doi:10.1016/j.compedu.2011.08.004

Jung, S., & Huh, J. H. (2019). An Efficient LMS Platform and Its Test Bed. *Electronics (Basel), 8*(2), 154. doi:10.3390/electronics8020154

Kadosh, R., & Dowker, A. (2015). *The Oxford handbook of numerical cognition* (2nd ed.). New York, NY: Oxford University Press. Retrieved from https://goo.gl/sD5vku

Karatas, H. (2015). Correlation among academic procrastination, personality traits, and academic achievement. *Anthropologist, 20*, 243–255.

Keengwe, J., & Kidd, T. T. (2010). Towards best practices in online learning and teaching in higher education. *MERLOT Journal of Online Learning and Teaching, 6*(2), 533–541.

Kehrwald, B. A., & Parker, B. (2019). Implementing online learning: Stories from the field. *Journal of University Teaching & Learning Practice, 16*(1), 1. Retrieved from https://bit.ly/2BQ5fvq

Keller, J. M., & Suzuki, K. (2004). Learner motivation and E-learning design: A multinationally validated process. *Journal of Educational Media, 29*(3), 229–239. doi:10.1080/1358165042000283084

Kemp, J. (1977). *Instructional design: A plan for unit and course development*. Belmont, CA: Fearon Publishers.

Kent, M. (2016). Adding to the mix: Students use of Facebook groups and blackboard discussion forums in higher education. *Knowledge Management & E-Learning: An International Journal, 8*(3), 444–463.

Kerby, M., Branham, K., Gayle, M., & Mallinger, G. (2014). Consumer-Based Higher Education: The Uncaring of Learning. *Journal of Higher Education Theory and Practice, 14*(5), 42–54. Retrieved from http://www.na-businesspress.com/JHETP/KerbyMB_Web14_5_.pdf

Khan, B. H. (1997). *Web-based instruction*. Englewood Cliffs, NJ: Educational Technology Publications Inc.

Kimmons, R., Hunsaker, E. W., Jones, J. E., & Stauffer, M. (2019). The Nationwide Landscape of K–12 School Websites in the United States. *The International Review of Research in Open and Distributed Learning, 20*(3). doi:10.19173/irrodl.v20i4.3794

Kitchen, R., & Berk, S. (2016). Educational technology: An equity challenge to the common core. *Journal for Research in Mathematics Education, 47*(1), 3–16. doi:10.5951/jresematheduc.47.1.0003

Klein, J., Endfinger, B., & Crumley, C. (2018, April 26). Leveraging instructional design effectively. In *Proceedings of the WSCUC Academic Resource Conference*. Academic Press.

Knowles, M. (2005). *The adult learner: The definitive classic in adult education and human resource development*. Burlington, MA: Elsevier. doi:10.4324/9780080481913

Kochhar-Bryant, C. A. (2016). Identity, commitment, and change agency: Bedrock for bridging theory and practice in doctoral education. In V. Storey, & K. Hesbol (Eds.), *Contemporary Approaches to Dissertation Development and Research Methods* (pp. 29-42). Hershey, PA: IGI Global. doi:10.4018/978-1-5225-0445-0.ch003

Koehler, M., & Mishra, P. (2009). What is technological pedagogical content knowledge (TPACK)? *Contemporary Issues in Technology & Teacher Education, 9*(1), 60–70.

Kop, R. (2011). The challenges to connectivist learning on open online networks: Learning experiences during a massive open online course. *The International Review of Research in Open and Distributed Learning, 12*(3), 19–38. doi:10.19173/irrodl.v12i3.882

Koran, M. (2017). 'It's Worse Than You Think': Teachers, Students Say Online Cheating Is Pervasive. *Voice of San Diego*. Retrieved from https://www.voiceofsandiego.org/topics/education/worse-think-teachers-students-say-online-cheating-pervasive/

Koutsabasis, P., Stavrakis, M., Spyrou, T., & Darzentas, J. (2011). *Perceived Impact of Asynchronous E-Learning after Long-Term Use: Implications for Design and Development.* https://pdfs.semanticscholar.org/b5c0/a7efb16813311139468 be68d9c8c47 a6b24d.pdf

Kozak, A. (2016) *The End of Solitude: Overtaken by Technology.* Quiet Review. Retrieved from https://www.quietrev.com/the-end-of-solitude-overtaken-by-technology/

Kreber, C., & Kanuka, H. (2006). The scholarship of teaching and learning and the online classroom. *Canadian Journal of University Continuing Education, 32*(2), 109–131.

Krentler, K. A., & Willis-Flurry, L. (2005). Does technology enhance actual student learning? The case of online discussion boards. *Journal of Education for Business, 80*(6), 316–321. doi:10.3200/JOEB.80.6.316-321

Ku, T. D., & Chang, C. S. (2011). The effect of academic discipline and gender difference on Taiwanese college students' learning styles and strategies in Web-based learning environments. *The Turkish Online Journal of Educational Technology, 10*(3).

Kuh, G., & Hu, S. (2001). The effects of student-faculty interaction in the 1990s. *The Review of Higher Education, 24*(3), 309–332. doi:10.1353/rhe.2001.0005

Kumar, R., Myers, J., Aytug, Z. G., & Presider-Houy, L. (2018). Purposeful assessment design: Aligning course-embedded assessment with program-level learning goals. *Business Education Innovation Journal, 10*(1), 6-15. Retrieved from http://www.beijournal.com/

Kuosa, K., Distante, D., Tervakari, A., Cerulo, L., Fernández, A., Koro, J., & Kailanto, M. (2016). Interactive visualization tools to improve learning & teaching in online learning environments. *International Journal of Distance Education Technologies, 14*(1), 1–21. doi:10.4018/IJDET.2016010101

Landers, R. N., & Reddock, C. M. (2017). A meta-analytic investigation of objective learner control in web-based instruction. *Journal of Business and Psychology, 32*(4), 455–478. doi:10.100710869-016-9452-y

Larbi-Siaw, O. & Owusu-Agyeman, Y. (2017). Miscellany of Students' Satisfaction in an Asynchronous Learning Environment. *Journal of Educational Technology Systems, 45*(4).

LaRose, R., & Whitten, P. (2000). Re-thinking instructional immediacy for Web courses: A social cognitive exploration. *Communication Education, 49*(4), 320–338. doi:10.1080/03634520009379221

Lattimer, H. (2008). Challenging history: Essential questions in the social studies classroom. *Social Education, 72*(6), 325–328.

Lawler, P. A., & King, K. P. (2000). *Refocusing faculty development: The view from an adult learning perspective*. Proceedings from AERC 2000: Adult Education Research Conference. Vancouver, BC, Canada: New Prairie Press. Retrieved from https://newprairiepress.org/cgi/viewcontent.cgi?referer=https://www.google.com/&httpsredir=1&article=2187&context=aerc

Lazowski, R. A., & Hulleman, C. S. (2016). Motivation interventions in education: A meta-analytic review. *Review of Educational Research, 86*(2), 602–640. doi:10.3102/0034654315617832

Lederman, D. (2017) *What Works in Blended Learning*. Inside Higher Ed. Retrieved from https://www.insidehighered.com/digital-learning/article/2017/07/26/researchs-clues-what-works-blended-learning

Lederman, D. (2017). Inside digital learning: Online education ascends. *Inside Higher Ed.* Retrieved from https://www.insidehighered.com/digital-learning/article/2018/11/07/new-data-online-enrollments-grow-and-share-overall-enrollment

Lederman, D. (2018). Online education ascends. *Inside Higher Ed.* Retrieved from https://www.insidehighered.com/digital-learning/article/2018/11/07/new-data-online-enrollments-grow-and-share-overall-enrollment

Lee, J., & Jang, S. (2014). A methodological framework for instructional design model development. *Educational Technology Research and Development, 62*(6), 743–765. doi:10.100711423-014-9352-7

Lee, M., Kim, H., & Kim, M. (2014). The effects of Socratic questioning on critical thinking in web-based collaborative learning. *Education as Change, 18*(2), 285–302. doi:10.1080/16823206.2013.849576

Lehan, T., Hussey, H., & Mika, E. (2016). Reviewing the review: An assessment of dissertation reviewer feedback quality. *Journal of University Teaching & Learning Practice, 13*(1), 4.

Lehan, T. J., Hussey, H. D., & Shriner, M. (2018). The influence of academic coaching on persistence in online graduate students. *Mentoring & Tutoring, 26*(3), 289–304. doi:10.1080/13611267.2018.1511949

Lehman, R. M., & Conceição, S. C. O. (2010). *Creating a sense of presence in online teaching: How to "be there" for distance learners*. San Francisco, CA: Jossey-Bass.

Lei, H., Yunhuo, C., & Zhou, W. (2018). Relationship between student engagement and academic achievement: A meta-analysis. *Social Behavior and Personality, 46*(3), 517–528. doi:10.2224bp.7054

Leong, P. (2011). Role of social presence and cognitive absorption in online learning environments. *Distance Education, 32*(1), 5–28. doi:10.1080/01587919.2011.565495

Leslie, H. (2019, June 14). Trifecta of student engagement: A framework for an online teaching professional development course for faculty in higher education. *Journal of Research in Innovative Teaching & Learning*. doi:. doi:10.1108/JRIT-10-2018-0024

Li, K., & Zhao, J. (2004). Principles and application models of blended learning. *E-education Research*, (7), 1-6.

Lim, J. (2016). The relationship between successful completion and sequential movement in self-paced distance courses. *International Review of Research in Open and Distributed Learning*, *17*(1). doi:10.19173/irrodl.v17i1.2167

Lister, M. (2014). Trends in the design of e-learning and online learning. *Journal of Online Learning and Teaching / MERLOT*, *10*(4), 671–679.

Liu, H., & Li, Q. (2014). Concepts exploration of Chinese MOOC and strategies for optimizing platform---A survey on Chinese MOOC platform. *Modern Educational Technology*, *24*(05), 81–87.

Liu, X., Magjuka, R. J., Bonk, C. J., & Lee, S. (2007). Does sense of community matter? An examination of participants' perceptions of building learning communities in online courses. *The Quarterly Review of Distance Education*, *8*(1), 9–24.

Livni, E. (2018, December 11). The science of "vibes" shows how everything is connected. *Quarz*, 2018. Retrieved from https://qz.com/1490276/the-science-of-vibes-shows-how-everything-is-connected/

Lombard, M., & Ditton, T. (1997). At the heart of it all: The concept of presence. *Journal of Computer Mediated Communications*, *3*(2). Retrieved from http://www.ascusc.org/jcmc/vol3/issue2/lombard.html

Lombardi, M. M. (2007). Authentic learning for the 21st century: An overview. *Educause Learning Initiative*, *1*, 1-12. Retrieved from http://net.educause.edu/ir/library/pdf/ELI3009.pdf

Long, P., & Siemens, G. (2011). Penetrating the fog: Analytics in learning and education. *EDUCAUSE Review*, *46*(5), 31–40.

Louwrens, N., & Hartnett, M. (2015). Student & teacher perceptions of online student engagement in an online middle school. *Journal of Open, Flexible & Distance Learning*, *19*(1), 27–44. Retrieved from https://goo.gl/P2jzXD

Lowenthal, P. R., Dunlap, J. C., & Snelson, C. (2017). Live synchronous web meetings in asynchronous online courses: Reconceptualizing office hours. *Online Learning.*, *21*(4), 177–194. doi:10.24059/olj.v21i4.1285

Mabrito, M. (2006). A Study of Synchronous Versus Asynchronous Collaboration in an Online Business Writing Class. *American Journal of Distance Education*, *20*(2), 93–107. doi:10.120715389286ajde2002_4

Maehl, W. H. (2000). *Lifelong learning at its best*. San Francisco, CA: Jossey-Bass.

Maguire, E. A., Gadian, D. G., Johnsrude, I. S., Good, C. D., Ashburner, J., Frackowiak, R. S. J., & Frith, C. D. (2000). Navigation-related structural change in the hippocampi of taxi drivers. *Proceedings of the National Academy of Sciences of the United States of America*, *97*(8), 4398–4403. doi:10.1073/pnas.070039597 PMID:10716738

Marzano, R. J. (2009). Teaching with interactive whiteboards. *Educational Leadership, 67*(3), 80–81.

Matos, N. (2016). *There's no such thing as asynchronous teaching.* Chronicle Vitae. Retrieved from https://chroniclevitae.com/news/1471-there-s-no-such-thing-as-asynchronous-teaching

Matthews-DeNatale, G. (2013). Are we who we think we are? ePortfolios as a tool for curriculum redesign. *Journal of Asynchronous Learning Networks, 17*(4), 41–55. doi:10.24059/olj.v17i4.395

Maurer, H. (2015). Is the Internet turning us into dummies? *Communications of the ACM, 58*(1), 48–51. doi:10.1145/2629544

Mayes, R., Luebeck, J., Ku, H. Y., Akarasriworn, C., & Korkmaz, Ö. (2011). Themes and strategies for transformative online instruction: A review of literature and practice. *Quarterly Review of Distance Education, 12*(3), 151–166.

Mayhew, M., Rockenbach, A. N., Bowman, N. A., Seifert, T. A., Wolniak, G. C., Pascarella, E. T., & Terenzini, P. T. (2016). *How college affects students: 21st century evidence that higher education works* (Vol. 3). San Francisco, CA: Jossey-Bass.

McDonald, D. (2016). *Asynchronous vs. Synchronous Communication in the Online Classroom. Center for Teaching and Learning.* Learning House. Retrieved from https://ctl.learninghouse.com/asynchronous-vs-synchronous-communication-in-the-online-classroom/

McMillan, D. A., & Chavis, D. M. (1986). Sense of community: A definition and theory. *Journal of Community Psychology, 14*(1), 6–23. doi:10.1002/1520-6629(198601)14:1<6::AID-JCOP2290140103>3.0.CO;2-I

McTighe, J., & Wiggins, G. P. (2013). *Essential questions: Opening doors to student understanding.* Gale Virtual Reference Library.

Means, B., Toyama, Y., Murphy, R., Bakia, M., & Jones, K. (2009). *Evaluation of evidence-based practices in online learning: A meta-analysis and review of online learning studies.* US Department of Education.

Means, B., Toyama, Y., Murphy, R., & Baki, M. (2013). The effectiveness of online and blended learning: A meta-analysis of the empirical literature. *Teachers College Record, 115*(3), 1–47.

Merchant, Z., Goetz, E., Cifuentes, L., Keeney-Kennicutt, W., & Davis, T. (2014). Effectiveness of virtual reality-based instruction on students' learning outcomes in K-12 and higher education: A meta-analysis. *Computers & Education, 70*, 29–40. doi:10.1016/j.compedu.2013.07.033

Merriam, S., & Bierema, L. L. (2014). *Adult learning: Linking theory and practice.* San Francisco, CA: Jossey-Bass.

Meyer, A., Rose, D. H., & Gordon, D. (2014). *Universal Design for Learning, Theory and Practice.* CAST Professional Publishing.

Mezirow, J. (2018). Transformative learning theory. In *Contemporary Theories of Learning* (pp. 114–128). Routledge. doi:10.4324/9781315147277-8

Michinov, N., Brunot, S., Le Bohec, O., Juhel, J., & Delaval, M. (2011). Procrastination, participation, and performance in online learning environments. *Computers & Education*, 2011, 243-252. Retrieved from http://primarythinking.net/EDGE/content/EDGE904/Activity%201%20-%20Reading%201a.pdf

Miertschin, S., Goodson, C., & Stewart, B. (2015). Time Management Skills and Student Performance in Online Courses. In *ASEE Conference and Exposition Proceedings*. Retrieved from 10.18260/p.24921

Mishra, P., & Koehler, M. J. (2006). Technological pedagogical content knowledge: A new framework for teacher knowledge. *Teachers College Record*, *108*(6), 1017–1054. doi:10.1111/j.1467-9620.2006.00684.x

Molnar, A., Kearney, R., & Molnar, A. (2017). A comparison of cognitive presence in asynchronous and synchronous discussions in an online dental hygiene course. *Journal of Dental Hygiene*, *91*(3), 14–21. Retrieved from http://search.proquest.com/docview/1962427939/

Montebello, M. (2018). *AI Injected e-Learning*. Cham: Springer. doi:10.1007/978-3-319-67928-0

Moore, D. E. Jr. (2018). Assessment of learning and program evaluation in health professions education programs. *New Directions for Adult and Continuing Education*, *2018*(157), 51–64. doi:10.1002/ace.20268

Moore, M. (1989). Three types of interaction. In M. Moore (Ed.), *Readings in principles of distance education*. University Park, PA: American Center for the Study of Distance Education.

Moore, M., & Kearsley, G. (1996). *Distance education: A systems review*. Belmont: Wadsworth Publishing Company.

Moskal, P., Dziuban, C., & Hartman, J. (2013). Blended Learning: A Dangerous Idea? *Internet and Higher Education*, *18*, 15–23. doi:10.1016/j.iheduc.2012.12.001

Muncy, J. A. (2014). Blogging for reflection: The use of online journals to engage students in reflective learning. *Marketing Education Review*, *24*(2), 101–114. doi:10.2753/MER1052-8008240202

Mupinga, D., Nora, R., & Yaw, D. (2006). The learning styles, expectations, and needs of online students. *College Teaching*, *54*(1), 185–189. doi:10.3200/CTCH.54.1.185-189

Murcia, J. A. M. (2016). Supported teaching autonomy support. *RICYDE. Revista Internacional de Ciencias del Deporte*, *12*(43), 2–4. doi:10.5232/ricyde2016.043ed

Mustea, D. (2016). The Role of Communication Skills in Teaching Process. In *The European proceedings of behavioral and social science*s (pp. 430-434). Academic Press. Retrieved from https://www.futureacademy.org.uk/files/images/upload/ERD2016FA052F.pdf

NACOL, North American Council for Online Learning. (2010, October). National standards for quality online teaching (ver. 2). Vienna, VA: *International Association for K-12 Online Learning.* Retrieved from http://www.inacol.org/research/nationalstandards/iNACOL_TeachingStandardsv2.pdf

Nagel, L., Blignaut, A., & Cronjé, J. (2009). Read-only participants: A case for student communication in online classes. *Interactive Learning Environments, 17*(1), 37–51. doi:10.1080/10494820701501028

Najmul Islam, A. (2016). E-learning system use & its outcomes: Moderating role of perceived compatibility. *Telematics and Informatics, 33*(1), 48–55. doi:10.1016/j.tele.2015.06.010

Nasser, R., Cherif, M., & Romanowski, M. (2011). Factors that impact the usage of the learning management system in Qatari schools. *International Review of Research in Open and Distance Learning, 12*(6), 39–62. doi:10.19173/irrodl.v12i6.985

National Center for Education Statistics. (2002). The traditional student defined. Retrieved from https://nces.ed.gov

National Educational Technology Standards for Students. (2015). *ISTE National Educational Technology Standards adopted by the Oklahoma State Department of Education.* Retrieved from https://goo.gl/fZ4uFR

National Middle School Association. (2010). *This we believe: Keys to educating young adolescents.* Westerville, OH: Author.

National Research Council. (2007). Rising Above the Gathering Storm: Energizing and Employing America for a Brighter Economic Future. Committee on Prospering in the Global Economy of the 21st Century: An Agenda for American Science and Technology. Committee on Science, Engineering, and Pub. Retrieved from https://s3.wp.wsu.edu/uploads/sites/618/2015/11/Rising-Above-the-Gathering-Storm.pdf

National Survey of Student Engagement. (2017). *Engagement insights: Survey findings on the quality of undergraduate education-annual results 2017.* Bloomington, IN: Indiana University Center for Postsecondary Research.

Newman, F. M., Marks, H. M., & Gamoran, A. (1996). Authentic pedagogy and student performance. *American Journal of Education, 104*(4), 280–312. doi:10.1086/444136

Nguyen, T. (2015). The effectiveness of online learning: Beyond no significant difference and future horizons. *MERLOT Journal of Online Learning and Teaching, 11*(2), 309–319.

Ni, A. (2013). Comparing the effectiveness of classroom and online learning: Teaching research methods. *Journal of Public Affairs Education, 19*(2), 199–211. doi:10.1080/15236803.2013.12001730

Nolfi, S., & Floreano, D. (1999). Learning and evolution. *Autonomous Robots, 7*(1), 89–113. doi:10.1023/A:1008973931182

Norberg, A., Stöckel, B., & Antti, M. (2017). Time Shifting and Agile Time Boxes in Course Design. *International Review of Research in Open and Distributed Learning*, *18*(6). Retrieved from https://files.eric.ed.gov/fulltext/EJ1155830.pdf

Northey, G., Bucic, T., Chylinski, M., & Govind, R. (2015). Increasing Student Engagement Using Asynchronous Learning. *Journal of Marketing Education*, *37*(3).

Northrup, P. T. (2002). Online learners' preferences for interaction. *Quarterly Review of Distance Education*, *3*(2), 219–226.

Nyysti, K., & Walters, K. (2018). Out of isolation: Building online higher education engagement. In A. Scheg & M. Shaw (Eds.), *Fostering effective student communication in online graduate courses* (pp. 179–192). Hershey, PA: IGI Global. doi:10.4018/978-1-5225-2682-7.ch010

O'Dwyer, L., Carey, R., & Kleiman, G. (2015). Learning theory & online learning in K-12 education: Instruction models & implications. In A. Kumi-Yeboah (Ed.), Curriculum design & classroom management: Concepts, methodologies, tools & applications (pp. 167–187). Academic Press. Retrieved from https://goo.gl/gsfV6H

Oakes, K. (2002). E-learning: LCMS, LMS—They're not just acronyms but powerful systems for learning. *Training & Development*, *56*(3), 73–75. Retrieved from https://goo.gl/FrNSdp

Online education trends report. (2018). Best Colleges. Retrieved from https://www.bestcolleges.com/perspectives/annual-trends-in-online-education/

Oosterhof, A., Conrad, R., & Ely, D. (2008). *Assessing learners online*. Upper Saddle River, NJ: Pearson.

Osterman, K. F. (2000). Students' need for belonging in the school community. *Review of Educational Research*, *70*(3), 323–367. doi:10.3102/00346543070003323

Osuna-Acedo, C., Marta-Lazo, C., & Frau-Meigs, D. (2018). From SMOOC to TMOOC, learning towards professional transference: ECO European project. *Comunicar*, *26*(55), 105–114. doi:10.3916/C55-2018-10

Ouzts, K. (2006). Sense of community in online courses. *The Quarterly Review of Distance Education*, *7*(3), 285–295.

Ozkan, S., Koseler, R., & Baykal, N. (2009). Evaluating learning management systems: Adoption of hexagonal e-learning assessment model in higher education. *Transforming Government: People. Process and Policy*, *3*(2), 111–130.

Oztok, M., & Brett, C. (2011). Social Presence and Online Learning: A Review of Research. *Journal of E-Learning & Distance Education*, *35*(3). Retrieved from http://www.ijede.ca/index.php/jde/article/view/758/1299

Oztok, M., Wilton, L., Lee, K., Zingaro, D., Mackinnon, K., Makos, A., ... Hewitt, J. (2014). Polysynchronous: Dialogic construction of time in online learning. *E-Learning and Digital Media*, *11*(2), 154–161. doi:10.2304/elea.2014.11.2.154

Paino, K. (2015). Learning Collaboratively and Globally, New York City. Retrieved from: https://bookcreator.com/2015/01/expand-students-horizons-global-collaboration/

Palloff, R. M., & Pratt, K. (1999). *Building learning communities in cyberspace: Effective strategies for the online classroom.* San Francisco, CA: Jossey-Bass.

Palloff, R. M., & Pratt, K. (2013). *Lessons from the Virtual Classroom: The Realities of Online Teaching.* San Francisco, CA: Josey-Bass.

Palloff, R. M., Pratt, K., & Stockley, D. (2001). Building learning communities in cyberspace: Effective strategies for the online classroom. *Canadian Journal of Higher Education, 31*(3), 175–178.

Palloff, R., & Pratt, K. (2005). *Collaborating Online: Learning Together in Community.* San Francisco, CA: John Wiley and Sons, Inc.

Palloff, R., & Pratt, K. (2011). *The excellent online instructor: Strategies for Professional Development.* San Francisco, CA: Augsburg University.

Palmer, D. H. (2008). Student interest generated during an inquiry skills lesson. *Journal of Research in Science Teaching, 46*(2), 147–165. doi:10.1002/tea.20263

Pappas, C. (2015). Synchronous vs. asynchronous learning—Can you tell the difference. Elearning Industry. Retrieved from https://elearningindustry.com/synchronous-vs-asynchronous-learning-can-you-tell-the-difference

Pascarella, E. T. (1980). Student-faculty informal contact and college outcomes. *Review of Educational Research, 50*(4), 545–595. doi:10.3102/00346543050004545

Pásztor, A., Molnár, G., & Csapó, B. (2015). Technology-based assessment of creativity in educational context: The case of divergent thinking & its relation to mathematical achievement. *Thinking Skills and Creativity, 18*(1), 32–42. doi:10.1016/j.tsc.2015.05.004

Perry, J. A. (2015). The Carnegie Project on the Education Doctorate. *Change: The Magazine of Higher Learning, 47*(3), 56–61. doi:10.1080/00091383.2015.1040712

Peterson, A., Beymer, P., & Putman, R. (2018). Synchronous and Asynchronous Discussions: Effects on Cooperation, Belonging, and Affect. *Paper presented at the annual meeting of the American Educational Research Association.* Academic Press. 10.24059/olj.v22i4.1517

Pew Research Center. (2017). U.S. students' academic achievement still lags that of their peers in many other countries. Retrieved from https://www.pewresearch.org/fact-tank/2017/02/15/u-s-students-internationally-math-science/

Phan, T. (2018). Instructional strategies that respond to global learners' needs in massive open online courses. *Online Learning, 22*(2), 95–118. doi:10.24059/olj.v22i2.1160

Phirangee, K., & Malec, A. (2017). Othering in online learning: An examination of social presence, identity, and sense of community. *Distance Education, 38*(2), 160–172. doi:10.1080/01587919.2017.1322457

Picciano, A. G., & Seaman, J. (2010). *Class connections: High school reform and the role of online learning*. Retrieved from http://www.babson.edu/Academics/Documents/babson-survey-research-group/class-connections.pdf

Picciano, A. G. (2009). Blending with purpose: The multimodal model. *Journal of Asynchronous Learning Networks, 13*(1), 7–18.

Pina, A. (Ed.). (2017). *Instructional design standards for distance learning*. Bloomington, IN: The Association of Educational Communications and Technology.

Pittman, L. D., & Richmond, A. (2008). University belonging, friendship quality, and psychological adjustment during the transition to college. *Journal of Experimental Education, 76*(4), 343–361. doi:10.3200/JEXE.76.4.343-362

Premack, R. (2018, September 15). Jeff Bezos said the 'secret sauce' to Amazon's success is an 'obsessive compulsive focus' on customer over competitor. *Business Insider*. Retrieved from https://www.businessinsider.com/amazon-jeff-bezos-success-customer-obsession-2018-9

Prior, D. D., Mazanov, J., Meacheam, D., Heaslip, G., & Hanson, J. (2016). Attitude, digital literacy & self-efficacy: Flow-on effects for online learning behavior. *The Internet & higher education, 29*, 91–97. doi:10.1016/j.iheduc.2016.01.001

Protopsaltis, S., & Baum, S. (2019). Does online education live up to its promise? A look at the evidence and implications for federal policy. Retrieved from https://mason.gmu.edu/~sprotops/OnlineEd.pdf

Pyke, J. (2010). A closer look at instructor-student feedback online: A case study analysis of the types and frequency. *Journal of Online Learning and Teaching, 6*(1), 110.

Quality Matters (QM). (2012). Why quality matters. Retrieved from https://www.qualitymatters.org/index.php/why-quality-matters/about-qm

Reigeluth, C. M. (1994). The imperative for systemic change. In C. M. Reigeluth & R. J. Garfinkle (Eds.), *Systemic change in education*. Englewood Cliffs, NJ: Educational Technology.

Reigeluth, C. M. (1997). Educational standards: To standardize or to customize learning? *Phi Delta Kappan, 79*(3), 202–206. Retrieved from https://goo.gl/56xLbS

Reigeluth, C. M., Beatty, B. J., & Myers, R. D. (Eds.). (2016). Instructional-design theories and models (Vol. 4). New York, NY: Routledge.

Reiser, R., & Dempsey, J. (2017). *Trends and issues in instructional design and technology* (4th ed.). Upper Saddle River, NJ: Pearson.

Renninger, K. A., & Hidi, S. E. (2016). *The power of interest for motivation and engagement.* New York, NY: Routledge.

Ren, Q. (2013). Theoretical framework for establishing and evaluating effective college English classroom environment. *Foreign Language Teaching and Research, 45*(05), 732–743.

Reynolds, R. B. (2016). Relationships among tasks, collaborative inquiry processes, inquiry resolutions, & knowledge outcomes in adolescents during guided discovery-based game design in school. *Journal of Information Science, 42*(1), 35–58. doi:10.1177/0165551515614537

Richey, R., Klein, J., & Tracey, M. (2010). *The instructional design knowledge base: Theory, research, and practice.* New York, NY: Routledge. doi:10.4324/9780203840986

Riggle, B. A., Wellner, L., Prager, E., & Hall, B. (2019, April). Professional practice doctorates: Rethinking the dissertation experience. In *Proceedings of the WSCUC Academic Resource Conference.* Academic Press.

Rios, T., Elliott, M., & Mandernach, B. J. (2018). Efficient instructional strategies for maximizing online student satisfaction. *Journal of Educators Online, 15*(3), 158–166. doi:10.9743/jeo.2018.15.3.7

Robertson, R. L., & Larkin, M. J. (2019). Developing an instrument to observe and evaluate assessment system maturity. *Journal of Educational Research and Practice, 9*(1), 55–80. doi:10.5590/JERAP.2019.09.1.05

Roberts, P., Maor, D., & Herrington, J. (2016). ePortfolio-based learning environments: Recommendations for effective scaffolding of reflective thinking in higher education. *Journal of Educational Technology & Society, 19*(4), 22–33.

Roberts, T. (2008). *Student plagiarism in an online world: Problems and solutions.* Hershey, PA: IGI Global. doi:10.4018/978-1-59904-801-7

Robinson, G., Morgan, J., & Reed, W. (2016). Disruptive innovation in higher education: The professional doctorate. *International Journal of Information and Education Technology (IJIET), 6*(1), 85–89. doi:10.7763/IJIET.2016.V6.664

Rodesiler, L. (2017). Sustained blogging about teaching: Instructional methods that support online participation as professional development. *TechTrends, 61*(4), 349–354. doi:10.100711528-017-0164-6

Rosenzweig, E. Q., Hulleman, C. S., Barron, K. E., Kosovich, J. J., Priniski, S. J., & Wigfield, A. (2019). Promises and Pitfalls of Adapting Utility Value Interventions for Online Math Courses. *Journal of Experimental Education, 87*(2), 332–352. doi:10.1080/00220973.2018.1496059

Rourke, L., Anderson, T., Garrison, D. R., & Archer, W. (1999). Assessing social presence in asynchronous text-based computer conferencing. *Journal of Distance Education, 14*, 51–70.

Rovai, A. P. (2001). Building classroom community at a distance: A case study. *Educational Technology Research and Development, 49*(4), 33–48. doi:10.1007/BF02504946

Rovai, A. P., & Jordan, H. M. (2004). Blended learning and sense of community: A comparative analysis with traditional and fully online graduate courses. *International Review of Research in Open and Distance Learning, 5*(2), 1–13. doi:10.19173/irrodl.v5i2.192

Rueda, R., Sundt, M., & Picus, L. O. (2013). Developing scholarly practitioners: Lessons from a decade-long experiment. *Planning and Changing, 44*(3), 252–265. Retrieved from https://eric.ed.gov/?q=Developing+Scholarly+Practitioners%3a+Lessons+from+a+Decade-Long+Experiment.&id=EJ1145925

Rushkoff, D. (2010). *Program or be Programmed. Ten commands for a digital age.* New York: OR books.

Russell, G. (2014). Absence of face-to-face communication is one of the benefits of online learning. *ValuEd.* Retrieved from http://blog.online.colostate.edu/blog/online-education/absence-of-face-to-face-communication-is-one-of-the-benefits-of-online-learning/

Russell, J., & Markle, R. (2017). Continuing a culture of evidence: Assessment for improvement. Princeton, NJ: Educational Testing Service. doi:10.1002/ets2.12136

Russell, S. S. (2006). An overview of adult learning processes. *Urologic Nursing, 26*(5), 349–353. PMID:17078322

Ryan, A. M., & Patrick, H. (2001). The classroom social environment and changes in adolescents' motivation and engagement during middle school. *American Educational Research Journal, 38*(2), 437–460. doi:10.3102/00028312038002437

Ryan, M. (1991). Intensive learning: An answer to the dropout crisis. *NASSP Bulletin, 75538*(538), 25–30. doi:10.1177/019263659107553805

Ryan, R. M., Lynch, M. F., Vansteenkiste, M., & Deci, E. L. (2011). Motivation and autonomy in counseling, psychotherapy, and behavior change: A look at theory and practice. *The Counseling Psychologist, 39*(2), 193–260. doi:10.1177/0011000009359313

Sachdeva, A. (1996). Use of effective feedback to facilitate adult learning. *Journal of Cancer Education, 11*(2), 106–118. PMID:8793652

Salmon, G. (2004). *E-moderating: The key to teaching and learning online.* London, England: Routledge Falmer. doi:10.4324/9780203465424

Salmon, G. (2013). *E-tivities: The key to active online learning.* New York, NY: Routledge. doi:10.4324/9780203074640

Salter-Dvorak, H. (2014). 'I've never done a dissertation before please help me': Accommodating L2 students through course design. *Teaching in Higher Education, 19*(8), 847-859. doi:10.1080/13562517.2014.934344

San Jose State University. (2018). High demand courses. Retrieved from http://online.sjsu.edu/teachingresources/nextstep_synchronous

Sánchez, A. M. (2010). Procrastinación académica: Un problema en la vida universitaria. *Studiositas*, *5*, 87–94.

Sandeen, C. C. E. (2013). Integrating MOOCS into Traditional Higher Education: The Emerging "MOOC 3.0" Era. *Change*, *45*(6), 34–39. doi:10.1080/00091383.2013.842103

Sandoval, Z. (2017). Asynchronous and synchronous sessions in online courses. Retrieved from https://www.academia.edu/35998401/ASYNCHRONOUS_AND_SYNCHRONOUS_SESSIONS_IN_ONLINE-COURSES_GRADUATE_STUDENTS_PERCEPTIONS

Saye, J. W., & Brush, T. (2002). Scaffolding critical reasoning about history and social issues in multimedia-supported learning environment. *Educational Technology Research and Development*, *50*(3), 77–96. doi:10.1007/BF02505026

Scalise, K., & Gifford, B. (2006). Computer-based assessment in e-learning: A framework for constructing "intermediate constraint" questions and tasks for technology platforms. *The Journal of Technology, Learning, and Assessment*, *4*(6).

Schaffhauser, D. (2018) Report: The real role of blended learning in instruction. *The Journal*. Retrieved from https://thejournal.com/articles/2018/03/28/report-the-real-role-of-blended-learning-in-instruction.aspx

Schmid, B., Miao, S. L., & Bazzaz, F. A. (2000). Student peer assessment. *Journal of Community & Applied Social Psychology*, *114*(5), 9–15.

Schreurs, J., & Dumbraveanu, R. (2014). A shift from teacher centered to learner centered approach. *International Journal of Engineering Pedagogy*, *4*(3), 36–41. doi:10.3991/ijep.v4i3.3395

Scruton, R. (2010). Hiding behind the screen. *New Atlantis (Washington, D.C.)*, *28*(Summer), 48–60. Retrieved from https://www.thenewatlantis.com/publications/hiding-behind-the-screen

Seidman, A. (Ed.), *(Year). College student retention: Formula for student success* (2nd ed.). Lanham, MD: Rowman & Littlefield.

Seifert, T., & Feliks, O. (2019). Online self-assessment and peer-assessment as a tool to enhance student teachers' assessment skills. *Assessment & Evaluation in Higher Education*, *44*(2), 169–185. doi:10.1080/02602938.2018.1487023

Selwyn, N., Banaji, S., Hadjithoma-Garstka, S., & Clark, W. (2011). Providing a platform for parents? Exploring the nature of parental engagement with school learning platforms. *Journal of Computer Assisted Learning*, *27*(4), 314–332. doi:10.1111/j.1365-2729.2011.00428.x

Serdyukov, P. (2015). Paradox of teacher and student in online education and societal culture. *Proceedings of Global Learn 2015* (pp. 713-723). Association for the Advancement of Computing in Education.

Serdyukov, P. (2017). Innovation in education: What works, what doesn't, and what to do about it? *Journal of Research in Innovative Teaching & Learning*, *10*(1), 4–33. doi:10.1108/JRIT-10-2016-0007

Serdyukov, P., & Hill, R. A. (2013). Flying with clipped wings: Are students independent in online college classes? *Journal of Research in Innovative Teaching, 6*(1), 50–65.

Serdyukov, P., & Serdyukova, N. (2006). *Adult learners in an online college class: Combining efficiency and convenience of E-learning. In Education for the 21st century: Impact of ICT and digital resources* (pp. 205–214). NY: Springer.

Serdyukov, P., & Serdyukova, N. (2009). Effective Communication in Online Learning. In *Proceedings of the 9th WCCE IFIP World Conference on Computers in Education*. Academic Press; Retrieved from http://www.wcce2009.org/proceedings/papers/WCCE2009_pap124.pdf

Serdyukov, P., & Serdyukova, N. (2012). Time as Factor of Success in Online Learning. *Journal of Information Technology and Application in Education, 1*(2), 40–46. Retrieved from http://www.jitae.org/paperInfo.aspx?ID=1203

Serdyukov, P., & Sistek-Chandler, C. (2015). Communication, collaboration and relationships in the online college class: Instructors' perceptions. *Journal of Research in Innovative Teaching, 8*(1), 116–131.

Sharp, J. H., & Huett, J. B. (2006). Importance of learner-learner interaction in distance education. *Information Systems Education Journal, 4*(46), 2–10.

Shatkini. (2018). Synchronous study sessions. Oregon State. Retrieved from http://blogs.oregonstate.edu/inspire/2018/1/05/synchronous-study-sessions/

Shea, P. J., Fredricksen, E. E., Pickett, A. M., & Pelz, W. E. (2004). Faculty development, student satisfaction, and reported learning in the SUNY Learning Network. In T. M. Duffy & J. R. Kirkley (Eds.), *Learner-centered theory and practice in distance education* (pp. 343–377). Mahwah, NJ: Lawrence Erlbaum Associates, Inc.

Shelton, K. (2011). A review of paradigms for evaluating the quality of online education programs. *Online Journal of Distance Learning Administration, 4*(1), 1–11.

Shepperd, R. (2002). *Predictors of Students' Success in Distance Education Courses* [Dissertation]. West Virginia University, Morgantown, WV.

Shroff, R. H., Deneen, C. C., & Ng, E. M. (2011). Analysis of the technology acceptance model in examining students' behavioral intention to use an ePortfolio system. *Australasian Journal of Educational Technology, 27*(4), 600–618. doi:10.14742/ajet.940

Shukla, V. K., & Verma, A. (2019, April). Enhancing LMS Experience through AIML Base and Retrieval Base Chatbot using R Language. In *Proceedings of the 2019 International Conference on Automation, Computational and Technology Management (ICACTM)* (pp. 561-567). IEEE Press. Retrieved from https://bit.ly/36pluhn

Simplicio, J. S. (2002). The technology hub: A cost effective & educationally sound method for the integration of technology into schools. *Education, 122*(4), 674–679. Retrieved from https://goo.gl/xy6ar7

Singh, H., & Reed, C. (2001). A white paper: Achieving success with blended learning. *Centra Software, 12*, 1–11.

Siragusa, L. (2006). Quality eLearning: An instructional design model for online learning in higher education. In *Western Australian Institute for Educational Research Forum*. Perth: Edith Cowan University.

Sivo, S. A., Ku, C.-H., & Acharya, P. (2018). Understanding how university student perceptions of resources affect technology acceptance in online learning courses. *Australasian Journal of Educational Technology, 34*(4), 72–91. doi:10.14742/ajet.2806

Smaldino, S., Lowther, D., Mims, C., & Russell, J. (2018). *Instructional technology and media for learning* (12th ed.). Upper Saddle River, NJ: Pearson.

Smith, K. S., Rook, J. E., & Smith, T. W. (2007). Increasing student engagement using effective and metacognitive writing strategies in content areas. *Preventing School Failure, 51*(3), 43–48. doi:10.3200/PSFL.51.3.43-48

Smith, P., & Ragan, T. (2004). *Instructional design* (3rd ed.). New York: John Wiley & Sons.

Smith, T. (2005). Fifty-one competencies for online instruction. *The Journal of Educators Online, 2*(2), 1–18. doi:10.9743/JEO.2005.2.2

Southard, S., & Mooney, M. (2015). A comparative analysis of distance education quality assurance standards. *Quarterly Review of Distance Education, 16*(1), 55–76.

Spady, W. (1970). Dropouts from higher education: An interdisciplinary review and synthesis. *Interchange, 1*(1), 64–85. doi:10.1007/BF02214313

Spector, J., & Ohrazda, C. (2004). Automating instructional design: Approaches and limitations. In D. Jonassen (Ed.), *Handbook for research for educational communications and technology* (2nd ed., pp. 685–699). Mahwah, NJ: Lawrence Erlbaum.

Stafford-Brizard, K. B. (2016). Building Blocks for Learning. Retrieved from https://www.turnaroundusa.org/wp-content/uploads/2016/03/Turnaround-for-Children-Building-Blocks-for-Learningx-2.pdf

Stefani, L., Mason, R., & Pegler, C. (2007). *The Educational potential of e-portfolios: Supporting personal development and reflective learning*. New York, NY: Routledge. doi:10.4324/9780203961292

Steiger, J. H. (1980). Statistically based tests for the number of common factors. *Paper presented in the annual meeting of the Psychometric Society*. Academic Press.

Stokes, P. (2012). In B. Wildavsky, A. Kelly, & K. Carey (Eds.), *What online learning can teach us about higher education? Reinventing higher education: The promise of innovation* (pp. 197–224). Cambridge, MA: Harvard Education Press.

Strayhorn, T. (2010). *The role of schools, families, & psychological variables on math achievement of black high school students*. The University of North Carolina Press. doi:10.2307/40865058

Su, D. (2013). Reorienting College English to Serve National Development Strategies and Cultivate Talents with International Visions. *Foreign Language Research*, (6), 90-96.

Su, F., & Beaumont, C. (2010). Evaluating the use of a wiki for collaborative learning. *Innovations in Education and Teaching International*, *47*(4), 417–431. doi:10.1080/14703297.2010.518428

Sung, Y. T., Chang, K. E., & Liu, T. C. (2016). The effects of integrating mobile devices with teaching & learning on students' learning performance: A meta-analysis & research synthesis. *Computers & Education*, *94*(1), 252–275. doi:10.1016/j.compedu.2015.11.008

Suskie, L. (2019, April 17). What is good assessment, revisited. Retrieved from: https://www.lindasuskie.com/apps/blog/

Sweller, J. (1988). Cognitive load during problem solving: Effects on learning. *Cognitive Science*, *12*(2), 257–285. doi:10.120715516709cog1202_4

Tan, C. T. (2013, September). Towards a MOOC game. *Paper presented at the 9th Australasian Conference on Interactive Entertainment: Matters of Life and Death*. Academic Press. 10.1145/2513002.2513040

Tauber, T. (2013). The dirty little secret of online learning: Students are bored and dropping out. *Quartz*. Retrieved from https://qz.com/65408/the-dirty-little-secret-of-online-learning-students-are-bored-and-dropping-out/

Taylor, B. (2016). The struggle is real: Student perceptions of quality in online courses using the Community of Inquiry (CoI) Framework. Retrieved from http://www.escholarship.org/uc/item/3qz4c14n

Terenzini, P., & Pascarella, E. (1977). Voluntary freshman attrition patterns of social and academic integration in a university: A test of a conceptual model. *Research in Higher Education*, *6*(1), 25–44. doi:10.1007/BF00992014

Terry, K. (2002). *The Effects of Online Time Management Practices on Self-Regulated Learning and Academic Self-Efficacy* [Doctoral dissertation]. Virginia Polytechnic Institute and State University, Blacksburg, VA.

Thalmann, M., Souza, A. S., & Oberauer, K. (2019). How does chunking help working memory? *Journal of Experimental Psychology. Learning, Memory, and Cognition*, *45*(1), 37–55. doi:10.1037/xlm0000578 PMID:29698045

The National Center on Universal Design for Learning. (n.d.). What is UDL? Retrieved from http://www.udlcenter.org/aboutudl/whatisudl/3principles

Thompson, P., Vogler, J. S., & Xiu, Y. (2017). Strategic tooling: Technology for constructing a community of inquiry. *Journal of Educators Online*, *14*(2), n2. doi:10.9743/jeo.2017.14.2.10

Throne, R., & Duffy, J. (2016, April 7). Situated Ed.D. dissertation advising in an online doctoral community of practice. In *Proceedings of the WSCUC Academic Resource Conference*. Academic Press.

Throne, R., & Walters, K. (2019, May 18). Doctoral research supervisor agency: Fostering engagement in guiding U.S. online practitioner doctorates. In *Proceedings of the 15th Annual International Congress of Qualitative Inquiry*. Academic Press.

Throne, R., Shaw, M., Fore, C., Duffy, J., & Clowes, M. (2015, November 2). Doctoral candidate milestone achievement: A philosophy for situated dissertation advising. In *Proceedings of the Eighth International Conference on e-Learning and Innovative Pedagogies*. Academic Press.

Throne, R. (2012). *Practitioner research in doctoral education*. Dubuque, IA: Kendall Hunt.

Tinto, V. (1975). Dropout from higher education: A theoretical synthesis of recent research. *Review of Educational Research*, *45*(1), 89–125. doi:10.3102/00346543045001089

Toffler, A. (1984). *The third wave*. New York, NY: Bantam Books.

Tomar, D. (2018). Synchronous or asynchronous online education: Which one is right for you? The Best Schools. Retrieved from https://thebestschools.org/magazine/synchronous-vs-asynchronous-education/

Topolka-Jorissen, K., & Wang, Y. (2015). Focus and delivery of doctoral programs in Educational Leadership. *International Journal of Educational Reform*, *24*(3), 212–232. doi:10.1177/105678791502400302

Topping, K. (1998). Peer assessment between students in colleges and universities. *Review of Educational Research*, *68*(3), 249–276. doi:10.3102/00346543068003249

Toppo, G. (2018, August 8). Defining 'Regular and Substantive' Interaction in the Online Era. Inside HigherEd. Retrieved from https://www.insidehighered.com/digital-learning/article/2018/08/08/new-debate-regular-and-substantive-interaction-between

Tu, C. H., & McIsaac, M. (2002). The relationship of social presence and interaction in online classes. *American Journal of Distance Education*, *16*(3), 131–150. doi:10.1207/S15389286AJDE1603_2

Tucker, B. (2009). The next generation of testing. *Educational Leadership*, *67*(3), 48–53.

Tucker, C. (2015). 5 tips for managing mobile devices. *Educational Leadership*, *72*(8), 25–29.

Tuckman, B. W. (1965). Developmental sequence in small groups. *Psychological Bulletin*, *63*(6), 384–399. doi:10.1037/h0022100 PMID:14314073

Turnbull, D., Chugh, R. & Luck, J. (2019). Learning management systems: An overview. doi:10.1007/978-3-319-60013-0_248-1

Tyler, R. A. (1949). *Basic principles of curriculum and instruction*. Chicago, IL: University of Chicago Press.

U.S. Department of Education NCES. (2017). Collaborative Problem-Solving Skills of 15-Year-Olds: Results from PISA 2015. Retrieved from https://nces.ed.gov/pubs2017/2017249.pdf

United States Distance Learning Association (USDLA). (2018). *Quality standards certification.* Washington, DC: United States Distance Learning Association.

University of Michigan. (n.d.). Asynchronous Learning. Retrieved from http://umich.edu/~elements/asyLearn/learning.htm

Vesley, P., Bloom, L., & Sherlock, J. (2007). Key elements of building online community: Comparing faculty and student perceptions. *MERLOT Journal of Online Learning and Teaching, 3*(3), 234–246.

Voelkl, K. (2012). School identification. In S. L. Christenson, A. L. Reschly, & C. Wylie (Eds.), *Handbook of research on student engagement* (pp. 193–218). New York, NY: Springer. doi:10.1007/978-1-4614-2018-7_9

Vygotsky, L. (1978). *Mind in Society: Development of Higher Psychological Processes.* Cambridge, MA: MIT Press.

Vygotsky, L. S. (1986). *Thought and Language.* Cambridge, MA: MIT Press.

Wang, H. (2009). Investigations on the teaching and teachers of College English. *Foreign Language World*, (4), 6-13.

Wang, P., Li, M., & Huang, H. Y. (2012). Promoting educational quality: challenges and way out for college English teachers take college English classroom education as an example. *Chinese College Education*, (10), 81-84.

Wang, S. (2012). Teacher development in the construction of college English course system. *Foreign Language World*, (4), 2-5.

Wang, Z. (2014). On effective teaching in the foreign English classroom: from a constructivist learning perspective. *Foreign Language World*, (4), 71-79.

Wang, C., Shannon, D., & Ross, M. (2013). Students' characteristics, self-regulated learning, technology self-efficacy, and course outcomes in online learning. *Distance Education, 34*(3), 302–323. doi:10.1080/01587919.2013.835779

Wang, P. (2011). Constructivism & learner autonomy in foreign language teaching & learning: To what extent does theory inform practice? *Theory and Practice in Language Studies, 1*(3), 273–277. doi:10.4304/tpls.1.3.273-277

Wang, Q., Quek, C. L., & Hu, X. (2017). Designing and improving a blended synchronous learning environment: An educational design research. *International Review of Research in Open and Distributed Learning, 18*(3), 99–118. doi:10.19173/irrodl.v18i3.3034

Wankel, C., & Blessinger, P. (2012). *Increasing student engagement and retention using online learning activities: Wikis, blogs, and webquests.* Boston, MA: Emerald Group Publishing. doi:10.1108/S2044-9968(2012)6_Part_A

Wanstreet, C. E. (2009). Interaction in online environments. In A. Orellana (Ed.), *The perfect online course: Best practices for designing and teaching* (p. 425). Charlotte, NC: Information Age Publishing.

WASC Senior Colleges and University Commission. (2013). *2013 Handbook of accreditation.* Retrieved from Western Association of Schools and Colleges.

WASC Senior Colleges and University Commission. (2014). *Meaning, quality, and integrity of degrees FAQ.* Retrieved from Western Association of Colleges and Schools.

Watson, C. E., Kuh, G. D., Rhodes, T., Light, T. P., & Chen, S. (2016). ePortfolios - The eleventh high impact practice (editorial). *International Journal of ePortfolio, 6*(2), 65-69.

Watson, R., & Watson, S. (2012). An argument for clarity: What are learning management systems, what are they not, & what should they become? *TechTrends, 51*(2), 28–34.

Wenglinsky, H. (1998). *Does it compute? The relationship between educational technology & student achievement in mathematics.* Princeton, NJ: Educational Testing Service.

West, R. (2018). *Foundations of learning and instructional design technology.* Montreal, Quebec: Pressbooks. Retrieved from http://lidtfoundations.pressbooks.com

Wiesenberg, F., & Stacey, E. (2008). Teaching philosophy: Moving from face-to-face to online classrooms. *Canadian Journal of University Continuing Education, 34*(1), 63–69.

Wiggins, G., & McTighe, J. (2005). *Understanding by design* (2nd ed.). Alexandria, VA: Association for Supervision and Curriculum Development.

Wilson, A., Watson, C., Thompson, T. L., Drew, V., & Doyle, S. (2017). Learning analytics: Challenges and limitations. *Teaching in Higher Education, 22*(8), 991–1007. doi:10.1080/135 62517.2017.1332026

Wong, S. S. (2016). Development of teacher beliefs through online instruction: A one-year study of middle school science & mathematics teachers' beliefs about teaching & learning. *Journal of Education in Science, Environmental Health, 2*(1), 21–32. doi:10.21891/jeseh.28470

Wood, D., Kurtz-Costes, B., & Copping K. (2011). Gender differences in motivational pathways to college for middle class African-American youths. *American Psychological Association, 47*(4), 961–968. doi:10.1037/a0023745

Woods, R., & Ebersole, S. (2003). Using non-subject-matter-specific discussion boards to build connectedness in online learning. *American Journal of Distance Education, 17*(2), 99–118. doi:10.1207/S15389286AJDE1702_3

Wrenn, V. (2016). *Effects of Traditional and Online Instructional Models on Student Achievement Outcomes.* Retrieved from https://digitalcommons.liberty.edu/doctoral/1135

Wu, T. (2018, February 16). The Tyranny of Convenience. *New York Times.* Retrieved from https://www.nytimes.com/2018/02/16/opinion/sunday/tyranny-convenience.html

Wubbels, T., den Brok, P., van Tartwijk, J., & Levy, J. (Eds.). (2012). *Interpersonal relationships in education: An overview of contemporary research* (Vol. 3). Springer Science & Business Media. Retrieved from https://www.springer.com/gp/book/9789460919398

Xu, J. (2015). Research on foreign language classroom: In retrospect and into the future. *Contemporay Foreign Language Studies,* (9), 1-6+76.

Xu, D., & Smith, S. (2013). *Adaptability to online learning: Differences across types of students and academic subject areas.* Teacher's College, Columbia University.

Yamagata-Lynch, L. (2014, April). Blending Online Asynchronous and Synchronous Learning. *International Review of Research in Open and Distance Learning, 15*(2). Retrieved from http://www.irrodl.org/index.php/irrodl/article/view/1778/2837

Yamagata-Lynch, L. C. (2014). Blending online asynchronous and synchronous learning. *International Review of Research in Open and Distance Learning, 15*(2), 189–212. doi:10.19173/irrodl.v15i2.1778

Yamagota-Lynch, L. (2014). Blending online asynchronous and synchronous learning. Irrodl. Retrieved from http://www.irrodl.org/index.php/irrodl/article/view/1778/2837

Yeager, D. S., Hanselman, P., & Dweck, C. S. (2019). A national study reveals where a growth mindset improves achievement. *Nature, 573*(7774), 364–369. doi:10.103841586-019-1466-y

Yin, R. K. (2014). *Case study research: Design and methods.* Thousand Oaks, CA: Sage Publishing.

You, J. (2016). Identifying significant indicators using LMS data to predict course achievement in online learning. *Internet & Higher Education, 29*(1), 23–30. doi:10.1016/j.iheduc.2015.11.003

Young, C., DeMarco, C., Nyysti, K., Harpool, A., & Mendez, T. (2019). The role of faculty development in online universities. In K. Walters & P. Henry (Eds.), *Fostering Multiple Levels of Engagement in Higher Education Environments* (pp. 260–275). Hershey, PA: IGI Global. doi:10.4018/978-1-5225-7470-5.ch012

Young, S., & Bruce, M. A. (2001). Classroom community and student engagement in online courses. *MERLOT Journal of Online Learning and Teaching, 7*(2), 219–230.

Young, S., Kelsey, D., & Lancaster, A. (2011). Predicted outcome value of email communication: Factors that foster professional relational development between students and teachers. *Communication Education, 60*(4), 371–388. doi:10.1080/03634523.2011.563388

Zhang, Q., & Yan, J. (2014). Phenomena of college English education going away from goals and strategies for correcting. *Modern College Education,* (6), 101-108.

Zhang, H., & Ma, J. (2015). The design and practice of flipped classroom under MOOCs—taking modern educational technology course as an example. *Modern Educational Technology, 25*(2), 53–60.

Zhao, C., Deng, W., & Gage, F. H. (2008). Mechanisms and Functional Implications of Adult Neurogenesis. *Cell, 132*(4), 645–660. doi:10.1016/j.cell.2008.01.033 PMID:18295581

Zhou, X., & Zhu, X. (2016). Criteria driven college English curriculum implementation and evaluation. *Foreign Language Learning Theory and Practice,* (3), 32-36.

Zhu, Y. (2013). Effectiveness of foreign language classroom teaching: A case study of an outstanding teaching episode in the third SFLEP national foreign language teaching contest. *Foreign Language World,* (2), 50-58.

Zilvinskis, J., Masseria, A. A., & Pike, G. R. (2017). Student engagement and student learning: Examining the convergent and discriminant validity of the revised National Survey of Student Engagement. *Research in Higher Education, 58*(8), 880–903. doi:10.100711162-017-9450-6

Zuckerman, M., Porac, J., Lathin, D., Smith, R., & Deci, E. L. (1978). On the importance of self-determination for intrinsically motivated behavior. *Personality and Social Psychology Bulletin, 4*(3), 443–446. doi:10.1177/014616727800400317

About the Contributors

Vaughn M. Bradley, Jr. received his B.A. degree in Biology Education from Hampton University in May of 1991, his M.A. degree in Administration/Supervision I from Loyola University in December of 1996, and his PhD degree in Education from Walden University in May of 2018. Dr. Bradley is a Middle School Assistant principal with 26 years of experience in successfully incorporating technology as a science teacher and school administrator. Dr. Bradley is also a peer reviewer for the *Journal of Educational Research and Practice.*

Joshua Elliott is an Assistant Professor and Director of the Educational Technology program at Fairfield University. Dr. Elliott has spoken at national and regional conferences, and is a ISTE Certified Educator, Google Educator, and Apple Teacher. He runs frequent professional development workshops structured to provide teachers with strategies for effective technology integration. Dr. Elliott's research and teaching goal is to help teachers improve their ability to incorporate technology into their teaching for optimal student learning.

Lesley Farmer, Professor at California State University (CSU) Long Beach, coordinates the Librarianship program, and was named as the university's Outstanding Professor. She also manages the CSU ICT Literacy Project. She earned her M.S. in Library Science at the University of North Carolina Chapel Hill, and received her doctorate in Adult Education from Temple University. Dr. Farmer chaired the IFLA's School Libraries Section, and is a Fulbright scholar. A frequent presenter and writer for the profession, she won several honors, including American Library Association's Phi Beta Mu Award for library education, the International Association of School Librarianship Commendation Award, and the SLA Education Division Anne Gellar Award. Dr. Farmer's research interests include digital citizenship, information literacy, and data analytics. Her most recent books are Library Improvement through Data Analytics (ALA, 2016) and Managing the Successful School Library (ALA, 2017).

Barbara M. Hall is the Director of Curriculum and Associate Professor in the School of Education at Northcentral University, where she serves on several committees, including the University Diversity Committee, Chair of the Curriculum Subcommittee of the Academic Affairs Council, and Co-Chair of the Governance Work Group. She earned her PhD in Education with a specialization in instructional design for online learning from Capella University in 2011. Prior to her arrival at Northcentral University in 2017, Dr. Hall worked has the Chair of the instructional design program at Ashford University. She continues to research, publish, and present around intersubjectivity in peer dialogue as she learns more about critical pedagogy. She has earned multiple recognitions throughout her career, including awards for innovative teaching, collaborative assignments, faculty research, and service to military service members and their families.

Carol Hall is a member of the University of Phoenix College of Doctoral Studies who serves as Lead Faculty/Area Chair (LFAC) for Doctoral Studies in Education, Subject Matter Expert, EdD and ACCESS faculty member, and dissertation committee member. Dr. Hall is a Certified Advanced Facilitator with many years' experience in teaching and administering in public, private, parochial, and international elementary schools and higher education. Dr. Hall received her Doctorate in Educational Administration from Baylor University. She obtained her master's degree from Texas Woman's University, and her undergraduate degree was earned at Centenary College of Louisiana.

Heather Leslie is an Instructional Designer at the University of San Diego. Heather has a background in online teaching, course design, and faculty professional development. She holds a doctorate in Strategy, an MBA, a Bachelor of Science in International Business and a Masters in Adult Education. Her research interests include the scholarship of online teaching and learning and trends in higher education. Heather's passion is collaborating with faculty to create engaging, innovative, and meaningful learning experiences for students that align with the University's mission and values.

Jamie Mahoney is an Assistant Professor in the Adolescent, Career, and Special Education Department at Murray State University. She teaches Special Education courses for dual certification Learning Behavior Disorder/ Elementary or Middle School undergraduate students and graduate students in the Alt. Cert, Master LBD, and Moderate Severe Disabilities programs. She has taught students with various disabilities in the areas of math, reading, and language arts for over 20 years in the elementary public school setting. She is certified in the areas of special education, general education, reading endorsed, assistive technology certified, and educational leadership certified. Her research interests include preparing preservice and in-service teachers to effectively teach students of all abilities using differentiated instruction methods, response to intervention and progress monitoring, increasing student engagement using technology, collaboration and co-teaching methods, and assessment methodologies.

Huda Makhluf is the Interim Director and Chief Academic Officer of the Precision Institute and former Chair of the Dept. of Mathematics and Natural Sciences at National University. She directs academic affairs administration for the Institute. She earned a bachelor of science degree in biology from the American University in Beirut, Lebanon, and a PhD in microbiology and immunology from the Medical University of South Carolina. She was a post-doctoral Fellow at Harvard Medical School and Baylor College of Medicine. Since 2007, she has been a visiting scientist at the La Jolla Institute for Allergy and Immunology and has worked in the Division of Vaccine Development for Dengue Fever and the Zika virus.

Erika Prager is the Director of Assessment and an Associate Professor in the School of Education at Northcentral University. She earned an Ed.D. in adult and post-secondary education from the University of Wyoming and has more than two decades of experience working in higher education. Her specialization areas include assessment, strategic planning, institutional effectiveness, and accreditation. For the last five years, Erika and her family have been living in Cali, Colombia where she works remotely.

Sladjana Rakich is an Assistant Professor of School Counseling at National University.

Miranda R. Regnitz is the Curriculum Project Manager in the School of Education at Northcentral University. She earned her Project Management Professional (PMP) certification from the Project Management Institute in 2019. In the same year, she was also recognized as a top contributor to the School of Education. Ms. Regnitz also earned an Innovation in Teaching award for her work on the holistic approach to integrating the ePortfolio in a master's degree program. Previously, she earned an MS in Organizational Leadership with a specialization in organizational training and instructional design from Colorado State University - Global Campus, where she served as Associate Director of Operations, Learning Technology Project Manager, Trainer, and Enrollment Advisor. Ms. Regnitz has also worked as the Director of Educational Services for Beyond Campus Innovations.

Andy Riggle has instructed graduate level students in face-to-face and online learning environments involving dissertation development, educational/organizational leadership, research methodology and design, statistical data analysis, educational foundations, scholarly writing and APA formatting, psychological and educational assessment, human resources, and school counseling. He has served as dissertation Chair and committee member for multiple online graduate level students as well as coordinated principal licensure programs. He has been involved with developing online dissertation and master level courses in research methodology and design, statistical data analysis, educational leadership, instruction and curriculum, special education, sport management, and served on various university committees. Dr. Riggle has served as a part-time faculty member, full-time faculty member, curriculum developer, Assistant Dean, and now Dean of the School of Education for Northcentral University. He regularly presents on Northcentral University's programs and unique one-to-one student engagement model.

Sonia Rodriguez is an Assistant Professor at National University, located in La Jolla, California. She currently is the Program Director for Educational School Counseling. She has 30 years of experience in social services and education. Her areas of expertise are educational leadership, school improvement models, school counseling, and bilingual/dual language instruction. Her research focus is the Latina leadership, superintendency, equity and social justice in education.

Peter Serdyukov is a Doctor of Pedagogic Sciences in Educational Technology Applications (Kiev State Linguistic University 1997), PhD in Structural and Mathematics Linguistics (Kiev State Pedagogic Institute of Foreign Language 1979). He is the Chair of the Department of Educational Technology and Informatics, Kiev State Linguistic University, Ukraine (1982-1998). Professor, Teacher Education Department, Sanford College of Education, National University, La Jolla, CA USA (2001-present). He is the author of 120 books, chapters, articles and conference presentations in educational technology, online learning, instructional methodology, global education, teacher preparation and adult learning.

Robin Throne, PhD, is a professor, research methodologist, and doctoral research supervisor. Her research agenda continues to consider doctoral researcher positionality, research supervisor agency, and voice and land dispossession for women and land-based cultures. She is the author of *Autoethnography and Heuristic Inquiry for Doctoral-Level Researchers: Emerging Research and Opportunities* (IGI Research Insight Series, 2019).

Laurie Wellner, Ed.D., is the Vice President of Academic Affairs at Northcentral University in San Diego, California and has worked in education for the past 24 years. Dr. Wellner specializes in issues regarding autism, special education and organizational leadership, ADHD, Educationally Related Mental Health Services, faculty development, course design and program development and the successful communication and collaboration with stakeholders for the improvement of the educational process. Dr. Wellner has served as an adjunct professor at Claremont Graduate University, and Touro College (New York). She has served on many committees pertaining to systems change in education. Dr. Wellner is the author of several articles, a meta-analysis of the literature in the area of trust theory, a curriculum guide for applied behavior analysis, as well as other writing, leadership, conferences and research projects. She regularly chairs and participates in committees for dissertation research at the doctoral level. She is a passionate advocate for the success of all.

Dai Zhaohui received his MA in Linguistics and Applied Linguistics in Shanghai University in 2005. Later, he received his PhD in English Language and Literature from Shanghai International Studies University in 2016. Since 1992, he has been working at Shanghai University as a college English teacher and is currently an associate professor and MA supervisor in English department, where has been working as a vice dean for more than ten years. He has published quite a number of research articles in the field of translation, language learning and information education and got Award for Outstanding Achievements in Training Students for Profession in 2004 and Second Class Prize of Teaching Achievement Award in 2009, issued by Educational Commission of Shanghai Municipality.

Index

A

Accessibility 2, 92, 160, 163, 173, 207, 226, 234, 242
ADDIE 111-112, 156-158, 173
Alignment 164, 173, 184, 186-188, 190, 213, 283, 285
AMOS 257, 270
Assessment Process 188, 192
Asynchronous Discussions 228
Asynchronous Learning 4, 7-8, 10, 14-15, 18-19, 40, 43, 46, 48, 52, 55, 57, 67, 69, 72, 114, 127, 182, 189, 225-228, 230-231, 236-237, 240-244

B

Backward Instructional Design 178, 182
Badging 204, 207, 224
Blended Learning 1, 22-23, 125, 131, 247-252, 254-257, 260-262, 264-266
Blogs 4, 6-7, 55, 57, 63-64, 83-84

C

Chunking 84, 277, 281, 289
Cloud-hosted platforms 207, 224
COI Model 111
Collaboration 3-4, 9, 12, 14-16, 18, 24, 40-41, 47, 59-60, 62-63, 66, 68, 70, 86, 89-90, 116-117, 136-138, 155, 194-195, 197, 204, 206, 221, 251, 263-264, 266, 273
College English 247-257, 261-266, 270
College English Education 248, 250, 263,

270
Communication 3-4, 6-10, 12-18, 23-24, 46-47, 54, 57, 60, 62, 66-67, 70, 78, 87, 89, 92-95, 108, 110, 115-117, 123-124, 127-128, 130, 137, 142, 149-150, 163, 166, 180, 184, 190-191, 196-197, 208, 226-228, 237-238, 243-244, 250, 263-264
Conferencing 35, 39, 52, 57, 59-60, 62, 86, 89-90, 113, 127, 174
Convenience 1-4, 6, 10, 16-17, 21, 25, 40, 47-48, 155, 165, 226
Cooperative learning 228
Course Design 36-37, 57, 111, 138, 155, 159-163, 166, 179, 195, 204, 229, 235-237, 250, 263, 266, 274, 280
Course Integration 271, 273, 280, 286

D

Data 38, 72, 80, 128, 130-131, 135-137, 154, 161, 166, 174, 181, 184, 187, 189, 191-195, 197, 202-203, 208, 210, 213, 217-218, 225, 230, 236-237, 250-252, 254-255, 257, 264-265, 280, 283
Digital Portfolio 224

E

Education Doctorate 179, 181, 184, 188-189
Educational Technology 138-140, 162, 165, 251, 277
Endogenous Variables 258, 270
Engineering a Mindset 213, 224

ePortfolio 206-207, 224, 271-286, 289
Exogenous Variables 258, 270

F

Fundamental Attribution 224

G

Growth Mindset 204, 216-218, 220-221, 224

H

Hybrid (course) 173

I

Icebreakers 109, 113, 117-118
Indicator 174
Innovation 180-182, 197, 204, 207, 219, 221, 250, 271, 273, 282, 284, 286
Institutional Assessment 182, 192, 194-195
Instructional Design 109, 111, 113, 116, 118, 151-169, 174, 178, 180, 182-183, 189-190, 194-197, 204, 235, 238, 251, 277, 281-283, 286
Interactive 1, 24, 48, 52, 57, 59, 62-63, 65, 68-69, 86, 89-90, 94, 133, 154, 160, 168, 174, 227, 230, 235, 250, 277, 279

L

Learner Autonomy 134-135, 149
Learning 1-10, 12-25, 34-41, 43, 46-48, 52-60, 63-73, 78-91, 93-96, 107-111, 113-118, 123-144, 149-169, 173-174, 178-195, 197-198, 202-211, 213-214, 216-217, 219-221, 224-232, 235-244, 247-248, 250-266, 270, 272-278, 281-286, 289
Learning Management System (LMS) 7, 161, 174, 194

M

Mapping 66, 90, 157, 165, 212

Mathematics 123, 131, 133-134, 139-142, 144, 219-220, 251, 274
Micro-Competencies 208-210, 224
Mindset 57, 202, 204, 213, 216-221, 224
MOOCs Philosophy 247, 249, 251-252, 255-256, 262, 265-266
Motivation 8-9, 41, 67, 78, 81-83, 85-87, 123, 131, 133-135, 138, 143, 150, 156, 202-203, 206, 214, 216-218, 220-221, 247, 249, 253, 256, 258-262, 264-265, 283

N

Needs Assessment 153, 174, 235
Netiquette 85, 107, 109, 113-115, 117-118

O

Online Course Design 155, 162
Online Education 1-3, 5-6, 15, 24, 35, 40, 48-49, 93, 96, 151-152, 155-160, 164-165, 167-169, 196, 203-204, 264, 266, 284
Online Instruction 22, 59, 123, 137, 149, 151, 154, 160-161, 163, 165, 169, 226-227, 235, 243, 249
Online Learning 1-7, 10, 14-22, 24-25, 35-36, 38, 41, 46-48, 52-53, 56-57, 59, 79, 88, 96, 107-110, 113, 117-118, 124, 128, 130, 132-133, 135-136, 139, 141-143, 149-151, 156, 158, 160-161, 164-165, 168, 173-174, 194, 204, 226-230, 242, 244, 250-251, 266, 277
Online Student engagement 131-132, 135
Online Teaching 21, 54, 78, 109, 113, 118, 139, 151-152, 154, 180, 204, 226, 238
Open-Source 127-128, 143, 150
Outcome 19, 139, 153, 160, 174, 180, 185, 189, 205, 209, 214-215, 249, 261

P

Pedagogue 229, 244
Peer learning 230
Portfolio 186, 204, 206-207, 224, 271-273, 285, 289

Practice-Based Research 180-182, 196
Precision 5, 202, 204, 206-210, 219-221, 224, 227
Precision Education Model or Precision Learning 224
Program Assessment 225
Proprietary 127-128, 143, 150, 159

Q

Quality Matters (QM) 159, 204
Questioning 86, 89, 204

R

Relevancy 202, 214

S

Scaffolding 180, 187-189, 191, 195, 271, 273-275, 280, 283-286, 289
Screencasting 52
Self-Efficacy 82, 109, 136, 150, 204, 214-215, 217, 224
SEM Modelling 270
Semi-Structured Interviews 131, 254, 270
Social Media 7, 39, 48, 115, 132, 135
Social Presence 9, 16, 24, 56, 59, 88, 93, 107, 109-110, 112-113, 116, 118, 228
Social presence construct 228
Socialization 3, 15, 24
Standards 114, 126, 138, 151-152, 154-156, 159-167, 169, 190-191, 213, 235, 273, 283, 285
Student Engagement 17, 77-81, 83, 85, 91, 95-96, 131-132, 135, 158, 160, 166, 204, 217, 221, 225, 227-228, 237-240, 244, 271, 273, 282-283, 286
Student Motivation 83, 131, 150, 206, 221
Student Success 18, 23, 59, 70, 77-78, 95, 154, 166, 202, 213, 221, 236-237

Synchronous 1-10, 12-16, 18-20, 22-25, 34-49, 52, 55-57, 59-60, 62-65, 71, 73, 77-78, 86, 89-91, 96, 108-109, 111, 113, 125-127, 135, 137, 140-141, 150, 182, 190, 192, 196-197, 225, 228, 231, 236-237, 241
Synchronous Learning 1, 5, 7-10, 14-15, 18, 20, 24, 43, 46, 48, 55, 59-60, 64-65, 71, 91, 109, 127, 228, 231

T

Task Analysis 274-275, 283, 289
Time 1, 3-4, 6-9, 12-24, 34-44, 46-49, 56, 59-60, 62-63, 65-68, 72, 87-92, 95, 108-109, 113-116, 118, 124, 126, 132, 140-141, 143, 149-151, 155, 160, 166, 168, 173, 185, 187, 189, 193-194, 203-204, 208-210, 213, 224, 226, 228-229, 237, 240-242, 255, 266, 272, 281, 285
Tutorial 276-281, 289
Twitter 2, 52, 57, 67, 73, 115

U

Ubiquitous Learning 260, 270

V

Value 6, 10, 12, 14-17, 34, 42, 46, 81-82, 133, 141, 181, 185, 203-204, 207, 210, 214-215, 217, 220, 254, 257, 264, 270, 275, 280-281, 283-285
Videos 6, 19, 37, 46, 52, 56-58, 60, 64-70, 83-84, 95, 164, 211, 214, 226, 242, 277, 280

Recommended Reference Books

Handbook of Research on

Assessment Practices and Pedagogical Models for Immigrant Students

ISBN: 978-1-5225-9348-5
© 2019; 454 pp.
List Price: $255

Premier Reference Source

Preparing the Higher Education Space for Gen Z

ISBN: 978-1-5225-7763-8
© 2019; 253 pp.
List Price: $175

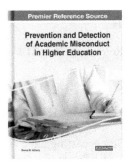

Premier Reference Source

Prevention and Detection of Academic Misconduct in Higher Education

ISBN: 978-1-5225-7531-3
© 2019; 324 pp.
List Price: $185

Premier Reference Source

Care and Culturally Responsive Pedagogy in Online Settings

ISBN: 978-1-5225-7802-4
© 2019; 423 pp.
List Price: $195

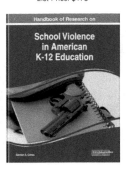

Handbook of Research on

School Violence in American K-12 Education

ISBN: 978-1-5225-6246-7
© 2019; 610 pp.
List Price: $275

Premier Reference Source

Critical Assessment and Strategies for Increased Student Retention

ISBN: 978-1-5225-2998-9
© 2018; 352 pp.
List Price: $195

Ensure Quality Research is Introduced to the Academic Community

Become an IGI Global Reviewer for Authored Book Projects

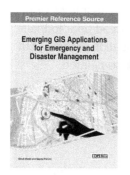

Premier Reference Source

Emerging GIS Applications for Emergency and Disaster Management

Premier Reference Source

Managerial Strategies and Green Solutions for Project Sustainability

Premier Reference Source

Comparative Approaches to Using R and Python for Statistical Data Analysis

Premier Reference Source

Solutions for High-Touch Communications in a High-Tech World

The overall success of an authored book project is dependent on quality and timely reviews.

In this competitive age of scholarly publishing, constructive and timely feedback significantly expedites the turnaround time of manuscripts from submission to acceptance, allowing the publication and discovery of forward-thinking research at a much more expeditious rate. Several IGI Global authored book projects are currently seeking highly-qualified experts in the field to fill vacancies on their respective editorial review boards:

Applications and Inquiries may be sent to:
development@igi-global.com

Applicants must have a doctorate (or an equivalent degree) as well as publishing and reviewing experience. Reviewers are asked to complete the open-ended evaluation questions with as much detail as possible in a timely, collegial, and constructive manner. All reviewers' tenures run for one-year terms on the editorial review boards and are expected to complete at least three reviews per term. Upon successful completion of this term, reviewers can be considered for an additional term.

If you have a colleague that may be interested in this opportunity, we encourage you to share this information with them.

IGI Global's Transformative Open Access (OA) Model:
How to Turn Your University Library's Database Acquisitions Into a Source of OA Funding

In response to the OA movement and well in advance of Plan S, IGI Global, early last year, unveiled their OA Fee Waiver (Offset Model) Initiative.

Under this initiative, librarians who invest in IGI Global's InfoSci-Books (5,300+ reference books) and/or InfoSci-Journals (185+ scholarly journals) databases will be able to subsidize their patron's OA article processing charges (APC) when their work is submitted and accepted (after the peer review process) into an IGI Global journal.*

How Does it Work?

1. When a library subscribes or perpetually purchases IGI Global's InfoSci-Databases including InfoSci-Books (5,300+ e-books), InfoSci-Journals (185+ e-journals), and/or their discipline/subject-focused subsets, IGI Global will match the library's investment with a fund of equal value to go toward subsidizing the OA article processing charges (APCs) for their patrons.

   Researchers: Be sure to recommend the InfoSci-Books and InfoSci-Journals to take advantage of this initiative.

2. When a student, faculty, or staff member submits a paper and it is accepted (following the peer review) into one of IGI Global's 185+ scholarly journals, the author will have the option to have their paper published under a traditional publishing model or as OA.

3. When the author chooses to have their paper published under OA, IGI Global will notify them of the OA Fee Waiver (Offset Model) Initiative. If the author decides they would like to take advantage of this initiative, IGI Global will deduct the US$ 1,500 APC from the created fund.

4. This fund will be offered on an annual basis and will renew as the subscription is renewed for each year thereafter. IGI Global will manage the fund and award the APC waivers unless the librarian has a preference as to how the funds should be managed.

Hear From the Experts on This Initiative:

"I'm very happy to have been able to make one of my recent research contributions, 'Visualizing the Social Media Conversations of a National Information Technology Professional Association' featured in the *International Journal of Human Capital and Information Technology Professionals*, freely available along with having access to the valuable resources found within IGI Global's InfoSci-Journals database."

– **Prof. Stuart Palmer,**
Deakin University, Australia

For More Information, Visit: www.igi-global.com/publish/contributor-resources/open-access or contact IGI Global's Database Team at eresources@igi-global.com

CPSIA information can be obtained
at www.ICGtesting.com
Printed in the USA
BVHW011025310321
603619BV00016B/138